Education for Peace and Disarmament: Toward a Living World

Education for Peace and Disarmament: Toward a Living World

DOUGLAS SLOAN, Editor
Teachers College, Columbia University

Teachers College, Columbia University
New York and London 1983

Published by Teachers College Press, 1234 Amsterdam Avenue, New York, N.Y. 10027

Grateful acknowledgment is made for permission to reprint the following material:

Page 28. Poem by Alia Johnson, "Why We Should Drop the Bombs." Reprinted by permission of *Evolutionary Blues*, Box 40187, San Francisco, CA 94140.

Page 29. Excerpt from "Speak, You Also," in *Paul Celan: Poems*, translated by Michael Hamburger. Copyright © 1980 by Michael Hamburger. Reprinted by permission of PERSEA BOOKS, INC., 225 Lafayette Street, New York, NY 10012, CARCANET PRESS, Manchester, England and Michael Hamburger.

Pages 211 and 214. Poetry from *Modern Arab Poets*, translated and edited by Issa J. Boullata. © Three Continents Press, Washington, D.C. Reprinted by permission of Three Continents Press, Inc., and Heinemann Educational Books.

Library of Congress Cataloging in Publication Data

Main entry under title:

Education for peace and disarmament.

Includes index.
1. Atomic weapons and disarmament—Study and teaching—United States—Addresses, essays, lectures. 2. Peace—Study and teaching—United States—Addresses, essays, lectures. I. Sloan, Douglas.
JX1974.7.E28 1983 327.1′74′07073 83-14469

ISBN 0-8077-2747-4

Manufactured in the United States of America

88 87 86 85 84 83 1 2 3 4 5 6

Contents

PREFACE

Toward an Education for a Living World

The totality, the finality, and the growing imminence of nuclear extinction are by now apparent to all who have eyes to see and the will to look. This collection of articles represents one attempt to seek ways whereby educators and education can join with others to avert the catastrophe of nuclear war, and to undo the forces that drive us toward it.

This attempt also grows out of the twofold conviction that the peace movement in general and education for peace in particular must not allow themselves to be impelled solely by fear, but must be grounded in a primary and positive vision of the fully human; and that, so grounded, education for peace is not a peripheral matter but lies at the heart of the educational venture. Before the enormity of the nuclear threat one reaction is simply paralysis and stupefaction; another is indifference born of fear (including that cool, academic nonchalance, which hides a deep despair and cynicism). Another reaction is panic; and, unfortunately, a large element of the peace movement appears still to be built primarily on fear, and an even larger element is constantly tempted to rely on fear as its main mode of persuasion. Obviously, in perilous times an unflinching ability to see what is in store for us, if we do not turn ourselves around, is absolutely essential. But if we are to take the necessary steps without faltering, there must be something to turn toward, and an awareness of the energies available for the turning. A movement built solely on fear is destined to founder, and in doing so may help bring about the very thing it fears most. As the great Russian philosopher Nikolai Berdyaev wrote:

> War is possible only in a certain psychological atmosphere and this psychological atmosphere is created in a variety of ways, sometimes in unnoticed ways. Even an atmosphere of fear of war can be favourable to war. Fear never leads to any good.[1]

The primary task of education for peace is, therefore, to reveal and tap the reality of those energies and impulses that make possible the full human capacity for a meaningful and life-enhancing existence. But this is what education in its inner essence has always been about, which is why an adequate understanding of education for peace is not something secondary to the real tasks of education, like, for instance, adding on to the rest of the curriculum a special course called "peace studies" (though it certainly may require at least that), but is integral to education in its deepest and fullest sense. However important the secondary tasks of education may be, and until now they have usually received primary emphasis, we can no longer avoid recognizing how terribly and truly deadly it is to ignore the heart of the matter.

However, we can be more specific still about the integral connection between education and the movement for peace. In the first place, the basic aim of educators is to provide for the healthy growth and development of children, and to create a culture worthy to receive them. The threat to the children that they should never grow up, and that in the interim the preparations for their destruction should impoverish and corrupt the world in which they now live, strikes at the foundation of the educational vocation.

In the second place, efforts for peace are intimately connected with education because they involve the ways in which we attempt to know and understand reality. And our ways of knowing directly affect the way we relate to the world and, hence, the kind of world we create for ourselves through our institutions, our technologies, and our conceptions of reality. The world we apprehend and live in is structured by our consciousness. It is here that education and the peace movement have the most to do with each other, and it is here that, so far, both have done the least.

The dominant modern view of how we know, of what we can know, and, therefore, of what life and the world and their potentialities hold for us has been shaped by the positivist assertion (in its various modern forms) that all knowledge is acquired only through "the positive data of science," which has meant, in effect, only through that which can be counted, measured, and weighed. The central positivist claim is that science provides our only way of knowing and our only source of genuine knowledge. This claim has its corollaries, namely, (1) that all problems are scientific and technological problems, including all human problems, which are to be cast exclusively in scientific and technological terms and dealt with accordingly; and (2) that quantitative science provides an adequate, all-embracing picture of the world—the so-called scientific and technological world view, a mechanistic, quantitative world in which there is no place for normative values, ethics, final causes, meaning, and above all qualities and the feelings, sensations, consciousness, and intangible, inner webs of relationships in which qualities inhere. The world that thus can be known and the world that results is one in which the only consideration is quantity—power.

True, it has become *au courant* in some philosophical circles to maintain that positivism is now at last being overcome; and increasingly fewer and fewer people show any desire to be regarded as positivists. Nevertheless, there remains everywhere more than a little of what Owen Barfield has humorously called RUP, "the residue of unresolved positivism," and in certain important areas, including those dominant in modern education (to say nothing of the military, the government, the corporate world, and the scientific establishment itself, despite some notable exceptions within the last), this residue is more on the order of a pervasive, conglomerated mass. That this is the case, and what it means, what momentously destructive consequences it has had for human beings and human community, why it is immediately relevant to the human search for justice and peace and for a living and livable world, become apparent with a little reflection.

As positivism, often without the name, has battened its hold on the modern mind, we have witnessed a steady, unremitting shrinking and narrowing of reason to its lowest, most elemental dimensions. For convenience sake, we may call it, as others have (though this is not an entirely satisfactory designation), technical reason. It is a reason skilled at calculation, but with no sense for beauty; a reason adept at taking things apart, but oblivious to the intangible and undergirding connections of the whole; a reason skilled in the perfecting of means, but void of meaning; a reason enamored of process, but bereft of purpose; a reason highly developed in efficiency, but dead to the richness of experience; a reason devoted to problems and programs, but without vision; a reason that while it is fragmenting, also drives to reassemble the parts it has created in homogenous, interlocking, closed, collective unities. It is the cultivation of this narrow reason that much of modern education has taken as its sole reason for being. That this technical reason is but the shadow of rationality in its fullest sense, there is in the modern world little inkling.

This technical reason, when set in the context of a larger, more capacious rationality, is of utmost importance and usefulness. But when allowed to define and determine the rational, technical reason by itself is ultimately destructive. An exclusive emphasis on technical reason strengthens the hands of those who control science and technology. Political, economic, and military centralization is the constant trend where only technical reason is recognized. The reductionism of technical reason parcels out knowledge in discrete, compartmentalized domains, which offer themselves to capture by powerful vested economic and political interests having no concern for the interrelatedness of knowledge or of nature or of human community. Nature is subjected to unrelieved dismantling and spoliation. Human community rooted in commitments to time, place, and persons is eroded and torn apart in the name of modernization and development. Considered public policy disappears in the tumult of interest-group politics. Crucial political, moral, and cultural issues and choices go unattended, and are decided by default, or by technological imperatives. And the further consolidation of social control in the hands of the already politically, economically, and technologically powerful proceeds apace. A purely quantitive, technical reason knows only power (by definition) and is, therefore, not neutral, but has a special affinity for power and for the powerful.

At the same time, often in panicky and fear-stricken reaction to the desolations wrought by a narrowed, fragmented, and fragmenting technical reason, there well up on every side all manner of dark, surging, destructive passions that pour out in dogmatisms, fundamentalisms, political ideologies, mass enthusiasms of every sort. When irrational passion and technical reason join forces, we begin to recognize familiar central characteristics of our modern situation: a highly refined, disciplined technical reason attuned only to its own imperatives and driven by irrational forces impervious or hostile to genuine human needs and concerns. In such a situation, calls for greater reason, when only technical reason is recognized and allowed, can only make matters worse; and attempts to restrain and redirect technical reason by placing it in the service of irrational commitments are usually worse yet. What is needed is a recovery of the breadth and depth of rationality in its fullness, a rationality that encompasses and can reconcile and reenliven the powers of both our calculative, technical reason and our deepest, most humane feelings and commitments.

One way to speak of this larger rationality is to speak of imagination and an education of imagination. It should be obvious that imagination here is not meant in the trivial sense of much modern education that loves to speak of "the creative imagination" but is really referring to the exercise of fancy as a necessary but essentially separate and minor prelude to technical logic and reason. In modern education the notion of imagination has become as thinned and fragmented as reason itself. We are here using imagination—and, perhaps, some such expression as Insight-Imagination might be more satisfactory—to refer to the activity of the whole person in knowing. Often a false contrast is made between rational thinking and irrational will, when the real contrast should be made between rational thinking and irrational thinking, rational feeling and irrational feeling, rational will and irrational will. In all knowing the whole person—the thinking, feeling, willing, valuing person—is involved. To ignore the feeling and willing capacities, and the development of all our sensitivities and sensibilities as potentially organs of cognition, is to restrict unduly the possibilities of knowledge, and to make all our thinking vulnerable to dead, habitual, and even brutal and psychotic impulses and energies. Must we not begin to seek ways to generate within ourselves, and to bring into our thinking, dynamic, living impulses and energies that can inform thinking and open up to it living and life-giving dimensions of reality?

Einstein's statement that the bomb has changed everything except our mode of thinking is more and more quoted, and with good reason. But it is then, in most instances, casually dropped, and other matters taken up. The radicalness of what Einstein there says is almost never taken note of, or pursued further. He says that the only way to avert "unparalled catastrophe" is to change our mode of thinking. To change our mode of thinking! Unless we assume that Einstein was merely tossing off a felicitous expression, must we not ask seriously what this means, and then attend to it urgently and with all our efforts and abilities? Whatever else it may imply, it cannot mean continuing on our present positivist, technicist path to catastrophe. In this light the task of developing an adequate education of Insight-Imagination is central to the peace movement and to every effort for a living world.

It is here that a dilemma confronts the peace movement. Events are moving quickly, and the looming threat of destruction requires action so immediate that we cannot wait upon a fundamental transformation of human nature and thinking to deal with them. At the same time, however, the potential for nuclear war is now with us, humanly speaking, forever. The knowledge of the bomb is available and can never be put back in the bottle. This evident fact is frequently hurled at the peace movement by its opponents as though it discredited the efforts for peace, rather than making them all the more urgent and necessary. So education faces a dual task: a short-term one of marshaling all available forces to turn the present situation around, and a long-range, permanent task of forming those structures of consciousness and of society that alone can make possible a just and sustainable peace. Both tasks are necessary and must be carried out simultaneously: the first making breathing room for the second, and the second more and more informing and strengthening the first. The difficulties in such a tension-filled undertaking are manifold; the necessity for it is inescapable.

In this light we can begin to sketch out in a most preliminary and incomplete way what to the editor seem to be some of the main dimensions of education for peace, knowing that some contributors to this issue might well disagree, and that all would probably draw a somewhat different picture.

The most immediate task of the peace movement requires the *relentless questioning and unmasking of officialdom.* It is at this point that the question most often posed to the peace movement must be faced. What about the Soviet Union? It will not do for the movement to focus its criticism only on Western governments, which, to their credit, are still relatively open and accessible to such criticism. Nor will its ultimate aims be served for the peace movement to soft-pedal the unattractiveness and brutishness of the Soviet state, sentimentally hoping that it will change for the better of its own accord. The peace movement has much to do in learning how to extend its growing international reach into the Soviet Union with the same effectiveness it is beginning to experience in the West. At the same time, however, the peace movement cannot permit Western governments self-righteously to cast the Soviet Union as the sole villain and only embodiment of evil in the world. And, above all, the peace movement in the West must be relentless in exposing the efforts of its own governments to generate fear among their people in order to gain their unquestioning compliance with official policies, all the more so as these policies contemplate the incineration of hundreds of millions of people. Not only does a successful playing on fear allow folly and criminality to go unchallenged, it elicits similar responses and hardening on the other side; and it locks out of consideration any recognition of real change, possibilities for change, elements of flexibility and even of self-interested realism on the other side, which can be the essential starting point for mutual relaxation of tensions all around.

A second reproach made to the peace movement is that, however well-intentioned its efforts, they endanger the mutual deterrence that has, it is claimed, prevented nuclear war for nearly four decades. But it is by no means clear that deterrence has worked: Rather, under cover of the doctrine of deterrence, the arms race has continued unabated. From only a handful of nuclear weapons in 1945 there are now approximately 50,000 in the world, and the United States and Russia alone are adding to this total three to five new bombs daily.[2] Arms-control agreements worked out in the context of a presumed deterrence doctrine have done little to stem this growth of destructive potential (and many knowledgeable analysts argue that each new arms-control agreement, while probably better than nothing, has served to ratify the desires of the military services, and of their scientific and technical weapons experts, for deployment of the next, new generation of weapons).[3] If these weapons go off in an exchange, then deterrence will have proved not to have worked; on the contrary, it will have been the flawed concept that actually led to disaster.[4] And all of this is to say nothing of the continued proliferation of nuclear weapons among nations that may or may not be concerned with deterrence at all.[5]

But it is now becoming clear that deterrence as such cannot even be said to be the policy of the two major superpowers. If it were, either nation could be satisfied with a relatively small number of weapons. On this point, Spurgeon M. Keeny, Jr., and Wolfgang K. H. Panovsky have written: "A devastating attack on the urban societies of the United States and Soviet Union would in fact require only a very small fraction of the more than 50,000 nuclear weapons currently in the arsenals of the two superpowers. . . . An exchange of a few thousand of these weapons could kill most of the urban population and destroy most of the industry of both sides."[6] Theodore Draper, commenting on their statement, has added that "no one has ever disputed what President Carter said in 1979 about 'just one of our relatively innumerable Poseidon submarines . . . that it carries enough warheads to destroy every large and medium-size city in the Soviet Union.'"[7] Clearly, a policy of minimum deterrence has long been abandoned.

What is most disturbing in this light has been an actual U.S. policy that has shown itself increasingly bellicose and insensitive to the dangers of nuclear war. President Reagan, while rattling the nuclear keys, has worked on the fears of Americans by belaboring Soviet strength in land-based ICBMs while ignoring U.S. and NATO superiority in submarine-based and airborne weapons. Plans were adopted to deploy a whole new generation of utterly destabilizing weapons—the MX missile, the Trident submarine and Trident II missiles, Pershing II missiles, cruise missiles, and the Mark 12-A Re-entry Vehicle. These are by all accounts destabilizing weapons, which only heighten insecurity by increasing pressures on the Soviets to adopt preemptive first-strike policies. Moreover, the new missiles for deployment in Europe have a three- to six-minute time span from launch to impact, the reality of which can compel the Soviets to adopt a launch-on-warning system, further increasing the possibilities of accidental nuclear exchange. (And with the scores of acknowledged U.S. computer errors that have already threatened accidental nuclear exchange, it is most disquieting, as several persons have observed, to contemplate the Soviets on a launch-on-warning system having to depend on their own more technologically backward computers.[8])

President Reagan's "zero option" and START proposals would not halt the deployment of any of these weapons, and it seems little wonder that Edward Muskie called START a "secret agenda for sidetracking disarmament."[9] Even these proposals, including the president's "interim proposal" for the Geneva negotiations on intermediate-range weapons, appear to have been prompted partially in response to public demands for some signs of genuine U.S. efforts to seek arms control. Still, little evidence is forthcoming—indeed, there is much to the contrary—to suggest that the administration has yet to develop and pursue a serious arms control policy.[10]

Moreover, the administration has been reinforcing the impression that the United States is adopting first-strike policies by its actual steps to reactivate civil defense (with all its absurdities), to rejuvenate attention to ballistic missile defense, to develop silo-busting and earth-burrowing warheads, to improve so-called C³I (Command, Control, Communications, and Intelligence) measures, and, amidst all the patriotic ballyhoo of a Fourth of July, to celebrate the conquest of space, and of the space program, by the military and the extension of its war preparations into earth orbit via space satellite.[11] It is true; the administration has not referred publicly to the policy set forth in a Department of Defense document released in 1982 of being able to conduct "protracted nuclear war" with the intention of "prevailing."[12] Neither, however, has it ever publicly repudiated such a policy, and one can only suppose that this policy continues to guide the administration's strategic planning.

Increasingly, the conclusion presses: The ability to project U.S. military power into Third World countries and other places of tension at will, backed up by the threat and use, if necessary, of nuclear weapons, has become more important to our policymakers than avoiding a nuclear war. Is it too little to ask them what could possibly justify such policy? To ensure uninterrupted supplies of oil from the Middle East, perhaps?[13] That an oil cut-off would be humanly and socially wrenching and tragic, especially given the energy extravagance of present American society, ought never to be denied. But it would not be the end of the world, which, if they are not altered, present military policies to secure those oil lines very probably, and literally, could be.

Also, in facing its immediate tasks, the peace movement finds itself constantly having to deal with the question of national security, and the meaning of real national security.[14] What contributes most to real national security: the continued amassing of nuclear weapons that threaten all life, or the creation of a strong, democratic society at home, the protection of the environment and the preservation of scarce resources—ground water, topsoil, our rivers and lakes, the building of community, the provision of meaningful livelihoods, adequate housing and medical care, and so forth? Government leaders speak of waging "a war of economic attrition" against Russia. The first image that comes to mind is Verdun, in which both sides embarked on a battle of "attrition" with the purpose of bleeding white the army of the other, only as each was drawn deeper into the conflict to discover that its own life's blood was hemorrhaging away. Military expenditures already seriously sap the economic health of both the United States and Soviet Union.[15] And the president's proposed $1.5 trillion military budget threatens to undercut the quality of American life even more severely. Jobs, housing, industrial productivity, medical research and facilities, the environment, agriculture, transit, education, and cultural health generally are being sacrificed to the build-up of arms that offer not greater security but ever more insecurity for the nation's and the world's peoples.[16] Furthermore, the administration's assault on the democratic rights and safeguards of its own citizenry—in its attempts for example, to unleash anew the CIA and to attack the Freedom of Information Act—undercuts the substance of that which is most precious to the West and ultimately is the source of its real security.

There is, finally, the haunting moral question that refuses to go away: What could possibly justify this or any nation's use of nuclear weapons against another's unarmed population of hundreds of millions of innocents, men, women, and children? Every attempt at justification sounds like a parody of Swiftian satire. If the only possible moral answer must be, "Nothing can justify it," can there be any moral grounds for building and possessing nuclear weapons, since doing so implies readiness to use them? The questions have yet to be faced forthrightly with all that they entail and all their devilish complexities made plain. Doing so, and helping the American and world's peoples do so, is one of the unavoidable tasks of the peace movement and peace education. It will require a greater moral and spiritual strength than is now apparent. In this light the work of such persons as Gene Sharp in investigating new options in conflict and defense (as represented in his article in this issue) assumes particular importance.

In his testimony to the Senate Foreign Relations Committee on May 13, 1982, the Noble Laureate physicist Hans Bethe said that two principles are essential to grasp:

—Our strategic forces are, if anything, superior to the Soviets;

—Our national security, and that of our allies, is most threatened by the grotesque size and continuing growth of both nuclear arsenals.[17]

From this vantage, real national security demands that alternatives to the present weapons build-up be given serious study and consideration. Among such alternatives are a return to minimum deterrence, a nuclear freeze, a comprehensive test ban, the establishment of nuclear-free zones, a no-first-use policy by the West, and the various proposals for bilateral arms reductions put forward or supported by serious and knowledgeable persons such as George Kennan, Jerome Wiesner, McGeorge Bundy, Hans Bethe, Admiral Noel Gaylor, and others. Not that there may not be problems with each proposal, or that all would prove acceptable, but serious proposals put forward by serious and knowledgeable persons deserve better than to be peremptorily rejected out-of-hand as has been the official response to date.[18] The short-term task of the peace movement, then, is urgent and itself many-sided and complex. It involves the relentless questioning of officialdom and of its myths and deceptions, and a demand that alternatives to the present path be seriously engaged.

The long-term tasks are just as important, and require immediate, simultaneous attention with the short-term. If it is to achieve its aims, it seems especially crucial to long-term peace and disarmament education that it extend its international outreach, in order that peace and disarmament education might both have the effectiveness it seeks and truly represent a global perspective. This is a difficult but urgent undertaking (one not made easier by the current falling off of cultural—and especially of academic—interchange between the United States and Russia). Peace and disarmament education must also recognize and take advantage of the educational functions of many different agencies and institutions: religious groups, schools, professional organizations, citizens' groups, the media, and a growing cadre of enlightened Wall Street leaders and their investors. The powers that be also recognize the educational potential of this diversity of agencies and can be expected to intensify efforts to draw them into an interlocking, total system of propaganda, surveillance, information control, and behavioral conditioning and reinforcement. The struggle between the truly educational and the pseudo-educational, propagandistic use of public institutions will turn in important part on having essential clarity about the difference between education and propaganda.

The long-term tasks of peace and disarmament education have basically two dimensions or orientations: those concerned, on the one hand, with the structures of society and, on the other, with the structures of consciousness.[19] Most peace and disarmament education has been primarily concerned with the first, with the structures of society—the institutions, the procedures and norms of institutional relationships, and the means of governance and regulation of them. There is a long and, in many respects, richly sophisticated tradition of studies, methods of analysis, and actual teaching and curricular practices that clusters around this pole of peace and disarmament education.

Space here permits only a summary glance, and an incomplete one at that, at some of the main areas of study in this regard.[20] Connected with peace and disarmament education has been the growing interest in global education and global community studies, although these do not always include specific focus on the problems of war itself. Of increasing importance has been the field known as "World Order Studies," which, largely through the work of the Institute for World Order, has attempted to develop a method of envisaging and assessing various workable alternatives to the present international systems, and to explore concrete ways for their realization. The little peace and disarmament education that actually takes place in many academic settings has often been associated with traditional strategic studies and studies in international relations and world politics. In the university these last approaches frequently run counter, or at least stand in ambiguous relationship, to peace and disarmament education, since much in strategic and international studies has been oriented toward bolstering the present system and even uncritically supporting specific national strategic policies. Another area of concern, more radical in some ways, has included those peace studies that have focused on nonviolent means of resistance, civil disobedience, and conflict resolution; the full weight of resources available in this approach of long standing has yet to be brought to bear on peace and disarmament education in other areas. Similarly, there is need for greater historical awareness and understanding in every field of peace and disarmament education.

Of particular importance is the urging by almost all persons deeply involved in peace and disarmament education that problems of war and peace be studied in connection with other related issues, such as economic development, the economic aspects of the arms race, social justice, human rights, ecological balance, and conceptions of a just world order. The interrelations among military spending, economic development, and human rights are fundamental and demand analysis and understanding. A peace not grounded in a just political and economic order, and impervious to ecological destruction, is unsustainable, and for the exploited, famished, and the oppressed is no peace at all.

Despite a long tradition, peace and disarmament education still remains on the edge of most educational undertakings today. Teacher education has been almost totally remiss in dealing with peace and disarmament education of any sort. As a result, many teachers first encounter peace and disarmament education as something peripheral to that which they have themselves been taught are the proper concerns of education. It is of crucial importance to demonstrate that peace and disarmament education has a fundamental place at the center of all education. Otherwise it will continue to be largely regarded as a side issue, or will be rendered innocuous by being relegated to specially insulated peace studies compartments in the curriculum.

Concern with the structures of society has received much more systematic and sustained attention among those involved in peace and disarmament education than has concern with what we have here called the structures of consciousness—with our ways of thinking and with the changes necessary in our ways of thinking. To be sure, peace education evinces a growing interest in the values, attitudes, and transformations of behavior deemed necessary for the full realization of just and peaceful social structures. In most cases, however, this growing interest in values, for example, does not begin to touch the deeper questions—ethical, epistemological, ontological—raised by the need for a fundamental change in our thinking. The thinking characteristic of the peace movement, and of most peace education, still tends to leave intact the modern dualistic split between subject and object, inside and outside, between institutions and attitudes, knowledge and values, and, consequently, reveals itself to contain more than "a residue of unresolved positivism." Even those who speak most about the need for global awareness and global relationships often do so (as Broughton and Zahaykevich argue in their article in this issue) in fundamentally positivist terms, cloaking in ostensibly organic, qualitative metaphors what remain essentially mechanistic, quantitative modes of thought and action. To the extent that this is done, unknowingly and with the best of intentions, all the greater are the dangers. It can only be self-defeating, and may redound with even more tragic consequences, for the peace movement to perpetuate the same ways of thinking, and conceptions and perceptions of reality, that shape the institutions and actions it wishes to change.

What might be some of the elements of a change in our ways of thinking that would at least begin to break the hold of positivism and of the narrow conception of reason, and of human possibilities, that has us in its grip?

A change in our way of thinking would, if nothing else, recognize and reorient itself, in method and substance, around the *reality of qualities*. Nothing would be more radical for our thinking than to see that qualities are not only subjective but also objective, and even more constitutive of reality than quantity. Power and might could no longer make claim to being the ultimate reality. Those scientific and technological world views that depict the universe as a dead, lifeless mechanism would be seen for the absurdities they are. Science would be forced to develop methods and concepts adequate to the realities of life, quality, and consciousness, rather than dealing with these, as now, exclusively in terms of the quantitative and inanimate (still the fundamental conceptual basis of even the so-called life-sciences). Or, failing this, the strict limits of quantitative science would be clearly apparent, and appropriately circumscribed. The qualitative enhancement of life and of culture would become more important than their quantitative manipulation and control.

A change in our mode of thinking could once again reinstate a recognition of *the fullness of the human reality*. The irreducibility of the central human problems would be recognized as essential to human dignity. The central human problems are not computable, and are, therefore, not amenable to technological solutions without a loss of the essentially human. We could also begin to come to grips with the deep, destructive impulses of the human psyche, to which a purely technical reason is as oblivious as it is to the sources of genuine creativeness. The persistence of a narrow reason within the peace movement does not enable it to recognize, much less to bring to light and deal with, the dark and deadly proclivities of the human heart. Nikolai Berdyaev has noted how war always presupposes the arousal of *erotic* conditions of love and hate. War seduces, it lures and beckons, hence the frisson of excitement that one detects even or, perhaps, especially in the attempts to portray its hideousness: War tempts with promises "to get us off the hook"; to enable us to surrender our human tasks and responsibilities; to obliterate the memory of past deeds, debts, and failures; to taste reality kept from us by the everyday routine of the OK world; to have the ultimate joy of a final paroxysm of sadism and ressentiment at the claims of existence, of the Other, and of all the others. A grasp of the fullness of the human being would be a first step in beginning to deal with the depths of our human involvement in war. But it would also enable us to begin to recover a healing awareness of the equally real beauty and higher potential of the human being, starting particularly with a renewed sense, almost lost in the modern world, of the beauty and nobility of the human form itself. That human beings would docilely hand over to a machine, to the silicon chips in a launch-on-warning system, the responsibility for their own final destruction is testimony to how complete has been our loss of any grasp of the full human reality. (And in this regard, we may very well ask of those educators who now try to outdo one another in recommending the adoption of computers in education just how they plan to do this without fostering further the illusions that all human problems are computable and human beings are justified in abdicating to the machine.)

A sense of the truly human would also help to restore a *respect for language*. That which is most unique about the human being is grasped primarily in language, and in the deeply human and numinous meanings expressed in language. Human commitments, community, and meaning all turn on a respect for language. Many observers have noted that the abuse and misuse of language is integral to government and military preparations for war. The lack of respect for language is nowhere more evident than in the use by officialdom of misleading language to describe nuclear weapons and nuclear strategy. Sanitized, detached, and deceptive phrases—"a wider menu" of "nuclear options," "preemptive deterrence," "surgically clean strikes," and so forth—seek to conceal and make palatable instrumentalities of death and destruction.[21] While the misuse of language reaches its heights in the current utterances of officialdom, the way for it has long been eased and prepared by those theories of language, often given the highest academic standing and sanction, that see words not as the bearers of intrinsic meanings, but only as signs to be manipulated at will; that see words not as meaning-laden symbols with their own integrity, but as one-dimensional labels useful for any arbitrary functional purpose. As Wendell Berry has eloquently shown, the degeneration of language and the degeneration of the human being and of human community go hand in hand.[22]

A change of thinking would also recognize that *a grasp of beauty* is essential to an adequate cognition of reality. A spreading and unchecked ugliness invariably accompanies an unrestrained technical reason. Toleration and awareness of this ugliness bespeak the widespread atrophy of sensitivities and sensibilities that, if fully formed, would make the contemplation of the destruction of this beauteous earth unbearable. It is probably no coincidence that the U.S. administration most given to entertaining the possibility of nuclear war is also the most heedless of the beauty and fragility of the environment. Winston Churchill has been quoted as saying, "The Stone Age may return on the gleaming wings of science." The meaning is twofold: the technology that carries the missiles on their way, and the scientistic world views of a purely quantitative, mechanistic universe that is dead already by definition and that, as it clamps itself on the modern mind, steadily dulls the capacity to perceive and respond to the living world really there. In contrast to Churchill's words is the affirmation of Dostoevski that "beauty shall save the world." Clearly more than that trivial aestheticism, which is about all of beauty left to the modern mind, can Dostoevski's meaning indicate anything less than what is revealed in a creative, imaginative grasp of qualitative reality and wholeness?

A genuine sense of beauty means a sense of reverence for life, a grasp of diversity in wholeness, of qualitative richness and reality, of newness and meaning. And it requires a new mode of thinking that is at once capacious and precise: Insight-Imagination, the involvement of the whole person in knowing. It is here that the artistic, the scientific, and the ethical come together in thinking and knowing. And its realization requires its own appropriate education: an education of imagination in which the development of technical reason takes place within the larger rationality revealed in color, sound, tone, movement; in a joy and immersion in the delights of words and the living images evoked by them; in calm and healing architectural, classroom, and community environments; in the aesthetic presentation of every lesson; in awareness and respect for the rhythms of growth and learning; in the direct presence and appreciation of living nature; and in meaningful social responsibilities and the presence of nourishing, trustworthy persons. From such an education could come support for the positive (not positivist!) transformation of our thinking needed for both the development of a humanly useful critical and technical reason, and for the establishment of lasting, just, and peaceful social structures. The very envisaging of the possibility of a genuine transformation in our ways of thinking can in itself begin to awaken within us awareness of the real grounds that exist for life-affirming hope and action.

A version of this volume first appeared as a special issue of *Teachers College Record* 84, no. 1 (Fall 1982). The editor takes pleasure in expressing his gratitude to Francis B. Simon and Glorieux Dougherty of the *Record* staff, whose devoted and expert work has made this volume possible.

DS

Notes

1 Nikolai Berdyaev, *Slavery and Freedom* (New York: Charles Scribner's Sons, 1944), p. 156.

2 Ruth Leger Sivard, *World Military and Social Expenditures, 1981* (Leesburg, Va.: World Priorities Inc., 1981), pp. 12–15.

3 Herbert Scoville, *MX: Prescription for Disaster* (Cambridge: The MIT Press, 1981), pp. 91–117; see also James Fallows, "Practical Sense," *The New York Review*, June 24, 1982, p. 16.

4 "Deterrence is not a stationary state, it is a degenerative state," writes E. P. Thompson (E. P. Thompson and Dan Smith, eds., *Protest and Survive* [New York and London: Monthly Review Press, 1981], p. 44).

5 See Sivard, *World Military and Social Expenditures, 1981*, pp. 11–12.

6 Spurgeon M. Keeny, Jr., and Wolfgang K. H. Panofsky, "Mad vs. Nuts: The Mutual Hostage Relationship of the Superpowers," *Foreign Affairs*, Winter 1981/1982, p. 293.

7 Theodore Draper, "How Not to Think about Nuclear War," *The New York Review*, July 15, 1982, p. 42.

8 See Charles Mohr, "A Scary Debate over 'Launch Under Attack,'" *The New York Times*, July 18, 1982, p. E4.

9 Quoted in *Disarmament Times* 5 (June 29, 1982): 2.

10 See, for example, Martin Tolchin, "4 Predecessors Assail Adelman on Missile Idea; Say ICBM Stand Could Hurt Talks in Geneva," *The New York Times*, June 23, 1983, p. 1.

11 See, for example, Tom Wicker, "The Real Star Wars," *The New York Times*, May 24, 1983, p. A25.

12 Richard Halloran, "Pentagon Draws Up First Strategy for Fighting a Long Nuclear War," *The New York Times*, May 30, 1982, p. 1; and "Revised U.S. Policy Said to Focus on 'Prevailing' over the Russians," *The New York Times*, June 17, 1982.

13 For example: "Some administration officials have said that they expect the Soviet Union to invade Iran within the decade because Soviet oil production will have begun dropping. In that event, United States strategy would be to threaten the Soviet Union with a direct military confrontation" (Richard Halloran, "Arms Outlay Rise in Soviet is Seen," *The New York Times*, July 21, 1982, p. A5).

14 See Richard J. Barnet, *Real Security: Restoring American Power in a Dangerous Decade* (New York: Touchstone, 1981).

15 Sivard, *World Military and Social Expenditures, 1981*, pp. 18–21.

16 Ibid. See also Emma Rothschild, "The Economics of the Arms Race," *The Arms Race and Us* (New York: The Riverside Church Disarmament Program, 1982), pp. 8–13.

17 Hans A. Bethe, "The Inferiority Complex," *The New York Review*, June 10, 1982, p. 3.

18 For the latest example at this writing, see Judith Miller, "U.S. Said to Decide against New Talks to Ban All A-Tests," *The New York Times*, July 20, 1982, p. A1; and idem, "U.S. Confirms a Plan to Halt Talks on a Nuclear Test Ban," *The New York Times*, July 21, 1982, p. A1.

19 See "U.S. Nuclear Strategy and World Order Reform: An Interview with Louis René Beres," *Macroscope*, no. 11 (Spring 1982): 3–6.

20 See ibid; Magnus Haavelsrud, *Approaching Disarmament Education* (Guilford, England: Westbury House, 1981), especially the chapter in this volume by Betty Reardon, "The Status of and Recommendations for Disarmament Education," pp. 114–28; see also "The Contribution of UNESCO to Disarmament since the First Special Session of the General Assembly Devoted to Disarmament," Report submitted by the Director-General of the United Nations Educational, Scientific and Cultural Organization to the Twelfth Special Session of the General Assembly, June 9, 1982.

21 See E. P. Thompson, "A Letter to America," in *Protest and Survive*, ed. Thompson and Smith, pp. 3–54; and Henry T. Nash, "Bureaucratization of Homicide," in ibid., pp. 157–59.

22 Wendell Berry, "Standing by Words," *The Hudson Review*, Winter 1980–1981, p. 399.

Beyond Nuclear Numbing

ROBERT JAY LIFTON
Yale University

It is a fact of the greatest absurdity that we human beings threaten to exterminate ourselves with our own genocidal technology. One must never lose that sense of the absurdity, the madness, the insanity of it. In fact, all work in nuclear areas has to combine a sense of that absurdity with a pragmatic, everyday struggle to do something about it. This struggle begins with our confronting the issue of what the bomb does to our minds and our mental ecology, and that includes the terrible question of the bomb's ability to impair our capacity to confront it.

In our universities, we have done virtually nothing to address the situation, to explore it as compassionate thinkers and scholars. This is an intellectual and moral scandal, and we should not forget that. A provost of a small college upstate who was also awakening to this idea recently wrote to me on just that score. He said, in effect: "I have a minor nightmare that in the year 2050 there will be some hypothetical survivors looking in disbelief at our 1980 and 1981 catalogs. It's as if, living on the edge of the cliff, the Academy seemed not to care." Now there are reasons for that. There are many reasons, but I think they all stem from a single basic matter. We are accustomed to teaching as a form of transmitting and possibly recasting knowledge. And in the service of that we form various narratives and interpretations of that information. But we have no experience teaching a narrative of potential extinction of ourselves as teachers and students, of our universities and schools, of our libraries and laboratories. So our pedagogical or teaching impulse instinctively and understandably shies away from such a narrative. Yet we do so at a terrible cost; we have no right to shy away from it. I will try to sketch in some of the dilemmas that we teach from, and also some of the possibilities for learning in our present nuclear predicament.

Today, many of us—perhaps even all of us—share a kind of confusion. Not just confusion about identity, or about formation of self in terms of the ordinary issues of selfhood that we all have to face, but doubts about being itself, about collective human existence. In that sense, teaching and learning in the nuclear age come from or touch a quality of despair. Yet it is also true that that despair, if confronted—and that is a big if—can be a powerful source of the finest kind of teaching and learning. This is a strange moment in our nuclear situation. One could depict it in broad strokes this way: On one hand, the danger of nuclear war is greater, perhaps, than it ever has been. Anybody close to the weapons situation more or less attests to that. This has to do with nuclear saber-rattling on our part and sometimes on the part of the Soviet Union. It has to do with the proliferation of nuclear weapons by the two nuclear superpowers. Of course there is proliferation in other countries as well, but it is impossible to restrict international proliferation if we do not first restrict it among the nuclear superpowers. Then there is the tense political climate and the threat and counterthreat that we see constantly emanating from these two camps, along with a massive tendency toward something like expectation of nuclear war. One has to face that tendency and confront it.

Each of us, looking at friends or inside himself, can see a pattern something like this: I let the bad news—the danger—in, because I cannot keep that actuality out for too long. Then I feel anxious, and one of the sources of anxiety is the inner question of whether I do anything about that very anxiety. The psychological temptation all too widespread is to move toward the safe ground of resignation or even cynicism—waiting for the bomb, expecting it, declaring that it is inevitable, and, of course, in that process contributing to its occurrence. The most sophisticated expression of this kind of pattern is found in our universities. I recently gave a seminar at a college and was talking informally afterward at a faculty luncheon. Somebody with a very sophisticated style of academic resignation said: "Well, look, what's so special about the human species? There's nothing in evolution that says a species has to last forever; other species have come and gone. So maybe the way to look at this is that our species may have come to the end of its reign, or the end of its story." What this faculty member was expressing is a kind of convoluted, intellectualized acceding to—something like the inevitability of—nuclear war. And again that kind of attitude contributes to the possibility of it.

Still, it is also true that at this time there is a partial breakdown in the denial and numbing. People are beginning to doubt the rationalizations put forward by our political and military leaders. People throughout the world are becoming more fearful and appropriately so of the threat of nuclear war. This growing concern has even become apparent in various public debates and presentations of the major networks in this country. Yet there is a call for more and greater denial on the part of our leaders, more and greater numbing. They do not want us to address this issue. It is as if our leaders have medieval attitudes in addressing postmodern technological and genocidal issues, and they call it an American Renaissance. There are struggles in all this between knowledge and refusal of knowledge, and that is a direct issue for us as teachers and students. And there are struggles between confrontation and denial, between feeling and numbing. Our task as teachers and students could possibly be put in a very simple phrase—to try to do what Martin Buber called "imagine the real." Can we imagine the real? Can we overcome the impediments to and the unprecedented demands on our imaginations in order to imagine the reality? And that is using *real* and *reality* very differently from the way in which some of our ostensible realists (who turn out to be wild romanticists—and dangerous ones at that) use it. Our task as teachers and students is to struggle toward imagining the real; that is a central question if we are to teach or learn anything, and if we are to act.

Here I want to emphasize that I do not mean teaching and learning as a substitute for action, but as a form of action that in turn leads to further action. I have been involved in the doctor's movement and have been trying to think about the healing imagination. Of the various issues and arguments we have put forward, the most important concerns whether a physician should step out of his one-to-one office situation or client situation with his patient in order to move into this difficult realm of addressing nuclear war. And we, of course, insist that this is the central issue for us as healers, and we hold to that in our doctors' movement. But the same situation applies to teachers: whether they can move from standard classroom habits toward this larger question. Perhaps this situation is epitomized by Dick Gregory's reply to someone at an antinuclear rally who asked him "What are you doing here? Why don't you just limit your efforts to Black Power?" "Hell," Gregory replied,"if I go to a Black Power rally in the morning and they drop a bomb at noon, won't be no Black Power rally in the evening to go to." There is a lot of wisdom in that, and it is the same for us as teachers.

I have also, I must confess, been very much influenced in thinking about these questions by recent work I have been doing on Nazi doctors during the European Holocaust. It is a very different situation, but one can see a certain similarity and draw lessons from the Nazi extremity, and especially the Nazi doctors. One very important lesson is that the Nazi doctors that I have interviewed were all very ordinary people. They teach us that it is possible for very ordinary men and women who are not inherently demonic to engage in demonic pursuits—for healers to become killers. And it can be said that among the Nazis, teachers and other professionals with pride in their professions could lend themselves to mass murder. The majority of teachers in the universities in Nazi Germany did not actively take part in mass murder, but they sat back and did virtually nothing, or accommodated themselves or went along. There is a lesson in that for us. Now. Here.

I want to address three areas central to any discussion of these issues. First, I want to convey something about Hiroshima and what that experience was like. Second, I want to consider the impact of the existence of nuclear weapons on us—even without their being used again; and third, I want to point to some hopeful developments, toward a change in consciousness.

But before I do all of that, I have to tell a story. One needs stories.This one is not exactly funny—in fact, it could be called gallows humor. It is about a Jew who is the only remaining survivor of a pogrom in czarist Russia. He is called before the czar and the czar says to him, "You look like a nice fellow, even though you are a Jew, and as a gesture of leniency, I'm going to give you your choice of how you wish to die." The Jew thinks about it for a moment and then answers: "Well, as an expression of gratitude for your leniency, and to save everybody trouble, I choose old age." That could be another central theme of this discussion: the desire for us all to reach old age, and to let our children and their children and so on to live to a rich old age.

I arrived in Hiroshima in the early spring of 1962, and the first thing I found there seventeen years after the dropping of the bomb was very simple. Here was one of the great and tragic turning points of human history, the first use of a nuclear weapon on an undefended population, and the problem of psychological effects had not been studied. There were studies of the physical aftereffects, and there had been some brief studies of psychological patterns, but there had not been an overall study of the psychological and social effects in a systematic way. I was able to stay and do that study, and from that experience I developed a rule of thumb, which is only slightly exaggerated if at all: The more important a subject is, the less likely it is to be studied in our academies or elsewhere. Why?

I think there are two reasons. One is that a subject like Hiroshima is very unpleasant; there are disturbing and threatening dimensions involved in studying it. But second, to study Hiroshima you have to alter your assumptions, your presuppositions, your conceptual apparatus. You have to change your way of looking at things as a professional, your way of looking at the world as a professional—and most professionals do not want to do that. They would rather not study these things. The same kind of question can be raised about teaching. Is it true that the more important a subject is the less likely it is to be taught? That may not always be true; there are teachers who teach very important subjects—but when you look at the nuclear weapons issue, it gives one pause.

What I found in Hiroshima can be summarized in four stages. The first stage has to do with death immersion. From that one moment, that split second of exposure to the atomic bomb on the hot summer morning of August 6, survivors experienced a lifelong encounter with death that is still very much with them. The first stage of that encounter with death had to do with being exposed to the grotesque scenes of the dead and near-dead and the sense people had that they would likely die, but also that everything was dying. As one survivor, a physics professor whom I interviewed, put it: "My body seemed all black. Then I thought, the world is ending." That sense of the end of the world, which we used to consider limited to some kind of mental aberration, something like psychosis, is now an all too understandable response to situations that we can create with our destructive technology. The second phase had to do with the experience people had days, weeks, months after the atomic bomb had fallen. People who had been initially untouched physically developed horrible and grotesque symptoms of bleeding from all of the body orifices, bleeding into the skin, loss of body hair, and the onset of severe diarrhea, weakness, high fever, and in many cases death. These symptoms were acute radiation effects but people were mystified by them. They did not know what caused them, and they thought it was some kind of strange epidemic or poison. Of course they were right. The ordinary people called it "invisible poison." Eventually intellectuals came to call it radiation. But it gave people the sense that this weapon not only killed and maimed on an unprecedented scale, but left something in your bones that could strike you down at any time.

The third stage occurred not months but years after the dropping of the bomb, with the discovery first made three years later that various forms of leukemia were increasing in incidence among survivors who had been significantly exposed to radiation. And then it was discovered over subsequent decades that various forms of cancer, including common forms (thyroid, stomach, lung, uterine), were increasing. The numbers were still relatively small, but this discovery generated a psychological effect of fear because of the survivors' sense that a poisonous substance left in the bones could kill years, even decades later. Increased incidence of cancer is still being discovered because the delay in cancer onset is very great and can be many decades. That fear, of course, extends into the next generation, because it is known that radiation effects can be transmitted genetically. Studies of comparative populations have not shown clear-cut increase of abnormalities in the second generation, but there are abnormal chromosomal effects that make one suspicious and worried. When I was back in Hiroshima a little over a year ago, and I spoke to people there, they said, "Well, maybe the second generation's all right, but we don't know about the third." In other words, the inner fear is endless; it goes on and on, and no reputable scientist or authority can say with assurance that there will not be subsequent effects. We do not know.

The fourth and final stage has to do with the lifelong identity one has as an atomic bomb survivor or *hibakusha,* as they are called by the Japanese. They have what I call symbolic reactivation when there are bomb tests or when various issues come up that relate to their experience of August 6, 1945. When such associations occur—and they are not infrequent—survivors are likely to reexperience all of the symptoms and fears that they had from the time of the first exposure. They can also retain various forms of guilt—questioning why they survived while others died, why they could not save more people, and also just a gnawing discomfort on the border of guilt that survivors often feel.

Even a description as brief and cursory as this can, I think, convey that the moment of exposure to this first "baby" bomb affected people for a lifetime. At the end of my study on Hiroshima, *Death and Life,*[1] I spoke of Hiroshima and Nagasaki as a last chance, a nuclear catastrophe from which we can still learn, from which we can derive the knowledge that could contribute to holding back, perhaps preventing, the even more massive extermination that these events seemed to foreshadow. That is our situation now; it is our opportunity as teachers and students. Hiroshima is important to us: It is a text for us and we must embrace it and learn from it.

Yet one must ask, where is Hiroshima being taught? Where are these images that are given to us from Hiroshima at such tragic cost to the victims seized upon, studied, learned from? Not too many places. And there are problems about Hiroshima too. I said it was a text for us. It is a text intellectually and morally in terms of what it can teach us about nuclear war, and it is a passionate narrative that we must learn from. But it is not an adequate text. We know very well that our weapons have 100 to 1,000 times the strength in both destructive power and radiation poisoning of those baby bombs dropped on Hiroshima and Nagasaki.

Despite that, there are important truths that we learn from the Hiroshima experience, and these are truths of the nuclear age. First, there is the totality of destruction from a single weapon, from a single plane. Tokyo was also leveled, as was Berlin, but by many hundreds of planes, many hundreds of weapons. Second, there is the unending lethal influence of the weapon—the radiation effects that go on and on with the accompanying fears that I have mentioned. Third is the sense of being identified as victims of an ultimate weapon that is not really a weapon but a force that threatens the species. Here one has to ask a question. Would foreknowledge help? If there were to be another nuclear disaster, would knowledge of what would happen in the disaster help people to experience the disaster? Ordinarily we would say yes. If you are experiencing a tornado or a flood, you want to imagine in advance what will happen in that situation and prepare yourself for how to act—that helps you enormously in terms of physical aid to others and psychological experience during the event. But not quite so for nuclear weapons. It would not help one to know all these things about the effects of radiation and massive destructive power.

Here we come to a mythical absurd trio of expectations, really illusions or falsehoods. One of them is that psychological preparation is useful for actual nuclear disaster. This is not true. The second is that civil defense will protect us from it—not true at all. The third is that medical help will restore survivors. This is the falsehood that we in the doctors' movement are trying to eliminate. We say we will not be around to patch you up after nuclear war. We will be dead and you will be dead and if there are any of us around, nobody in the band of survivors living at a stone-age level will be in a situation where healing is possible. Those are three central illusions one has to address in teaching and learning. At the heart of the difference between Hiroshima and the present is the illusion of limit and control. It is a simple fact that once the weapons are used, they are uncontrollable and without limit to their destructiveness; there are enough to literally destroy life on earth, human and most animal. The fact is that at Hiroshima there was an outside world to come in and help. One bomb leveled the city, and it is quite true that there was a total breakdown of the social and communal structure of Hiroshima. The whole web of institutions and arrangements necessary to the functioning of any human group disappeared. But because of the intervention of an outside world, that social breakdown could be temporary and Hiroshima could indeed be rebuilt, and has been rebuilt. People rushed in from nearby areas of Japan and offered help, including medical help. Some help, though little and late, came from the American Occupation. Can one really be sure or even think it possible that there will be an outside world if there is nuclear genocidal exchange of any level given our present nuclear arsenals? Of course not.

Much of our teaching and learning must involve questioning false assumptions about nuclear war and what would happen. The concept of limited nuclear war is not new; it began with the very development of the weapons. Some of the earliest discussions of limited war were written about twenty years ago by Edward Teller and Herman Kahn. Teller, for instance, in his extraordinarily misleading book *The Legacy of Hiroshima*, writes that "rational behavior consists of the courage to use nuclear weapons where tactically indicated," and that is still of course our present policy with so-called limited nuclear war. It then follows, in Teller's argument, that "being prepared to survive an all out nuclear attack is what we should strive for."[2] I must say to Teller that this kind of rational behavior—notice the use of the word *rational*, as he defines it—is nothing more than the logic of madness, and really deadly madness at that.

Similarly, Herman Kahn in his book on thermonuclear war calls for a reasonable or "non-hypochondriacal" response to nuclear war, and says that we should be prepared to experience nuclear war with some equanimity, that we will not be exposed to much more risk than we are in peacetime. He goes on to say that in order to prevent—"undo" is his word—the fear of radiation in a nuclear attack, each person should be supplied with an individual Geiger counter-like radiation meter so that his radiation level can be recorded. Kahn explains that "if somebody is complaining of feeling weak or not feeling too well, you look at his meter and say 'You've only received 10 roentgens—why are you vomiting? Pull yourself together and get to work.' "[3] He actually wrote that. Here we must, as teachers and scholars, tell Herman Kahn that nuclear weapons make either corpses or at best hypochondriacs of us all, that this wishful scenario of nuclear recovery has little to do with the way people behave, and that the psychological assumptions here are as faulty as the moral ones. So whether we are psychological professionals or scientists or humanists, it is our task to look into these false assumptions, to take note of the bootlegging of psychological and physical assumptions about nuclear war and about the way in which people would behave and combat them.

In 1945, a new image came into the world, an image of extinguishing ourselves as a species by our own hand, with our own technology. It is what I call the imagery of extinction. That image derived primarily from the atomic bombing of Hiroshima and Nagasaki and from the Nazi Holocaust in Europe. Since World War II, that image has combined with images of possible future holocausts and with apocalyptic kinds of imagery around such things as the possible destruction of our environment (because we know that our environment is susceptible to our technology of destruction) and the drying up of resources such as food and energy.

Some technological prophets had such imagery and there are possibilities for the humanistic imagination at times to anticipate scientific possibilities. For instance, in H. G. Wells's *War of the Worlds,* the novelist wrote about an atomic bomb. It is ironic—and a lesson for us as teachers and students—that Leo Szilard, who was a great scientist and an active antibomb, antinuclear voice for many years, first realized that he and his colleagues could indeed make an atomic bomb by reading Wells. Of course, he knew a lot about physics and it was this knowledge that he connected immediately with what Wells wrote.

But what happens to us in the face of this imagery of extinction? What impact do these weapons have without even being used? As I mentioned earlier, addressing these questions requires us to change or question our basic assumptions. I myself have been changing the way I look at psychological experience because of that 1962 Hiroshima study and have begun to evolve an entirely different model or paradigm around symbolization of life and death. I think that all of us, as teachers or scholars, acknowledge that our ideas and concepts derive, to some degree, from the historical situation in which we live because we are agents, we are children of history. Yet if these concepts are to have any power, we must struggle toward something like universality or at least some generalizing possibility beyond the historical moment. In this sense I think our ideas about nuclear weapons and the entire constellation of physical, psychological, and social experience around them can teach us a great deal about everyday life, about psychology, history, and humanistic endeavor in our contemporary moment. If one begins to ask how these weapons have affected us just by their existence and how this imagery of extinction has affected us, I would say something like this: We need first of all a model of psychological behavior that looks not only at the nitty-gritty everyday experience, what I call proximate experience, but also at larger or ultimate experience—at the connections of the self beyond the self, or what I take to be an ordinary human requirement of feeling connected to those who have gone before and those who will go on after our finite limited life span. That need is not always fully conscious, but it is there. Ordinarily this imagery of larger connectedness, what I call the symbolization of immortality, is expressed in five general modes. There is the biological (or biosocial) mode, the sense of living on through or in one's sons and daughters and their sons and daughters in an endless chain of biological attachment that can come to include group, tribe, organization, people, nation, or even species. A second mode is theological, the idea of transcending death through spiritual attainment, whether or not including specific imagery about life after death. The third mode is the creative, the sense of living on in one's work or works, whether notable artistic or scientific creations or more humble human influences. A fourth mode involves living on in nature itself, as part of the theme of "eternal nature" emphasized in all cultural traditions. Finally, there is the mode of a different order: experiential transcendence, a psychic state so intense that time and death disappear. It is the classical mode of the mystics, involving principles of ecstasy or "losing oneself."

The presence of nuclear weapons makes us begin to doubt all these modes, because from the age of five or so, we are exposed to imagery of extinction. Who in our culture can be sure of living on through our children or our works when we can imagine the possibility of the extermination of everything in nuclear holocaust? Even eternal nature is susceptible to our pollution and our weapons. That is one reason we so desperately embrace the experience of transcendence in a direct way. This experience too, traditionally made available to cultures, has been denied in postindustrial cultures, but now it is seized upon with desperation whether in the drug revolution or in the search for altered states of consciousness. The issue here is a radical sense of futurelessness, and we need a sense of human future if we are to function not only in the future but in our everyday lives right now. It is a part of a normative psychological need, and we can see consequences of this need's being unfulfilled. We see projections of space colonies as a substitute for a destroyed earth, or of new religions, or of a new return to nature. In other words, in each of these modes we see some desperate effort to break out of what we take to be an interruption of a continuous process that we require. It is as if everything that happens is in some degree a product of our nuclear age, although nothing can be explained totally by nuclear weapons—we still go through struggles with people we love, and we have ambitions that we seek to achieve, but every issue arises within the context of this double dimension. Here again is where teaching and learning and genuine scholarship should enter to a much greater degree.

There are also direct political problems of great importance for us to begin to look at, and for those who study political problems to study and teach. For one thing, all political issues are infused with a desperate intensity because they could lead to some type of nuclear confrontation no matter where they start, and that has to affect the ways in which leaders address nuclear issues. Jonathan Schell, in his book *The Time of Illusion,*[4] proposes the interesting theory that the entire Watergate experience can be largely explained by confusions about so-called nuclear credibility. He suggests that nuclear credibility is never quite credible and that therefore the leaders develop a near-paranoid fear of those who begin to doubt American policy. Whether or not one accepts his argument, Schell's questions about the way in which nuclear weapons imagery infuses our politics are important.

Difficult issues of secrecy and security are also raised by nuclear weapons. Much of McCarthyism and earlier witch hunts had to do with the struggle around secrecy—with the illusion that one can keep the secret of mass destructive capability from one's ostensible enemy. The concept of national security and the illusions around it are similar. I would say the beginning theme here should be the reverse of what is generally said: More weapons do not bring more security; they bring less security to everybody, especially to those who hold them. We will not have a relevant politics in this country until some political leaders have the courage to say that and just that. And we have to start saying it in our teaching and learning. We still have the freedom to do this in the universities. We can teach and learn along lines that we wish. We have to use that freedom.

An important study was done by Michael Carey, a former assistant of mine and a freelance writer with a background in psychology and history. It confirms on a direct empirical level some of the psychological issues raised by the imagery of extinction. He interviewed people of his generation when they were in their late twenties or early thirties about the nuclear air raid drills held in schools throughout the United States in the 1950s.[5] Carey has collected an extensive library of records and photographs, many of which have been published in a series of articles in the *Bulletin of the Atomic Scientists*. I am sure that many of us can recall those quaint experiences, in which the general tone was: There is the big, bad atomic bomb, but with American know-how and cooperation we can defeat it. The way to defeat it was not to look out the window—that might hurt your eyes—and to take some paper and put it over your head as protection against radiation fallout; if that doesn't work, hide under your desk. Of course, the kids were too smart to believe that and were confused. Carey demonstrates in his work that many were overwhelmed with anxiety. A pattern of fear, nightmares, and terror evolved early on followed by a kind of suppression or numbing toward the whole experience. The effects come out later, when there are nuclear threats in different parts of the world, or during a period of trauma or of loss in one's own life.

From Carey's work and other evidence, certain thematic processes of the greatest importance become apparent. One is the confusion, even equation, of ordinary death with grotesque massive annihilation. This happens just as a child is learning the terrible truth that death is final; you cannot go to sleep and wake up again as a child wants to believe at first. At this time he is also inundated with imagery of extinction, or meaningless death, in which children, adults, and old people all die together without reason. As the idea of dying with dignity becomes a cruel joke, the already difficult matter of coming to terms with one's own mortality is made still more difficult, and that is a grave psychological issue. That is why I called my most recent book *The Broken Connection*.[6] The threat to the connection between living and dying, between the idea of death and the continuity of life, is a major issue for us today.

A second theme is that nothing can be depended on. There are pervasive doubts about the lasting nature of anything. We do not have faith that anything will last, and this lack of faith has contributed to the development of a new ephemeralism. This can be seen in some of the shifts in attitudes toward work, for instance—the hippie attitude in the late 1960s or early 1970s that work is meaningless. Also, there is the present seeming reversal that everybody wants to be a doctor or a lawyer in a safe job haven. I think that they are both part of the same social process in which we are uncertain about what lasts and what work has meaning.

A third perception that can be drawn directly from Carey's work is the theme of craziness. Certainly there is craziness in the situation of the two great world powers waiting to drop these bombs and threatening to exterminate each other and the rest of the world in the process. Of course, that is crazy in a collective sense. It does not require individual psychosis. It is ordinary people who are doing it—and one must remember that. There is also craziness in the remedies suggested to children by the authorities during the drills. There was a perception of craziness in the great explosion of absurdity and mockery that was expressed, sometimes very brilliantly and appropriately, during the uprisings of the 1960s and 1970s.

A fourth theme found in Carey's work and in other parts of the culture is a less healthy one. It has to do with an all-powerful identification with the weapon itself, identifying with its power, or wanting to see it dropped—getting it over with, so to speak, in a Strangelove-like syndrome of waiting for the bomb to go off and wanting to overcome all the anxiety of waiting.

Finally, there is a theme that is perhaps the overriding theme for all of us, since these themes are not solely the possession of those who went through the nuclear drills. This fifth theme is the double life we live in the nuclear age. On the one hand we know that a series of bombs could be dropped that within a moment would destroy us—all of us, everything we have known, loved, or struggled with in our lives, and on the other hand we go about our lives with business as usual as though no such threat exists. To some extent we have to do that, we have to get through the day and take care of our daily tasks. But when we do so in an absolute way it is at a great cost, and I sometimes think of this as not so much an age of anxiety as an age of numbing, because there is an increasing gap between knowledge and feeling.

A lot of numbing or diminished feeling disseminates from this fundamental issue, and that is something we have to address. The category of psychic numbing is useful, I think, because it is so central to what we confront in our age. Although we have psychoanalytic concepts such as denial and repression, it is helpful to have one overall term for all kinds of diminished feeling. I developed that concept from survivors who experienced the bomb in Hiroshima. They described to me how right after the bomb fell they saw people dying around them, they knew they were dying, they knew something horrible was happening, but they suddenly ceased to feel, underwent what one woman writer described as a "paralysis of the mind." I began to see psychic numbing as a defense mechanism necessary to them, but then I began to wonder about the people who make the bomb and about the rest of us. And of course numbing to a greater or lesser degree, by physicist or engineer, is absolutely necessary to the making of the bomb. The same holds true for political and military leaders who consider the projected use of those bombs, but also for the rest of us as the constituency of these people who do not do enough to prevent it from happening. Numbing has to do with exclusion and there are two ways of looking at it. One is the blockage of images because they are too painful, as in the case of Hiroshima survivors and many of us around nuclear weapons. The other is a related but different kind of issue: the inability to imagine, to imagine the real, because we have no precedent for it. We have never experienced anything like a nuclear holocaust so it is very hard for us to imagine what it would be like. It is why visual experience like slides of Hiroshima or the Hiroshima experience in general—despite its representing a baby bomb rather than the bombs we now have—still has enormous value for our teaching and learning in the nuclear age. And of course the numbing extends to our professions, to students and teachers as well. It is necessary, I think, to break out of the numbing and begin to teach and learn about these issues.

The worst kind of development, and perhaps the most obscene dimension of the nuclear age, is nuclear fundamentalism or nuclearism. It has to do with the worship, literally the deification, of the very agents of our potential destruction.

If we study the history of Protestant Fundamentalism in this country, we find it is essentially a twentieth-century movement that had its origins in a concern that the fundamentals of the Christian faith were being lost. However, there is a more general principle here. When fundamentals are threatened, you embrace something called fundamentalism in which you concretely put forward as absolute dogma those tenets that are being threatened. We see nothing less than a worldwide epidemic of fundamentalism right now, in this country with many of the religious or pseudo-religious cults, and certainly on all sides in the Middle East and in other parts of the world. Fundamentalism is dangerous because it responds to the failing symbolization of connectedness, or symbolic immortality, with an absolute claim of truth and of a single path and a beginning claim to have the right to destroy all those who do not agree with it. Moreover, some of the fundamentalist groups can even embrace the Armageddon of nuclear weapons as part of their own cosmology, by creating the illusion that somehow they will survive out of some kind of elite spirituality that they claim for themselves.

Fundamentalism and its relationship to nuclear weapons is a central issue. But the most disturbing form of fundamentalism is the fundamentalism around the weapons themselves. I call this nuclearism, the worship of the weapons as deities, deities that of course can destroy all but that also can presumably create, as any deity worth his or her name must do. This may sound extreme, but just read some of the literature on the reactions of people who have watched a nuclear test or those who received the news of the nuclear explosions on the two Japanese cities. There is a kind of awe and an effort to evoke Biblical imagery and then an admiration of the beauty. You see nuclearism carried out when the weapons are used in attempts to win diplomatic games that cannot be won. Nuclearism then becomes a form of the worship of technology as a source of obtaining force that we seem to have more difficulty attaining in more direct human terms.

Here again I have to invoke Edward Teller. He wrote in *The Legacy of Hiroshima*[7] that radiation from test fallout is very small and its effect on human beings is so little that if it exists at all it cannot be measured. It might be slightly harmful to humans or it might be slightly beneficial, and it might not have any effect. What I am trying to convey is how nuclearism, the worship of the weapons themselves, can distort a mind as great as Teller's and make him say utter nonsense. This worship can lead to a glorification of the bomb, an embrace of the bomb, and a dependency on the bomb, a sense of the bomb as a diety that can destroy and also create—which is one of the reasons, for instance, we are so loath to give up so-called nuclear energy for peaceful purposes, even as we see its danger and its absurdity in terms of economics. So nuclearism, the worship of these weapons, which is not limited to the United States or to the Soviet Union—all countries that seek a bomb are infected by this process, is the most indecent, the most grotesque corruption of power in our time. We have to examine it, explore ways in which it occurs, and confront it.

Despite all these troubling psychological aspects, something positive and hopeful is happening, and I would characterize the situation now as both desperate and hopeful. Both of those dimensions are needed, I think, to address it properly. John Dunn, the contemporary Notre Dame theologian, asks: What story are we in? What he means by that is, what happens to us and what do we become? It is a story of the human imagination, and one thinks of Yeats's words, "Oh Lord, let something remain."

At the heart of the story and the struggle is our quest for awareness—awareness is the key. What is awareness? One meaning of it is being cognizant of danger, being wary. The other side of it, however, the more recent meaning, is insight, understanding, illumination that takes one beyond what is given. That is what we must seek; that is what is involved in imagining the future and imagining the real, and this is beginning to happen. Today we see a groundswell from within our culture with grass-roots elements, but why has it taken so long? Obviously, the threats and the dangers we have heard about are awakening people to danger. Another way of looking at it is that the tired, numbing process collectively maintained is itself under duress, and well that it is, because we need a beginning degree of tension bordering on anxiety to motivate us to take action. Again, as teachers and students these are issues we have to explore.

There is a significant individual step that each of us must take, the movement from that destructive and self-destructive stance of resignation and cynicism toward a stance of addressing the problem, of seeing oneself as responsible to the problem of joining with others and taking a stand. It is often a significant personal watershed, and it is one that one has to think about, because awareness includes self-awareness. This partly includes something I am beginning to think of as a form of faith, even a form of secular faith. One has to have the faith to imagine a human future without nuclear war, and then to feel power, authenticity, and vitality in that active imagination in teaching and learning and action; yes action, and strong action.

People are hungry for truth because they feel the threat and the tension. They want to hear what is going on underneath to cause that threat and, as we found in the doctors' movement, they are more responsive than ever. That can take place in our professions, in our teaching and learning, and we can then, I think, return to ourselves as true teachers, as true students, because the scholarship and teaching are of a central moral concern, as they always should be. It is what gives them power. Even from pure professional self-interest we ignore these issues at our peril, because if we numb ourselves to the forces that threaten the existence of our individual group and species, how can we call ourselves students of humankind, how can we call ourselves teachers with any kind of wisdom? We cannot. Strangely enough, and maybe not so strangely, when we begin to address and confront these grim issues of death and holocaust it also has the effect of putting us more in touch with what we most value in life—with love and sensuality and creative realization and the capacity for life projects that have meaning and significance for us. So my call, our call, is not for a death trip, but really quite the opposite. It is to affirm the personal and professional and intellectual efforts that we need to make on behalf of this wondrous and fragile entity that we call human life.

I want to close with two poems, because the poets can say this better than any others. The first is a painfully ironic statement by a gifted young poet, "Why We Should Drop the Bombs," by Alia Johnson:

It would be so exciting,
It would be so powerful,
It would punish us for our sins
Things wouldn't be so boring any more.
We would get back to basics
We would remember who we love.
It would be so loud,
It would be so hot.
The mushroom clouds would rise up.
We could start over.
We wouldn't have to be afraid
  of it anymore.
We wouldn't have to be afraid anymore.
We would finally have done it.
Better than Raskolnikov.
It would release our anger in the ultimate
  tantrum and then we could rest.[8]

Then, finally, some words of Paul Celan, who is one of the great Holocaust poets of Europe:

Speak, you also,
speak as the last,
have your say. . . .

Look around:
look how it all leaps alive—
where death is! Alive![9]

Notes

1 Robert Jay Lifton, *Death and Life* (New York: Simon & Schuster, 1967).

2 Edward Teller with Allan Brown, *The Legacy of Hiroshima* (Garden City, N.Y.: Doubleday, 1962), pp. 244ff.

3 Herman Kahn, *On Thermonuclear War* (Princeton, N.J.: Princeton University Press, 1961), p. 86.

4 Jonathan Schell, *The Time of Illusion* (New York: Alfred Knopf, 1976).

5 See Michael J. Carey, "The Schools and Civil Defense: The Fifties Revisited," pp. 115–27 of this volume.

6 Robert Jay Lifton, *The Broken Connection* (New York: Simon & Schuster, 1979).

7 Teller with Brown, *The Legacy of Hiroshima*.

8 Alia Johnson, "Why We Should Drop the Bombs," *Evolutionary Blues* 1, no. 1 (1981).

9 Paul Celan, "Speak, You Also," *Paul Celan: Poems*, trans. Michael Hamburger (New York: Persea Books, 1980), p. 85.

Teaching Peace

RICHARD J. BARNET
Institute for Policy Studies, Washington, D.C.

The teaching profession has failed to prepare young people to live in the nuclear age. We do not have courses that explain the most important fact of our era—that ours is the first generation in human history with the theoretical capability to end human history. Only recently, in works such as Jonathan Schell's *The Fate of the Earth,* has the general public had even an intimation that this stunning possibility sets our time apart from the rest of human history. So much official talk about nuclear war has a sedative purpose. It calms, placates, and immobilizes public opinion. The self-protective instincts of our species are numbed by nuclear-speak. Officials talk of megaton weapons almost as if they were bows and arrows, and our citizens are ill equipped to evaluate what they say, to ask the pertinent questions, and to respond.

Teachers of history and civilization have been unable to convey the special character of the time in which we live. Our young people do not see their generation within its historical context, and therefore they cannot grasp either the unique dangers or the unique opportunities of their own time. No one should enter high school without having had instruction on the characteristics of nuclear weapons and their effects. Citizens must have a realistic understanding of these weapons. But the information should be imparted in a way that does not breed hopelessness and despair. The only way this can be done, it seems to me, is to put the present security system based on the nuclear threat beside alternative security systems, for example, increased reliance on international law, conventional weapons, nonviolence, and so forth, so that students may encounter other visions of how collective security could be organized.

We also need courses on the history of warfare that would trace the evolution of weapons of mass destruction and the doctrines for their use. When and why did humankind embark on a project of reducing the cost of mass destruction of which the hydrogen bomb is the culmination? Why have we equated political power with the capacity for mass destruction? Is this development related to the emergence of modern democracy? Of mass-consumption culture? No one has a very good theory about this, but we are unlikely to get the theory to enable us to understand the destructive impulses of the species until we begin asking the pertinent questions at a deeper level.

We should be teaching diplomatic history as case studies of the war system in operation. Why has there been, so far, only one use of nuclear weapons in war? Why has the bomb not been used deliberately to incinerate people since Nagasaki? In what way has it been used for political purposes? Students should be familiar with the historical circumstances surrounding nuclear threats made by the United States in the Korean War, the Vietnam War, the Berlin Crisis, and the Cuban Missile Crisis, and they should become familiar with Khrushchev's nuclear diplomacy. The historic turning points ought to be pondered. Why did the United States at the end of the war fail to implement either of the two strategies that might have avoided the arms race? It did not elect to carry out a "preventive war" on the USSR. Why not? Nor did it choose a serious disarmament strategy. What were the assumptions of our leaders behind their decision in effect to choose an inevitable arms race? Students should be encouraged to speculate on these matters. They need to think of the dilemma of their generation as the consequence of specific human decisions, not as a mysterious, inexorable historical process.

Case histories are important because the subject we are dealing with is political pathology. There is much evidence that leaders have chosen the disastrous course of the nuclear arms race with their eyes open. We ought to study the prophets of the nuclear arms race, beginning with the nuclear scientists themselves—such as Leo Szilard, who predicted with remarkable accuracy what would happen in weapons development and what the impact on national security would be. It would be interesting to pit the predictions of the disarmament advocates against those of their adversaries. The record will show a consistent complacency among the latter group about the "natural" limits of the arms race, the possibilities of limiting nuclear war or "winning" it. There is a body of expert analysis and prediction over almost forty years to explain why unilateral restraint to stop the arms race was necessary and what the consequences would be if such action were not taken. The ignored counsel of James Franck, Leo Szilard, Henry Stimson, J. Robert Oppenheimer, Herbert Scoville, Paul Warnke, and many others should be examined. Their picture of reality should be put up against the picture that prevailed. The evidence challenging the prevailing national security strategy is not known by most students.

The facts of the arms race must be taught. The few courses that deal with this material at all are inadequate on two grounds. First, they tend to emphasize the complexity of the arms competition rather than its essential simplicity. It is not hard to find the data about the numbers of warheads, missiles, tanks, that are available to the Soviet Union and to the United States and its allies. It is hard to know what to make of it. Young people are not being equipped to ask the essential simplifying questions about weapons inventories, military budgets, and posture statements that citizens must be able to ask if they are to exercise any control over military or national security policy. Increasingly in business courses students are being taught to read balance sheets and profit-and-loss statements with great sophistication. They are given the tools to protect them from being mystified by numbers. We ought to teach the defense budget in the same way, since for many of us it is our single biggest family investment. The basic questions about whether particular military spending increases or decreases security are quite simple. The popular instinct "enough is enough" that is behind the freeze campaign is healthy, but citizens need to be immersed sufficiently in the data and the tools for understanding the data to bring their intellectual understanding, their instincts, and their moral vision together. One must master enough complexity to understand the essential simplicity of the arms race.

The second inadequacy of the current national security courses I have encountered is that they teach nuclear strategy as if it were scholastic philosophy. Students are encouraged to enter the arcane world of the nuclear strategists and then to follow the debates within the system without questioning the premises on which the whole body of knowledge is based. It is legitimate to debate the relative virtues of "credible first strike posture," "minimum deterrence," "superiority," "parity," and the like, but not without examining the very assumptions behind deterrence theory or delving into its intellectual history. Two generations have grown up believing that something called "deterrence" is an inevitable basis of security without being conscious of the fact that the atomic bomb preceded deterrence theory. The way we think about weapons is influenced by the accidents of weapons development. We need to know more about where these ideas come from. How are they tested? Who benefits from them? Who loses? In other words, we should be using available intellectual tools such as the sociology of knowledge to help disenthrall ourselves from destructive myths of great power. Ideas about the achievement of security have greater impact on this society than does any other set of ideas. Most of our public money is spent implementing them. The peace of mind of our people depends on them. Yet we examine them little.

More and more the arms race is being fought on so-called psychological principles. Weapons are procured not so much to produce a physical impact, for more weapons are not needed to accomplish the theoretical end of everything, but rather for psychological effect. If the reality of "falling behind" is now meaningless, when a thousand missiles more or less make no difference, weapons procurement is defended as a way of changing "perceptions" of reality. If we have more weapons, we will not be so afraid to use our power. Military spending and deployment project national attitudes and these in turn elicit favorable behavior from the adversary. The psychological principles behind such official reasoning appear to fly in the face of much knowledge about human behavior learned from interactions at levels below interstate conflict. At the very least the citizen ought to be exposed to the psychological assumptions behind security strategy and have some basis for evaluating it. We have a great deal of experience with which to evaluate the "bargaining chip" theory of negotiation—that the more you scare the adversary with an arms buildup the more forthcoming he will be in arms negotiations. The evidence as I read it suggests that the theory is as silly as it sounds. But the contrary view should be taught too, along with the supporting evidence.

As important as it is to have a deeper understanding of the arms race as a technological and psychological phenomenon, it is insufficient for deepening our understanding without the study of "the enemy." When I was at college the courses then taught on the Soviet Union were known popularly as "Know Your Enemy." The trouble was and is that such courses, taught from ideological bias, actually make it more difficult to gain understanding of the huge land empire with which we are fated to share the planet or blow it up. Studying the USSR in America in a cold-war climate is extremely difficult, just as studying the United States in Russia in a serious way is, to put it mildly, a formidable task. We need to provide information that will encourage empathy with the Soviet people, yes with Soviet leaders too, without falling into the trap of becoming apologetic or naive. There is a huge body of information to master. Soviet behavior in the arms race, which has been largely imitative of ours, is on the record and that record needs to be known. There is some information about the Soviet military-industrial complex and the role of the military in setting foreign policy. Comparisons of the institutions behind the arms race within the two societies are helpful. Americans need to acquire some sense of the evolution of Soviet society. How does the USSR differ in its foreign policy from czarist Russia? From the Russia of Stalin's day? Where is the Soviet Union going? What impact does our policy have? What are the pressures on Soviet leaders? The more it is possible to study them as rational political figures seeking to juggle many conflicting interests to preserve their power, the more empathy can be developed for them. Without a certain empathy, practical policies of coexistence are not possible. That does not mean sympathy or support for outrageous policies, but increased understanding. For example, it makes a great deal of difference whether the Soviet Union invaded Afghanistan in a defensive reflex to stabilize their frontier or, as the Carter Administration publicly charged, as a first step in the march to the Persian Gulf. Completely different security strategies are dictated in the two cases.

The more we can learn about the Soviet Union, even its oppressive and dangerous policies, the better the prospects of coexistence. Even the facts of the gulag, espionage, repression in Poland, or other inflammatory information are less destabilizing of our relationship than the myths about Russia that have been internalized in our culture. Nothing has engendered more support for militarism in this society than the endless repetition of certain "facts" about the Soviet Union. Their ideology, like Hitler's, requires them to "take over the world." Their leaders have threatened to "bury" us. They will lie, cheat, and steal for their goals because they have no morality. They never abide by their agreements. They cannot be trusted. This is not the place to argue with these "facts," which, a variety of public opinion polls suggest, are after almost fifty years of repetition deeply embedded in the consciousness of our people. But they should be examined and set against bodies of knowledge available about the Soviet Union. Psychologically, we operate in two different planes. We gather "objective" information in an academic setting, but often it does not touch our prejudices. It is the task of good teaching to bridge this gap.

If I had been asked to write this article fifteen years ago, I would have included a similar discussion of China. Of course studying China is useful, but the intensity of feeling about China has disappeared in this country. Yet not so long ago China was more of an "enemy" than the Soviet Union. They were the poor, brutal, fanatical communists with whom, unlike the Soviet Union, we had fought an actual war in the nuclear age—and lost. (In the Korean War, it will be recalled, the Chinese chased General MacArthur from the Yalu River.)

The swift transformation of China from enemy into near ally suggests that not only must we study actual countries that are perceived as adversaries so that we can see them as human beings instead of devils but we must look at the concept of "the enemy." "The enemy" is a classic political organizing principle about which Elias Canetti and others have written perceptively. Recently in the Falkland Islands war we have seen how marvelously useful instant enemies are to harried political leaders. The arms race is maintained as much by political myths that pacify and confuse the public as by the self-serving institutions of the military-industrial complex. In a democracy political leaders could not sell a crippling and hazardous arms race unless public attitudes supported it. It is in fact true that many congressional representatives have supported more militaristic policies than they personally liked because of a fear of being branded "soft" by a political opponent who could whip up public anxiety about "the enemy." If we are to reverse the arms race, we need to understand better the mechanisms by which we are manipulated to support it.

To prevent nuclear war we need to have a better understanding of what I have called the roots of war. What are the forces inside our society and other societies that impel us toward arms races and military confrontation? Students need some insight into the psychological climate of bureaucracies that encourages "toughness" and makes the counseling of restraint a matter of personal and professional risk. The climate inside bureaucracies and deliberative bodies reflects that of the society as a whole. Why is it that there are men sitting in the U.S. Senate today who have counseled dropping the atomic bomb in the Korean and Vietnam wars who remain respected members of the community, while someone like Billy Graham, long on the "most admired Americans" list, must battle to save his reputation as a result of having come out for disarmament and peaceful coexistence with the Soviet Union? There is not much good theory available with which to answer these questions. Citizens are going to have to develop some of the theory themselves, at least some working hypotheses. The important task of teachers is to get them thinking about the structures and the myths that are leading us to nuclear war. Perhaps the most powerful of these myths is patriotism. What constitutes a healthy love of country in a world that has outgrown the national state?

We also need to reflect on two important notions that emerged at the end of World War II. One was the idea that "wars begin in the minds of men." The Cold War has been explained and justified as ideological warfare. Is the Cold War and the military confrontation with the Soviet Union really about freedom? Have we gained or lost freedom in fighting the Cold War? Or are we really fighting for the idea of private property? If so, what are the economic effects of permanent mobilization? There is growing evidence that the military economy distorts the job market, is far less able to generate jobs than almost any other alternative investment, and is inflationary. The emergence of the national security state has fundamentally changed the relationship between business and government. The simple notion that military spending is good for the economy or even good for business in general needs to be examined. We need some clarity about the ideas for which we are supposedly fighting. Much of the support for the arms race is generated by appeals to deep but vague feelings of citizens that in arming we are protecting something precious that we would otherwise lose. Deep anxieties about the collapse of civilization are being enlisted in the service of militarism, the greatest threat to civilization. The illusion that you can fight ideas with weapons is a very old one. Students ought to be introduced to some of the ideological crusades of the past and their consequences. They need to consider the costs of a permanent war economy and national security state in terms of the values that we seek to protect. The "garrison state" thesis of Lasswell, for example, ought to be examined anew.

The second body of thought that ought to be revived is the doctrine of personal responsibility that was developed in the Nuremberg trials. Throughout history statesmen have been able to act out their power fantasies with relatively little personal risk. The gulf between private morality, in which individuals are punished for killing, and state morality, in which the most efficient killers reap the rewards of power, is immense. The idea behind Nuremberg was a practical notion that if leaders could be sure that they would feel the same disastrous consequences as their subjects they would not be so ready to start wars. I would personally favor an international criminal code that would make it a crime for any individual to threaten the use of nuclear weapons. But the issue of personal responsibility for participating in the arms race is a broader one. What are the obligations of scientists, businessmen, teachers, bureaucrats, and so forth, to eschew the short-term career rewards offered by the war system in order to play a role in ending it? What should the individual citizen do? How do we change the social climate so that individuals need not be heroes in order to confront the war system?

The most important function of teaching with respect to nuclear war is to enable men and women to confront that possibility and to participate in a historic process to change the war system. To communicate in such a way as to enable rather than to immobilize is an enormous pedagogical challenge. The two psychological attitudes that perpetuate the arms race are denial and resignation. The mechanisms of denial are protected by an exceedingly thin shell. The sharp increase in the flood of information about the consequences of nuclear war has for millions of people already broken through this psychological defense against horrifying reality. More people than ever know about the consequences of nuclear war and admit that they care.

But immobilization is a far more difficult problem. The very flood of statistics, sickening pictures of atomic victims, and recitals of the horrors of nuclear war that have been marshaled to combat official fantasies about "survival" have the effect of reinforcing deep feelings that nothing can be done. Once people outgrow the complacency of official wisdom they are often overcome by the sheer enormity of the forces that are propelling the world to disaster. It is important also to marshal the evidence that people's actions can make a difference because they have made a difference in the past. Perhaps the closest historical anology to the contemporary antiwar movement is the abolitionist movement that ended slavery. There too an obsolete institution that mocked the professed morality of the day and undermined the economic efficiency of society was supported by powerful interests and powerful myths, but in a relatively short time, as history is reckoned, slavery was ended by the intervention of ordinary men and women. We ought to spend more time studying the heroes of our civilization.

How can teachers speak to the problem of passivity? One way is to encourage students to dream creatively about building an alternative security system. Students should be encouraged to look at conflict areas of the world that could touch off a nuclear war and consider how those conflicts could be demilitarized. How do we broaden people-to-people contact so as to diffuse the image of the enemy? Ideas for promoting peace from Plato to Kant to Roosevelt ought to be studied in preference to the details of wars on which our students spend so much time.

Teaching peace requires familiarizing students not only with a range of practical disarmament ideas but also with the extensive literature on creative nonviolence. Nonviolent resistance has obvious limitations as a security strategy but it is, arguably, considerably less utopian than security strategies based on a nuclear suicide pact. Citizens, young and old, ought to have the opportunity to let their minds play with a range of more hopeful and less destructive security strategies, for the preservation of hope is perhaps the single most important contribution education can make to the preservation of peace.

Finally, a course of study to equip citizens to develop the moral and intellectual strength to participate in the historic movement to abolish the war system must encourage self-examination. The arms race and the war system are deformed answers to the genuine human need for security. There is a connection between feelings of personal insecurity and susceptibility to war propaganda. It takes a secure individual to be able to envisage a future different from that which the leaders are holding out. For a nation to choose peace, its citizens must become peacemakers. For a peace ethos to replace a war ethos, individual citizens need greater insight into their own aggression and greater awareness of the private uses of patriotism and nationalism. It has been said that the institution of war will not be eliminated until human nature is transformed. That is a hypothesis we cannot afford to test, for we do not have the time. The collective madness of war must be addressed at the level of social organization and at the level of the individual, for a nation cannot be secure until its citizens feel secure.

Teaching about Reversing the Arms Race

SEYMOUR MELMAN
Columbia University

In 1972 a major textbook publisher invited me to prepare several chapters on the arms race for an introductory text in political science for college students. The manuscripts that I submitted were sent for review to political science faculty in various American universities and their unanimous judgment was that this material was definitely unsuited for their purposes. The publisher returned my text, together with a check for the work done. In a subsequent telephone conversation, one of the editors explained that the reason they could not accept my manuscript material was that it would render their entire textbook virtually unsaleable in an important part of the projected market.

What was contained in the manuscripts on the arms race that I had prepared? The following were among the principal points of data and analysis that were presented:

pre-World War II U.S. military expenditures amounted to 12 percent of the budget; post-World War II spending ranged between 40 and 60 percent of the federal government's administrative budget;

ways in which the fear and hate engendered by the Cold War contest fueled an arms race;

the policy factors that have determined the main design of U.S. armed forces;

the composition of the military budget;

the nature and composition of U.S. Strategic forces and General Purpose forces;

limits of military power;

location of U.S. military bases and armed forces around the world;

the military assistance programs of the U.S. government;

the role of military assistance in developing countries, and its effects on economic development;

the braking effect of the arms race on economic development;

consequences of the arms race for rule of law;

how General Dwight D. Eisenhower initiated the "military industrial complex";

introduction of the corporate form of central office to the Pentagon under McNamara;

the characteristics of the central office form of management;

characteristics of the U.S. military economy;

effects of a permanent military economy on industrial research, industrial productivity;

who needs a war economy;

twenty economic consequences of the war economy for American society;

effects of the permanent war economy on the character of the U.S. government;

the politics of military power;

the parts of American society that are potential opponents of a permanent military economy.

I think it was significant that neither the publisher nor the various reviewers in departments of political science were prepared to challenge the validity of any particular statement of fact or indicate that any point of generalization was other than a warranted inference from the data that were presented. What then was the source of the manifest discomfort my manuscript aroused? The arms race was not presented as simply an American defensive response to Soviet aggression. Furthermore, the arms race was diagnosed as being a race that could not be won, that in fact was self-defeating: in the short run by its economic effects; and over a longer period owing to the prospect of a nuclear war, which would surely cause indescribable havoc everywhere.

Against the background of this experience, it was no surprise to me to discover, in 1980, from several collections of course outlines dealing with war, peace, defense, and international relations—all in major American universities, that in only seven places in the United States was there a record of courses that mentioned the term *disarmament*. Of those seven courses, two treated the subject for at least two weeks of the semester.

By 1982, the overwhelming majority of the American public was no longer accepting the arms race, the nuclear arms race in particular, as an immutable part of public life. The movement to stop the nuclear arms race (the freeze) has opened up the issue of reversing the arms race with an intensity unseen since the dramatic debates about bomb testing and nuclear fallout that led to the test ban treaty of 1963. But the American public and its principal institutions like the press, the schools, and the government have become ill-equipped for addressing the halting or reversing of the arms race. The chief reason for this is that for twenty years, from 1962 to 1982, serious discussion about reversing the arms race has been strongly discouraged.

In 1962, the U.S. government's Arms Control and Disarmament Agency (ACDA), which had formal responsibility for such planning, formulated—for the last time—a comprehensive proposal for reversing the arms race. That proposal was never negotiated because in October 1962 the Cuban missile crisis cast a pall over such discussion. The key leaders and advisers of the U.S. government at that time emerged from the Cuban missile crisis with the judgment that they had learned how to play nuclear "chicken" and win. In that atmosphere of nuclear-armed euphoria there was no room at all for discussion about reversing the nuclear arms race—which had just been won.

In short order, thereafter, the disarmament section of the U.S. Arms Control and Disarmament Agency was essentially dismantled. At the same time, private foundations and government agencies proceeded to withdraw research support from any topics about reversing the arms race. The conduct of the arms race and ways of regulating it (arms control) became the new fashion in funding. That emphasis has endured to the present day with the result that for twenty years there has been virtually no systematic address in the United States to problems of reversing the arms race. With rare exception, academics and graduate students accepted the Establishment decision: Expertise on disarmament is no path to success.

That fact, at the side of a formidable apparatus of conventional belief about the arms race, is the major hurdle that must be overcome if the growing wish of the American people to stop the arms race is to be fulfilled. I am convinced that American schools, at all levels, can make a major constructive contribution to reversing the arms race. What is required is, above all, a willingness to address afresh and with critical intelligence the array of beliefs that legitimate the arms race.

Textbooks on American history and American government teach that the United States wins wars. Indeed, the history of the United States is made to appear as a procession of military victories. The idea that the United States might not win a war is never discussed. Accordingly, the arms race, seen in that context, is just another race to be won. Since every race is presumed to be winnable, and since the United States has won all the previously described military contests, it is only reasonable for the student to infer that the present arms race, including its nuclear component, can also be won. (During a lecture at one of the schools of the U.S. government's Defense University, I stated that U.S. armed forces had lost the war in Vietnam. An indignant officer rose, declaring: "The United States Army did not lose in Vietnam." To this I replied: "Well, it did not succeed." The idea of losing was clearly uncomfortable to the point of being undiscussable among these well-educated senior officers.)

The United States is a large and rich country. But it is not omnipotent. Nevertheless, omnipotence is precisely the assumption that is constantly implied as the Pentagon's main institutions decline to discuss any part of the large field of subject matter titled "limits of military power." However, an understanding of the main idea of limits of military power is a precondition for giving serious consideration to the idea of reversing the arms race. Here are some of the key ideas that are involved.

LIMITS OF MILITARY POWER

The immense military forces deployed by the U.S. government are nevertheless under constraints owing to factors that are both inherent in nature and manmade.

1. Owing to the unprecedented concentration of energy release with nuclear weapons, it has become possible for the first time to destroy, swiftly, entire communities and entire societies. The nuclear weapon that destroyed Hiroshima (equal to 20,000 tons of TNT) was carried by one airplane. If B-52s were to transport an equivalent of conventional explosives to the same point, 700 planes would be required and the explosive force released would extend over a considerable period of time and be somewhat dispersed geographically rather than occurring at one moment at one place. The Hiroshima-sized nuclear weapon is now considered "tactical" in size, with true strategic weapons ranging up to 1,000 times the power of the Hiroshima weapon. For all that, this capability comes up against a limiting condition: It is not possible to destroy people or a community more than once. Therefore the increasing size and quantity of nuclear weapons yields no definable military advantage.

2. A community or society that is destroyed cannot be politically dominated. Insofar as one traditional objective of military power in foreign policy was to make possible sustained political control of another society, that kind of objective is frustrated by the destructive capability of nuclear weapons.

3. The concentration of energy release made possible by even single nuclear weapons has frustrated the defense side of military operations, in the sense of a shield against attack. For example: During the Battle of Britain in World War II the British won the air war against the German Luftwaffe by their ability to shoot down 10 percent of the attacking planes, for this meant that one plane and its crew were good for an average of ten missions. The Luftwaffe generals were defeated because a plane and its crew could not do enough damage in ten missions to make it worthwhile to expend them at a 10 percent rate.

When equivalent planes carry nuclear weapons, even highly successful defense—even 90 percent of attacking planes brought down—would not constitute an effective shield. Even a few planes coming through with nuclear weapons mean in each instance the destruction of an entire community.

4. Owing to the frustration of traditional military defense, following the availability of nuclear weapons in quantity, military men proceeded to drop the idea of defense as a shield and replaced it with defense as a threat system. *Deterrence* was the name given to the threat system, meaning that the threat of

destruction would suffice to cause the leaders of a hostile state to veto offensive acts against the deterring power.

5. Once nuclear offensive capabilities extend into the overkill range, it is no longer feasible to improve on military effects of the system as a whole by numerous improvements on components of military systems. Before the advent of nuclear weapons in quantity, it was meaningful to improve military systems by a better rifle, a better bullet, a better artillery shell, a better truck, a better tire, a better food ration. The expectation was that all these subimprovements would yield net improvement of capability of armed force as a whole. Once offensive power extends into the overkill range, that classic strategy of "suboptimization" is frustrated because the theoretical capability for destroying something more than once is not a meaningful "improvement."

6. The usefulness of nonnuclear (General Purpose) forces to nuclear-armed states is restricted in the *direct relation of nuclear-armed states to each other.* Insofar as the military commanders of nuclear states are indoctrinated to win, when two such commanding groups face each other in a military contest it is reasonable to expect a swift escalation of the range of weapons destructiveness, for both commanders cannot win at the same time. If officers are indoctrinated to bring up greater firepower to prevent defeat, then greater firepower includes nuclear weapons.

7. The World War II model for the use of nonnuclear weapons for subduing an opponent is not necessarily transferable where an opponent operates by the strategy and tactics of guerrilla warfare. The experience of many countries during this century supports the conclusion that guerrilla warfare can be successful under three conditions: (a) where people are prepared to sacrifice even their lives for a common purpose; (b) where the military-political effort is supported by a part of a surrounding population or a part of a government; (c) where the military-political opponent of the guerrillas finds it difficult to differentiate the guerrilla operative from the surrounding population. Under these conditions even superbly equipped armed forces that wield immense firepower, as the U.S. forces did in Vietnam, cannot necessarily overcome the opponent.

All these factors combine to limit possible uses of military power in foreign relations.

American folk mythology about military omnipotence is matched by a parallel set of beliefs about economic omnipotence. Here are some key propositions: The United States has indefinitely large resources of every sort; the United States can afford guns and butter at the same time; military spending and activity contribute to the general economy (in effect, guns *create* butter). As in the case of military power, it is essential to appreciate the limits of economic power. In March 30, 1982, testimony at the Special Hearings on Economic Implications of the Military Budget (Congressman Ronald Dellums), I presented a statement that included the following analyses and data on limits of production resources in the American economy.

LIMITS OF PRODUCTION RESOURCES

Capital resources used for military budgets. In ordinary industrial-management usage, capital is conventionally understood as composed of "fixed" and "working" capital. The fixed component includes land, buildings, and machinery. The working-capital component comprises the tools, fuel, raw material, purchased components, and working hours of every sort required to conduct production on a sustained basis. Military budgets are important in relation to fixed and working capital because a modern military budget sets in motion precisely the sorts of resources ordinarily understood as the capital of modern industry. A modern military budget is a capital fund.

From 1946 to 1980 the Department of Defense (DOD) budgets totalled $2,001 billion. The planned DOD budgets from 1981 to 1986 are $1,600 billion. One way of appreciating the magnitude of resources involved here is to compare the sum of military budgets, $3,601 billion from 1946 to 1986, with the money value of the reproducible national wealth of the United States (as of 1975), $4,302 billion. This latter sum refers to the money value of all structures, machinery, public and private facilities, business and personal inventories. The money value of the land is not included here. The sum of military budgets 1946–1986 is a quantity of resources amounting to about 83 percent of the estimated money value of everything manmade on the surface of the United States.

Another way of appreciating the size and effects of U.S. military budgets is by comparing the military budgets of the United States and other countries with some indicator of major new capital resources in an economy. For this purpose we can contrast the military budgets of a single year with the gross fixed capital formation achieved by economies during the same period. The latter category is a measure of all new civilian (private and public) structures, machinery, and equipment added to an economy during a given year.

For 1977 (the last year of available data compiled by the United Nations), we observe that for every $100 of gross fixed capital formation in the United States, $46 was separately expended for military purposes. The ratio of military spending to each $100 of new fixed capital formation was $18.90 in Germany and $3.70 in Japan. Obviously, the German and Japanese economies have reaped a benefit from the concentration of their capital-type resources in civilian capital formation.

Within the American economy access to capital resources is limited for industrial managements by their ability to wield finance capital, the money representation of production resources. We are indebted to President Eisenhower for calling attention, in his farewell address of January 17, 1961, to the fact that "we annually spend on military security more than the net income of all U.S. corporations." From 1951 to that date the annual budget of the Department of Defense had, each year, exceeded the net profits of all corporations. That has continued from 1961 to 1981. Hence, the federal managers of the U.S. military economy have wielded, for thirty years, the largest single block of finance capital resources in the American economy.

This concentration of capital resources in behalf of military economy necessarily limits their availability for civilian economic purposes of every sort. Two conditions control this effect. The first is a limitation conferred by nature itself: Materials or energy used in one place cannot, at the same time, be available at another place. A second limitation derives from the character of the products of military economy: Whatever other usefulness may be assigned to them, military products do not add to the ordinary goods and services of consumption or to capability for further production.

As production resources (capital) of every kind were preempted for the military, that became a major spur to deterioration in the U.S. industrial system and its infrastructure. All this was first discussed in detail in my book *Our Depleted Society.** The following is from the opening paragraphs.

> The United States now is the scene of a drama different from that implicit in her confident ideology. A process of technical, industrial, and human deterioration has been set in motion within American society. The competence of the industrial system is being eroded at its base. Entire industries are falling into technical disrepair, and there is massive loss of productive employment because of inability to hold even domestic markets against foreign competition. Such depletion in economic life produces wide-ranging human deterioration at home. The wealthiest nation on earth has been unable to rally the resources necessary to raise one fifth of its own people from poverty. The same basic depletion operates as an unseen hand restricting America's relations with the rest of the world, limiting foreign-policy moves primarily to military based initiatives. . . .
>
> The price of building colossal military power and endlessly adding to it, has been the depletion of American society, a process now well advanced in industry, civilian technology, management, education, medical care, and the quality of life. The prospect of "no future" has become a permanent part of government security policies that depend mainly on the threat of using nuclear weapons. Never before were men made to feel so powerless, so incapable of having a voice over their own fate. . . .
>
> Americans have believed that our nation is so wealthy and so productive that there is no possible contradiction between massive military buildups and growing affluence for all. The United States can

**New York: Holt, Rinehart and Winston, Dell Books, 1966. The reader may wish to follow the development of these lines of analysis. See my* Pentagon Capitalism *(New York: McGraw-Hill, 1970), and* The Permanent War Economy *(New York: Simon & Schuster, 1974).*

afford guns and butter; besides, doesn't defense spending put money into circulation? This was learned from three years of U.S. involvement in World War II—an experience different from twenty years of Cold War. The contradiction between guns and butter is now real and measurable. Our able young men cannot, at once, be trainees for the Atomic Energy Commission and physicians in training; they cannot be teaching the young and also designing missile components. The salary money spent by the missile builder goes into circulation, but that does not in the least add to the stock of talent available for civilian work that needs to be done. "Guns" take away from "butter" even in the United States.

In sum, it is my judgment that an appreciation of the limits of military and economic ability in the United States is a vital precondition for addressing reversal of the arms race.

In order to develop a serious understanding of how the present arms race can be reversed it is essential to go back to several official publications of the U.S. government that are, all of them, dated 1962.* That date must be used as a beginning because it was at that point that the U.S. government formulated, for the last time, a comprehensive proposal for reversing the arms race. The idea of reversing the arms race must be differentiated from ad hoc proposals, however meritorious, such as a freeze that would put a halt to new arms production; a reduction of 50 percent in nuclear weapons that would still leave massive overkill on all sides and leaves the "conventional" military forces untouched; developing agreement for a complete (above-ground and below-ground) prohibition on nuclear explosions; barring the production and deployment of particular major weapons systems—MX, cruise missiles,

*In 1961-1962 the newly created U.S. Arms Control and Disarmament Agency was charged with preparing American proposals designed to achieve general disarmament. The agency staff, headed by William C. Foster, had the important support of an eminent advisory committee headed by John J. McCloy, who had but recently retired from the presidency of the Chase Bank. During 1961, McCloy developed, with V. Zorin, the Statement of Principles that, a year later, was used by the ACDA staff to develop the U.S. plan. McCloy wielded his considerable prestige as a leading figure of the American Establishment on behalf of the disarmament principle in addresses to business and political groups. The agency published a series of booklets remarkable for their clarity of advocacy of the disarmament principle: *Disarmament: The New U.S. Initiative,* Publication 8, General Series 5, September 1962—six addresses by senior officials on disarmament; *Toward a World Without War, A Summary of United States Disarmament Efforts—Past and Present,* Publication 10, General Series 6, October 1962—an overview of early post-World War II disarmament efforts and an explanation of the U.S. 1962 disarmament plan; *Blueprint for the Peace Race: Outline of Basic Provisions of a Treaty on General and Complete Disarmament in a Peaceful World,* Publication 4, General Series 3, May 1962—full text of the U.S. disarmament plan with a statement by President Kennedy; *Nuclear Testing and Disarmament,* Publication 3, General Series 2—text of radio-television address made by President Kennedy on March 2, 1962.

neutron bombs. Any one or several of these steps, if implemented, would make some improvement to the alternative of an all-out unrestrained arms race, but as long as the political, economic, and technical dynamics of the arms race are permitted to continue, the only prudent understanding is that we are in for multiplied hazard to the continuance of the human race.

The main desirable criteria for reversal of the arms race include the following. The plan must be comprehensive with respect to all classes of armament and armed forces. That is essential because there is major variation in the composition of armed forces among the great powers. Hence, only an across-the-board formulation of reversal can begin to be politically acceptable. The reversal process must be so designed as to not change the relative relation of armed forces on the way down. The reversal process must include reliable means for inspection and verification. A reversal process requires parallel development of dispute-settling mechanisms of an international character, for it is unreasonable to suppose that a reversal of armament and armed forces will, by itself, eliminate sources of dispute among nation-states. Finally, a reversal process must include some enforcement mechanisms, including appropriate formation and plans for operation of international peace-keeping forces.*

I am sure that it will come as a surprise to many Americans in 1982 to know that the formal proposal for reversing the arms race advanced by the government of the United States in 1962 was deliberately designed to be achieved during a period of about ten years and was framed with the objective of taking down national armed forces to the level of residual internal policing competence. Thanks to the initiative of Congressman Ted Weiss (Dem.) of New York City, the full text of the U.S. proposal for reversing the arms race (1962) was reprinted in the *Congressional Record* of May 25, 1982.

A competent national policy for reversal of the arms race must include provision for coping with conversion from military to civilian economy. There are, after all, about 5.5 million persons on direct military-type payrolls. These include the 2 million members of the uniformed armed forces, 1 million civilian employees of the U.S. Department of Defense, and 2.5 million employees in military-serving industries in the United States.

A sophisticated strategy for economic conversion of factories and military bases—planning and implementation—is reflected in a proposed bill (HR 6618) introduced in the U.S. House of Representatives by Congressman Ted Weiss in the Spring of 1982. The text of this bill reflects a policy designed for comprehensive, decentralized, and economically sound conversion planning. The main components of this legislation include the following.

*I have attached to the present article a short bibliography on disarmament topics. If it appears to be mostly "dated" it is because the whole subject of reversing the arms race has been remarkably unattended during the last twenty years.

Every military-serving factory and base is required to establish an alternative-use committee: 50 percent management nominees, and 50 percent from among the working people. The alternative-use committees are charged with preparing blueprints for changing over the facilities and the people to civilian work, when and as required. The same bill establishes the Defense Economic Adjustment Council, composed of the appropriate members of the Cabinet and representatives of management and labor, and charged with distributing information to facilitate the functioning of alternative-use committees and encouraging the preparation "of concrete plans for non-defense-related public projects addressing vital areas of national concern (such as transportation, housing, education, health care, environmental protection and renewable energy resources) by the various civilian agencies of the government, as well as by state and local government." The bill includes provisions for one-year advance notification of contract termination, and provides funds and machinery for facilitating the retraining of military-industrial employees and relocating these as civilian job opportunities may require.*

In sum, my judgment is that teaching about reversing the arms race requires unlearning some of the main popular preconceptions about unlimited American military and economic power. Second, it requires a thoughtful examination of the comprehensive proposals that have been formulated by or for the U.S. government, and of how these might be improved in keeping with the intensified condition of the arms race in 1982.

Selected Readings

Barnet, R., and Falk, R., eds. *Security in Disarmament.* Princeton, N.J.: Princeton University Press, 1965.

Epstein, W., and Toyoda, T., eds. *A New Design for Nuclear Disarmament.* London: Bertrand Russell Peace Foundation, 1977.

McVitty, M. *A Comparison and Evaluation of Current Disarmament Proposals.* New York: Institute for World Order, 1964.

———. *Preface to Disarmament: An Appraisal of Recent Proposals.* Washington, D.C.: Public Affairs Press, 1970.

Melman, S., ed. *Disarmament: Its Politics and Economics.* Boston, Mass.: American Academy of Arts and Sciences, 1962.

Myrdal, A. *The Game of Disarmament: How the United States and Russia Run the Arms Race.* New York: Pantheon, 1977.

Noel-Baker, P. *The Arms Race.* London: Atlantic Books, 1958.

———. *Disarmament.* New York: Garland, 1971 (original, 1926).

Osgood, C. *An Alternative to War or Surrender.* Urbana, Ill.: University of Illinois Press, 1962.

United Nations. *Disarmament, A Selected Bibliography, 1967–72.* UN Publ. E.73.I.14.

*The text of this bill may be obtained from the office of Ted Weiss in Washington, D.C., or from the office of SANE, 711 G. St. SE, Washington, DC 20003. See references on economic conversion listed below.

———. *The United Nations and Disarmament, 1945–1970*. UN Publ. 70.IX.1.

———. *The United Nations and Disarmament, 1945–1965*. UN Publ. 67.I.9.

Wong, C. *Economic Consequences of Armament and Disarmament (A Bibliography)*. Los Angeles, Calif.: Center for the Study of Armament and Disarmament, California State University, 1981.

World Law Fund. *Current Disarmament Proposals*. New York: Institute for World Order, 1964.

Wright, M. *Disarm and Verify*. New York: Praeger,1964.

Wright, Q., Evan, W., and Deutsch, M., eds. *Preventing World War III: Some Proposals*. New York: Simon & Schuster, 1962.

Selected Readings on Economic Conversion

Cambern, J.R., and Newton, D.S. "Skill Transfers: Can Defense Workers Adapt to Civilian Occupations?" *Monthly Labor Review*, June 1969, pp. 21–25.

The Conversion Planner. Bimonthly newsletter of action on economic conversion. SANE, 711 G. St. SE, Washington, D.C. 20003. Subscription: $5.00 per year.

Disarmament Commission, Soviet Peace Committee. *Socio-Economic Problems of Disarmament*. Vienna: International Institute For Peace, 1979.

Dumas, L.J. "Economic Conversion, Productive Efficiency and Social Welfare." *Journal of Sociology and Social Welfare* 4, nos. 1–2. March 1977.

The Economic Impact of Reductions in Defense Spending. Summary of Research Prepared for the U.S. Arms Control and Disarmament Agency, Publication 64, July 1, 1972.

Elliott, D. *The Lucas Aerospace Workers' Campaign*. Young Fabian Pamphlet 46, Civic Press Ltd., Civic St., Glasgow, G4 9RH, November 1977.

——— et al. *Alternative Work for Military Industries*. Richardson Institute for Conflict and Peace Research, 158 North Cower St., London NW1 2ND, August 1977.

Jobs from the Sun, Employment Development in the California Solar Energy Industry. A report by the California Public Policy Center, February 1978. (From California Public Policy Center, 304 S. Broadway, Room 224, Los Angeles, California 90013.)

Lucas, An Alternative Plan. IWC Pamphlet no. 55. Institute for Workers' Control, Bertrand Russell House, Gamble Street, Nottingham NG7 4ET, 1977.

Melman, S. "Beating Swords into Subways." *The New York Times Magazine*, November 19, 1978.

———, ed. *Conversion of Industry from a Military to Civilian Economy*. A series in six volumes. Frederick Praeger Special Studies, New York: Praeger, 1970: M. Berkowitz, *The Conversion of Military-Oriented R&D to Civilian Uses;* J.E. Lynch, *Local Economic Development after Military Base Closures;* A. Christodoulou, *Conversion of Nuclear Facilities from Military to Civilian Uses;* S. Melman, ed., *The Defense Economy;* J. Ullmann, ed., *Potential Civilian Markets for the Military-Electronics Industry;* D.M. Mack-Forlist and A. Newman, *The Conversion of Shipbuilding from Military to Civilian Markets*.

———. "Inflation and Unemployment as Products of War Economy: The Trade Union Stake in Economic Conversion and Industrial Reconstruction." *Bulletin of Peace Proposals* 9, no. 4, 1978.

———. *Our Depleted Society*. New York: Holt, Rinehart and Winston, and Dell Books, 1965, chaps. 10–14.

———. *The Permanent War Economy*. New York: Simon and Schuster, 1974, chaps. 8 and 9.

———. *Planning for Conversion of Military-Industrial and Military Base Facilities*. Washington, D.C.: U.S. Department of Commerce, Economic Development Administration, Office of Technical Assistance, 1973.

———, ed. *The War Economy of the United States*. New York: St. Martin's Press, 1971, chaps. 26–33; see also bibliography on conversion, p. 244.

Sense about Defence: The Report of the Labour Party Defence Study Group. Quartet Books Ltd.,

27 Goodge St., London W1P 1FD, 1977. (Note: includes a major listing of studies on the UK military economy and conversion prospects and problems.—S.M.)

U.S. Department of Defense, Office of Economic Adjustment. *Economic Recovery: Community Response to Defense Decisions to Close Bases,* 1976.

Wallensteen, P., ed., *Experiences in Disarmament: On Conversion of Military Industry and Closing of Military Bases.* Report no. 19. Uppsala University, Department of Peace and Conflict Research, June 1978. (Note: contains major review article on conversion literature, papers on the United States, the United Kingdom, and Sweden, and bibliographic appendices. —S.M.)

For a copy of the outline of a war economy course, write to: Professor Seymour Melman, Room 304, Mudd Building, Columbia University, New York, NY 10027.

Investigating New Options in Conflict and Defense

GENE SHARP
Southeastern Massachusetts University and Center for International Affairs, Harvard University

UNSOLVED PROBLEMS

Severe dangers still face humanity. Efforts to improve the human condition have often failed. Specifically, we must face the fact that we have failed to solve the four problems of dictatorship, genocide, war, and systems of social oppression. Strong forces work to create a world very different from that which most people want.

In our century we have seen the development of the most extreme forms of dictatorship, including the Nazi and Stalinist varieties. We have seen the rise of modern war with the most destructive forms of weaponry yet to be developed. We have experienced a widespread sense of personal and political powerlessness. We have seen the efforts of social reformers to achieve justice produce very limited results, or even disaster, as they created societies which were (as in Russia) more tyrannical than the old ones. We have seen genocide, which had happened before, conducted massively by a supposedly civilized country. We have seen terror used both to maintain systems and to change them. We have observed and experienced increasing attacks and restrictions on anything that approximates freedom.

Many attempts based upon established political assumptions and policies to solve these problems have been made. Nevertheless, we have not moved significantly toward their resolution. The future prospects in these areas can give us little comfort. The dangers are likely to continue to increase in the coming years. What is happening to the technological capacity of modern weaponry is scarcely imaginable. Future dictators will have far greater means at their disposal for controlling human societies and individuals than did Hitler and Stalin, for example. The technical capacity to kill off people *en masse* is even now much more developed than the means that Hitler's henchmen had.[1]

These problems have become even more serious as the institutionalized and

I am grateful to Robert Irwin and Gregory Bates for suggestions and criticisms for this article. This article was originally published jointly by the Teachers College Record *and* Social Alternatives *(Australia).*

technical capacities for such violence and controls have increased. Yet the means at the disposal of governments to wield violence and to dominate continue to be developed to an extreme degree. As the perception that improvements are possible recedes, individuals and whole societies increasingly see such problems as insoluble and perceive themselves as powerless to shape their futures. Their resulting inaction passes as apathy.

These problems are, however, human problems, created and continued by human beings. Therefore it is within our capacities to reverse direction and to solve them. New thought, greater knowledge, and increased understanding about such problems are needed to help us develop policies and chart a course of action to change this situation.

SEEKING SOLUTIONS

Our task is at least two-fold: first, to find out what is the nature of those problems and what may be required to face all of them collectively (because they may mutually reinforce each other), and then, to learn what are the steps to chart a strategy for change in the face of these four problems. The development of strategies for change for the coming decades will be determined by our view of the basic causes of those problems and therefore what is required to correct them. There are, of course, other grave problems—including those of environment, water, food, population, and destruction of nonliterate cultures—which lie outside this discussion but require attention and action as well, and whose solution would be aided by resolution of the four problems on which attention is focused here.

Those four problems can be viewed as possessing two broad characteristics. One is the capacity for the large-scale use of political violence by relatively small groups of people in command of political machines of internal and international violence. The other characteristic is that much of the population in these countries, and most clearly the victims of this violence and domination, have experienced a widespread and deep sense of powerlessness. Two key parts of the problem are therefore how to remove that violence, or keep it controlled, and how to empower people so that they will be able to gain and maintain control of their own lives and destinies, despite severe threats.

These four problems—dictatorship, genocide, war, and systems of social oppression—are perhaps not separate problems for which separate solutions are required, or even possible, as we have usually assumed. It may be that they are tied together, that they are four expressions of a single problem: the use of organized violence for political purposes.

Political violence here means physical violence used or threatened for political purposes. That includes imprisonment, war, torture, assassinations, *coups d'etat*, terrorism, guerrilla war, beatings, riots, and other forms. The capacity for such violence becomes institutionalized in such forms as prison systems, concentration camps, military forces, militia, political police, and assassination squads.

Without institutionalized political violence, dictatorship, genocide, war, and systems of social oppression could not exist. How could one maintain an oppressive social system without the capacity to arrest the discontented, without facilities to imprison them, or ability to send in troops to put down unrest? How could one have a dictatorship without capacity for internal violence to hold down the enslaved population? Without political violence, major international conflicts would take other forms than modern war. One could not commit genocide without the capacity to kill large numbers of people.

As institutionalized political violence, this violence is not the spontaneous outburst of "aggression" or "frustration." It is the systematic, deliberate organized use of violence by institutions which have been established deliberately to be able to apply that violence. That creates a severe danger which has gone largely unrecognized: when an institution is set up to use political violence for one purpose—even a good one—that same institution can be used for a different purpose. For example, an army organized to defend a country from foreign attack can attack its own government and replace it by a *coup d'etat,* or be shifted to suppress movements for greater internal freedoms or social justice. The institutions of political violence are not tied to a particular purpose, even to their original designated task. Their capacity may be shifted to other uncontemplated or unwanted purposes, sometimes under orders and sometimes autonomously.[2]

Violent sanctions for political objectives are, therefore, integral to some of the most serious problems of our time. At the same time, however, they are intrinsic to modern governments and the State apparatus as requirements for enforcing rule and law internally and for maintaining sovereignty and interests internationally. Violent sanctions are believed to be needed because of the perception that they are the most powerful means of action available.

At the same time, however, grounds for dissatisfaction with violence as the ultimate sanction exist: (1) the destructive capacity of violence has reached unacceptable levels; (2) satisfactory ways to deal with certain types of political violence—such as terrorism, genocide, and nuclear weapons—have not been found; (3) reliance on violence to struggle against an opponent with continued superior capacity for violence tends to force submission, self-destruction, or defeat by attrition; and (4) there are undesirable long-term structural consequences of political violence as the society's ultimate sanction, related in part to the interchangeability of the purposes for which it may be used but rooted also in other factors.[3]

SANCTIONS AND POLITICAL VIOLENCE

If modern political systems depend on political violence to maintain themselves, is it not then impossible to lift this reliance on political violence, and hence impossible to eliminate those four problems?

Clearly, sanctions cannot simply be abolished or renounced. Any society requires some kind of final sanctions. (Sanctions are understood here as means of applying punishment or reprisals for failure to behave in the desired manner.) Within a society people, groups, and the society as a whole require some final sanction to deal with acute conflicts, to enforce certain minimal standards of human behavior, some means of dealing with very destructive and violent acts within a society, and to prevent internal usurpations and suppression. Internationally, a society faces conflicts in which important issues are at stake. The dangers are often very real. Countries do get invaded, even small "innocent" ones striving to be neutral in a wider conflict, and people who were no provocation to anybody have been oppressed, enslaved, and exterminated by foreign attackers.

Sanctions are relied upon either to hold in reserve to facilitate the successful operation of more routine procedures, or to wield directly in face of opposition when regular procedures have failed, are closed, or are inappropriate. Sanctions are used by States to help enforce the obedience of the populace, by the citizenry against the State, by certain nongovernmental groups against others, and by States against each other. Sanctions in domestic and international politics are usually a key element in political power. Most violent sanctions are applied basically as punishments for disobedience or violation of expectations and not primarily to achieve the aim of the original command or wish. But some violent sanctions and more often nonviolent sanctions may be used with the primary intent of achieving the original objective which has been withheld or refused. In many situations simply the capacity to wield, or the threat to apply, sanctions may induce the desired behavior.

Serious issues are often involved in acute domestic and international conflicts. Failures to wage conflicts, or failures to do so successfully, are often of lasting and fundamental significance, as much of the history of the twentieth century demonstrates. When large groups of people and whole countries lack adequate sanctions, they are unable to resist domination by foreign aggressors, internal dictators, or economic oppressors.

There is, then, a legitimate need for some kind of sanctions, some means of protecting against external dangers and of meeting certain internal needs. This need is widely recognized and underlies the support for institutionalized political violence including war. The need for sanctions for at least certain minimal purposes—on which opinions may differ—is such a basic societal need that it cannot be simply removed or renounced. This applies irrespective of the type of social, economic, or political system.[4]

Most people and regimes are confident that in extreme situations in domestic and international politics, political violence—threatened or applied—provides the only available realistic sanction, *the* ultimate sanction offering reasonable chances of effectiveness. This does not mean that political violence has always been welcomed as a positive good. Mostly it has been accepted only as a necessary evil. Recognition of its dangers has led in liberal democracies to legal and constitutional restrictions or prohibitions on the use of political violence. That has not, however, solved the problem since the institutions of political violence can always ignore or defy the restrictions or prohibitions. We have assumed that we had to rely on violence as the only available ultimate sanction, although we did not always like it, although we tried to modify it and make it just, although we tried to restrict it in various ways. People and societies have thus placed their confidence in the very phenomenon which has contributed to such tragic and fundamental consequences.

But is it true that political violence is the only available set of sanctions capable of effectiveness in crises?

ALTERNATIVE NONVIOLENT SANCTIONS

Contrary to the common assumption, a very different type of sanctions also exists which have been widely applied instead of violent sanctions, both domestically and internationally by individuals, groups, social movements, whole societies, and governments in diverse conflict situations. Internationally, nonviolent sanctions have included noncooperation, economic embargoes, diplomatic boycotts, and even nonviolent invasions. Domestically, they have included civilian insurrections, civil disobedience campaigns, strikes, economic boycotts, civil liberties struggles, minority rights campaigns, mutinies, and even nonviolent sanctions for law enforcement. These nonviolent sanctions have been used in widely differing periods of history, cultures, and political conditions, and also for a wide variety of purposes.[5]

This group of sanctions is called the technique of nonviolent action. It includes many types of nonviolent "weapons," or penalties and other pressures, used to oppose or to achieve given objectives. At least 198 specific methods of action have been identified. Actions included in the technique range from methods of mild symbolic protest, through the potentially paralytic forms of social, economic, and political noncooperation, to the large group of diverse disruptive forms of nonviolent physical, psychological, social, economic, and political intervention.[6]

The methods of nonviolent noncooperation include diverse forms of economic boycotts, strikes, and political noncooperation which, when applied with other methods under appropriate circumstances, can produce paralysis of the institutions against which they are directed. These methods can make it impossible for a hostile regime to achieve its objectives. This type of struggle does not, and must not, use violence, for a major part of its working is produced by political *jiu-jitsu* in which violent repression operates to undermine support for the opponent and to increase that for the nonviolent side.

This type of action is based on the view that political power derives from cooperation and assistance of people and institutions. This help may be provided, restricted, or refused to any given institution, policy, or regime. Contrary to popular assumptions, people using the nonviolent technique can operate successfully against a violent, repressive regime *without* needing to shift to violence. The technique has defeated and even destroyed dictatorial systems. Nonviolent action can at times not only alter people's beliefs and opinions, but also gain objectives by the mechanisms of accommodation and nonviolent coercion.[7]

Nonviolent sanctions using noncooperation operate by directly cutting off the sources of power of the opponent. This is possible because all regimes, including the most dictatorial ones, are dependent for the sources of their power upon the people they rule; when obedience and cooperation are withheld or withdrawn, those sources of power are restricted or severed, and in time the regime is thereby disintegrated. Change by accommodation and nonviolent coercion can be achieved because with this technique the population is able to mobilize its own sources of social, economic, and political power and also to undermine the availability of the sources of power of hostile regimes and oppressive rulers. These means, when developed and applied skillfully, can be more effective for social and political goals compatible with popular participation and freedom than is political violence.

These nonviolent means have in particular instances, defeated Nazis, frustrated Communist rulers, undermined dictators, disintegrated empires, battled foreign invaders, and dissolved *coups d'etat*. These nonviolent sanctions and forms of struggle have been applied in many cultures and parts of the world by people who never were, and never became, believers in "nonviolence." Yet, these "common" people were capable not only of great courage but also great power to determine their own present and future.

Therefore, despite the violence of our age, we are not without resources for developing alternatives to political violence. There is a vast history of people and institutions applying nonviolent sanctions on which we can draw as our heritage. This we ought not simply to imitate. We can regard past nonviolent struggles as primitive prototypes of what could be. These have been cases of actions carried out by people drawing upon inspiration, intuition, and improvisation. With the benefit of what they have accomplished, we can if we want apply ourselves to learn how to multiply the effectiveness of this type of struggle. We would then have revealed before us a power capacity which is not merely equal to political violence but far greater.

Nonviolent sanctions have the potential to be applied as substitute sanctions in place of political violence. This could enable us simultaneously to oppose major political oppression and international aggression, and in the long run reduce the total *quantum* of institutionalized political violence. That could have highly beneficial consequences.

In order to develop and evaluate the potential of nonviolent sanctions, two important tasks are required: (1) research and policy studies and (2) educational work. These will differ in significant ways from established "peace research" and "peace studies." The focus in these would be primarily (1) on the nature and potential of nonviolent sanctions, as compared to violent ones, and (2) on the four problems which require institutionalized political violence for their existence and which nonviolent sanctions would be intended to remove.

RESEARCH AND POLICY STUDIES

In the past, the concern that research should be used to help prevent war and other violence has been expressed in peace research programs and institutes and even national peace research institutes or academies. Whether such research efforts are highly useful, only moderately so, a waste of resources, or actually harmful is to a large degree determined by their orientation and the tasks which they are given. The choice of orientation and tasks is therefore crucial and will require careful thought.[8]

Such programs ought to avoid two dangers: (1) acceptance of military assumptions, and (2) acceptance of the assumptions of a variety of peace groups. If military assumptions are accepted, not only would one be duplicating much existing work but also would be building on assumptions that have failed to bring world peace and contributed to the present extreme dangers. If peace group assumptions are accepted, one would also be building on approaches which have failed to abolish war, at least in part because of failure to face fully the need for effective means to wage acute conflicts and resist hostile forces.

Research and policy studies are urgently needed which do not fall into the trap of accepting either set of assumptions but which do face fully the reality of conflict, the need for sanctions, and the gravity of domestic and international dangers of aggression, usurpations, dictatorships, genocide, systems of social oppression, terrorism, and political violence in general.

Various other approaches to peaceful resolution of conflicts—such as negotiation, arbitration, conciliation, mediation, and similar means involving compromise—have certain merits and utility; these comments are not intended to belittle them. Many of these can make important future contributions to resolving those conflicts in which the issues are not fundamental to the direction of the society or to its moral principles, and in which one is not facing an opponent ready to apply organized violence to achieve an objective. Issues exist, however, on which compromise is properly morally and politically unacceptable. In such cases those approaches to conflict resolution which rely on willingness to compromise (such as arbitration and conciliation) are inappropriate. Resort has commonly been had to violence in these situations. Almost without exception, the traditional approaches to peace have failed to address the need for sanctions by which to struggle on issues which are not suitable for compromise. Peace proposals which ignore the need for sanctions suffer from a fatal flaw. Similarly, researchers who accept the assumption that violent sanctions are required without rigorous investigation of alternatives irresponsibly help to perpetuate the grave problems, including war, which follow inextricably from that assumption.

Therefore, a responsible approach to research and education on the problems of conflict and peace needs to face the most important and difficult issue blocking the way to the abolition of war: the need for sanctions in conflicts in which compromise is unacceptable or impossible. Prime attention is then needed to alternative nonviolent means of waging conflict.[9]

We do not know enough about these alternative nonviolent sanctions, including their problems and potentials in extreme conflicts—such as defending against foreign invasion or internal usurpation. Such knowledge is vital in order to wage such struggles most effectively, and confidence in the potential for effectiveness is essential for widespread, permanent, adoption of nonviolent sanctions. Such limitations on knowledge, effectiveness, and confidence have a predictable result: few people are willing to give up reliance on political violence (including war) for facing attacks on the society's constitutional system and independence. The consequent resort to political violence threatens in such internal conflicts widespread civil disorder and even civil war, while in international conflicts it brings the danger of massive war and annihilation.

Other conflicts, in which lesser issues are at stake on which compromise is possible and acceptable, are also important; efforts to resolve them peacefully are also needed. However, the acute conflicts are by far more serious. Therefore, it is crucial that financial, institutional, and intellectual resources be primarily concentrated on those acute conflicts, rather than on the lesser ones which can be resolved by better skills in negotiation and similar means involving compromise. It is in the acute conflicts in which people and governments believe military action and other political violence are required that we lack sufficient knowledge of nonviolent sanctions and adequate alternative policies based upon them to enable skeptics to accept alternative nonviolent sanctions. Therefore, the primary task of studies aimed to prevent war and ensure peace and to remove political violence should be on research and policy studies about nonviolent sanctions.

As in other fields, we can gain greater knowledge of nonviolent sanctions by basic research into their practice and workings. We can help make them more effective than in the past by applying the results of problem-solving research, policy studies, and by preparations and training. We can expand their future utility in place of military means by policy studies designed to adapt deliberate and prepared nonviolent struggle to destroy dictatorships, defeat *coups d'etat,* and defend against international aggressors. This advance development of viable nonviolent alternatives would make possible a choice to use them instead of war and other political violence.

The broad areas for basic research include:

- the nature and dynamics of nonviolent struggle;
- its requirements for effectiveness;
- its mechanisms of change;
- principles of strategy and tactics;

- case studies of past nonviolent struggles;
- weaknesses of dictatorships; and
- requirements for establishing and preventing control by usurpers.

Problem-solving research is required into these and other areas:

- how best to mobilize, prepare, and train a population for using nonviolent sanctions rather than military ones;
- how to increase the effectiveness of nonviolent sanctions;
- how people can better persist in their nonviolent resistance despite violent repression;
- how the problems of leadership and diffusion of responsibility among all participants can be solved;
- how weaknesses in the usurper's regime and society may best be utilized to help bring success to the nonviolent defenders;
- how temporary defeats can be prevented from producing demoralization; and
- how a series of successes can be transformed into full victory against the attack.

Policy studies need to deal with such tasks as these:

- the degree of adequacy or inadequacy of policies relying upon nonviolent sanctions in place of violent ones for national defense against foreign invaders and internal usurpers;
- the potential of such civilian means of defense to meet the defense needs of present U.S. allies so that they would become more self-reliant without contributing to dangerous military arms races and nuclear proliferation;
- how these nonmilitary means can best be used to liberalize or disintegrate established dictatorships by actions of their own populations;
- how people living under extreme social oppression can use nonviolent sanctions to establish a more just social system instead of using guerrilla warfare and single-party dictatorship;
- how a society can structure its institutions in order best to be able to use civilian-based defense against hostile attacks while maximizing the humane qualities of its own society;[10]
- how attempts to commit genocide can best be prevented and if launched defeated;
- how the general population and the independent institutions of the society can best become willing and able to apply these alternative means of national defense in place of military means; and
- how such a program of transarmament—the transition to the new policy—can be carried out with maximum economic benefit to the society.

These examples illustrate a wider range of topics which need investigation.[11] Institutions established to conduct such studies ought to communicate relevant results of research and policy studies on alternatives to military preparations and action to both nongovernmental bodies and to governmental ones—legislative, executive, military, and others—which will make decisions whether in crises to resort to military action or to nonviolent sanctions. Research centers with this orientation and these projects could make major contributions to the resolution of the great problems of our time.

EDUCATIONAL OPPORTUNITIES

In addition to research and policy studies, deliberate educational efforts are urgently required on alternative nonviolent sanctions and the four identified problems. This focus differs from "peace studies." "Peace studies" or "nonviolent studies" seem generally to be far more diffuse. They often give major attention to the evils of war and the merits of conciliation, arbitration, compromise, and social change, while largely neglecting nonviolent struggle. They almost always exclude or give minimal attention to dictatorships, genocide, internal usurpations, and international aggression. Instead, a focus on nonviolent sanctions in the context of the four identified problems is more directly relevant to major crises and to the decision how to wage struggle in acute conflicts.

A widespread interest now exists in alternatives to violence generally, and a much greater interest than ever before in learning specifically about nonviolent sanctions and their potential for defense and other purposes. Yet there are grossly inadequate educational opportunities and resources available to meet this need. Development of new educational opportunities and resources and improvements in existing ones, are therefore urgently needed in this field throughout the whole range from popularized forms to rigorous academic approaches. These will include efforts within formal educational institutions from grade school through universities, adult education programs, and informal study groups. Additional efforts are needed by the media of public communication.

It is highly important that such educational efforts be as unbiased and as high in quality as is achievable; the purpose is to provide knowledge and understanding to assist thought and fair evaluation, not to indoctrinate people to accept a particular view or policy.

We need a general public education program on the nature of civilian struggle and nonviolent forms of action so that people come to understand what it really is, instead of all the misconceptions which are common. This program could include such means as books, newspaper articles, fiction, historical novels, adult education courses, television drama series, radio programs, videotapes, magazine features, and the like.

Study groups on nonviolent sanctions and their potential can be a very useful educational format. They can be used by small numbers of people, or the groups can multiply so that very large numbers of people participate. There is flexibility in their scheduling and timing, and, with adequate literature, videotapes, and the like, "experts" are not required as leaders. Study groups can be completely independent, or can be associated with other such groups, or with an organization with broader or different interests. There are now indications that a remarkable number of people are ready to join study groups on nonviolent sanctions. Development and dissemination of good educational resources and knowledge of how to organize and conduct such groups are therefore highly important.

In schools and colleges, we need curriculum changes to introduce into regular courses and disciplines specific information of a suitable academic type about nonviolent forms of struggle. For example, this information may include the role it has played in various historical situations, how it operates, its psychological dynamics, and other dimensions. In colleges, on the high school level, and perhaps even earlier, we need specific courses on nonviolent struggle. This means developing curriculum materials, textbooks, videotapes, films, and other resources.[12]

Where courses on nonviolent sanctions are already offered, there is usually room for improvement. For example, efforts might be made to improve the variety and quality of such courses, to increase their academic rigor, to add new resources, to deepen the understanding and knowledge offered and sought, to improve the balance and fairness of presentations, and to expand the offerings of those and related courses.

In colleges and universities special programs of study may be launched. Normally a specific phenomenon such as nonviolent sanctions would not be the focus of a special department or program. It would instead be examined repeatedly in the context of the studies of the regular departments and programs. We face here, however, an unusual situation: a vast and highly significant field of human experience, in many countries, societies, and historical periods, has usually been left out of our historical studies and our research and teaching in social psychology, sociology, political science, and the like. With unusual exceptions, nonviolent struggle is not among the phenomena studied in those fields, and their faculties are inadequately familiar with this specific subject matter. The problem is compounded by a whole series of gross misunderstandings and erroneous assumptions which are part of the popular perceptions of "nonviolence."

Therefore, special attention is required which can only be provided by special programs with trained faculty. Such special programs, however, must collaborate closely with existing departments and disciplines, and students will need to undertake major studies in them.

Such steps as the following can be taken to improve education about nonviolent alternatives in schools and colleges:

- preparation for grade schools and high schools of courses and curriculum materials on alternative sanctions and the problems of dictatorship, genocide, war, and systems of social oppression;

- preparation of guides and suggestions for instructors in courses in this field at various educational levels, including both recommendations which could be implemented directly, and also encouragement to modify them, or to create new courses and approaches;
- selection and development of historical studies which provide corrective treatment to the past relative neglect of nonviolent struggle;
- preparation of new texts, study guides, and other printed curriculum materials focusing on alternative sanctions and the four selected problems, and their opposite positive conditions, providing sound informational backgrounds and balanced presentations, and raising new questions about all of these;
- development of table games for home and classroom use as learning and problem-solving tools in the evaluation and use of nonviolent sanctions in acute conflicts;
- preparation of new films, dramatized and documentary television programs, videotapes, and the like about these phenomena and problems;
- exploration of participatory educational methods for possible use in courses on nonviolent alternatives designed to stimulate and facilitate the learners' active involvement in their own educations;
- establishment of grants to provide (1) aid to educational institutions to develop and expand undergraduate and graduate programs in these fields; (2) scholarships and grants to graduate students wishing to specialize in this field including support for writing their doctoral dissertations; and (3) support for researchers and educators to prepare educational resources—textbooks, syllabi, films, video programs, and others—and to make educators aware of their availability;
- development of interdisciplinary programs of undergraduate studies on nonviolent sanctions and the four identified problems;
- offering of individual graduate courses, seminars, and dissertation supervision, and the like, on nonviolent sanctions and the four problems within established departments and programs;
- development of interdisciplinary graduate studies, courses, seminars, dissertation supervision, and the like in this area in cooperation with established departments and programs;
- offering special summer courses on alternative sanctions and the identified problems for (1) visiting students from other universities, (2) high school teachers leading courses in this field, and (3) college and university faculty from other institutions leading courses on these phenomena and problems (courses (2) and (3) may focus both on substance and on educational methods and approaches);
- assistance in the establishment of quality M.A. and Ph.D. programs to train future researchers, policy analysts, and educators in the study of alternative sanctions and the four related problems;

- encouragement of the expansion or development of small and large libraries focused on the whole area or on specific phenomena and problems; and
- development of formal and informal networks through which educators, students, and researchers working in this field in various institutions may consult with each other and share their problems, experiences, and insights.

CONCLUSION

A great variety of opportunities and tasks lie before us in learning more about the nature and potential of nonviolent sanctions for resolving some of our most serious problems. These tasks require the assistance of a great variety of people and institutions. This work will help provide the knowledge and understanding needed to evaluate the potential contribution of alternative nonviolent sanctions. These studies may help us better to understand our world, our problems, and our options, and may also help us to deal with and resolve some of our most serious problems. The effort is needed.

Notes

1 These four problems are examined in much greater detail in Gene Sharp, *Social Power and Political Freedom* (Boston: Porter Sargent, 1980). Other relevant material on strategy for liberation from oppression and related ethical questions can be found in idem, *Gandhi as a Political Strategist, with Essays on Ethics and Politics* (Boston: Porter Sargent, 1979), especially chap. 12, "Morality, Politics, and Political Technique."

2 This analysis of the role of institutionalized political violence draws on "The Societal Imperative," chap. 11 in Sharp, *Social Power and Political Freedom*, pp. 285–308.

3 On the structural consequences of violent and nonviolent sanctions, see "Popular Empowerment," in ibid., pp. 325–56.

4 See also "The Societal Imperative," in ibid., pp. 291–93.

5 See Gene Sharp, *The Politics of Nonviolent Action* (Boston: Porter Sargent, 1973), especially "The Nature and Control of Political Power," chap. 1, pp. 7–62; and "Nonviolent Action: An Active Technique of Struggle," chap. 2, pp. 63–105. Many additional historical examples are cited and described in the remainder of the book.

6 On these methods, see "The Methods of Nonviolent Action," part 2, in ibid., pp. 107–445.

7 On these mechanisms, see "Three Ways Success May Be Achieved," ibid., chap. 13, pp. 705–76.

8 This discussion draws heavily on my written testimony "Recommendations on a 'National Peace Academy'" presented to the U.S. Commission on Proposals for the National Academy of Peace and Conflict Resolution, meeting in Boston, Massachusetts, June 2, 1980. A passage from my oral testimony is included in *To Establish the United States Academy of Peace: Report of the Commission for the National Academy of Peace and Conflict Resolution to the President of the United States and the Senate and House of Representatives of the United States Congress* (Washington, D.C.: U.S. Government Printing Office, 1981), p. 133.

9 For a list of the major components of a multifaceted program for research, education, and consideration of nonviolent sanctions see, "Twenty Steps in Development and Evaluation of Nonviolent Sanctions," Appendix B in Sharp, *Social Power and Political Freedom*, pp. 383–90.

10 For some studies on this policy, see "For Further Reading" at the end of this article.

11 For listings and brief descriptions of areas for research and policy studies on alternative nonviolent sanctions, see Gene Sharp, *Exploring Nonviolent Alternatives* (Boston: Porter Sargent, 1970), "Research Areas on Nonviolent Alternatives," chap. 4, pp. 73–113; and idem, "Research Areas on the Nature, Problems and Potentialities of Civilian Defense" in *Gandhi: Theory and Practice, Social Impact and Contemporary Relevance: Proceedings of a Conference*, ed. S. C. Biswas (Simla: India Institute of Advanced Studies, 1969), pp. 393–413.

12 The first such videotapes for educational use are now available: *Alternatives to Violence: A Video Series*, funded by the Fund for the Improvement of Postsecondary Education, U.S. Department of Education, through the University City Science Center, Philadelphia. Enquiries to: W.T.L. (Distribution), Box 351, Primos, Pa. 19018.

For Further Reading

ON NONVIOLENT STRUGGLE

Sharp, Gene, *The Politics of Nonviolent Action* (Boston: Porter Sargent, 1973). Available in paperback in three volumes: *Power and Struggle, The Methods of Nonviolent Action*, and *The Dynamics of Nonviolent Action* (Boston: Porter Sargent, 11 Beacon St., Boston, Ma. 02108, 1974).

ON CIVILIAN-BASED DEFENSE

Atkeson, Edward B., "The Relevance of Civilian-based Defense to U.S. Security Interests," *Military Review* 56, no. 5 (May 1976): 24–32, and no. 6 (June 1976): 45–55.

Boserup, Anders, and Andrew Mack, *War Without Weapons* (New York: Schocken, 1975; London: Francis Pinter, 1974).

Roberts, Adam, ed., *Civilian Resistance as a National Defense* (Harrisburg, Pa.: Stackpole Books, 1968. Also published as *The Strategy of Civilian Defence* (London: Faber, 1967).

Sharp, Gene, "Civilian-based Defense: A New Deterrence and Defense Policy," in *Strategic Doctrines and Their Alternatives*, ed. Yoshikazu Sakamoto and J. Saxe-Fernandez (Paris: UNESCO, forthcoming). Includes an extensive multilanguage bibliography.

———, *Exploring Nonviolent Alternatives* (Boston: Porter Sargent, 1970). Out of print, but can be found in libraries. See especially, "Research Areas on Nonviolent Alternatives," pp. 73–113.

———, "Making Europe Unconquerable: Civilian-based Deterrence and Defense." Booklet. (New York: Institute for World Order, 777 United Nations Plaza, New York, N.Y. 10017, 1982). Includes an extensive multilanguage bibliography.

———, "Making the Abolition of War a Realistic Goal." Pamphlet. Wallach Award Essay. (New York: Institute for World Order, 1981).

———, National Security Through Civilian-based Defense, forthcoming. Information about it may be obtained from the Association for Transarmament Studies, 3636 Lafayette Avenue, Omaha, Ne. 68131. This group has opened its membership to persons outside of Nebraska, and will be issuing a newsletter on civilian-based defense from September 1982.

———, *Post-Military Defense* (Princeton, N.J.: Princeton University Press, forthcoming).

———, *Social Power and Political Freedom* (Boston: Porter Sargent), especially "'The Political Equivalent of War'—Civilian-based Defense" and "Seeking a Solution to the Problem of War," pp. 195-261 and 263–84.

ON RELATIONSHIPS BETWEEN THE "FOUR PROBLEMS" AND NONVIOLENT STRUGGLE

Sharp, Gene, *Social Power and Political Freedom* (Boston: Porter Sargent, 1980).

ON MORAL NONVIOLENCE, NONVIOLENT SANCTIONS, AND POLITICAL ETHICS

Sharp, Gene, *Gandhi as a Political Strategist, with Essays on Ethics and Politics* (Boston: Porter Sargent, 1979), especially Part Two, "Essays on Ethics and Politics," pp. 201-309.

A Nuclear Freeze and a Non-interventionary Conventional Policy

RANDALL FORSBERG
Institute for Defense and Disarmament Studies, Brookline, Massachusetts

The nation-state system, the world's economic structure, and the arms race are not static but changing and evolving phenomena. In working to reverse the nuclear arms race we therefore need to think not of a static goal, but rather of a process of change. Thinking in these terms, I shall try to show that, by gradually confining the military more and more to defense, narrowly defined, and by doing this while other changes are taking place the world's economic and political structure, we can move over the long term to a world in which nonviolent means of solving conflicts are feasible and practicable.

In order to understand the possibility of such a change, it is first necessary to understand how military forces are used today.

CURRENT MILITARY POLICIES

WORLD MILITARY SPENDING

Surprisingly, only about 20 percent of the U.S. military budget goes to nuclear weaponry—that is, to design, develop, and manufacture and to field and train men to operate our nuclear forces.

Eighty percent of the U.S. military budget goes to conventional armaments, that is, to ground troops, naval forces, and tactical air forces. The same, roughly speaking, is true of the Soviet Union.

On a worldwide basis, only about 12 percent of military spending goes into the nuclear arms race. Another 10 percent goes into conventional armaments in developing countries. (All of Latin America, Africa, the Middle East, South Asia, and the Far East, excluding China and Japan, have armaments that account for only 10 percent of the total arms budget of the world.)

What remains is the biggest chunk of world military spending. This chunk, not only quantitatively but also in political and psychological terms, is the heart of the arms race, the root of the problem. This is the approximately 80 percent of world military spending that goes to the conventional armed forces of the industrialized countries in the northern hemisphere: the United States, Europe, the Soviet Union, China, and Japan.

This article is based on a speech given at Princeton University in September 1980.

What are the functions of these conventional forces—forces that are virtually ignored amidst the current alarm over nuclear weapons?

THE ROLES OF CONVENTIONAL ARMED FORCES

There are three major functions of the conventional arms of the industrialized countries. The first is to deter another devastating conventional world war like World War II.

It should be noted that one of the functions of nuclear weapons is to prevent the large conventional forces focused on Europe from being used. Yet the purpose of those conventional forces, in turn, is usually presented as providing an alternative to the use of nuclear arms. So, in a circular manner, we maintain nuclear weapons to make sure that we do not use our conventional forces, and we maintain conventional forces to make sure that we do not use our nuclear forces. Each rationalizes the other indefinitely, in a perverse and risky manner of avoiding what is, after all, a great danger.

World War II claimed scores of millions of lives. Avoiding another such war is an important, constructive function. But the manner in which we are doing it—in the image that John Kennedy used, holding a sword of Damocles over our own heads by a thread so slender that any pressure will bring down total destruction—is not rational. Surely this manner of avoiding a major, devastating conventional war need not be permanent. Surely if we act with the degree of responsibility we normally attribute to adults, we will be able to change from a peace maintained through fear, a precarious deterrence that rests on the threat of imminent obliteration, to a stable, disarmed, and truly secure peace.

The second function of conventional armed forces in the northern hemisphere is internal repression. This is marked and well known in Eastern Europe. It may also obtain in the West, however. When the socialist and communist parties in Italy and France appear to come near to winning free elections, there are statements by people like Henry Kissinger that, if they were to come to power, the West should be prepared to use military force to oust them. Thus, in a subtle and muted way, preventing democratic movement toward socialism may be one of the functions of the NATO alliance and of the U.S. troops stationed in Europe.

The third major function of the conventional forces of the industrialized countries, most particularly of the United States and secondarily of the Soviet Union, is to provide the capability to intervene in "local" conflicts in the Third World. This is not a defensive function. It is an aggressive function. It means imposing our will, our view of the world and of desirable political systems, on smaller, weaker, less technologically advanced countries, in areas where we do not face militarily equal opponents. It does not mean defending anyone from external aggression of major dimensions, but rather committing such aggression: using superior technology, greater wealth, and manpower in the tens or hundreds of thousands to serve as cannon fodder to tip the balance in someone else's war. The aggressive character of such action is the same whether the conflict is about the availability of natural resources or about the political and economic system that will prevail, maintaining an open door for capitalism or a foothold for socialism.

The interventionary role of conventional armed forces is "where the action is" in the modern world in the use of force. This is the arena in which the power-politics competition between the United States and the Soviet Union takes active military form. It is also the issue that, ultimately, drives the nuclear arms race. It is therefore important to be familiar with the interventionary conventional forces of the United States and the Soviet Union and with the history of intervention on the part of the two superpowers.

DISTINGUISHING BETWEEN DEFENSIVE AND INTERVENTIONARY FORCES

Of the U.S. conventional armed forces, about half are oriented primarily toward helping defend Western Europe in the event of a war with the Soviet Union. These include the army's armored and mechanized divisions, which are heavily equipped with tanks and artillery and require an operating area with an extensive road network and industrial infrastructure.

They also include what the navy calls its "sea-control" forces. One mission of the U.S. Navy is to send convoys from the United States to Western Europe with supplies of tanks, artillery, ammunition, oil, and so on, in the manner of World War II. In order to prevent the United States and NATO from being able to mount a permanently sustainable attack against the East, the Soviet Union has developed a very large force of antiship submarines, whose role is to come out into the North Atlantic and sink the convoys. In response to this Soviet submarine force, the United States and the Western countries have developed extensive antisubmarine warfare capabilities, which form the main part of the sea-control component of the navy. These capabilities include antisubmarine submarines (submarines designed to go after other submarines); antisubmarine patrol aircraft; and surface ships (cruisers, destroyers, and frigates) that escort the convoys, providing antisubmarine and antiaircraft point-defense in case Soviet submarines and aircraft penetrate the earlier barriers.

The remaining U.S. conventional forces are oriented more toward fighting in developing countries than toward defending Western Europe (or any other part of the world) against an attack by the Soviet Union. These forces include the marines and the army's infantry, airborne, and paratrooper divisions. In comparison with the Europe-oriented divisions, these ground troops are more lightly equipped. They can fight in difficult mountain, desert, or jungle terrain, where there are few roads. They can be brought in by air, together with their relatively light equipment; or they can land, as the marines do, over the beach. They are not well prepared to stand against Soviet tank armies. They are well prepared to fight against the weaker, poorly equipped forces of developing countries.

On the naval side, what the navy calls "power-projection forces" are designed to project U.S. military power to distant parts of the world. This part of the navy is organized around two main types of ship. First there are the aircraft carriers, large floating airfields. These ships are like a skyscraper turned on its side. They have a crew of 5,000 men and they carry 100 military aircraft, including about 80 supersonic fighter and attack planes. The attack planes are designed to bomb shore-based or naval targets; the fighter planes are designed to fight off enemy aircraft.

The United States has thirteen aircraft carriers. Each carrier is surrounded by a group of surface ships that give the carrier antiaircraft and antisubmarine defense. In addition, the carriers are supported by "underway replenishment ships," unarmed transports that resupply the carriers with airplane fuel, ammunition, and, in the case of carriers that are not nuclear-powered, the fuel to keep the carriers themselves going. These underway replenishment ships, in turn, have their own escorts to provide antiaircraft and antisubmarine defense. As a result, each single carrier with the ability to place 100 planes in any remote region of the world involves a task force of 10–15 ships, built at a total cost $10–15 billion.

Because of this tremendous expense, the United States is the only country in the world that operates a fleet of aircraft carriers with modern supersonic aircraft.

The Soviet Union has recently started building some smaller carriers, about half the size of the U.S. carriers. They carry twenty-five helicopters and fifteen vertical-takeoff-and-landing (VTOL) planes, which fly at subsonic speeds and cannot be used against an enemy with supersonic aircraft. These helicopter carriers are mainly oriented toward antisubmarine warfare. They provide the Soviet Union with about one-twentieth of the offensive power-projection capability that the United States has.

The other major type of ship in the U.S. power-projection force is the amphibious assault ship, which lands marines and their equipment. Like aircraft carriers, amphibious assault ships give a country the ability to sit offshore and launch an attack in a place where it does not have access to enough popular support to be able to use an ordinary ground base or dock facility. The carriers make it possible to bomb from the air. The amphibious assault ships make it possible to land ground troops over the beach.

The United States has five amphibious assault ships that are gigantic: Like small carriers, they weigh 40,000 tons and carry twenty-five helicopters and fifteen VTOL planes. The United States has another forty amphibious landing ships that weigh over 10,000 tons. The size of the ship determines its range, that is, how far away and how long it has the fuel and supplies to operate.

With one exception, the largest amphibious landing ships in the Soviet Union weigh 4,000 tons. These small ships are designed to carry landing craft in the enclosed seas near the Soviet Union: the Baltic, the Mediterranean, the Sea of China, and the Sea of Okhotsk. They make it possible for the Soviet Union, in the event of a conflict on one of its borders, to come around behind the action and make a beachhead in support of that conflict. Without larger carriers and amphibious assault ships, it is not possible for the Soviet Union to go down to South Asia, Africa, or Latin America and launch a large-scale assault against a developing country.

This difference in U.S. and Soviet naval power means that the United States is free to operate in an interventionary manner in any part of the world, while large-scale, direct Soviet military operations are constrained to areas contiguous to Soviet borders, which it can support through direct overland routes or short, well-protected air routes.

THE HISTORY OF INTERVENTION

Since World War II, the United States has been involved in two major interventions in developing countries: Korea and Vietnam. In both places the intervention involved about 500,000 men. That is approximately the scale of the "swing" forces that the United States maintains permanently in peacetime in order to be able to fight in any part of the world, out of a total standing armed force of two million men.

The Soviet Union has about twice as many men under arms as the United States. However, most Soviet troops are occupied on two fronts. About two-thirds are oriented toward Europe, where the Soviet Union faces not only a major commitment by the United States, but also three very powerful U.S. allies: West Germany, France, and the United Kingdom, each with armed forces of around 500,000 men. (The other NATO countries and the Soviet allies in the Warsaw Pact have armed forces numbering 200,000 or less, and they roughly counterbalance.)

Most of the remaining third of Soviet armed forces are based in the Far East, facing Chinese forces that outnumber them in manpower but are about evenly matched in tanks, artillery, and other heavy equipment.

The Soviet Union has not maintained a large "swing" force for direct large-scale military intervention in the Third World. The common myth is that communism spreads through Soviet military aggression. However, the manner in which the Soviet Union has supported nationalist, socialist, and communist revolutions in developing countries has been, until Afghanistan, not through large-scale, direct military intervention with its own troops, but rather through the flow of funds, arms, and training. This type of small-scale, indirect intervention is, of course, paralleled by military aid and arms supplies emanating from the West.

This has been the main style of Soviet involvement in African countries. In

Angola, Mozambique, Somalia, and Ethiopia, there have been at most a few thousand Soviet military advisors. The largest foreign presence in Africa is the Cuban contingent of 12,000 troops in Angola. (One of the many ironies of the Cold War is that the Cuban presence in Angola is apparently sanctioned by Gulf & Western Oil, because the Cuban troops prevent a recurrence of the civil war in Angola and, thus, make it possible for Angola to continue to export oil smoothly.)

This point needs to be stressed, not because it is unimportant to counter indirect involvement and pressure by the two superpowers on Third World countries, but rather because it is impossible and irrelevant for either side to counter such influence by means of maintaining large conventional forces of its own. The appropriate response to small-scale pressure, influence, and supplies is either something of the same kind or else, preferably, nonmilitary political and economic aid, which is more attractive and useful to the populations of the countries involved.

In terms of direct, large-scale intervention in a developing country, using military strength to make sure that the "communist" side wins a local conflict against a "noncommunist" side—that is, the mirror image of what the United States did or tried to do in Korea and Vietnam, Afghanistan represents the first example of such action for the Soviet Union. The Soviet troops in Afghanistan number about 85,000, a much smaller intervention than that of the United States in Korea or Vietnam, but still quite large in comparison with past Soviet military involvement in the Third World.

The Soviet intervention in Afghanistan and the very slight recent build-up of power-projection capability in the Soviet Navy reflect what may be a long-term trend in the Soviet Union to expand in the direction of the precedent that the United States has set over the last thirty years. Each decade, Soviet armed forces become somewhat less oriented toward territorial defense and somewhat more capable of projecting military power at a distance. But a major threat of this kind still remains far in the future. Ending the conventional arms race is still a feasible way to avoid the Soviet acquisition of long-range power-projection capabilities—and it may well be the only way of doing so.

THE CONNECTION BETWEEN NUCLEAR AND CONVENTIONAL FORCES

What is the relationship of the nuclear arms race to the various roles of conventional military forces? Most people in the United States believe that the purpose of U.S. nuclear weapons is to deter a nuclear attack on the United States by the Soviet Union by threatening retaliation in kind. This is undoubtedly one of the functions of U.S. nuclear weapons, but it is not the only function, nor the function that motivates the continuation of the nuclear arms race between the United States and the Soviet Union.

The purpose of the on-going nuclear arms race, to the extent that there is any rational purpose, is to back up U.S. uses of conventional armed forces overseas and to deter such uses of Soviet conventional forces. This connection between the roles of nuclear and conventional military forces is illustrated throughout the history of the nuclear arms race.

Initially, the United States developed nuclear weapons because we believed that there might be a nuclear program in Germany during World War II. We wanted to be able to respond to a potential nuclear threat with a nuclear response. However, toward the end of the World War II it became clear that Germany did not have a nuclear program, and that there was no nuclear threat to the Western allies. At that point the U.S. nuclear program did not end, but continued with great momentum.

During the four-year wartime Manhattan project, the United States produced enough fissionable uranium and plutonium to make just three nuclear bombs. We tested one of them in the desert, and we used the other two on Hiroshima and Nagasaki. This use of nuclear weapons had nothing to do with deterring a nuclear attack on the United States or anyone else. The United States used the nuclear weapons that had been produced for two reasons. One was to end a conventional war with, it was argued, less loss of life than would occur if the war continued. It was claimed that it might take 500,000 American lives to recapture all of the Pacific islands from the Japanese, in bloody, over-the-beach warfare. The bombs dropped on Hiroshima and Nagasaki killed, immediately, about 100,000 persons each. So nuclear weapons were seen as a means of decreasing death and violence and ending the war more quickly. They were intimately interrelated with the pursuit of conventional warfare goals.

The second reason probably played a great role in the dropping of the second bomb, on Nagasaki, for the bomb on Hiroshima should have been enough (if even that was needed) to make the Japanese sue for total surrender, the only terms that were allowed to them. The function of the second bomb, if not the first, was to intimidate the Soviet Union: as a precedent for the postwar environment, to make clear that the United States not only had a nuclear monopoly, but was prepared to use it. The demonstration was intended to show that, if the Soviet Union used its conventional forces in a manner objectionable to the United States, the United States would not hesitate to respond with nuclear weapons. Thus, again, nuclear policy was inextricably intertwined with conventional war and power politics.

THE POSTWAR NUCLEAR ARMS RACE AND NUCLEAR POLICIES

During the period from 1945 to 1955, the United States continued to have a virtual monopoly on nuclear weapons. U.S. policy in this period was called "massive retaliation." Its purpose was to deter Soviet uses of conventional military force by threatening simply to wipe out the major cities of the Soviet

Union in response. In 1950 the United States had 300 nuclear bombs on 300 propeller-driven planes. Those were all the nuclear weapons in the world. They were not very many by present-day standards, and they might well have been used against population targets because they were, relatively speaking, so few in number.

By 1960, the Soviet Union had acquired nuclear weapons and the means to deliver them to the United States. It had at that time 150 strategic bombers that could reach this country, together with several hundred nuclear missiles and about 500 bombers that could reach Western Europe.

In the interval, the United States had deployed 2,000 strategic bombers, loaded, ready to go, and aimed at the Soviet Union: 600 B52s and 1,400 shorter-range B47s stationed at overseas bases. The United States had also built up a force of about 10,000 tactical nuclear weapons. These are short-range nuclear weapons aimed primarily at military targets: antiaircraft missiles with nuclear tips; antisubmarine torpedoes with nuclear tips; and surface-to-surface missiles to use on the battlefield against oncoming enemy tank formations, including missiles with a range of 400 miles that would go from West Germany to East Germany, as well as missiles with a range of 70 miles, missiles with a range of 30 miles, and even 8-inch howitzers with a range of 15 miles, for use on the battlefield in West Germany. (The neutron bomb is an antitank weapon that is designed to emit enough radiation not merely to kill the men driving the tanks but to make them die in a matter of minutes or hours rather than days or weeks.)

Accompanying its deployment of tactical nuclear weapons, the United States maintained the policy in effect since the end of World War II of posing a threat of first use of nuclear weapons. If the United States became involved in a conventional war with the Soviet Union, and the war was going against this country, we would be ready (on someone else's territory) to escalate up to the use of our tactical nuclear weapons against Soviet conventional forces.

Until the mid-1960s, the United States still had such a marked superiority in both intercontinental and Europe-oriented nuclear weapons that it could continue to pose this threat with some confidence. The United States built up its original strategic missile force much sooner than the Soviet Union did. Both on land and on submarines the main force of invulnerable U.S. missiles was deployed between 1960 and 1967. At that time, the Soviet Union was still relying on its few intercontinental bombers and on 200 vulnerable ICBMs. Neither the Soviet bombers nor the ICBMs were ready to launch, and both could have been destroyed in a preemptive strike.

The Soviet Union first began to acquire nuclear forces that gave it an invulnerable, second-strike deterrent in 1965. This is when the USSR started building ICBMs in steel-reinforced concrete underground silos. The Soviet Union deployed 1,400 such ICBMs over the period 1965–1971. It started building submarines with long-range missiles deployed in range of the

United States only in 1967; and it built up a force of 62 strategic submarines between 1967 and 1977.

Thus, it is only in this last fifteen years that U.S. cities have become unavoidably hostage to a Soviet missile strike that could take place in half an hour. It is only because we failed to stop the arms race in 1960 that we are exposed to this threat today.

During the last decade there has been widespread recognition of parity between the United States and the Soviet Union in nuclear forces. What this means is not that the Soviet Union can match all the esoteric nuclear capabilities of the United States, but that, for the first time, it can match the all-important "bottom-line" second-strike capability: It can retain the forces to obliterate the United States in a second strike, no matter what sort of counterforce attack the United States undertakes first.

While the Soviet Union was still building up its main generation of strategic missiles, betwen 1970 and 1977, the United States took out most of the missiles that it had on land and on submarines and replaced them with new missiles with multiple nuclear warheads or MIRVs (multiple, independently targetable re-entry vehicles).

In 1976, in a program that was perfectly predictable, the USSR started doing the same thing: replacing its main ICBM and submarine-launched missiles with new MIRVed missiles. The Soviet MIRV program has now been completed on land but is still under way on submarines, where it probably will not be completed until 1985.

FUTURE COUNTERFORCE DEVELOPMENTS AND THEIR POLICY IMPLICATIONS

The response of the United States to Soviet acquisition of an invulnerable deterrent force over the last fifteen years is to try to recapture the clear superiority that it had until the mid-1960s. The attempt to do this is being made by developing and deploying the MX missile, which will have the ability to destroy Soviet ICBMs in their silos, and by adding a new submarine-based missile, the Trident II, and a new type of missile, the cruise missile, which will provide thousands of additional nuclear warheads with precision-attack capability.

In addition to these new offensive nuclear forces, the United States already has an extraordinary antisubmarine warfare (ASW) capability, built, as described earlier, in response to Soviet conventional submarines. The U.S. ASW capability has been strengthened for operations against strategic submarines. The United States has large sonar towers off the coast of Norway, off the Azores, and off the Japanese islands. These are attached by cable to a giant computer processing center, which can dampen out all of the other noises in the ocean and leave in only the noises of Soviet submarines. Under good conditions, Soviet submarines can actually be tracked all the way across the Atlantic by means of these sonar towers. Soviet submarines come out of narrow port exits. They are rather poorly designed and noisy. The port exits are surrounded by U.S., Japanese, and British antisub submarines and aircraft.

As a result of this ASW capability, when the United States acquires the MX in the late 1980s, it will be back in a position similar to that of the 1950s and 1960s, when it could threaten a preemptive strike against most Soviet medium-range and intercontinental nuclear forces.

There will be very important differences, though, between the earlier situation and that in 1990. When the United States threatened a preemptive strike earlier, the number of targets (airfields and missile groups) that it would strike was relatively small, a few hundred; and the Soviet Union had no capability to launch its missiles on warning of an incoming attack. Today and in the future that will not be the case. The Soviet generals can now launch their missiles, just as the United States can, when their radar screens show that the opponent's missiles have been launched. In addition, current U.S. counterforce attack scenarios provide for the use of several thousand nuclear warheads against the large Soviet missile forces. The Soviets could send back to the United States a retaliatory attack of equal magnitude.

The effect of even a limited counterforce exchange between the two superpowers, with nuclear warheads directed against the nuclear forces of the opposing side, has been calculated to be between three and twenty million dead in the United States and a like number in the USSR, simply from downwind fallout of the explosions on missile sites. This is the most easily predictable effect. No one has the faintest notion of what would happen to the global ecology if 4,000–8,000 nuclear weapons were exploded in a very short space of time. The ozone layer would be blown away. The fallout would increase the background level of radiation and darken the sky worldwide. Tremendous firestorms would be created. These things combined would create changes in the world's climate that could be cumulative and synergistic.

For all these reasons, counterforce uses of nuclear weapons are not really thinkable—and yet they remain U.S. strategy. It remains U.S. official policy to say that this country would be willing to use nuclear weapons first in a conventional conflict; to maintain large numbers of tactical nuclear weapons for use locally, on someone else's territory; and, with the new generation of weapons, to hold out the possibility, if the war escalates, of an intercontinental attack on the other side's nuclear and other military forces.

The U.S. nuclear policy of developing improved counterforce capabilities and posing an increased threat of nuclear escalation from conventional war is not intended to deter an out-of-the-blue attack on American cities. If anything, it actually increases the risk of such an attack, as the final consequence of escalation. This policy is maintained, as I said at the outset, to back up U.S. uses of conventional force overseas and to deter Soviet uses of conventional force.

The main region for nuclear deterrence of conventional war is Europe. But this is a very stable region, in which conventional war between East and West is highly unlikely: Both sides have too little to gain and too much to lose. Where conventional war remains quite likely and, thus, where the nuclear backup may actually be believed to play an active role in shaping the course of events is in the Third World. In this sense, the purpose of the ongoing nuclear arms race is, from the point of view of the United States, to give the United States greater freedom to intervene in developing countries without risking a conventional challenge on the part of the Soviet Union, and to inhibit Soviet conventional intervention. From the point of view of the USSR, the purpose of trying to match U.S. nuclear developments is to nullify the nuclear factor in global power politics.

The U.S. generals calculate that, if they can show on paper that a direct conventional confrontation between the two superpowers could escalate to a local or intercontinental nuclear exchange that would leave the United States ahead by some measure, then the Soviet generals will not risk sending in conventional forces in the first place; nor will they feel free to intervene themselves in developing countries where Western stakes are high, which was not the case in Afghanistan.

THE GOAL OF ARMS-CONTROL EFFORTS

STOPPING THE NUCLEAR ARMS RACE AND ENDING INTERVENTION

The SALT negotiations, as they have been conducted over the past ten years, have not been directed at stopping the nuclear arms race nor at changing U.S. nuclear policy. They have not moved toward getting rid of our tactical nuclear weapons, our first-use, escalatory policy, or our counterforce nuclear potential. They have been directed at seeing to it that neither side buys weapons that, from a military point of view, are wasteful, excessively expensive, and foolish. They have been directed at "managing" an ongoing arms race. Even the modest goal of avoiding "destabilizing" (counterforce) developments has not prevailed when it conflicted with planned military programs. Thus, room was made in the SALT II treaty for the United States to acquire the counterforce MX missile. A continued competition for military advantage was preferred to a mutual halt with the Soviet Union on new ICBMs on both sides.

Rather than merely supporting a continuation of arms race management, we should be aiming, over the next five years, first of all, for a total halt in the production and deployment of nuclear weapons by both the United States and the Soviet Union. The United States should not build the MX to threaten improved Soviet SS-18s that may threaten U. S. ICBMs. We should be arranging an agreement for neither side to build such weapons. This is not, at present, one of the objectives of the U.S. government.

The United States should not be introducing new counterforce missiles into Western Europe in response to the Soviet SS-20s. There, too, we should be working for a halt on both sides. The United States should not be introducing the Trident II missile, which we do not need, nor the cruise missile, which we do not need, merely to expand the size of our arsenal and provide more "nuclear warfighting," countermilitary options to the military.

If the United States and the Soviet Union were to stop the nuclear arms race right where we are today, this would represent only a slight decrease in the backup potential of existing nuclear forces to support conventional objectives in the manner that they do today. The United States would still have 30,000 nuclear weapons—20,000 tactical local nuclear weapons and 10,000 intercontinental weapons. The United States could still threaten to fight "local" nuclear wars and to undertake counterforce first strikes.

Stopping the nuclear arms race would not by itself be enough to change the nature of U.S. nuclear policy, but it would be a dramatic signal of intent that we plan to change, that we are going to restructure international relations so that they are not to be based indefinitely on fear and genocidal hostage relationships. It would show that we intend not to continually raise the risk of nuclear warfare as a means of supporting intervention in developing countries; that we plan gradually to lessen our reliance on nuclear weapons.

A freeze on the nuclear arms race should be accompanied by efforts to constrain and eventually eliminate direct, unilateral military intervention by the big powers in developing countries. If the Soviet Union intervenes in Afghanistan, this does not justify U.S. intervention in Saudi Arabia. On the contrary, the more clearly and explicitly the United States prepares to intervene in the Middle East—as current plans for the Rapid Deployment Force make clear we are doing—the more free the Soviet Union will be to intervene in areas that it considers to be of interest and value.

The appropriate response to intervention by either superpower in any war where the other is not directly involved with its own troops (which is a practical definition of aggression in the modern world) is to work against it in each individual case. We should be working hard and consistently to avoid any interventionary use of U.S. military forces. We should be working in the international arena for sanctions against the Soviet intervention in Afghanistan. Further, we should be working to develop international standards—codes of behavior that are held up clearly to the superpowers, to the developing countries, and to the other industrialized countries—that absolutely forbid such uses of military force. We should also be emphasizing to those who are reluctant to abandon the option for intervention that it must be abandoned if we are to get a handle on the nuclear arms race, for what drives the nuclear arms race is, ultimately, the continued aggressive potential and use of conventional force on the two sides.

A VISION FOR THE FUTURE

After the nuclear arms race has been halted and intervention in developing countries stopped, there are other major steps of deescalation in the military confrontation between East and West that we must take before the armed forces of the industrialized countries will really be oriented to national defense.

First, the enormous, mutually deterring conventional forces of the NATO and Warsaw Pact blocs, and of the Soviet Union, China, and Japan, must be very substantially reduced before the potential enemies will believe that their opponents no longer pose an offensive threat. These forces must be cut to a fraction of their present size in order for it gradually to become clear that it is, in fact, possible to maintain a stable, demilitarized peace in the northern hemisphere.

Second, we must stop technical innovation not only in nuclear weaponry, but also in conventional armaments: developments in fighter aircraft, tanks, ships, and missiles that create instability and uncertainty about the future.

If these steps were taken in successive stages—first, stopping the nuclear arms race; second, ending conventional military intervention by the superpowers in developing countries; third, reducing the large conventional military forces of East and West and of the Soviet Union and China; and fourth, stopping innovation in conventional weaponry—then the conventional military forces of the countries in the northern hemisphere would look rather like those in the southern hemisphere today. There would no longer be a tremendous military preponderance in the northern hemisphere. There would no longer be the sense of an impending threat of war between East and West or between North and South. At that point, we could reduce the enormous nuclear arsenals of the United States and the Soviet Union not only marginally, but down to a level at which they could no longer cause a global, civilization-destroying holocaust.

Only when there is no longer pressure for nuclear superiority to influence the use of conventional armaments, only when conventional military policies are truly defensive and when this constraint is firmly embedded in the hearts and minds of most people, will we be in a position to move to the abolition of nuclear and conventional armaments and to reliance on nonviolent modes of conflict resolution as a replacement for military modes.

Movement toward a demilitarized future is possible. The stages that I have outlined are plausible. They do not involve instability. They do not involve insecurity. They do not involve loss or sacrifice.

They do, however, require clear understanding of the actual roles of military force in the modern world. They also require strong action on the part of the public to transform the cynical attitudes that prevail among the decision-making elites of the industrialized countries into moral, defensively oriented attitudes. The elites, I fear, will not make such a change if left to their own devices. They would rather perpetuate the nuclear arms race until a holocaust occurs than permanently relinquish all use of armed force, the ultimate tool of power.

Only when we have widespread public education, debate, and understanding of the nature of our military forces and their role in the world, as well as a social consensus on transforming that world, will it be possible to achieve meaningful arms control and arms reduction.

Teaching in a Nuclear Age

ROBERT K. MUSIL
SANE Education Fund, Philadelphia, Pennsylvania

Nuclear weapons are a cultural problem. Of course, they are incredibly destructive, and there is a growing likelihood that they may go off sooner than we think.[1] But nuclear weapons are produced by a particular culture. If we are to renounce the bomb and rid ourselves of it at last, we must share with our students and with the public what we discover about the deep, tangled roots of society's most prolific and most poisonous growth. Indeed, the culture and ideology of nuclear weapons threaten to destroy the fabric of our society whether or not we ever witness the final nuclear conflagration.

For teachers the problem of nuclear weapons has been looked at in several ways. Probably the most common is to assume that our job is simply to hand on the best of Western culture, to liberally educate our students. So armed, it is up to them to live as best they can in a world bent on destruction.[2] The other approach is to offer specialized courses on arms control, often in political science or in history or, occasionally, in conflict resolution or even peace studies.[3] Such courses and teaching are essential. But we need to move beyond them; we need to make the study of nuclear weapons culture and the search for nuclear disarmament central to our curriculum in the many humanistic disciplines, in the sciences, and in interdisciplinary offerings as well.

Several years ago, I began to trace the bomb throughout American life for SANE's National Endowment for the Humanities-funded radio documentary series, "Shadows of the Nuclear Age: American Culture and the Bomb."[4] The story of the bomb and its cultural effects led me relentlessly across disciplinary terrain. Ultimately, over one hundred prominent Americans—in history, government, religion and ethics, film, literature, language, economics, and other fields—were interviewed for the project. And we but began to chart the territory. It is in such a spirit of exploration that our teaching about nuclear weapons must continue with students. There are no easy answers; the old ones obviously have proved inadequate to our present dilemma. Insights into the nuclear age, especially its cultural dimension, are bound to come from unlikely places.

For me, one of the seminal ideas for "Shadows" came while teaching the course "Power and Politics in Washington, D.C.: Issues in National Security." I had worked at the Center for National Security Studies in Washington, D.C., on Watergate-related issues during 1974-1975. Many of the issues so characteristic of the Nixon administration—secrecy, abuse of executive power, the obsessive desire to maintain an image of rigid control—came sharply into focus through an insight from Jonathan Schell in his Watergate book, *The Time of Illusion.* Foreshadowing his powerful work *The Fate of the Earth,* Schell linked the madness of the Nixon White House with the bomb. The war in Vietnam was finally a struggle to maintain the image of American credibility.

> The doctrine of credibility, however, was rooted firmly in the experience of the modern period. It was rooted in the doctrine that formed the basis for all strategic thinking in the nineteen-sixties—the doctrine of nuclear deterrence. For it was in the credibility of the nuclear deterrent that the United States had placed its hopes for survival in the nuclear age. The government hoped that by creating a formidable impression of national strength and will in the minds of the nation's adversaries it could deter them from launching a nuclear attack. . . . Thus, according to the doctrine of credibility, the United States was engaged in a global public relations struggle in which a reverse in any part of the world, no matter how small, could undermine the whole structure of American power.[5]

One of the main results of living with nuclear weapons, then, is the way in which "deterrence"—the notion that we must be prepared, or look like we are prepared, to launch a nuclear war at any moment—seeps into all our thinking. Such a permanently belligerent posture has a number of deleterious effects. And it is a pose that will be with us so long as there are nuclear weapons. Without the appearance of readiness to launch the ultimate holocaust, any number of officials have told us, the deterrent effect of our nuclear weapons would be lost. But this macho pose—hand always dangling, lightly curled, near the nuclear hip—is not limited to executive behavior. E. P. Thompson, the British historian now devoting himself to European Nuclear Disarmament (END), has put it best:

> Deterrence has repressed the export of violence towards the opposing bloc, but in doing so the repressed power of the State has turned back upon its own author. The repressed violence has backed up, and has worked its way back into the economy, the polity, the ideology and the culture of the opposing powers. . . . Imagination has been numbed, language and values have been fouled, by the postures and expectations of the "deterrent" state.[6]

The task for educators should be to get to the root of those cultural distortions arising from and maintaining the nuclear arms race. But that is not enough. Suppose, for a moment, that George Kistiakowsky is correct when he says that he expects to see a nuclear war within his lifetime.[7] We educators have lived since the 1950s with images of the final holocaust. Somehow it always occurs during classroom hours. As we huddle under our desks, what final words will be fused to our blackboards? We must offer to our students information, attitudes, values, methodology, and rigorous research that will help stave off nuclear war, not merely comprehend it. The bomb has shattered many of the traditional ways of thinking and acting in our culture. In teaching courses about nuclear war we must be equally bold and innovative. And we must interest far greater numbers of students than a few potential specialists in arms control. The bomb has captured the popular imagination in film, literature, and music. If we follow the bomb where it leads, students in various disciplines—artists, musicians, writers, economists—will become involved in ways they surely will not in courses that center primarily around nuclear strategic theory.

WHAT KIND OF COURSE?

Follow with me for a moment the impact of the bomb as we might encounter it at the beginning of a semester's course. Then we can sketch in just a few elements for understanding the culture of the nuclear age. Our course will inevitably be interdisciplinary, humanistic, value-centered. It will rely heavily on imaginative works in literature and film, and on critical analysis of language, symbols, and logic. Finally, it must contain some real research, useful in stopping the arms race, carried out by the students themselves. The method, as I have said, must be open, feeling, creative, and humble. It is too easy for the professor and a few key students to "know more" about facts and figures, the nuts and bolts of the nuclear arms race. I do not advocate ignorance of these things. But surely they are not enough. Consider the "facts" of the first atomic explosion.

As the world's first atomic explosion rent the predawn sky at Trinity site near Alamogordo, New Mexico, in July 1945, the story is told of a drunken military policeman who, having fallen asleep in the desert, was awakened by the light Robert Jungk has called "brighter than a thousand suns." There was a roar audible and palpable for many miles around. The very earth tremored as our MP reeled tipsily to his feet. He stared at the roiling luminescent purple, red, and yellow clouds, and is reported to have screamed in astonishment and awe, "My God! The longhairs have let it get out of control."

Several atomic scientists told me this story, with some amusement. There had been rumors and concern that the first blast might ignite all the nitrogen in the atmosphere, thereby destroying the earth. But a number of quick calculations had put this idea, for the scientists at least, almost completely to rest. Nevertheless, the image of our Everyman crying in the desert is an apt symbol for our own primal reaction to the bomb. Compare his elemental human reaction with that of General Leslie Groves, commander of the Manhattan Project. After the blast, General Groves was driven in his jeep out to Ground Zero to inspect the results of the world's first atomic explosion. As he approached Ground Zero, he could see that the floor of the desert had been lowered approximately nine feet in all directions. The desert sands had been fused into glass. General Groves paused, looked around, and commented, "Is this all?"

In between Everyman and the military mind lay the scientists themselves. Their deep ambivalence about atomic creation marks a central theme of the nuclear age. George Kistiakowsky and Robert Oppenheimer clapped each other on the back and closed a wager. And yet, even as they shared the glow of success, Kistiakowsky thought, "In the last millisecond of time, mankind will see something like this," and Oppenheimer too sensed the apocalypse. He drew on the now famous words of the Bhagavad Gita, "I am become death the destroyer of worlds." Later Oppenheimer would exclaim, "Scientists have now known sin."

Even as the blast wave from the first bomb passed over the bunkers where scientists were huddled, Enrico Fermi, ever curious, inventive, and cool, ripped tiny bits of paper and measured how far they were blown by the nuclear wind. He calmly and quickly calculated the explosive power. It was about twenty kilotons. Another figure—a GI drafted for work on the secret project—would not have much reaction to the bomb until a generation later. In 1945, Ted Lombard carried and worked with weapons-grade uranium without protective gear as he literally helped to fashion the first bomb. By 1979, with the wave of revelations about the health hazards that over 200,000 American GIs had been exposed to during nuclear tests, Lombard realized that his own health disabilities and the defects of his children and grandchildren could be traced back to that fateful day at Trinity site.[8]

And, finally, we should note the one atomic scientist who had left the project by the time of Alamogordo. Joseph Rotblat, like other atomic scientists, was driven to help create the bomb by the fear that the Nazis might be the first to do so. By late 1944, however, thanks to Project Alsos, an intelligence penetration into Germany after D-Day, the Allies knew that Hitler would not be able to build the bomb. Yet Rotblat was the only one to draw the obvious conclusion. The need to work on such a horrendous weapon had been removed. Despite the displeasure of security personnel, Rotblat simply resigned.[9]

And so, even the very first atomic blast in history requires of us as teachers a careful interdisciplinary reconstruction of experience in the style of *Rashomon,* a sensitivity not just to the facts, but to the whole moral tableau—religious imagery and moral questions, scientific calculations and medical effects, psychic numbing and guilt, the military uses of the bomb, incipient protest, and more. The language is worth careful study, too. I asked Hans Bethe whether it had ever bothered anyone that the first blast occurred on a Sunday at "Trinity" site. No one had raised the issue of blasphemy, currently resurfaced in the controversy over naming a nuclear submarine "Corpus Christi." But, Bethe told me that yes, he had been bothered by it all along.[10]

Another pattern emerges as we examine some of the cute code words first used for the bomb, a pattern of mechanization, depersonalization, and sexism. The boys' club atmosphere of nuclear culture is clear from its genesis. When the first atomic reactor was activated under Stagg Field at the University of Chicago, there was again the element of uncertainty, the fear of an uncontrolled critical reaction. Tellingly, before the fateful event, Leona Libby, the sole woman scientist in the Chicago Met lab project, was asked to leave the room. Whether it is "the Gadget," "the Super," "The X Division" (explosives), or the "Little Boy" and "Fat Man" that leveled Hiroshima and Nagasaki, the language obscures reality and feeling. Edward Teller, the so-called father of the H-bomb, has said, "The woman's liberation movement will never forgive me for my telegram to Los Alamos when I learned of the first successful H-bomb test in the Pacific. The full text was, 'It's a boy.'"[11]

This confusion of life with destruction, the linkage of power and paternity, the cute telegraphic response to an event that GIs who witnessed it described in terms of horror, reveal that we must look critically at the scientific method and sexism if we are to understand the forces behind the bomb.

The bombing of Hiroshima and Nagasaki also demonstrates the same need to reevaluate our experience, our received national tradition. One image that comes to mind is that of Secretary of War Henry Stimson, pillar of the Eastern Establishment, choosing which of five potential target cities in Japan to destroy with the first atomic bomb. During his service in the Wilson administration, Stimson, a Yale man, had said of spying, "Gentlemen don't read each other's mail." By 1945, he was able to pick the destruction of Hiroshima because he wanted to spare the cultural treasures of the ancient Japanese city of Kyoto.[12]

It is this bifurcation of mind and soul that is at the heart of the nuclear age. Whether it is a cultured secretary of war or the "good and bad" Nixon, moral schizophrenia is the essence of deterrence theory. It is the primary contradiction in postmodern thought that gives it its characteristic mode—a-moral absurdity.

VALUES AND THE CLASSROOM

Such a divorce of thought from feeling, the willingness to countenance incredible evils without guilt in the name of military necessity and deterrence, means that any approach to the culture of nuclear weapons must be humanistic and value-centered. The recent outpouring of concern about the nuclear arms race, for example, is primarily moral concern. But it is usually labeled by those in power as merely emotionalism. We need, however, to carefully examine the connection between feeling and moral sensitivity concerning nuclear weapons. Take the reaction of President Harry S Truman on hearing the news of the successful atomic bomb test at Alamogordo. He blurted out, "This is the greatest thing in history!" Later, even more revealingly, after Robert Oppenheimer tearfully talked to him in the Oval Office about guilt and the bomb, Truman said "I never want to see that cry baby in here again."[13] The literal barricading of one's moral sensibility, the compartmentalization of feeling—all by presumptively Christian postwar presidents—is another central theme of the nuclear age. How does it come about?

After the explosion of the first Soviet atomic bomb in September 1949, President Truman called on a committee of three men to counsel him whether to proceed with a crash program to build "the Super," a hydrogen fusion weapon with destructive power a thousand times that of the atomic bomb. The three men were Secretary of State Dean Acheson, Defense Secretary Louis Johnson, and Atomic Energy Commission Chairman David Lilienthal. Lilienthal was the sole dissenter to the decision, though a cautious one. A scientific panel headed by Oppenheimer had recommended against building the H-bomb, primarily on pragmatic grounds, though the immorality of such a weapon was mentioned. Lilienthal then told Truman that he dissented, but only on the pragmatic grounds that had been carefully laid out for him by the scientists. Before his death, I asked David Lilienthal why, as one of three people with the president's ear on the occasion of one of the most fateful of human decisions, he had not expressed his personal moral revulsion at the new weapon. He told me, "I would have simply been disregarded."[14]

Similarly, George F. Kennan, in charge of State Department Policy Planning immediately before the H-bomb decision, wrote a long policy memorandum to Dean Acheson opposing the H-bomb. In true bureaucratic fashion, Kennan's views did not reach as high as the president. Nor did they move Acheson, who was the one person actually capable of swaying Truman. I asked George Kennan why he had been unable to move Acheson. He replied, "He simply regarded me as an idealist and naive about power."[15]

At each pivitol stage in the nuclear arms race, the counsel of morality and restraint, of diplomacy and decency, has been disregarded. During the Cuban Missile Crisis, Adlai Stevenson incurred the wrath and disdain of a number of ExComm participants. He had suggested that diplomacy and an exchange of U.S. missiles in Turkey be used to avoid a military confrontation. With diplomacy foregone, the moral poles then revolved around Robert Kennedy, who opposed an *immediate* invasion ("I don't want to be another Tojo"), but counseled a naval blockade, itself an act of war, and those like Dean Acheson who said, "I know how to deal with the Russians, they only understand force. We need to bomb them."[16]

Within this milieu, John Kennedy and Ted Sorenson did talk about destruction, and Dean Rusk played a kind of bureaucratic, conciliatory role. But the crisis marched forward because a military solution was the only course left open. I asked Dean Rusk whether any of the participants discussed the religious or moral issues in confronting possible thermonuclear annihilation. He told me, "There was no need to discuss it, we were all civilized men. We shared a common set of values."[17] Yet even the cool Rusk found his old boss Acheson "out of touch with the reality of the nuclear age." Sorenson found the words of Acheson and others "callous." John Kennedy mourned the possible destruction. But the momentum, the deadly logic of nuclear deterrence prevailed. We went eyeball to eyeball with the Russians and, as Rusk put it, "the other side blinked."

Such blunting of emotion and moral sensitivity by the logic of deterrence is demonstrated again and again. Perhaps the most interesting direct response is from President Carter's national security advisor, Zbigniew Brzezinski. In a 1977 interview in the Baltimore *Sun,* Brzezinski was asked directly about his personal feelings on using the bomb: You have three small daughters and are a Christian, a reporter asked; could you turn the key to launch a nuclear war? "I would have to," was Brzezinski's unblinking reply.

THE CORROSION OF DEMOCRACY

The response of Brzezinski, the actions of national security planners in the executive branch, all reveal not only blurred moral vision because of deterrence and the bomb, but also a serious corrosion of our democracy. The bomb has accelerated and exacerbated the modern tendency toward centralized executive power, secrecy, and the corresponding diminution of congressional power and public opinion. In his journals, David Lilienthal muses about what the workmen outside a Dumbarton Oaks window would make of the historic atomic decisions being made by the men inside.[18] Lilienthal is troubled by the lack of democracy, but he does not act on his perceptions. Dean Rusk told me that he disapproves of the elitism involved in crisis decision making. But he, too, sees it as unavoidable. Eventually the small deceptions necessary to maintain secret decision making (such as Kennedy's returning to the White House from a campaign appearance during the Cuban Missile Crisis "because of the flu") become routine. McGeorge Bundy speaks in the Pentagon Papers of "orchestrating" public opinion; Lyndon Johnson plans for a Gulf of Tonkin incident and resolution even as he campaigns on a platform of peace and "no wider war."

The corrosion of true democracy by the ideology of deterrence was played out powerfully during the attempted assassination of President Reagan in March 1981. Recall the scene. The president steps toward his limousine outside the Washington Hilton. Smiling, he turns in a familiar gesture waving to the small crowd behind press lines to his left. Then there are rapid popping noises. The grin beneath the pompadour slides into a grimace, and, suddenly, the United States is in the midst of a policy crisis.

The chaos that ensued in the next few seconds outside the Hilton was replayed on television countless times that day. Each time, I was struck by the figure who shouted, "Get that bag out of here!" A small black bag was rushed away, even as a Secret Service agent and a policeman lay wounded, and presidential press secretary James Brady twitched unattended.

That black bag, known as the "football," contains the codes capable of launching a thermonuclear war. It follows the president wherever he goes. With the president wounded, the drama over that black bag continued throughout the day. On the one hand, we witnessed the calculated and calm dispensation of medical bulletins, reducing fears over the president's safety. On the other hand, we caught glimpses of confusion and tension over just who did control that black bag and the nuclear forces of the United States when the president is under anesthesia and the vice president is unavailable. Alexander Haig tried, in a flushed and halting attempt, to reassure the country that someone was in control of the government and, by inference, the nuclear forces.

What was implicit in the behind-the-scenes dispute between Haig and Defense Secretary Caspar Weinberger over the lines of national command authority was the assumption that in a nuclear age Congress and the citizenry are basically irrelevant to governance. They have become mere audiences to be stroked. Military power and central command authority, the question of who is commander in chief, have preempted the nation's definition of security.

THE BREEDING OF CYNICISM

It is no wonder, then, that citizens and our youth have become cynical about voting, the democratic process, and their elected representatives. The logic of deterrence also leads to seemingly bizarre, schizophrenic, even absurd behavior on the part of our leaders. They are by turns pacific and bellicose. As Alexander Haig put it in a recent speech, "From the dawn of the nuclear age, these weapons have been the source of grave concern to our people and the focus of continuous public debate. Every successive President of the United States has shared these concerns."[19]

What Haig did not add is that every successive president has added to the nuclear arsenal and threatened nuclear disaster even while expressing desires for peace and disarmament. What is someone like Lilienthal's workman to make of this? Consider the administration of Jimmy Carter. How do we explain a president who entered office awash in populist symbolism—peanuts and overalls in his campaign spots, fireside chats and sweaters, and a black choir, Martin Luther King, Sr., and a stroll down the street at his inauguration? It was Jimmy Carter who pledged to cut $5 to $7 billion from the defense budget, Jimmy Carter who shouted in his high southern drawl at the inaugural, "We will work toward our ultimate goal—zero nuclear weapons."

Yet, by midterm, Carter had launched a new generation of counterforce nuclear weapons, was giving militaristic speeches from the deck of the *Eisenhower*, allowing Brzezinski to assure the press that he was really "tough,"[20] and shockingly, after Walter Pincus discovered it buried in the Department of Energy budget, pushing a new device called the neutron bomb.

James Fallows, a former speechwriter for Carter, described to me some of the pressures on a president from the institutionalized structures of the arms race that create such seeming schizophrenia. Earlier, Carter had cancelled the B-1 bomber after careful analysis of the data and the merits of the system. But his decision to proceed with a new, powerful, mobile ICBM, the MX, was entirely different:

> When the MX decision came around, it was not decided on its merits in the same way. Rather, it was judged by the fact that Jimmy Carter was being just constantly attacked from the right for his weakness on defense policy. He was the man who had cancelled the B-1 bomber, who had waffled on the neutron bomb. So he felt he couldn't afford to add one more item to the litany of things he had done to destroy America's strength. He was facing near mutiny from the Air Force which felt its cherished B-1 bomber was in the toilet, and now they wanted the MX.[21]

BEGINNING IN THE CLASSROOM

For many of our students, much of this analysis and interdisciplinary exploration will be new. Frances FitzGerald examined recent American history textbooks in *America Revised.* Sometimes, she found, there is a stray photograph of a mushroom cloud, or a passing reference to the atomic bomb's hastening the end of World War II. But nothing substantive is ever said of nuclear strategy, the power and effects of nuclear weapons, or the cultural fallout from the bomb.[22] Given the kind of psychic numbing Robert Jay Lifton has described elsewhere, this is perhaps to be expected. But when a lack of information is combined with fear, cynicism, and despair and the myth of expertise needed to deal with nuclear questions, we need to approach our subject and our students with sensitivity.

NUCLEAR CONSCIOUSNESS-RAISING

One of the best ways to begin borrows from the techniques of women's consciousness raising. A number of psychiatrists, psychologists, and counselors in the past few years have explored ways of allowing people to share "nuclear stories," to overcome their feelings of despair and numbness over the bomb, to face what for all of us somewhere in our psyche is a terrifying reality. Carol Wolman of the University of California Medical School, Joanna Macy of Washington, D.C., and others are linked in a nationwide network called Interhelp. They offer workshops in coping with despair and powerlessness in a nuclear age.[23]

If, as teachers, we begin our explorations in this way, by sharing nuclear stories and fears, we accomplish a number of important things. First, we necessarily drop the authoritative (and occasionally authoritarian) pose of the professor dispensing truth. We demonstrate clearly that we, too, are terrified of nuclear war, that we do not have all the answers, that the thoughts and perceptions of our students matter—indeed, are crucial for the solution of our common dilemma. We set a tone of openness, for nuclear war is a subject, you will discover, that wants to slip constantly back into abstract discussion—into numbers, physics, throwweights, yields—discussions that can quickly become male dominated, given to displays of arcane knowledge, and replicas of the government approach to nuclear arms.

Such an opening exercise also emphasizes the need for *change*—both in society and in individual students—something that seems to me essential on the brink of nuclear destruction. Mere accumulation of knowledge—let alone credits—is not enough. For these reasons, I share with students my own nuclear story, a story that parallels the history of the nuclear arms race.[24]

My earliest recollection of things nuclear was a souvenir brought to me by my parents after they toured the atomic facilities at Oak Ridge, Tennessee, on a business trip to the South around 1950. Within a small cardboard box lay a somewhat amber-colored piece of glass. It was a small piece of that molten desert from Alamogordo, the very site where General Groves had asked, "Is this all?" I was by turns fascinated and somewhat horrified by that little piece of glass and the magical power for good or evil that it symbolized. I fantasized about a blissful future with nuclear energy, told amused adults that I wanted to become a nuclear physicist. And, at the same time, I worried about the bomb.

By the time of the Cuban Missile Crisis in October 1962, I sat in absolute horror at Yale as John Kennedy announced on television, "We do not seek worldwide thermonuclear war. The fruits of victory would be but ashes in our mouths. But neither will we shrink from it at any time it must be faced." Images of collapsing buildings, fireballs, dead and injured students and faculty, family and friends flooded my mind. My response—appropriately absurd in retrospect—was to contemplate changing my major. Suddenly, the works of Shakespeare, Milton, and Chaucer that I was studying seemed futile and ridiculous, a future as a college professor absurd. I decided briefly to be an opthalmologist—images of melting eyeballs, of blinded victims needing help haunted me for days. What did not occur to me then, and grew only slowly in my consciousness, was to do something concrete about the arms race itself.

My fear and confusion changed to anger and activism as the nuclear arms race and war impinged on me more and more. After graduate school, while a captain in the Army, I was appalled during training at Ft. Benjamin Harrison by a film of Hiroshima blandly offered to our class as mere evidence of "weapons effects." This was followed by a class in which two chrome-helmeted, field-grade officers burst into our classroom hurling M-60 training firecrackers. Blam! Blam! Blam! Blam! Music swells. Overhead projector switches on. Officers snap to attention. "Gentlemen, welcome to your 4-hour block of instruction on nuclear weapons!"

Such a Yippie scene was a clear shove in the direction of protest. It helped convince me, too, that the problem of nuclear weapons involved deep-seated attitudes and culture, not just technology and treaties.

As students tell their stories, a host of fears will come up—the lack of a real future, the fear of having children in such an insane world, the sense of helplessness, powerlessness, and dread. These perceptions are the beginning of the construction of an alternative reality—a new way of seeing the nuclear era, which, we are usually told, is designed to make us feel secure. Once the fundamental contradictions of the nuclear age are deeply felt, students can compare and expand their feelings with works of literature, film, art, music.

I have long since concluded that it was partly because of my interest in literature that I felt the Cuban Missile Crisis so deeply. Whatever our discipline, we must awaken the imagination and empathy of our students. My own initial reaction to abandon literature and the arts as trivial in the face of nuclear terror was not only absurdly inappropriate—it was also wrong.

LITERATURE AND IMAGINATION IN A NUCLEAR AGE

Kurt Vonnegut has wrestled a lifetime with images of total destruction and nuclear war. Much of his work is, in effect, an attempt to tell his own story of holocaust, to work out imaginatively the dread of the nuclear age and thus overcome it. As a prisoner of war, Vonnegut lived through the firebombing of Dresden, one of the most awful events of human history. Only the kind of black humor for which he is famous allowed him to convey such an experience at all. Black humor is, in fact, characteristic of much of the literature of the nuclear age. In his study of American culture in the 1960s, Morris Dickstein discusses Vonnegut and Joseph Heller:

> Earlier writers had been able to approach World War II with a certain moral simplicity; here after all was a "just war" if there was ever one. But after fifteen more years of continuous cold war and the shadow of thermonuclear war, all war seemed morally ambiguous if not outright insane; in the prolonged state of seige the whole culture seemed edged with insanity.[25]

Since Vonnegut had experienced Dresden firsthand, the government's secrecy about that bombing and Truman's explanations of Hiroshima all struck him as lies—insane lies. The culture that led up to such lies seemed askew as well. In his youth, Vonnegut had trained as a chemist; his brother Bernard actually became a noted atmospheric chemist. He believed deeply in technology and scientific progress. He spent hours sketching futuristic inventions, rockets and planes. But his wartime experience, Hiroshima, and a tour as a public relations man at General Electric convinced Vonnegut of the absurdity of such notions, of their immorality, and of the official mendacity of governments. "George Orwell was talking about euphemisms. Now governments just lie."[26]

Cat's Cradle captures the essential lunacy of inventing materials that can end the world. Dr. Felix Hoenniker, Vonnegut's fictional father of the A-bomb, spends practically twenty-four hours a day in the laboratory inventing ice-nine, a substance that instantly freezes whatever water it comes into contact with. This is so the Marines will not have to train in mud or swamps. The lack of imagination, of moral sensitivity, and the hermetically sealed existence of such thinkers is captured brilliantly by Vonnegut's simple reworking of one of the famous Oppenheimer stories. The narrator asks Newt Hoenniker for biographical information concerning his father and the bomb. Newt replies:

> Do you know the story about Father on the day they first tested a bomb out at Alamogordo? After the thing went off, after it was a sure thing that America could wipe out a city with just one bomb, a scientist turned to Father and said, "Science has now known sin." And do you know what Father said? He said, "What is sin?"[27]

Vonnegut's naive observers, simple style, and black humor often allow us to see as bizarre things that we ordinarily fail to notice because in our sophistication we are so inured to them. One of Hoenniker's colleagues, Asa Breed, gives a commencement address in which he tells the graduates that "the trouble with the world was that people were still superstitious instead of scientific . . . if everybody would study science more, there wouldn't be all the trouble there was."[28] It takes the superstitions of Bokonon and his religion of *Foma* or lies to point up the distortions of such a purely rationalist view. Or it takes a *naïf* like Miss Pefko, a secretary who expresses profound truths similar to those of our Everyman MP in the Alamogordo desert.

> I take dictation from Dr. Horvath and it's just like a foreign language. I don't think I'd understand—even if I was to go to college. And here he's maybe talking about something that's going to turn everything upside-down and inside-out like the atom bomb.[29]

And so it goes. We laugh at Vonnegut's portrayals, but we must also remember that when some scientists did protest the decision to drop the atomic bomb, they did so only at the Met Lab at the University of Chicago where work pressures had subsided. They had some time for reflection on the consequences of their work. But at Los Alamos, where scientists were under intense pressure to finish the atomic test in time for the Potsdam meeting, there was no such time or inclination to weigh the moral and political issues. Recall that only Joseph Rotblat quit the Manhattan Project once it was clear that the Nazis would be unable to build a bomb. Felix Hoenniker lives.

Black humor is also central to what is perhaps the most successful nuclear war movie of all time, *Dr. Strangelove; Or How I Learned to Stop Worrying and Love the Bomb*.[30] The title, *Strangelove*, is a play on perversion, in this case the twisted macho needs of General Jack D. Ripper (Sterling Hayden), named appropriately after a British sex criminal, General Turgidson (George C. Scott), whose mistress calls him at the war room ("I thought I told you never to call me here!"), and Colonel Kong (Slim Pickens), who rides the phallic bomb, cowboy hat in hand, to the ultimate orgasm. Aside from all the fun and verbal games in the film, Stanley Kubrick and scriptwriter Terry Southern are on to something here about the nuclear age, as the more conventional Hollywood drama *Fail-Safe* is not. Terry Southern has said that he was called in by Kubrick to work on the screenplay because a straightforward treatment could not capture the absurd horror of a red alert or the insanity of the institutions producing one.[31] With its zany and at times scatalogical humor, the film allows viewers to absorb and contemplate what is otherwise a chilling, unfathomable, almost unbelievable scenario—the end of the earth. Just as important, it discredits the well-meaning liberal, deterrent notions, the rationalistic poses that underlie and actually maintain the nuclear arms race.

President Muffley, played by Peter Sellers as a sort of hapless Adlai Stevenson figure, full of good intentions, is as ludicrous as the macho gorillas with whom he works. He is, appropriately, never in control of the situation in the way that Henry Fonda's composed, liberal president in *Fail-Safe* usually is. All the values and mannerisms that have become absurd in the face of nuclear war are best captured in the hilarious hotline conversation with the Soviet premier, as Muffley meekly apologizes. "I'm sorry, too, Dmitri. Think how I feel."

LANGUAGE AND NUCLEAR WAR

The emptiness of such conventional clichés is revealing and laughable in a nuclear black comedy. But we witness the perversion of language constantly in thinking and talking about surviving nuclear wars. Examples of Orwellian language are so abundant that it makes an excellent group project to collect and analyze them, or perhaps even to make a nuclear glossary, translating into plain, stark English the homey but deadly terms like "silo" or "nuclear exchange."

Consider the examples that abound in a film like *Panic in Year Zero,* in which Ray Milland[32] portrays a mild-mannered father-knows-best type who resorts to violence and vigilantism in the countryside beyond Los Angeles after a nuclear attack. *Panic* is not a good film, but its incredibly camp air allows students to laugh and engage in lively classroom discussion in a way that the horrors of *Hiroshima* or *The War Game* sometimes foreclose. Milland descends the ladder of decency slowly. He motors along with his teenage son beside him (Frankie Avalon plays the son who will discover manhood amid nuclear peril). Mom and Sis ride dutifully in the back seat, acting helpless throughout. Milland eventually punches out a service station attendant for gas, holds up a general store for provisions, and then with his son guns down the teenage hoods who have raped his daughter when she strayed too far from their nuclear hideout. All this occurs as Milland mouths platitudes about "saving law and civilization," and someone having to uphold "morality."

The climactic moment comes when the family car is halted by a commanding voice behind glaring headlights. What perils now? The family cringes until the camera pans back on an Army jeep with mounted machine gun. They cry, "We're saved! It's the Army!" The ensuing dialogue reveals that the Army has been busy putting down troublesome elements and that martial law has been declared. Such "salvation" is a fitting ending for the values of patriarchy and authoritarianism displayed throughout the film. The conclusion of *Panic* ranks with the infamous comment by an Army officer in Vietnam, "We had to destroy Ben Tre in order to save it."

Panic is based, however, in social reality. It dates from the heightened Cold War tensions and fallout-shelter craze of about 1961-1962 when John Kennedy attempted to implement the policies advocated by Cold War intellectuals during the Eisenhower years in the Gaither and Rockefeller reports. Now such thinking about limited nuclear wars, civil defense, survival, and the rest is once again official policy. Thus it is hard to distinguish between the craziness of *Panic* and official policy. At one point in the film, Ray Milland hurls a flaming oil drum of gasoline into the bumper-to-bumper traffic fleeing Los Angeles. The multicar crash that follows allows him to safely proceed with his family. Neglect for a moment the callousness of such a homicidal act. Try rather to imagine that such car scenes are advocated under the "crisis relocation" plans of the Federal Emergency Management Agency (FEMA).

The Orwellian nature of the title "FEMA" is self-evident. It used to be called "civil defense"—itself a euphemism, but at least one that we learned to associate with nuclear war. The effect of such civil defense language on actual thought and behavior, however, is of interest. I interviewed at length the director of planning of the California Office of Emergency Planning about a nuclear war in California.[33] Jim Watkins is a handsome, blond-haired young chemistry Ph.D. from the University of California at Davis. He is friendly, open, concerned, and an idealist. "I've always wanted to help people," he told me, "and this job allows me to do that." Watkins does not lose sleep worrying about nuclear war. He simply tries to plan for it thoroughly, carefully, and logically. When asked if his plans for mass evacuations of cities, distribution of food, and the like will work, he answers, "Yes. And they damned well better work." During crisis relocation, Jim Watkins told me, millions of residents of Los Angeles and San Francisco will drive calmly out of their cities, obeying the authorities. They will willingly share extremely limited rations and water supplies at their "relocation centers" because "the necessity of such measures will have been carefully explained to them." Having recently driven by literally miles of lettuce near Salinas, I wanted to know where the food will come from when a nuclear attack does occur. Watkins is again calm and logical, "That's no problem. We will simply wash off the contamination from the lettuce and then distribute it to the centers." The National Guard will, of course, be in charge, but not to round up troublemakers, only "to keep order and assist people." Jim Watkins has seen *The War Game,* Peter Watkins's mock documentary produced for BBC that was so searing they refused to show it. But the problems raised there, he assured me, are all "exaggerated."

As in *Panic in Year Zero,* the poison of radioactive fallout is not a problem for Jim Watkins and other planners who perceive nuclear war solely through numbers and sanitized language. Watkins believes that all the scenarios of the "postattack environment" calculate "too high a proportion of ground-burst nuclear weapons to air-burst weapons." If nuclear weapons are exploded in the air, there is no fallout; most incoming weapons, Watkins believes, will be airburst, so the problem of radioactivity is "manageable."

All of this planning does not make nuclear war more thinkable and hence more likely according to Watkins—only more survivable. Jim Watkins sincerely believes that it is those who decry nuclear war planning—planning that might save lives—who are immoral. And Watkins's office staff does not just sit back and plan either. They actively promote their views, distributing films and educational materials such as the book *Your Chance to Live,* prepared by the Defense Civil Preparedness Agency in 1972. The book was designed for children, under contract to the Far West Laboratory for Educational Research and Development, whose "mission is to create new and better opportunities for children to learn." *Your Chance to Live* is filled with cute graphics and language that seems written by Kurt Vonnegut rather than by a group formally sponsored by the California Regents, the California State Board of Education, and other state educational associations. Given the recent controversy over the comments by T. K. Jones that we should use shovels to prepare for nuclear war, direct quotation from *Your Chance* about shelter from fallout seems in order:

> If you are caught short, improvise. Pile protective materials around yourself: piles of newspapers, furniture, sacks of grain. Create your shelter area in an inner room or closet. You can also improvise protection by digging a trench in your yard and covering it with lumber (or a door) and earth.[34]

Civil defense planners have some theological backing for these views, backing that is based in similar distortions and language and thought.

Ernest Lefever caused considerable controversy over his defense of the sale of infant formula to the Third World before the failure of his nomination as assistant secretary of state for human rights. But Lefever, an ordained minister and a graduate of Yale Divinity School, believes that we must plan for fighting nuclear wars. In a nuclear age "there can be such a thing as a just war, a just nuclear war." Lefever and others of this school of deterrence theology are able to conceive of "just nuclear wars" precisely because of a lack of imagination and distortions of language not much different from those of Felix Hoenniker or *Panic in Year Zero.* Lefever firmly believes that "even after a full scale nuclear exchange, there would be pockets of will, of culture, of civilization from which we could rebuild, not to mention the Southern Hemisphere which would scarcely be touched."[35]

Even discounting the blithe disregard by Lefever and others of governmental studies like *The Effects of Nuclear War* or persuasive journalistic accounts like Jonathan Schell's *Fate of the Earth,* what we observe here is a definition of "culture" that equates a lapse into barbarism with the survival of freedom. Surely Lefever has missed films like *The Planet of the Apes,* with their popular and realistic depiction of "survival" that includes genetic transmutation, human slavery, and the Statue of Liberty buried in the sand.

The closed linguistic, imaginative, and moral system of nuclear planners that Watkins, Lefever, and others epitomize has been carefully described by Henry T. Nash, a former Air Force civilian target analyst.[36] Nash and his colleagues chose a number of significant targets in the Soviet Union for nuclear destruction and then "nominated" them for the honor of inclusion in the "bombing encyclopedia," a sort of perverse reference tool containing fifty word descriptions of key facilities to be "taken out" in the event of nuclear war. The analysts vied to have their nominations included, Nash says, and were able to do so because of the numbing effect of such language, the division of labor and responsibility, and the sense of the elite quality of their group; they were closed off from ordinary citizens by security clearances and special jargon. Just as important, Nash told me, was the fact that none of the analysts, in his recollection, discussed much else, even socially. There was little talk of the arts, literature, or film, no play of the imagination, and certainly no awareness of protest. Nash and his colleagues who were busy picking Soviet targets to destroy in the 1950s and 1960s did not even bother to watch films like *On the Beach, Fail-Safe,* or *Dr. Strangelove.*[37]

The Orwellian use of language to support nuclear war has extended to public policy, too. Even Dwight Eisenhower urged in a memorandum that the public be kept confused about the difference between "nuclear" and "thermonuclear" weapons. James Fallows told me that White House speech writers must never refer to the destructiveness of nuclear war in such vivid, concrete terms as people being "fried."Instead, the language used must be cool and bureaucratic. President Carter was one of the few presidents to describe even briefly the destructiveness of our weapons in a speech. He referred to the ability of a single nuclear submarine to destroy 160 Soviet cities. Even this rather brief, psychologically distant reference, Fallows reports, caused controversy for Carter inside the government.[38]

Most recently, the Reagan administration offers examples of sanitized language and psychological numbing that range from the early campaign statement of George Bush that nuclear war is winnable to President Reagan's and former Secretary of State Haig's comments about limited nuclear war and demonstration nukes in Europe. We are also bound to witness leaps in public cynicism as President Reagan simultaneously calls for deep reductions in nuclear arms and defends plans to go ahead with over $180 billion worth of new nuclear weapons systems, including the first-strike Trident D5 warhead, the MX, and thousands of new cruise missiles. Political pressures arising from European protests and the spectacular rebirth of the American antinuclear movement compel him to proffer democratic, peaceful gestures and rhetoric, but the iron logic of deterrence and credibility demands that the production line of nuclear warheads grind on.

The elaborate "doomsday" game played during the winter of 1982 with a complete test of the command system during simulated nuclear war is the kind of cauterizing practice necessary to contemplate an actual attack. Meanwhile, the public is to be reassured that our military command functions even if the president is dead. Thus is the Republic saved. But such war-gaming contains another kind of language—a provocation of the other side, which must view such "games" as evidence of intent to wage nuclear war. Thus, within one exercise we have the absurdity, the black humor, of the good-and-bad president again. At home, the administration cares about peace, deterrence, our survival; abroad it sends messages of aggressiveness and annihilation. The same double message is contained in civil defense planning currently budgeted at $4.2 billion. Jim Watkins may see civil defense as benign, but when the Soviets carry it out, we take it as evidence of their intent to wage and win a nuclear war.

BREAKING THE CYCLE—RESEARCH FOR DISARMAMENT

I began by asserting that in teaching about these distortions of our democracy and culture, as well as other aspects of the nuclear arms race, teachers must go beyond mere analysis. If all we do is point out, however ingeniously, the horrifying effects of living with the bomb—not to mention the well-known physical, medical, environmental, and economic dangers—we may only further numb our students. I have had students tell me that their friends will not take a course on nuclear war "because it's too depressing." If we are successfully to educate about nuclear war, we must do as the verb *educare* says, lead our students out of this mess. To do this, we must demystify nuclear weapons and policy planning, and pierce the veil of secrecy and obfuscation that surrounds them. And, without doubt, we must offer our students serious work to do that may concretely affect the outcome of the nuclear arms race. We must remind our students that there is hope, not false or cheap hope, but a recognition that the nuclear age has spawned protest, revulsion, new ways of thinking, and even partial victories that must not be overlooked. I have alluded to the impact of current nuclear protests on the Reagan administration. Students should discover, too, that advances like the Limited Test Ban Treaty were the result of a long period of public pressure similar to the one we are now witnessing. From 1957 to 1963 groups like SANE in the United States and the Campaign for Nuclear Disarmament in Britain created a climate that eventually affected the views of Eisenhower and even

John Foster Dulles.[39] And it was the actions of only a few individuals, including Dorothy Day of the Catholic Worker Movement, that launched a massive civil disobedience campaign in New York against nuclear air raid drills. Eventually, thousands joined Day in refusing to take shelter. The drills became a laughingstock, and civil defense was downplayed until today.[40]

In examining previous protests and the scope of the nuclear arms industry, students will need to do rigorous, original research using a variety of resources including oral interviews, ephemeral primary sources, government documents, corporate reports, the business press, and so forth. Their goal must be to discover and fill in those blanks that Frances FitzGerald discovered are all that currently exist in our collective educational histories of the nuclear age.

Howard Morland's research into how H-bombs are made offers an excellent case study of the ill effects of government secrecy and the social therapy of breaking it. Morland set out to trace in detail the entire H-bomb production process.[41] Along with other peace researchers, he has helped to put on the map places previously unknown—Rocky Flats, Savannah River, and Pantex. Without knowing the elements and design of the bomb, where components are produced, shipped, and assembled, Morland figured correctly, it would be impossible to assess nuclear environmental hazards and potential for accidents, or even to meaningfully mount local protests or organize workers.

Bishop Leroy T. Matthiessen, Roman Catholic Bishop of Amarillo, Texas, for example, spent thirty years within four miles of the Silas and Mason-run Pantex plant near Amarillo where all U.S. nuclear weapons are assembled. Bishop Matthiessen did not even know it was there. When he spoke out in the summer of 1981 against the building of nuclear weapons as sinful and urged that workers at Pantex quit their jobs, he made headlines. But few traced the more complex origins of such a moral pronouncement. Matthiessen's attention was drawn to the Pantex plant by the arrest of the Pantex 6, a group of religious activists.[42] They included an Oblate priest, Larry Rosebaugh, who had served time in prison for draft resistance during the Vietnam War as one of the Milwaukee 4. Uncovering how and where H-bombs are made, protest and risk on the part of committed Christians and other protestors, were all essential prior steps that led to the *education* of Bishop Matthiessen and eventually the public.

In fact, some of the best research on nuclear weapons is done outside the academy and can be emulated by students in any discipline. In Philadelphia, I recently spoke to Bob Smith, a member of the Brandywine Peace Community and one of the GE 5, another group of religious activists related to the Pantex 6, the Berrigan's Plowshares 8, and similar nonviolent communities. Smith had just had charges against him and the rest of the GE 5 dropped for pouring blood inside the headquarters of the General Electric Re-entry Division. The Re-entry Division is where the MK12A warhead, an essential component of counterforce strategy, is manufactured. Smith and his cohorts had worked, studied, protested, prayed, and kept vigil for over three years in an attempt to alert Philadelphians to the dangers of the MK12A. It is a warhead capable of carrying up to ten multiple independently guided reentry vehicles (MIRVs) that can strike separate targets with an accuracy of 100 meters. Finally, they took the serious risk of pouring their blood.

The prosecution eventually dropped charges against the GE 5 that totaled fifty-two years in prison. But Bob Smith is not ready for a vacation. Instead, he enthusiastically described to me his latest projects. He and others are researching the Defense Satellite Communication System (DSCS III; pronounced "discus") being produced by General Electric at its Space Division in Valley Forge.[43] In the Orwellian world we have explored, it should not be surprising that DSCS is actually an essential part of the Reagan administration's strategy of controlled nuclear war fighting. Along with increased cruise missiles, the MX, Trident submarines, the Pershing II, and neutron bombs, the administration is also investing heavily in enhancing the survivability and flexibility of nuclear command, control, and communication or "C^3."[44]

DSCS will provide integrated communication between all parts of our strategic triad and is designed to facilitate the kind of nuclear war fighting *in extremis* envisioned in the recent "doomsday" war game. Now Bob Smith is busy telling people and GE stockholders' meetings just what good things are being brought to life. Like other activists/researchers, Smith relies only on unclassified materials. He regularly consults with the National Action/Research on the Military Industrial Complex (NARMIC), scours the business press, and seeks information from corporate publications.[45] Then the information on GE is interpreted by, among others, Bill Whistler, a member of the Brandywine Peace Community and a former GE aerospace engineer who worked on ICBMs and satellites.

In addition, the Brandywine Peace Community has obtained an actual surplus MK12A warhead casing and its transporting barrel. They use it as a real-life visual aid and teaching tool at meetings and peace fairs, and in discussions with journalists and researchers. The warhead casing is a black cone that is over four feet high. It contains a slot about two and one-half feet long that holds a thermonuclear warhead with 350 kilotons of yield.[46] American warhead casings are designed with a special carbon-carbon graphite exterior to burn up on reentry, absorbing heat as they descend. Thus, they are far lighter and more accurate than Soviet ones, which still use heavy heat reflecting and shielding devices for reentry. Seeing an actual MK12A warhead casing is an education in itself, one that breaks through all the nuclear jargon. The small space for a bomb that can destroy a city is especially chilling. And just as shocking are the words carefully printed on the barrel for shipment from Valley Forge to Pantex, where the bomb will be installed. "Handle with care. Do Not Destroy."

Students can carry out similar research. An excellent way to begin might be to research your own local area and create a slide show on the nuclear arms race and its effects. Such a collective effort breaks the mystique of weapons research and teaches students the value of collective effort in understanding and changing something as vast and complex as the nuclear arms race. During Ground Zero week, I gave a workshop at Southwestern University in Memphis, Tennessee. Within two hours, a diverse group of college, secondary school, community, labor, and religious educators had outlined the script, basic research, and tasks necessary for a Memphis nuclear arms race slide show. They had even begun to assess talents and assign research, interviewing, photography, audio, editing, and the like. Tom Schlesinger of the Highlander School in Tennessee was also in the workshop and shared research he had already begun on the military in Memphis. Incredibly enough, part of the nuclear arms race is carried out there by inmates at the federal prison. In 1981, for example, the prison received a Department of Defense contract totaling $4.69 million for work on gun parts, fire control equipment, and nuclear missile launcher components.[47] Many campuses are also deeply involved in the nuclear arms race. I undertook a study of Pentagon spending in Philadelphia that not only revealed work on the MK12A warhead at GE, but also, a few blocks away, work on the Trident missile at the University of Pennsylvania.[48] Such research at universities is on the upswing as military research and development continues to blossom. According to Steve Burkholder:

> From 1979 to 1980 (the most recent years for which complete figures are available), higher education's share of the military R&D budget rose from $574 million to $652 million. . . . While the military's vast network of in-house labs received a piece of the basic research pie equal to higher education's a few years ago, the school's share of such funding now surpasses the Pentagon's own labs by almost $50 million.[49]

Once the students have thoroughly researched military contracts and facilities in their area, they can move on to civil defense planning and proceed to map out the destruction that a typical H-bomb would cause.[50] They can then explore with community groups the economic and social effects that excessive military spending causes in the area. Finally, they can begin to suggest and plan alternatives for conversion to peaceful uses and alternative technologies. As they interview and gather photographs and documentation, they will begin building networks in the community that will lead to further education and, eventually, to action.

Action begets hope. Even small actions such as the production of an original slide show or pamphlet that becomes part of the regular curriculum of local high schools, colleges, or community groups staves off that fatal numbness, the sense that learning is unreal, that the future is uncertain, that nothing can be done. Something can and must be done about the threat of nuclear war and its corrosive cultural effects. As educators it should be our job, whatever our discipline, to make sure that it happens.

Notes

1 Franklin Griffiths and John C. Polyani, ed., *The Dangers of Nuclear War* (Toronto: University of Toronto Press, 1978).

2 Albert Furtwangler, "Growing Up Nuclear," *The Bulletin of the Atomic Scientists* 39, no. 1 (1978): 44-48.

3 A manual containing the syllabi of twenty-one courses on disarmament is available from Carolyn Stephenson, Director, Peace and World Order Studies Program, Colgate University, Hamilton, N.Y. 13346. Also see *Peace and World Order Studies: A Curriculum Guide,* 3rd ed. (New York: Transactional Academic Program/Institute for World Order, 1981) (available from IWO, 777 United Nations Plaza, New York, N.Y. 10017). Also COPRED, Consortium on Peace Research, Education, and Development, Center for Peaceful Change, Stapler Hall, Kent State University, Kent, Ohio 44242, for a network of peace educators.

4 A complete set of audiocassettes, transcripts, and a seventeen-page study and discussion guide for all thirteen half-hour "Shadows of the Nuclear Age" documentaries are available for $97.75 from the SANE Education Fund, 5808 Greene Street, Philadelphia, Pa. 19144.

5 Jonathan Schell, *The Time of Illusion* (New York: Vintage Books, 1976), p. 9. Also, generally, pp. 7-14.

6 E. P. Thompson and Dan Smith, eds., *Protest and Survive* (Middlesex: Penguin Books, 1980), pp. 54, 56.

7 Interview, George Kistiakowsky, on file at the SANE Education Fund. All uncut interviews from "Shadows of the Nuclear Age" are on file and will be deposited in the SANE Education archives, Swarthmore College Library Peace Collection.

8 Interview, Ted Lombard, broadcast on "Consider the Alternatives." Transcript available fron SANE Education Fund. Also see generally: Howard L. Rosenberg, *The Atomic Soldiers: American Victims of Atomic Experiments* (Boston: Beacon Press, 1980); Michael Uhl and Tod Ensign, *The GI Guinea Pig* (New York: Playboy Press, 1980); and Harvey Wasserman and Norman Solomon, *Killing Our Own: The Disaster of America's Experience with Atomic Radiation* (New York: Delta Books, 1982), with an introduction by Dr. Benjamin Spock.

9 Interview, Joseph Rotblat, "Shadows," transcript and file.

10 Interview, Hans Bethe, "Shadows," file.

11 Interview, Edward Teller, "Shadows," transcript and file.

12 Martin J. Sherwin, *A World Destroyed: The Atomic Bomb and the Grand Alliance* (New York: Vintage Books, 1977), pp. 230-31.

13 Interview, Robert J. Donovan, "Shadows," transcript and file.

14 Interview, David Lilienthal, "Shadows," file. See also Herbert F. York, *The Advisors: Oppenheimer, Teller and the Superbomb* (San Francisco: W. H. Freeman, 1975).

15 Interview, George F. Kennan, "Shadows," file. See also George F. Kennan, *Memoirs, 1925-1950* (New York: Bantam Books, 1969), pp. 497-501; and Dean Acheson, *Present at the Creation* (New York: Signet Books, 1970), pp. 452-53. George Kennan's memorandum has been declassified since the publication of his *Memoirs* and is available in Thomas H. Etzold and John Lewis Gaddis, eds., *Containment: Documents on American Policy and Strategy, 1945-1950* (New York: Columbia University Press, 1978), pp. 373-81.

16 Interview, Dean Rusk, "Shadows," file. Also in Theodore Sorenson, "Shadows," file. See also Theodore Sorenson, *Kennedy* (New York: Harper & Row, 1965), p. 685.

17 Interview, Dean Rusk, "Shadows," transcript and file.

18 David Lilienthal, *The Journals of David E. Lilienthal, Vol. II, The Atomic Energy Years, 1945-1950* (New York: Harper & Row, 1964), p. 29.

19 Alexander Haig, *New York Times,* April 7, 1982.

20 Robert K. Musil, "Carter as Commander-in-Chief: The Rising Cost of U.S. Defense Policies," *Christian Century* 95, no. 16 (May 3, 1978): 466-69.

21 Interview, James Fallows, "Consider the Alternatives," transcript.

22 Interview, Frances FitzGerald, "Shadows," transcript and file. See also Frances FitzGerald, *America Revised* (Boston: Little, Brown, 1979).

23 Interhelp can be contacted at Interhelp, Box 4448, Arcata, Calif., 99521.

24 See also Robert K. Musil, "Growing Up Nuclear," *The Bulletin of the Atomic Scientists* 39, no. 1, (January 1982): 19.

25 Morris Dickstein, *Gates of Eden: American Culture in the Sixties* (New York: Harper Colophon, 1977), p. 106.

26 See Robert K. Musil, "There Must Be More to Love and Death: A Conversation with Kurt Vonnegut," *The Nation* 231, no. 4 (August 2-9, 1980): 128-33.

27 Kurt Vonnegut, *Cat's Cradle* (New York: Dell Books, 1970), p. 21.

28 Ibid., p. 25.

29 Ibid., p. 31.

30 See Charles Maland, "Dr. Strangelove (1964): Nightmare Comedy and the Ideology of Liberal Consensus," *American Quarterly* 31, no. 5 (Winter 1979): 697-717.

31 Interview, Terry Southern, "Shadows," file, and interview and lecture, Terry Southern, February 20, 1981, Philadelphia, Pa.

32 See Jack G. Shaheen, ed., *Nuclear War Films* (Carbondale: Southern Illinois University Press, 1978), for a brief description of *Panic* and other nuclear war films. The most comprehensive guide for teachers is John Dowling, *War/Peace Film Guide* (Chicago: World Without War Publications, 1980), rev. ed. (available from World Without War Publications, 67 E. Madison Street, Suite 1417, Chicago, Illinois for $5.75). Professor Dowling will also send a computerized update to the guide for $2.00 (John Dowling, Department of Physics, Mansfield State College, Mansfield, Pa. 16933).

33 Interview, James Watkins, "Consider the Alternatives," file.

34 Defense Civil Preparedness Agency, SM 3-12, 1972, *Your Chance to Live* (Washington, D.C.: U.S. Government Printing Office, 1973), p. 82.

35 Interview, Ernest Lefever, "Shadows," transcript and file.

36 See Henry T. Nash, "The Bureaucratization of Homicide," *Protest and Survive* (Middlesex: Penguin Books, 1980), pp. 62-74.

37 Interview, Henry T. Nash, "Shadows," transcript and file.

38 Interview, James Fallows, "Consider the Alternatives," transcript and file.

39 Interview, Robert A. Divine, "Shadows," transcript and file. See also Robert A. Divine, *Blowing on the Wind: The Test-Ban Debate, 1954-1960* (London: Oxford University Press, 1980).

40 Interviews, Jim Peck, Grace Paley, "Shadows," file. See also Lawrence S. Wittner, *Rebels against War: The American Peace Movement, 1941-1960* (New York: Columbia University Press, 1969), p. 265.

41 See Howard Morland, *The Secret That Exploded* (New York: Random House, 1981). See also Morland's original articles and discussion in *Time Bomb: A Nuclear Reader from the Progressive,* ed. James Rowan (Madison, Wis.: The Progressive Foundation, 1980) (The Progressive Foundation, 315 West Gorham Street, Madison, Wis. 53703).

42 Bishop Leroy T. Matthiessen, speech at Riverside Church Conference, November 1981, "Consider the Alternatives" file.

43 See Robert M. Smith, "GE and the Permanent War Economy," *Brandywine Peace Community Newsletter,* April 20, 1982 (available from Brandywine Peace Community, 51 Barren Road, Media, Pa. 19063).

44 See "Preparing for Nuclear War: President Reagan's Program," *The Defense Monitor* 10, no. 8 (1982) (available from the Center for Defense Information, 303 Capital Gallery West, 600 Maryland Avenue, SW, Washington, D.C. 20024).

45 NARMIC is the research division of the American Friends Service Committee (1501 Cherry Street, Philadelphia, Pa. 19103). It is also part of the Nuclear Weapons Facilities Task Force. See, for example, "Makers of the Nuclear Holocaust: A Guide to the Nuclear Weapons Complex and Citizen Action, 1981 (available from the Nuclear Weapons Facilities Project, Fellowship of Reconciliation, Box 271, Nyack, N.Y. 10960).

46 For a diagram of a similar nuclear reentry vehicle, see Coalition for a New Foreign and

Military Policy, "First Strike War Fare" (available from the Coalition, 120 Maryland Avenue, NW, Washington, D.C. 20002).

47 Tom Schlesinger, unpublished manuscript (available from the Highlander Center, RR 3, Box 37, New Market, Tenn. 37820).

48 Robert K. Musil, *The Pentagon in Philadelphia: The Economic and Social Effects of Military Spending in Philadelphia, 1968–1977* (Philadelphia: The SANE Education Fund, 1978) (available from SANE Education Fund, 5808 Greene Street, Philadelphia, Pa. 19144).

49 Steve Burkholder, "The Pentagon in the Ivory Tower," *The Progressive,* June 1981. Available in reprint from Nukewatch, an organization that researches military contracts on academic campuses. Contact the Progressive Foundation, 315 West Gorham Street, Madison, Wis. 53703.

50 An excellent resource for student activity is "The Nuclear Mapping Kit" (available from the American Friends Service Committee, Peace Education Division, 1501 Cherry Street, Philadelphia, Pa. 19103, or New York AFSC, 15 Rutherford Place, New York, N.Y. 10003).

Education as a Five-Letter Word

MICHAEL N. NAGLER
University of California, Berkeley

Think about the kind of world you want to live in. What do you need to build that world? Demand that your teachers teach you that.

—Peter Kropotkin

I do not want to live in the world if it is not to be one world.

—M. K. Gandhi

A recent article on peace education starts with a strong quotation from H. G. Wells: "Human History becomes more and more a race between education and catastrophe."[1] Education of a kind has been giving us an edge on catastrophe since long before we attained our human status. Birds teach their young to fly; wolves must learn to hunt in packs and to eat their prey. Homo sapiens living in small bands teaches its children the myths and norms that help them cope with their environment. The most important factor in the struggle of Third World peoples for physical survival today has been found to be not food, or medicine, or housing, but education.[2]

I hold, with Wells, that for our industrialized civilization, and the wider global network dragged along with us, education is likewise the key to our continued physical survival. I hold that since Wells's day catastrophe is gaining ground—a claim few dispute—and that, as he implied, education furnishes both the best set of terms in which to understand the present crisis and the tools to deal with it.

War is the single greatest threat to our survival in the present era. Clearly "war" may not be the right term for what will happen to us if either some Americans or some Soviets lose control of the emotional, political, economic, and technical nuclear threat system by which each seeks to maintain some illusion of restraint over the other's threatening behavior. Nonetheless, sufficient numbers on both sides still *think* of nuclear warheads as weapons and may provoke a fight with them, though the results of such a fight would be far different from any war, or indeed any experience the human race as a whole has ever undergone. Mentally, which is what counts for the present purpose, we are almost at war.

Now it is often said that the first casualty in time of war is truth. One thinks immediately of the concealment of casualty figures, the inaccuracies of propaganda, the diplomatic falsehoods and other misrepresentations that inevitably accompany hostilities. But the statement is more deeply true than that: War is inherently a lie-in-action. It denies the unity of mankind and the fact that all human beings can find ways of communicating short of violence—two fundamental truths.[3]

But if these fairly obvious truths hold, it follows ineluctably that war and education must be deeply incompatible. There is a sense in which this must be true of any helping profession: Medicine and war, law and war, both consort ill together, as do (let it be emphasized) statecraft and war, albeit all of these professions as presently practiced, education included, seem to be tied to war. To the extent that they are, they take us away from whatever help they were inherently designed for. Yet education seems conspicuously jarring on this list. Socrates said long ago that one cannot properly "learn" something that is not true, and this implies that education worthy of the name in our age has got to lead away from war both for the philosophical reason that war is so "untrue" and for the reason that war would now violate our chances for survival, which it has been the age-old function of education to extend.

How can education regain its edge over this particular catastrophe? Pruning the profession of its gross abuses—ROTC, the connection of the university with the national weapons laboratories, and so forth—would be the minimum that intellectual honesty demands, but one feels that in reality the problem is much deeper. Therefore, I would like to speak here to the individual educator and to concentrate on what can be done within our own professional domain. By what practices can education overtake catastrophe? Teaching how horrible war is has never worked and will not work now simply because war has become more horrible. And yet there is something about the newly awakening awareness of that horror that can, surely, be put to some advantage. Here I find Jacques Ellul's concise description of the present crisis useful: *"Ceci n'est point," he says, "l'âge de la violence, mais celle de la conscience de la violence"*[4] (This age is not the age of violence, but the age of awareness of violence). There is not more violence now than ever, Ellul holds (a disputable, but not a cardinal point); what is different is that we are more *aware* of it. It is present to our *conscience*—both "consciousness" and "conscience"—in a new way. Scholars (like Arendt, Ellul, Girard) have discovered violence as a subject fascinating in its own right, and—more to the point—it touches some new moral sensitivity in all of us: Other things being equal, we feel now that violence is illegitimate.

This change of consciousness-and-conscience may seem small comfort, surrounded as we are by so much overt violence, but it is potentially a very important fact. In the ancient world, for example, where neither slavery nor war aroused either theoretical interest or moral debate, their presence as institutions went unchallenged.[5] As soon as slavery did arouse theoretical interest and moral reaction, its days were numbered as a social institution.[6] So it was with dueling and many such obnoxious institutions. As Kenneth Boulding pointed out, this is how social evolution works: "Error can be found out, truth cannot. Evil when detected is rejected; good when detected is not."[7]

Yet here is a paradox in our age: the "error" of violence, as Ellul says, has been found out. We have reached that evolutionary moment when a critical mass of individuals can "see" that most forms of violence, particularly war, are retrograde or somehow wrong—yet we have not been able to discard them.[8] That paradox has landed us in a nightmarish tangle of irrationalities. Here in America one state throws out the death penalty and three others bring it back; we seek détente with the Soviet Union but do everything possible to antagonize them; we prepare for war with the rationale that we are securing peace; finally, as George Kennan says, we are prepared to "risk suicide for fear of death."[9] Society as a whole is like a snake that has swallowed a big frog it can neither get down nor give back. Some, having known violence for what it is without being able to discard it, only plunge deeper into violence, attempting to forget what they have seen.

Why do we not discard it? This is a deep question, but we get somewhere near the heart of it by saying that we simply see no convincing alternatives. If I know no other way to stop a mugger from attacking me, I will surely shoot him. If society as a whole can conceive of no other way of protecting itself from "criminals," it will surely arrest, imprison, punish, and even kill them, especially if criminal activities are steadily increasing. Even those who know—and it is a fact[10]—that punitive measures by and large increase the alienation that causes criminality will, if they see no alternative, keep on applying them. By the same principle, so long as we as a nation cannot think out loud about any other way to defend ourselves against perceived threats from the Soviet Union we will go on threatening to counter-destroy them, monstrous dangers and paradoxical absurdities to the contrary notwithstanding.

There *are* viable alternatives to all these categories of violence. The most important, most effective, and most overlooked set of alternatives is to live in such a way that, in George Fox's words, we "take away the occasion" of the violence: create social structures that do not breed criminality, enter into paths of energy use that do not force us to exploit the earth and its inhabitants, learn noncompetitive economic styles (and reformed national perspectives) that do not inevitably create hostility between our own and other national blocks. The next set consists of strategies for resolving conflicts when they do occur: mediation by third parties, armed and unarmed peacekeeping, recourse to improved systems of international law, negotiation and diplomacy.[11] Finally there are measures of last resort like nonviolent civilian-based defense (not to be confused with "civil defense," a part of the war-threat system) by which armed invasions have been neutralized, frustrated, and defused. This is not speculation. At all three stages, specimen attempts at corresponding but alternative strategies have been found to work. Here and there—as with third-party mediation in the thirteenth century—they have been made to work reliably.[12] This is a matter of historical record.

The existence and efficacy of these alternatives makes the question of the role of education in preserving peace absurdly simple: Teach them. Why teach history as if these episodes did not exist, or did not far outweigh in their significance what they lack in frequency? We have been studying the hole instead of the doughnut, or as Gandhi said, the breakdowns of the process of history, not history itself.[13] In history, in political science and anthropology, in many humanistic and social science disciplines, we could study how societies stay together instead of how they have fallen apart, make alternatives to violence thinkable, and thus construct an education that is at once more accurate and more effective at rescuing contemporary societies from disaster.

And yet, of course, the process of salvation will not be so simple. Human nature is such that the longer one is committed to an irrationality—and the irrationality of the Cold War is deeply ingrown by now—the less willing one becomes to throw off that irrationality at the mere sound of reason. In the glare of violence, not even the outlines of nonviolence are seen, and, educators and students alike, we live in that glare. Before the average student gets to school, he or she has seen over 20,000 acts of brutal violence on television. The "news" we watch and read has been selected by that bias; add to this the recent discovery of mass media by ideologues of a proviolent persuasion.[14] In short, we teachers face a classroom, and behind that a population, that already entertains serious delusions about the structure of reality. The higher reality I am suggesting that we teach will find no place to land.

For some this means that there is little an educator can do. I would prefer to interpret the fact as broadening the mandate of the educator. If it is not our responsibility to alleviate irrationality, what is? Let us look briefly at the situation of teaching in society at large.

In the "developed" world, education has been suffering a long decline (another reason Western educators think that there is little they can do). We can best understand the reasons from an occasion when the decline was—apparently—reversed, the public boost to education following Sputnik in 1957. Yet this was not a boost to *education;* rather, it reflected one purpose that one sector of the public thinks education is designed to serve: to enhance state power, to supply technology to keep us "winning" in our global competition with the Soviets. This is the reason Johnny should learn; indeed, it is for no small fraction of the population a mission of mythological proportions. The genius must be identified and schooled full time, wrote Max Rafferty, a former superintendent of public education in California, for our enemy is "a race of faceless, godless peasants from the steppes of Asia."[15]

I would argue that our response to this ideological context must be threefold. Before we are teachers we are citizens, and before citizens, people—human beings. (I often think, in fact, that excerpts from Emerson's *American Scholar* should be read at every graduation and every department meeting.) Therefore our first job is to extricate ourselves as individuals from the prevailing framework of irrationality, which continues putting peace beyond the planet's grasp. The second task is to exercise responsible citizenship whenever and wherever we still have the chance. The third (and the only phase I propose to comment on in this context) is for us both as individual teachers and as members of the teaching system to do what education can—and there is evidence that it could do a lot[16]—to communicate a sense of the reality and accessibility of peace.

When Sputnik went up and the Soviets threatened to slip out of the faceless peasant horde mythologem we had prepared for them, government and public agencies did not come flocking to Sovietologists to ask if our mythologem was wrong. They did not seek out philosophy professors to ask them *whether* there should be a relationship of competition with these people. They came exclusively for technical assistance. They see us as Sophists, for whom the task is not to help society formulate an appropriate ideology (Plato, *Republic* 6.493) but to help it prop up whatsoever ideology it forms. And, I am afraid, that is how too many of us see ourselves. The problem is much more than just political. We are following an inherently wrong control model, as Plato said;[17] government simply is not competent to dictate the purposes of education, and if it does so, both must fall. Nor is the solution to the problem just political (as that word is usually defined). We are in an age of twofold tragedy, when the purposes of society are particularly shallow and misguided—"winning" is meaningless as a human goal—and education is particularly vulnerable because it has no purpose of its own.

Education is losing prestige, and doing so most rapidly where it seems to gain prestige, because it has become the servant of a rudderless society. Might it not become the guide, and rescue both? If we would have it do so, we must face the most shunned question in the educational profession today: What is the *purpose* of education—and, by extension, of society at large? Why should Johnny learn?

Here we might be tempted to supply the answer: for our survival. And while there is a sense in which survival is indeed a purpose of education and always has been, there is also a sense in which mere survival is entirely inadequate. Survival is not a *goal,* any more than competition is. It is of course a base condition that makes it possible to entertain thoughts of a goal. As an end of human life, however, it is necessary but not sufficient, hardly capable of galvanizing the leap of imagination, the increment in rationality, required to address our present needs.[18]

Instead, let us take a clue from discarded institutions of the past—slavery, piracy, race prejudice, colonialism, dueling (I am well aware that they have not been utterly discarded everywhere in practice). What did all these institutions have in common? They were all stumbling blocks to the inherent fellowship of human beings. By his very nature, Augustine points out, man feels compelled to seek fellowship and, as far as in him lies, peace with his fellow man (*City of God* XIX.10). When, for reasons it would be fascinating to understand, particular ways of enslaving, dominating, or exploiting one's fellow man or woman were suddenly understood to block the progress of this fellowship, people made efforts to discard them, sometimes even though a good part of a society's economy or a good part of its organizational structure seemed to depend on them.

Now, when Comenius decreed that education should be accessible to everyone "unless God denied him sense and intelligence," the good bishop placed education squarely in the forefront of this dynamic process. And when a modern educational critic (and foe of Comenius) demands, as he should, that education give us "access to reality," he is really making the same claim.[19] For what more important reality can education serve than this—improving human sociability, answering to the desire for planetary integration that is so deeply rooted in our nature? Recently "citizenship" served as a less than thrilling but valid enough interpretation of that goal. But now students and faculty alike can think of nothing better to demand than that pathetic shadow of relevancy, "marketable skills." Citizenship was not such a bad idea, only we abandoned it in the wrong direction. Students have rejected citizenship because it left self-realization out of account, only to adopt a version of self-fulfillment that leaves the world out of account. Socially we have reduced citizenship to consumerism. Instead, we should upgrade it: *world* citizenship, a concept for which we lack a well agreed upon and sensible definition, would, with such a definition, orient the individual toward his chance to play a meaningful role in history. Education with this goal in view would train a student to "think globally, act locally" (in René Dubos's prophetic formula) and come perhaps as close as formal education can to putting students in the way of personal fulfillment. This it would do not at the expense of society, as modern "meism" does (while actually ruining the individual's chances of happiness in the bargain) but in the highest service of society. That is, it would not serve society's perceived interests—which, as Heraclitus said, would do society no favor—but turn out individuals equipped to help society perceive where its true interests lie.

It hardly need be said that they do not lie in war. War now would be not an obstruction but an obliteration of whatever hope remains for unifying humankind. If war, as we have claimed above, is a falsehood in action, peace is truth-in-relationships, perhaps their highest truth. Therefore peace has a strong claim to be, at least in this creaky hinge of history if not inherently, the goal and substance of education, if that term is meaningfully defined. Peace and global social integration are two sides of but one coin, and the coin is very thin. We realize each day a bit more clearly how these two concerns, which between them synergistically define the proper goal of education, resonate one with the other. Now we can turn to some of the nuts and bolts of how an education that responded to this compound goal would look.

In 1977 a group of Soviet and American teachers joined together to give each other an opportunity to criticize the way their countries were presented in the other country's textbooks. The results were bracing. Russian teachers found it insulting to be lumped together with fascist Italy and Nazi Germany as "totalitarian," while U.S. teachers, strange to say, felt the same way about finding their country lumped together with Nazi Germany and others as "imperialist." Some results were much more unpredictable, and the group produced an interim report showing that both nation's texts "are self-serving, ideological, erroneous in part, stress differences between the two countries [I return to this point] and are guided by cold-war points of view."[20] Unfortunately, the joint session where these biases were to have been corrected was prevented from occurring by a U.S. ban on large official meetings between Americans and Soviets. This gives an idea, though, of the exhilarating room for improvement that a world-order perspective (if not a general desire for truthfulness) identifies and how a perfectly accessible combination of political action and the improvement of curricular materials could work some such improvements. Let me mention, to continue the sampling, a different kind of recent development.

Since around 1948, American colleges and universities have been adding courses, and in some eighty cases programs or majors, designed to help students deal specifically with the huge issues of peace and world order.[21] Sometimes adopted quietly, these programs have more often found themselves posing a regular configuration of challenges to prevailing educational practises at many levels: profound reorganization of traditional educational compartments, explicit concern for the forbidden area of values (here the neo-Piagetan revolution associated with Lawrence Kohlberg is of interest), assumption of a mandate to do not only planning *for* the future, as Burns Weston says, but planning *of* the future.[22] Most radically of all, by their very coming into being these studies challenge the entrenched "Manichaean" presupposition that war and conflict are real, while cooperation and peace are not.

This regular pattern of a fundamental alteration of expectations has led some educational theorists to see these programs as part of a "paradigm shift" of major, perhaps millennial proportions that is now affecting not education only but civilization as a whole.[23] Be this as it may, the new curricula certainly are to the entire academic enterprise what ecology is, for example, to the "pure" disciplines of natural science—or more indistinctly, religious studies to philosophy, ethnic studies to the humanities, and so forth: The moment they exist you realize they should have been represented in, if not been made the heart of, their respective units all along.

Now that peace studies have come out from under the carpet, it is by no means clear that they should be given a separate room. Creating yet a new compartment in which the most responsible (as opposed to "pure"?) students and faculty can function has no philosophical or educational justification. Nonetheless, at campuses where the assumption that "you can't teach peace" has sunk deep into the woodwork and continues to influence the shape of educational development, or lack of it, from that advantageous position, somebody may have to teach that very thing, labeled as such, until the balance of perceived legitimacy is shifted. Better a marginal existence for peace, most of us feel, than none at all.

Whether it be from the margins or from central locations or diffused throughout the curriculum, there must begin a strong campaign against the American student's and American public's illiteracy with regard to peace. Of all illiteracies to be identified in recent years, this should be most distressing, for why Johnny cannot conceive of peace is ultimately more dangerous than why he cannot read. It would be our ultimate, perhaps our final irresponsibility to continue sending students out into this violent world—a world we have prepared for them—who do not know about the history of peace attempts in the East and West, the role of altruism in evolution, world-order theory, what Gandhi said and did, some history and theory of nonviolence, civilian-based defense, mediation, third-party peacekeeping in both its "top-down" and "bottom-up" manifestations (U.N. armed peace forces and grass-roots efforts from Gandhi's Shanti Sena to today's Peace Brigades International), prospects for formal education and training in conflict avoidance or conflict resolution (the International Peace Academy, the U.S. Academy of Peace and Conflict Resolution), and where all these and similar efforts have worked and failed.[24] Anyone who leaves school today, with whatever "major," without a good working knowledge of these subjects will be a menace to self and society. Therefore to continue passing this content over (or to "cover" it in such a way that its significance remains beyond reach of normal students) constitutes an error of omission the effects of which on American policy and decision making are becoming critically more dangerous. No one renounces any violence he has relied on for defense, assertiveness, or what he perceives to be the legitimate fulfillment of his aims who does not know an alternative defense, assertiveness, or fulfillment. There are such alternatives. We are obligated to learn and teach them.

And yet, as we have seen above, the problem is much more than a lack of knowledge. At a recent New England meeting on the proposed bilateral nuclear weapons freeze one man blurted out, "Give up our weapons and we'll just be lying down letting them grab us by the throat!" At such a time, telling him about the theory of nonviolent defense or even how it worked in Czechoslovakia in 1968 (assuming that anyone even knew this), reciting the heroism of the Norwegian schoolteachers during the Occupation, would only have landed on ears deafened by long-standing panic. What could have made him understand that other relationships between two roughly equal countries can exist besides deadly competition—that there might be another model applicable than that of snarling dogs? We have to think not only about our facts but of how we select, organize, and present them.

For example, anyone who took "geography" in my generation will immediately recognize the syntax of an expression like "Bolivia is a source of tin." But is this what Bolivia *is*? We were being educated for colonialism. To educate for pan-ecumenism we must retain and quicken the natural impression children have that Bolivia must be a country where human beings like ourselves live, play, work, love, and weep.

> My conventional education [writes Norman Cousins] taught me to recognize easily and instantly the things that differentiate one place or one people from another. Geography had instructed me in differences of terrain, resources, and productivity. Comparative culture had instructed me in the differences of background and group interests. . . . In those respects my education had been more than adequate. But what my education failed to do was teach me that the principal significance of such differences was that they were largely without significance.[25]

This was an untruthful education and, as my example of Bolivia might indicate, not without dangerous significance. We who learned unconsciously to "target" places like Bolivia for exploitation would soon enough learn to target cities of the Soviet Union in a more sinister sense—and have ours targeted by them in turn.

This brings us to a very basic issue. When that education for differences of which Cousins spoke goes on too long, it cannot but result in the ultimate differentiation of the other that we call dehumanization. Think for a moment about that piece of jargon from cold war mentality which we have just isolated: to target a city. On a technical level—and no less potent for being more subliminal—targeting a city means thinking about it as a target, which means mentally deleting from our horizon the fact that human beings live there. For us, the city and all its life has been reduced to a mere cipher in our mind's game of win-or-lose.

Nothing could be more basic to human conflict than the dynamic of dehumanization we are now considering. For human beings to wage war on one another, a behavior virtually unknown in the "lower" orders of evolution, they must deny their "enemy" the status of a cospecific by a mental process Eibl-Eibesfeldt calls "pseudospeciation."[26] The "systematic dehumanization" of the Soviet leadership that we Americans, as Kennan says, have carried on as an unstated policy is just that mental process.

Quite apart from the obvious danger that such a process may lead us into a horrendous conflict with real people who scarcely fit our mental image, there is a subtler danger with which every one of us should be intimately concerned: Dehumanization has seriously unhealthy repercussions on the dehumanizer. For reasons that may have to remain mysterious, any dehumanization of an "other" leads to a depreciation of human life in general, from which the dehumanizer himself cannot be extricated. "It is terrible, an inexorable law that one cannot deny the humanity of another without diminishing one's own."[27] And this is exactly what we have done. In a process that begins by maintaining a devil theory of another country, by targeting their cities, by conceptualizing their population as "faceless . . . peasants from the steppes of Asia" in educator Rafferty's words, we move by inexorable links to a mentality where weapons take on a weird life of their own—drawn from our own.[28] In the economy section of the *San Francisco Chronicle,* October 12, 1981, we read that President Reagan's policies were going to "revitalize the Nation's strategic nuclear deterrent . . . provide a torrent of profits . . . rain down orders." The B-1 bomber project was "revived" by President Reagan after being "killed" by President Carter. The imagery of life is transferred to the machinery of death. From here it is but a short final step to a mental world where we ourselves are no longer people who want to live, cry, love, work, relate to one another, but ciphers in a game of "population survivability," weapons in a weird mental environment of total war.

It follows that moving human life back onto the center of the stage and reinvesting the high potential of human life with the highest value—in a word, rehumanization—must be the guideline of every decision that constructs an education for living. And following this guideline we are sooner or later led to consider not just content, not even how content is selected and organized, but the fabric of the educational process itself.

It was not until a friend who had been out of the country for several years pointed it out to me that I realized how many of our classrooms have "troublemakers" sitting by themselves in the back. As Tolstoy learned at Yasnaya Polyana,[29] the society that isolates and stigmatizes pupils who are hard to deal with will try to use the same approach toward its "criminals"—and, we might add, hold a similar "strategic vision" (to use the lofty words of Defense Secretary Weinberger) of the geopolitical community as well: Get rid of communists, isolate political troublemakers, and the remaining world order will be stable. That will never work on the global scale any more than it has solved hyperactivity in the classroom or crime on the streets. All three domains—and they are equally important—are arenas in which reconciliation must be learned. And this learning occupies a higher mode than that which deals with information transfer; reconciliation must become the way we behave as well as the content of our teaching. For all important purposes, "example is the school of mankind," Burke said somewhere, "and he will learn at no other."

Ivan Illich has argued that institutionalized education has itself become outmoded and should be disestablished.[30] What I am arguing for here—conscious attention to the goals and methods of the entire process—is probably more difficult and would undoubtedly be more effective. We must remember that society at large already contains potent "educational" or value-shaping forces: We have mentioned television, that mass system for inculcating learning disability;[31] the United States supports an advertising industry, inimical to truth, of $34 billion a year. And the military uses more and more of its mushrooming funds to influence the schools and "instill military values," as one pamphlet says, in schools and colleges. These systems are practicing education without a license. No traditional mechanism of society exists to check or balance them. We who *are* licensed to practice education, strange idea though that may be, cannot subcontract our responsibility to such a system.

Nor is it necessary for educators, acting as such, to seek influence in government circles. Let the groves of academe stay "pure" in that sense of the word. But education is deeply involved in the underlying value system that predisposes people toward certain policies; and from *this* involvement it cannot escape. The way a "dissident" is handled in the classroom, whether a science teacher piths a frog, how much we teach by human contact rather than through television or computers (so that whatever else they learn, our students learn to learn from *people*)—all these acts and choices presuppose values and transmit them. There really does not seem to be any way around this, and, as the mist of "value-free education" slowly lifts, we see the one choice we really do have: to be responsible—to all of humankind—for the values that we hold and teach.[32]

In Marin County, California, milk cartons have become a medium for public service messages. Our milk cartons have been saying, "Schools are our most valuable national resource." It is a benevolent exaggeration: Children are our most valuable resource, here or anywhere. Schools are one place where that precious resource can be managed. My position has been that for *good* management of this vital link to our future existence and our present meaning we must realize two things. The first is that education is the social system least able to function without an overriding purpose. Kant meant this when he said, "Everything in education depends upon establishing correct principles."[33] The second is that it is not really obscure what those principles, what that purpose now should be. It is no coincidence that Gandhi, Freire, Dolci, Montessori, and Kohlberg, in a word most of our foremost educational inventors, have had a foot in two camps, educational reform and peace reform, at once. Peace is what we should teach more *about* because it is what all of us are teaching *for*—peace, and the reconcilation of the whole sphere of life.

Notes

1 Burns Weston, "Contending with a Planet in Peril and Change: An Optimal Educational Response," *Alternatives* 5, no. 1 (1979): 59.

2 Cf. John Ratcliffe, "Social Justice and the Demographic Transition: Lessons From Kerala State," *International Journal of Health Services* 8, no. 1 (1978): 129-31.

3 René Girard commenting on a passage from John (8:43-44), says, "Être fils de Satan, c'est hériter du mensonge. Quel mensonge? Le mensonge de l'homicide lui-même." Killing is "une source inépuisable de fausseté" ("To be a 'son of Satan' means to have inherited a lie. And what lie is that? The lie that is homicide itself. Killing is an inexaustible source of falsehood"); cf. *Des choses cachées depuis la fondation du monde* [On things hidden since the beginning of the world] (Paris: Grasset, 1978), pp. 184f.

4 Jacques Ellul, *Contre les violents* [Against the violent ones] (Paris: Le Centurion, 1972), p. 7.

5 Cf. Yvon Garlan, *War in the Ancient World,* trans. Janet Lloyd (London: Chatto and Windus, 1975), pp. 16–18.

6 A good account of this change of consciousness and how it became institutional change is found in Terence Brady and Evan Jones, *The Fight against Slavery* (New York: W. W. Norton, 1975).

7 Kenneth Boulding, *Stable Peace* (Austin: University of Texas Press, 1978), p. 122. Boulding goes on, "It is this asymmetry which gives evolution a direction, a time's arrow. In our time the arrow points clearly and unequivocally toward peace."

8 Cf. Girard, *Des choses cachées depuis la fondation du monde,* pp. 158, 219; and Boulding, *Stable Peace,* p. 69. An important aspect of this in the present crisis is pointed out by Richard Barnet: "The United States has had the misfortune to come to its moment of greatest imperial expansion just as the postimperial era began . . . at the very moment the number one nation has perfected the science of killing, it has become an impractical instrument of political domination" (*The Roots of War* [New York: Atheneum, 1972], p. 21). The "impracticality" of the instrument is entirely due to the awareness of its illegitimacy. Gandhi played a key role in this awareness; cf. William Shirer, *Gandhi: A Memoir* (New York: Simon & Schuster, 1979), pp. 11f.

9 This apt phrase of Mr. Kennan is from his address on accepting the Grenville Clark Prize, Hanover, New Hampshire, November 16, 1981.

10 Cf. William J. Bowers and Glenn L. Pierce, "Deterrence or Brutalization: What is the Effect of Executions," *Crime & Delinquency* 26, no. 4 (October 1980): 453–84.

11 For a good bibliography on civilian defense and some of the other alternatives, see Gene Sharp, *Exploring Nonviolent Alternatives* (Boston: Porter Sargent, 1970); and Charles Walker, *A World Peace Guard* (forthcoming).

12 Cf. Roscoe Balch, "The Resigning of Quarrels: Conflict Resolution in the Thirteenth Century," *Peace and Change* 5, no. 1 (1978): 33–38.

13 M. K. Gandhi, *Hind Swaraj* (Ahmedabad: Navajivan, 1938), p. 130. See also chap. 5 of Michael N. Nagler, *America without Violence* (Covelo, Calif.: Island Press, 1982).

14 For some light on this development, cf. Karen Rothmeyr, "The Mystery Angel of the New Right," *Washington Post,* July 12, 1981.

15 Quoted in Ken Macrorie, *Uptaught* (New York: Hayden, 1970), p. 39. I discuss a similar observation made by Tolstoy in Nagler, *America without Violence,* p. 71.

16 Cf. Howard Tolley, *Children and War: Political Socialization to International Conflict* (New York: Teachers College Press, 1973). Tolley's studies led to the conclusion that "schools play a prominent if not preeminent role in socialization to war" (p. 48) and that they have succeeded at times in doing the reverse, as during the Vietnam conflict (p. 136).

17 Plato's remarks come in the context of his famous model of the well-run state for the well-ordered soul, or individual. Like Plato, though I confine most of my remarks to the external and public level, I believe that unwarranted influence of appetitive, power-oriented drives in society arises from a comparable usurpation in the individual—and can be overcome there.

18 The fact is that the "other side" equally claims that survival is its goal; the Institute of Strategic Studies calls its journal *Survival.* If the peace movement has the same basic goal, is it a different movement?

19 Cf. Ivan Illich, "In Lieu of Education," in *Toward a History of Needs* (New York: Pantheon, 1978), p. 86: "Access to reality constitutes a fundamental alternative in education to a system that only purports to teach about it."

20 Reported in *Peace and Education* (journal of the Women's International League for Peace and Freedom), May 1981, p. 16.

21 Cf. *Peace and World Order Studies: A Curriculum Guide,* 3rd. ed. (New York: The Institute for World Order, 1980), and other IWO publications; also M. Andrew Murray, *Peace and Conflict Studies as Applied Liberal Arts* (Huntingdon, Pa.: Juniata College Peace and Conflict

Studies Program, 1980). For up-to-date information on these developments, teachers may join the Consortium on Peace Research, Education and Development (COPRED), Center for Peaceful Change, Kent State University, Kent, Ohio 44242.

22 Burns Weston, "Peace and World Order Education: An Optimal Design," in *Peace and World Order Studies,* p. 69.

23 Cf. James Baines, "The Peace Paradigm," *The Whole Earth Papers* 1, no. 1 (Fall 1977): 1-8; and Michael N. Nagler, "Peace as a Paradigm Shift," *Bulletin of the Atomic Scientists* 37, no. 10 (December 1981): 49-52. I incline to the view that the impending shift is millennial (as does Girard, *Des choses cachées depuis la foundation du monde,* p. 158), while most world-order theorists think of it as "merely" epochal. I differ most from most of both groups, however, in taking an analytical but not predictive position: History has no automatism beyond human engagement. This particular transition, which would seem to require an unusually high degree of intentional human engagement, will not happen by itself.

24 There is a vast but scattered bibliography on these deeply synergistic efforts. In addition to the two works cited in note 11, note that membership in COPRED (see note 21) includes a subscription to *Peace and Change,* in whose pages much of this history and theory is discussed.

25 Norman Cousins, *Who Speaks for Man?* (New York: Macmillan, 1953), p. 217.

26 Irenäus Eibl-Eibesfeldt, *The Biology of Peace and War,* trans. Eric Mosbacher (New York: Viking, 1979), *passim.* See also Robert Jay Lifton, *Home from the War* (New York: Simon & Schuster, 1973).

27 James Baldwin, *Fifth Avenue Uptown,* reprinted in William Smart, *Eight Modern Essayists* (New York: St. Martin's, 1973), p. 343.

28 In the strategic jargon, which we are all learning, you "kill" a silo; oncoming missiles that destroy one another are committing "fratricide." Truly, as Jonathan Schell points out, "strategic theory seems to have taken on a wierd life of its own, in which the weapons are pictured as having their own quarrels to settle, irrespective of mere human purposes" ("Reflections, *The Fate of the Earth,*" *New Yorker,* February 1, 1982, p. 71).

29 Leo Tolstoy, *On Education,* trans. Leo Wiener (Chicago: University of Chicago Press, 1972), p. 241.

30 Illich, "In Lieu of Education."

31 Not content to be the "first curriculum" children learn before they get to school, commercial television has now penetrated the schools; cf. Natalie Rothstein, "The Third Grade Has Been Brought to You By. . . ," *The Food Monitor* 26 (March-April 1982): 27-28.

32 For an interesting experiential account of such a "conversion," cf. Glenn Paige, "On Values and Science: The Korean Decision Reconsidered," *The American Political Science Review* 71 (1977): 1603-09. As Paige's example shows, and Kohlberg and Gandhi both argued in different ways, accepting responsibility for values is practically synonymous with enhancing them. In this connection see also Douglas Sloan, ed., *Education and Values* (New York: Teachers College Press, 1980).

33 Immanual Kant, *Education,* trans. Annette Churton (Ann Arbor: University of Michigan Press, 1964), p. 108.

The Schools and Civil Defense: The Fifties Revisited

MICHAEL J. CAREY
Fairbanks, Alaska

Memories of war are very like memories of childhood.
—George Bernanos, *A Diary of My Times*

We are now almost as far from the beginning of President Eisenhower's first term as his inauguration was from the death of Warren Harding. The fifties have been consigned to history except as an object of nostalgia, yet one of the most salient features of the decade remains as powerful today as it was in the past—the threat of nuclear war.

The bomb's presence is particularly ominous to the former school children of the fifties, who, as they grew to maturity, watched nuclear weapons proliferate in number, variety, and destructiveness. They discovered at an early age and never forgot that the United States could be destroyed by a nuclear holocaust in a few minutes. How these children of the fifties learned about the bomb is a special chapter in American education's history, special because this generation had a formal bomb-threat education: civil defense training, conducted by principals and teachers, that taught young people where to hide from the bomb and how to protect themselves from its deadly if mysterious forces.

The rudiments of this education are still vivid to many ex-students. "First of all, the [school] gong would go off," a New York teacher remembered of his childhood, "and the teachers would tell everybody to get under the desks. You could feel the tension in the air, fear. The kids are fidgety and jumpy and talking—whispering—but then there would be absolute silence. You never knew if it was a drill—a test—or the real thing."[1] A Pennsylvania laborer similarly recollected instructions to hide under his desk in case of a nuclear attack. "And I can also recall the stupid instruction, if you can't get under the desk, then get in the doorway. I heard that Pittsburgh would be wiped off the map, and I said, 'Wow, so will we because we're not that far from Pittsburgh.'" In Minnesota, a clerk explained, the teachers led the students to the basement of the school for protection in the air raid drills. "It was kind of scary, but it was a different kind of frightening thing. It was not like somebody was going to come and get you, but if an attack actually did happen, it would be so terrible."

Like the Pennsylvania laborer and the Minnesota clerk, many young people reached a simple conclusion that was inconsistent with the purposes of bomb-threat education: Hiding did no good. "Why are they bothering?" a New York psychologist remembered asking himself after hearing instructions about how to protect himself from the bomb. "There is no way we can survive. Because it's kids get under the desks, face away from the windows so the glass doesn't get in your eyes, close your eyes so the blinding flash doesn't blind you, close your ears so the deafening noise doesn't deafen you. You'd be at least deaf or blind aside from crippled—they didn't talk about the [bomb's] impact and being crushed."

Worldly adults quickly confirmed a California cab driver's youthful suspicions about an enemy attack on his school. "If it happens, it happens. They drop it, then we are blown away, and that's it. Only the young, the naive, and the school teachers were fooled by the drills."

American schools conducted three types of air raid drills in the fifties. These drills typically were held once a month, although never with such precision that there were no variations across the country. Los Angeles, for example, had them once a week in 1951, while some communities, especially small towns that seemed remote from military targets, had them infrequently. A study of school civil defense activities by the Research and Statistical Standards section of the Office of Education in 1952, however, revealed that 95 percent of 437 elementary schools sampled in cities of 50,000 or more people taught civil defense education, as did the overwhelming majority of secondary schools.[2]

The most common air raid drill—and the most widely remembered today—was called "duck and cover," for protection if the enemy attacked without warning. In this drill, students dropped to the floor or crawled under their desks at the teacher's command and took what a professor of education called "the atomic head clutch position": backs to the windows, faces buried between their knees, hands clasped on the backs of their necks, ears covered with their arms, and eyes closed (as the New York psychologist accurately recollected). The "atomic clutch" was supposed to protect children from the bomb flash, flying glass, and falling timbers, from what a civil defense proponent called "life in a meatgrinder," and the National Education Association warned teachers to have their students take the atomic clutch position immediately if a "sudden dazzling light" appeared outside the school to herald the bomb's arrival.[3] A Los Angeles school administrator explained that this emergency position was approved as medically sound by doctors because "it provides the desired protection for the back of the neck. . . . It compresses to some degree the organs of the abdomen, decreasing the effects of the blast on these organs."[4]

Advance warning drills, popularly known as "shelter drills," presupposed that teachers and students had enough time to hide in the school's basement, hallways, or other areas that civil defense and school authorities believed were strong enough to withstand a bomb blast. After the principal sounded an alarm throughout the school to begin the drill, the teachers commanded the students to rise, line up in an orderly manner, and proceed to the designated shelter, where everyone sat close to the walls, which were believed to offer the most safety. Sometimes students were required to take the atomic head clutch position for added protection. In response to those who questioned the value of this activity, Detroit educators replied with more the appearance than the substance of logic, "It is obvious that any particular building may be distant from any particular blast. Hence, any particular bomb may produce only light damage or no damage. . . (though there is a significant chance it will destroy your area.) *Hence, even light protection may yield appreciable security.*"[5]

The third form of drill, the dispersal drill, assumed that there would be enough time for children to get home safely before the enemy struck. At the end of the school day, teachers simply told students that an air raid drill was about to begin and asked them to go home as fast as possible. Only New York and a few other eastern cities had dispersal drills, for school officials soon realized that they had no control over the children and could not be sure that any warning would be sufficient to guarantee they would get home prior to an attack.

But bomb-threat education was not confined solely to air raid drills. Schools gave teachers civil defense education materials to provide students with information about facing the bomb's immense power. Comic books such as *The H-Bomb and You* taught that "we Americans must get used to the threat of war as a new way of life. It is not our choice but it IS our duty to be constantly prepared if our country is to survive."[6] Films such as *Inside the Atom, Our Cities Must Fight,* and *Survival under Atomic Attack* were also available to help teachers educate students, as were filmstrips such as "Up and Atom," "How to Live with the Atom," and "You and the Atom." ("You and the Atom" taught what must be the indisputable essence of civil defense wisdom: "The Atomic Energy Commission says the best defense against an atom bomb is to BE SOMEWHERE ELSE when it bursts."[7])

Probably the most popular educational tool was the story "Duck and Cover," created for wide distribution in print, film, and filmstrip in the early fifties by the Federal Civil Defense Administration and the National Education Association. A ten-minute film, *Duck and Cover* was the first attempt to explain on the screen what children should do in case of an atomic attack. Part live action, part animation, the film revolved around a friendly cartoon character, Bert the Turtle, who ducked and covered when danger appeared and did not uncover until it was gone. The atomic bomb, Bert explained, is a new danger. "It explodes with a flash brighter than any you have ever seen. Things will be knocked down all over town. . . . YOU must be ready to protect yourself." Real students were shown huddled under their desks, and cartoon teachers and students were depicted under their desks when the bomb blew out their school's windows. The film warned, "But sometimes

—AND THIS IS VERY IMPORTANT—the Bomb might explode and a bright flash come without any warning."[8] To reassure parents who wondered if children would find *Duck and Cover* unsettling, a New York City Board of Education representative emphasized the film's "mental hygiene approach, its underlying qualities of cheerfulness and optimism."[9] Today, Norman Key, National Education Association staff director for the project, says, "I thought it did good, but then it became obsolete as the civil defense emphasis changed."[10]

What was the official civil defense policy for U.S. schools during the fifties? Why were teachers given the role of civil defense educators? Why did bomb-threat education become an accepted part of school life—and why did it virtually disappear in the sixties?

Civil defense, its fifties advocates argued, is as old as the first American settlements. The farmers of New England who dropped their plows and picked up their rifles when Indians appeared were engaged in civil defense, as were the pioneers on the Oregon Trail who circled their wagons when they saw smoke signals. "Civil defense is synonymous with survival," a federal civil defense official wrote in 1957. "It might be said that any endeavor which seeks to preserve and further our life, liberty, and pursuit of happiness can be considered a form of civil defense. . . . It is our way of life."[11]

The Japanese attack on Pearl Harbor fixed in American minds the kind of attack that could be expected from an aggressor—unprovoked, unheralded, unjust—and the Soviet explosion of an atomic device in August 1949 demonstrated that the only potential postwar aggressor the United States faced had a weapon that could flatten its cities and set its farms ablaze. In less than a decade, the isolation that President Eisenhower called America's "unique physical security"[12] had disappeared before the modern weapons of war. "In the event of a future war," a civil defense planner advised, "all the people, all the facilities and all the skills and energies of the nation must be utilized to the fullest extent. To successfully carry out the program will require the cooperation of every man, woman, and child in this nation."[13]

A consensus emerged among policymakers in Washington that education had a crucial role to play in developing Americans with sufficient inner resources to meet the Soviet challenge. "Education," President Truman said in 1949, "is our first line of defense. In the conflict of principle and policy which divides the world today, America's hope, our hope, the hope of the world is education." The major weapon on the front line of defense was "the unfettered soul of free men, a spiritual defense unconquered and unconquerable."[14] The U.S. Education Policies Commission's 1951 report *Education and National Security* maintained a similar emphasis on the soul, declaring that "the schools must educate for moral and spiritual values" because "the problems that now most urgently require solution are not physical and technical, but moral and social."[15] These moral and spiritual values were not religious, however, but the secular values of the American democratic tradition, which every child was expected to learn through what Commissioner of Education Earl James McGrath called the three Rs of democratic citizenship, "Rights, Respects, and Responsibilities."[16] When the physical threat to the United States became the most dangerous in its history, those who made educational policy turned inward. "The inner citadel of our safety lies in the hearts and minds of our people,"[17] stated the *Ladies Home Journal* in a perfect reflection of this policy. Future conflicts with the Soviet Union would be decided by the quality of the American character, and American schools were expected to prepare the young in the spirit of the Duke of Wellington's maxim that the Battle of Waterloo was won on the playing fields of Eton.

Nonetheless, the burden placed on education was brutally practical. As early as 1946, Harry Gail of the University of Chicago alerted his fellow educators, "A new and critical responsibility has been imposed on education by the military application of atomic energy and other horizons of destruction revealed during the war. Let us call this the responsibility for survival."[18] When the Korean War broke out in June 1950, the responsibility for survival involved such questions as: Who would take care of American children if an enemy attacked during school hours? How would parents react if their government failed to establish procedures to protect their children? What would happen to the postattack morale and productivity of American workers if they had no confidence that their youngsters were receiving proper care and nurture? William R. Wood of the U.S. Office of Education cautioned, "Our future as a free people may well be determined by the skill and promptness with which our system of education is able to respond to the conditions that make necessary the development of civil defense education."[19]

It now was the responsibility of the schools to teach what Jack Johnson, provost of Hofstra College, called "protective citizenship," and throughout the country, state and local civil defense plans stressed the crucial link between physical protection against the bomb and good citizenship. New York State's civil defense message to its schools was typical. It outlined the fundamentals of air raid training but also insisted, "Our country will grow and prosper and will overcome its obstacles only if our children are properly trained and become adjusted to their future responsibilities as citizens, and in their growth acquire the moral fiber, the stature and strength of character that ensures greatness of mind and soundness of purpose."[20]

At the heart of every school civil defense program stood the classroom teacher. "The teacher," wrote the Colorado supervisor of public instruction, "is the key person in the civil defense program of the schools because upon him is placed the direct responsibility for the safety and welfare of his pupils."[21] The facts of nuclear war were not to inhibit "the resourceful teacher," explained the Michigan Department of Public Instruction, "who will view civil defense as an opportunity for learning experiences within the everyday classroom experiences."[22] Educators across the country reiterated the Indiana Department of Public Instruction's conclusion: ". . . few persons compare with the teacher in his or her opportunity to reflect confidence, maintain a calm atmosphere, and renew the courage of the children."[23] The duck-and-cover drills were "the hardest thing to face," but all would go well if the teacher trained "herself to say 'Take cover' as calmly as she says 'Good morning, children.'"[24]

Teachers were to prepare students so that, in the words of the Georgia Civil Defense manual, *"All will know exactly what to do* if a bomb falls."[25] "Responses," wrote Federal Civil Defense Training Officer James Ridgway, "should be drummed in until they are nearly automatic to forestall the possibility of 'freezing' in the event of an attack."[26] As the New York City Board of Education explained in a policy statement, it was essential that "the child should know what to do in school, at home, in the street, or in the playground," adding in the spirit of the frontier, "He should be trained in self-reliance, imbued with faith in his ability to survive, no matter what the danger."[27]

School administrators understood that effective air raid protection required cooperation from communities and parents. "We realized from the outset," said John W. Pritchard of the Detroit Public Schools, "that the effectiveness of our preparation depended on close working ties with city officials on civilian defense, to whom all our directives are submitted for approval."[28] The Midland, Michigan, school district did not follow Detroit's example—and discovered during an air raid drill that five other community organizations expected to use its schools in an attack.[29]

Many school districts sent letters home to explain civil defense activities and reassure parents. A Los Angeles letter said, "We in the schools are in direct contact with Federal, State, County, and City defense organizations. As devastating as the atomic bomb is, there is no evidence to justify a feeling of hopelessness in the event of such a bombing. Relatively slight obstacles offer considerable protection and the type of construction used in our schools is a definite item in our favor." The letter closed with a guarantee that the school district's plan had been developed by "competent experts in the atomic defense field."[30] In Colorado, a similar letter asked parents to let their children talk about civil defense activities and explain what they had learned. "Remember, they will be watching you closely to observe your reaction. Your attitude will largely determine theirs. If you are calm, they will be calm. If you are sensible, they will be sensible."[31]

Fear could not be allowed to weaken America and leave it vulnerable to foreign aggression. Civil Defense Administrator Val Peterson warned that panic, not the bomb, might be the ultimate weapon: "Like the A-Bomb, panic is fissionable. It can produce a chain reaction more deeply destructive than any explosive known." Peterson observed that between 1947 and 1952 the word *panic* increased in the press by 1,447 percent.[32]

A New York psychiatrist cautioned against creating an atmosphere in which the "atomic jitters" were prevalent, where children could emotionally experience thousands of atomic explosions before the first blast took place.[33] Fear was an invisible, highly toxic illness that could be carried by what a New York physician called "uncontrolled radio and television sets" that presented "new frightening prospects."[34] According to Missouri Civil Defense, fear was a communicable disease, and the New York Board of Education warned that in the presentation of civil defense material "the attitude of adults is infectious."[35] No cure was prescribed—only the strongest preventive medicine, such as the Pennsylvania Council of Civil Defense's admonition: "In teaching the essential facts and procedures necessary for self-protection, it is important to teach children *without frightening them.*"[36]

Everyone agreed that children should not be frightened, but there was disagreement about whether they actually were frightened. Thomas J. Durrell, New Jersey Assistant Commissioner of Education, told a 1951 conference of educators and civil defense officials, "Our experience in the public schools has shown that many children in the kindergarten and primary grades have been upset by mismanaged air raid drills, some of them to such an extent that they were afraid to go to school."[37] A Michigan educator wrote in 1952, "We had several drills last year, but this year we haven't had drills due to the fact that the drills caused so much tension among students."[38] Newspapers carried stories about a teacher who had students "take cover" whenever they were unruly; principals were asked to protect children from "the few teachers who resolve their own problems by pushing other people around"; and a professional education journal expressed shock at the press's pictures of "teachers standing grimly over children in air raid drills."[39]

In New York City during the early 1950s, the Committee for the Study of War Tension in Children, an antidrill group, contended that civil defense activities were doing more harm than good and labeled the film *Duck and Cover* "inadvisable" as "it can only create fears in children with which their resources are inadequate to deal." More specifically, a young father told a psychiatrist, "Doc, they're scaring the life out of my kid at school. At home he sticks real close to his mother or me, and every night he cries out in his sleep and comes running to our bed."[40]

These expressions of concern were a minority opinion. Professional educators for the most part concluded with satisfaction that American students had weathered the air raid drills without turmoil. New York Assistant Commissioner of Education Edwin Van Kleeck admitted in his article "A is for Atom, B is for Bomb" that he feared "the emotional mental health problem," but in his experience, "the pupils, almost without exception—and with upwards of three million school children there were bound to be exceptions—have taken the drills in their stride."[41] Detroit's John W. Pritchard expressed similar confidence, saying "Fear, we have found, is not commonly generated when we explain why we have air raid drills," and a New York high school principal argued that the proper explanation of civil defense activities to parents would reduce fears and complaints unless "subversives" were at work.[42]

Professional educators appealed to medical authority for approval of school civil defense. Dr. Jean A. Thompson, acting director of the New York Bureau of Child Guidance, explained that the twelve psychiatrists employed by the New York Board of Education assured her that while children had learned New York was an enemy target, secure children did not demonstrate undue fear. As proof, she cited the case of a "well-adjusted" twelve-year-old boy who, hearing an explosion, looked out the window of his home and remarked casually, "No mushroom cloud" before "he returned to his homework with a pleasant and reassuring smile at his mother."[43]

Perhaps a mental health professional could conclude that a twelve-year-old's immediate association of an explosion with an atomic bomb was perfectly normal only in an era when a pleasant and reassuring smile amounted to federal policy. Postwar security was designed to keep the secrets of the bomb from the American people—and fear was treated as one of the bomb's secrets. Fear was a controlled substance managed by responsible government officials so that it did not cause trouble. The *New York Times*'s military columnist Hanson Baldwin wrote, "Only a strong and enlightened Government leadership can penetrate the subconscious of American public opinion with the frightful facts of such a new weapon as the hydrogen bomb," but the government had no desire to spread such "frightful facts."[44] In 1953, President Eisenhower, following a suggestion from a panel chaired by Robert Oppenheimer, considered "Operation Candor" to tell the American people about the threat of nuclear war. Eisenhower's closest advisors believed, however, that frankness would scare the American people at home and be interpreted as weakness abroad. They had an alternative acceptable to the President: Operation Wheaties, a public relations effort to produce some momentum for his "Atoms for Peace" proposal, which championed the virtues of nuclear power and downplayed the bomb threat.[45]

President Eisenhower conceded in an October 1953 speech, "It is awfully hard to awaken people to a sense of responsibility without trying to create hysteria."[46] Whether anyone was "trying" to create hysteria, extreme emotionalism could be the result of too much talk about the bomb. It was far better to give the American people Ike's pleasant and reassuring smile.

But the nuclear threat was changing fast and making even the well-adjusted uncomfortable. In 1954, Civil Defense Administrator Peterson said, "The alternatives are to dig, die, or get out; and we certainly don't want to die."[47] The Soviet hydrogen-weapon tests confirmed the Atomic Energy Commission's conclusion that it is best to be "someplace else" when the bomb falls. During the middle of the decade, evacuation became a vogue word in civil defense, and plans were drawn up to evacuate America's largest cities, but actual school evacuation was attempted only briefly. In 1955, for example, Mobile, Atlanta, and Savannah launched major school evacuation exercises in which hundreds of cars and buses transported thousands of children into the countryside. Mobile's "Operation Kids" deposited 37,000 children beyond what local officials labeled the danger zone in seventy-five minutes, but evacuations were cumbersome and chaotic even in peacetime. Seven thousand pupils were left behind because of the uneven distribution of cars; they were theoretical casualties.[48] As former Office of Education official William R. Wood explained in a recent interview, "We got to the point that we couldn't get the kids out of town. After all, look what happened in Europe during World War II when people tried to flee before foreign armies."[49]

The school civil defense program began to lose credibility as nuclear weapons grew larger and the time for defensive preparation grew shorter, but the schools themselves, which had been under attack by critics of progressive education throughout the decade, suffered bitter blows after the appearance of Sputnik in October 1957. Education, the critics complained, had failed to keep us ahead of the Soviets in the weapons race during the first half of the decade, and now our rival had passed us in the space race. Admiral Hyman Rickover, one of the most vocal critics, led a retreat from moral and spiritual education, calling for the technical education that Commissioner of Education McGrath downplayed in 1950. Quoting the Atomic Energy Commission in his 1958 best-seller *Education and Freedom,* Rickover warned, "We are in a battle for brainpower," and another well-known critic, former Senator William Benton, thundered after a tour of Russia, "Russian classrooms and libraries, her laboratories and teaching methods may threaten us more than her hydrogen bombs."[50] If Rickover and those who shared his sentiments had their way, American youth would no longer hide from the bomb. They would receive a technical education that would enable them to build weapons—more, bigger, better—and create the absolute security that moral and spiritual education could never attain. Rickover envisioned a kind of scientific Sparta in which American students would rise up from beneath their desks and humble the Russians with weapons born of their technically sharpened minds.

Alva Myrdal, one of the most perceptive students of the arms race, has written, "People rightly should have become more startled and fearful as the nuclear arms race went into swing. It is a psychological riddle how people everywhere conditioned themselves to live with fear without mobilizing vigorous opposition."[51] The history of school civil defense contributes significantly to the riddle's answer.

American school children of the fifties were taught by their elders that it was not normal to fear the bomb. School civil defense was presented as a ritual, an unquestioning series of gestures before the most awesome weapon ever devised. Many students, like those quoted at the beginning of this essay, saw through the ritual of their bomb-threat education, but their fearful reaction was private and difficult to communicate, even embarrassing. "The Bomb," suggested a New York social worker, "probably embarrassed my parents, and they sort of communicated it to me. Like sex, like death, like God, like certain things in my parents' past that they did not want to talk about."[52]

The ritualization of civil defense often took the form of elaborate play for adults too, as in the mock attacks on major cities. Philadelphia, for instance, conducted a civil defense exercise during 1951 in which two imaginary atomic bombs were "dropped" on the city, "killing" 241,000 people and "injuring" another 293,000. Civil defense officials were pleased to report that city agencies tackled their problems with the "great ingenuity, skill, and know-how" characteristic of good Americans.[53] This was ritualized play to tame the gods of war, but it had no more bearing on reality than what an experienced teacher discovered in her classroom.

> I found a group of seven-year-olds constructing an atom bomb factory with their blocks. Small cylindrical blocks were used for bombs. "What is the difference between an atom bomb and a regular bomb?" one of the children asked.
>
> "An atom bomb explodes in a different way," I said. "It makes a louder bang." The children seemed satisfied and returned to rolling the cylinders down the long ramp they had built. "Easy," they cautioned. "We don't want them to explode before we are ready."[54]

What happened to the air raid drills and civil defense education? "What happened to your old car?" asked the National Education Association's Commission on Safety Education in 1966, replying to the same question. "Some of us still have that model and find it useful for certain purposes," continued the Safety Commission—but in fact most schools had sent the "old car" to the scrap heap.[55]

The 1950s model of civil defense education collapsed before the reality of the nuclear threat, and the schools could not find a satisfactory new "model." They succumbed to the apathy toward the bomb typical of the rest of the country. This apathy masked two apparently unanswerable questions. How do you influence government policies to make the bomb's use less likely? How do you hide from the bomb?

Education was never our first line of defense, as President Truman rhetorically claimed, and it could never guarantee absolute security, as Admiral Rickover believed. The schools had been called on to perform a task for which they were clearly inadequate.

Notes

1 These comments and subsequent remarks on school civil defense drills by former students are taken from interviews conducted from 1974 to 1977. This work has been reported in "Psychological Fallout," *Bulletin of the Atomic Scientists,* January 1982, pp. 20–24.

2 U.S. Office of Education, "Civil Defense Education Activities in School and Colleges, A Report on a Questionnaire Survey," June 1952, pp. 8–9. For an earlier study, which highlights the lower level of participation in smaller schools, see "Schools and Civil Defense: Report on a

Questionnaire Survey," prepared by the Research Division of the National Education Association, April 1951.

3 James A. Ridgway, "School Civil Defense Measures," *Elementary School Journal*, May 1954, pp. 501–03.

4 Raymond E. Pollich, "The Defense Program of the Los Angeles City Schools," *The National Elementary Principal*, June 1951, p. 22.

5 Detroit Public Schools and Wayne University Joint Committee on Civil Defense, *Civil Defense in the Schools* (Detroit, Mich.: Board of Education, 1956), p. 8. Italics in original.

6 Original script of *The H-Bomb and You*, Commercial Comics, Inc., September 3, 1954, p. 11.

7 "You and the Atomic Bomb," filmstrip (Suffern, N.Y.: Visual Sciences, n.d.). Writer Jeff Greenfield says of the air raid drills and filmstrips in his memoir *No Peace, No Place* (Garden City, N.Y.: Doubleday, 1973): "One of the clearest memories of a 1950's childhood is the 'take-cover' drill, practiced weekly, it seemed, in elementary school. . . . The A-bomb, we were taught in an assembly film strip, was identifiable by a sudden flash of light, the signal to 'take cover'" (pp. 30–31).

8 "Duck and Cover," Archer Productions, 1952.

9 *New York Times*, January 25, 1952.

10 Telephone interview with Dr. Norman Key, Washington, D.C., April 2, 1982.

11 Gayle Starnes, "Schools and Civil Defense," *School Board Journal*, August 1957, p. 21.

12 *Newsweek*, October 19, 1953, p. 35.

13 Russell J. Hopley to Secretary of Defense James Forrestal, May 1948, in U.S. Office of Civil Defense Planning, *Civil Defense for National Security* (Washington, D.C.: U.S. Government Printing Office, 1948), p. 5.

14 "Education is Our First Line of Defense," *School Life*, April 1, 1949, p.1.

15 As quoted by Henry Perkinson in his *The Imperfect Panacea: American Faith in Education, 1865–1965* (New York: Random House, 1958).

16 "Citizenship Begins with Children," *School Life*, March 1951, p. 84.

17 "Civil Defense Begins at Home," *Ladies Home Journal*, August 1951, p. 41.

18 "Some Educational Implications of Atomic Energy," *Education*, April 1947, p. 463.

19 As quoted by Clyde W. Meredith in "Civil Defense and the Schools," *School Life*, April 1952, p. 99.

20 "Protective Citizenship—Its Educational Implications," *School Life*, September 1953, p. 150; and New York State Civil Defense Commission, *Civil Defense and the Schools* (Albany: New York State Civil Defense Commission, 1953), p. vii.

21 Colorado State Department of Education, *Organizing Colorado Schools for Civil Defense* (Denver: Colorado State Department of Education, 1953), p. 5.

22 Michigan Department of Public Instruction, *Civil Defense in the Classroom: A Handbook for Teachers* (Lansing: Michigan Department of Public Instruction, 1955), p. 21.

23 Indiana Department of Public Instruction, *Civil Defense for the Schools of Indiana* (Indianapolis: Indiana Department of Public Instruction, 1952), p. 1.

24 Ruth Korey, "What Can We Do about School Defense?" *The Instructor*, April 1951, p. 82. A New York telephone installer suggested in an interview how routine an air raid drill could be for the students. "It was like getting up in the morning. It was a natural thing."

25 Georgia Civil Defense, *Civil Defense Manual for Georgia Schools* (Athens: Georgia Civil Defense, 1952), p. 8. Italics in original.

26 Ridgway, "School Civil Defense Measures," p. 504.

27 City of New York, Board of Education, *Civil Defense: A Curriculum Unit for the New York City Schools* (New York: Board of Education, 1953–1954), p. 3. School children could also be a source of inspiration for the rest of the public. In the New York State Civil Defense Newsletter of October 27, 1951, State Civil Defense Director Clarence Huebner reported "how effective was the work accomplished through school children, who are by far the most understanding of all the people who are approached on Civil Defense." He cited the schoolchildren of Baltimore, who recruited 5,000 adult volunteers for civil defense.

28 John W. Pritchard, "Disasters from the Air," *The Nation's Schools,* April 1951, p. 34.

29 Ibid., p. 13.

30 National Education Association, National Commission on Safety Education, *Civil Defense Plans for School Systems* (Washington, D.C.: National Education Association, 1951), p. 11.

31 Colorado State Department of Education, *Organizing Colorado Schools for Civil Defense,* p. 21.

32 Val Peterson, "Panic: The Ultimate Weapon," *Collier's,* August 21, 1953, pp. 100–01.

33 George S. Stevenson, "The Antidote for Atomic Jitters," *New York Times Magazine,* May 13, 1931, p. 55.

34 George Goldman, "Childhood Fears Today," *Child Study,* Fall 1951, p. 26. Goldman was equally alarmed about "adults who are so afraid of this danger that they consciously or unconsciously radiate their fears onto their children" (p. 26).

35 City of New York, Board of Education, *Civil Defense,* p. 3; and Missouri Department of Education and Missouri Civil Defense Agency, *Missouri Civil Defense: A Plan for Schools* (Jefferson City: Missouri Department of Education, 1952), p. 21.

36 Pennsylvania State Council on Civil Defense, *Civil Defense for Schools* (Harrisburg: Pennsylvania State Council of Civil Defense, p. 1952), p. 8. Italics in original.

37 State of New York, "Proceedings of the Institute on Mental Health Aspects of Civil Defense," June 21, 1951, p. 48.

38 U.S. Office of Education, "Civil Defense Education Activities in Schools and Colleges, A Report on a Questionnaire Survey," p. 9.

39 Howard A. Lane, "What Are We Doing to Our Children?" *National Elementary Principal,* June 1951, p. 7.

40 *New York Times,* November 21, 1952; and Lane, "What Are We Doing to Our Children?" p. 4.

41 *The National Elementary Principal,* June 1951, p. 25.

42 Pritchard, "Disaster from the Air," p. 37; and Mary Meade, "What Programs of Civil Defense Are Needed in Our Schools?" *The Bulletin of the National Association of Secondary School Principals,* March 1952, p. 183.

43 "The Impact on the Child's Emotional Life," *The National Elementary Principal,* June 1951, p. 31. Dr. Wilfred C. Hulse, psychiatrist at Mt. Sinai Hospital in New York, drew an entirely different conclusion after observing children in an air raid drill. He reported "a marked increase in thumb sucking, nail biting or other repetitive behavior that represents defense against anxiety" (*New York Times,* June 13, 1951).

44 *New York Times,* January 20, 1953.

45 Ibid.; Robert L. Branyan and Lawrence Larsen, *The Eisenhower Administration 1953–1951,* vol. I (New York: Random House, 1965), pp. 188–94; and Robert Gilpin, *American Scientists & Nuclear Policy* (Princeton, N.J.: Princeton University Press, 1962), pp. 127–28.

46 *New York Times,* October 2, 1953. According to a story in the April 11, 1982, Washington *Post,* the National Security Council's senior advisor Richard Pipes is the latest exponent of the reassuring smile. "He says the current probability for nuclear war is roughly 40 percent. But, he adds with a reassuring smile, nuclear war won't happen, provided we build up our strength some more."

47 "All Plans to Evacuate Cities Face Staggering Difficulties," *Life,* April 12, 1954, pp. 30–31.

48 James Ridgway, "School Evacuation Plans," *School Board Journal,* March 1957, p. 31.

49 Interview with Dr. William R. Wood, Fairbanks, Alaska, November 9, 1981.

50 As quoted by Hyman G. Rickover, *Education and Freedom* (New York: Dutton, 1959), p. 186; and Perkinson, *The Imperfect Panacea,* p. 214.

51 Alva Myrdal, *The Disarmament Game* (New York: Pantheon, 1976), p. 84.

52 See note 2 above.

53 "The Philadelphia Civil Defense Exercise," *The American City,* April 1951, p. 103.

54 Korey, "What Can We Do about School Defense," p. 82.

55 National Commission on Safety Education of the National Education Association, "Current Status of Civil Defense in Schools with Guidelines for Action" (Washington, D.C.: U.S. Government Printing Office, 1966), p. 17. The Safety Commission documented the decline in civil defense education in its study "School Involvement in Civil Defense Preparedness, 1964–65" (Washington, D.C., 1965). Less than 15 percent of about 25,000 school districts still had air raid drills.

Education and Disarmament

MAXINE GREENE
Teachers College, Columbia University

I want to begin by quoting from three people who remember a day in 1945. They all lived in Hiroshima, and their words are collected in the book *Unforgettable Fire,* along with pictures they have drawn.

> Standing on the hill I could see the shrine at its foot engulfed in flames and Shukkeien Garden burning between two branches of the Ota River. The fire extended to the Hiroshima Castle. Above the city was a mushroom cloud from the Atomic Bomb.[1]

> A girl was standing in the middle of the road staring vacantly. . . . She was eight years old. The wound on her head looked like a cracked pomegranate. Silently I carried her on my back. . . . Then I heard a girl's voice clearly from behind a tree. "Help me, please." Her back was completely burned and the skin peeled off and was hanging down from her hips.[2]

> The next morning at 7:30 I started from school toward the ruins of my house. . . . There were few people to be seen in the scorched field. I saw for the first time a pile of burned bodies in a water tank by the entrance to the broadcasting station. Then I was suddenly frightened by a terrible sight on the street 40 to 50 meters from Shukkeien Garden. There was a charred body of a woman standing frozen in a running posture with one leg lifted and her baby tightly clutched in her arms. Who on earth could she be? The cruel sight still vividly remains in my mind.[3]

I read these accounts of what they remember; I stare at the drawings; and I think that this was all the doing of ordinary human beings in positions of power—presumably decent, patriotic human beings caught up in strategic and technical thinking, *choosing* to drop an atomic bomb. I recall John Dewey talking about an "unregenerate Adam" in each living person, of Dostoevski's Ivan Karamasov declaring that "anything is possible." There is no way of demonstrating that cruelty and sadism and distancing are unnatural or even nonhuman. Nor are there any guarantees that an address to people's "better nature" or what is generalized as "conscience" or even their intelligence will avert atomic war or institute justice on the earth.

That is why education is so crucial; and by education I do not necessarily mean schooling, although I still believe that the public schools have the potential for becoming places where persons can be released to think, communicate with one another, discover what it might be like to live in a community with an enlarging circle of human beings, all grounded in the same world, but each a distinctive subject with a distinctive life story and a voice of his or her own. The fact that public schools so rarely succeed in this today has, I believe, a great deal to do with the same situation that makes a special issue on disarmament necessary. There are too many violations in this society; too many instances of neglect; too many acceptances of presumably deserved inequities; too many stock responses to a crucially altered world.

In my view, education ought to be thought of as the kind of activity that releases all sorts of human beings to reach out from their own places, their own locations in the world, to make sense of what they live and what they encounter around themselves. I put great emphasis on the importance of persons' being present to the educative situation—personally present, empowered to interpret (with the aid of the schemata, the constructs provided by their predecessors and contemporaries) their experience. Reality, as I understand it, *is* interpreted experience; and I would want to put much more stress on the process of interpretation than is ordinarily done, so that young people become to some degree self-reflective about the ways there are of making sense. When I speak of schemata and constructs, I am thinking of the modes of explanation and ordering derived in large measure from the disciplines: history and geography and physics and mathematics and the rest. I am thinking of the concepts that offer clusters of meaning as well, concepts that have their own history.

Let me give one example of what I mean by reflectiveness with respect to interpretation and sense-making. As very young children, we were all introduced to the concept of discovery, one of the principles of explanation common in American history. Today, most of us are aware that the term "discovery" is highly questionable. We know that when Columbus landed on Hispaniola, human beings with a highly developed culture already lived there, although he was incapable of ascribing to them any humanity or even language; and we know that his aim was not truly to discover but to extend the European quest for territory and exploitation to what he thought was the Far East. Surely it is necessary today, not only to make this clear to children, but to enable children to reflect on the terms in use for describing and explaining what happened in the past, and obviously in the present too. To talk of nations or structures instead of people; to use words like "victory" and "defeat"; to talk about a "great war"; to deal uncritically with "heroism" and "martial law": All this is to distort and to falsify, if attention is not drawn to the interpretive process itself.

But there is more. I happen to be much impressed by Hannah Arendt's words about "newcomers'" becoming part of a plurality or community,[4] and I have been moved to see the process of learning in terms of beginnings rather than in terms of end points and objectives, in large measure because the notion of beginnings carries with it a notion of initiatives freely taken and of freedom to imagine future possibility. I believe that, in peace education, the idea of beginnings is especially important. This is partly because it focuses attention on living human beings, feeling their particularity and concreteness, reaching out from their own situations, their own vantage points, to make sense of their lived worlds. At the horizon of those lived worlds, I like to think, is the larger world: and there must be some sense of continuity between the lived and the conceived if people are not to become purely technical thinkers. To be a technical thinker is to posit a wholly objective, "given" reality outside the self, a reality that is there to be exploited and manipulated, that is not susceptible to human reconceptualization and renewal. In some degree, I am talking about a ground for the learning process, an awareness of personal responsibility for the pursuit of meanings and truths. It seems crucial to me that young people become reflective about the fact that all knowledge—be it the precise knowledge of the natural sciences that makes predictions possible, be it the less precise knowledge of the social sciences—is gained from a particular location in the world, gained by a particular human being or a group of human beings responding to certain kinds of human interests. It seems crucial that they come to realize that no living being is capable of absolute certainty, because all knowing is perspectival, and no description or rendering can be absolutely final or complete. I also have in mind the need to resist positivism, or the modeling of all knowing after empirical knowing, the split between subject and object, the division of values from facts.

Of course clarity is important, as are regard for the evidence, and the hypothetical attitude, and critical responsiveness. But there is an overriding tendency in these days, ever since science lost its innocence and linked up in so many ways with an ever-expanding technology, to connect what we used to regard as open-ended experimental inquiry to the interest in technical control. When this, in turn, is associated with a spurious ideal of neutrality, when values are set aside and social consequences disregarded, it becomes all too easy to train an entire public in predominantly technical thinking. When this is done, it becomes a simple matter for the mass to use as criteria such norms as effectiveness and payoff and, after a while, to accept such notions as that of Alexander Haig when he opposes self-interest and military efficacy to human rights or technical superiority to what he calls our "feelings" about apartheid.

Although I was asked to write about the "fundamental objectives of disarmament education," I find it more meaningful to discuss ways of seeing, ways of knowing, ways of being located in the world. I am more interested in educating critical and self-reflective men and women, with commitments to values, than I am in equipping them with certain competencies, skills, even certain kinds of information. It is the way of being in the world and engaging with the world that is important. The danger lies in people's becoming accommodated to the idea of an objectively existent reality, defined by others, usually official others, and taking that reality for granted. Why else are people so ready to accept the mapping of the world into superpower spheres of interest? Why is it so hard to see alternatives to a superpower confrontation over the Falklands, let us say, or Nicaragua, or El Salvador?

Related to the idea of critically reflective interpretation is the idea of interconnectedness, of the totality of things. There is a kind of specialization, as we well know, that fragments the world and compartmentalizes vision. It is the kind that makes it increasingly difficult to envisage the overlaps, the connections, the consequences that make all the difference. Wendell Berry, for one, speaks eloquently about the connections between mindless exploitation of the land, neglect of civil rights, military thinking, and technical approaches to the problems of life.[5] The *New Yorker* some time ago provided an example of the same ways of thinking when the writer of "Notes and Comments" took issue with the Reagan administration's notion of states' rights and David Stockman's comment that he could not see why a Michigan taxpayer should pay for subways in New York. After talking about the ills of the subways, the writer remarked that "they might have been cured easily at an early stage and now require major surgery." He went on:

> The profit from the newly "deregulated" industry is paid for with the illness of the people whose health is ruined by the resulting poisonous emissions. The person who is thrown off the food-stamp rolls shows up again on the welfare rolls. The town that is being polluted today has to be evacuated twenty years from now. The student who drops out of college because his loan was cancelled is less productive in his work for the rest of his life.[6]

And, at the end of the comment, the writer said: "Somewhere along the line, the very idea of society seems to have got lost, and one is left with a picture of the country as a collection of wholly self-interested, wholly rivalrous individuals, who are unacquainted with any notion of the common good." There is an interesting suggestion here that there is a connection between value consciousness and the ability to see things in interrelationships. It seems to me that what is now being said about the importance of a core curriculum connects with this, if that core curriculum is pervaded by some sense of worthwhile questions and if it is geared to the understanding of the lived situations of those being empowered to learn. There is no place for what C. P. Snow called, in another connection, "two cultures" when the consequences of technical decisions are so likely to affect the very lives of human beings all over the world. At the very least, there must be some understanding of what nuclear war signifies and some comprehension of the possibility of arms control.

I happen to be particularly interested in the role of the arts, especially encounters with the arts, in the learning process. One reason is that informed awareness of works of literature or paintings or plays provides a heightened sense of place, a sense of being in the world. In addition, engagement with a

Melville work of fiction or a Goya painting or a Tom Stoppard play may offer a sense of alternative realities, a recognition that things can be other than they are. Another reason is that aesthetic experiences may lead to a recovery, as one writer put it, of a person's lost spontaneity—meaning that they may enable us to see through our own eyes, to break with stereotypes and stock responses and automatisms. There is also the fact that we have to be present, personally present, to works of art if we are to constitute them as meaningful; and that is likely to overcome the abstractness as well as the passivity that is fostered by so many of the forces in our time. And, indeed, to see things in their interconnectedness, to put the severed parts together, to create patternings and networks in experience, is also a charge to break with passivity, with the terrible receptivity that is being fostered by the media. We are all aware that the passive gaze has become the hallmark of our time. The incapacity to deal critically with media makes even war movies and science fiction films in some manner mystifying: They oversimplify drastically; they feed our illusions of attaining total control. I want to see persons becoming agents rather than consumers. I want to see them becoming engaged in action, not behavior. I want them to initiate their own integrations, to identify relationships and consequences, to endow their own worlds with meaning and thus give purpose to their lives.

I remember Reverend William Sloane Coffin talking about the connections between defense spending and the loss of an urban job corps, and of what might follow from increasing adolescent unemployment in the cities. I see connections between the desire to pile up nuclear arms and unnecessary cruise missiles and, oddly enough, the campaign against abortion in Congress and the cuts in spending for mental health research and education and integration and bilingualism. It is only as we see the connections (in the light of imagined alternatives) that we will be able to bring persons together to struggle against all the violations that are being perpetuated: violations of human rights, violations of the right to choose, violations of civil liberties. They are all related, and we are false to ourselves if we do not enable young people to discover that this is so, to question, to interrogate—even the easy lives they feel entitled to live. David Stockman, you recall, has questioned the claim that the poor are "entitled" to support and financial aid. He and his associates have never questioned the taken-for-granted sense of entitlement that pervades the nation: the belief that we are entitled to eat more, consume more, use more energy, live better than any other people on earth.

The relation between self-understanding and understanding of these larger issues reminds me of something Jean-Paul Sartre wrote, when he was discussing the importance of self-awareness and the consciousness of the self as something more than an object. Rather, he said, it is the source of a particular way of seeing, of confronting the objectness of the world. He stressed the fact that the meanings of things are always generated by consciousness. It is not simply that "it is I who confer on the alarm clock its exigency" (that I apprehend the alarm as a summons because it refers to my possibility of going to work). "It is man," he wrote, "who renders cities destructible, precisely because he posits them as fragile and as precious and because he adopts a system of protective measures with regard to them."[7] Unlike earthquakes and eruptions, he was saying, destruction is a human thing. I find this to be of enormous significance, especially when I hear people treating bombs or invasions or instances of starvation as if they were natural occurrences, or when people ask (when reminded how important it is to pay heed to the napalmed child or the bombed schoolhouse or the bodies strewn in a town square) whether they are to bleed for every person killed in the Italian earthquake or some such catastrophe. Somehow it has to be made clear that nature is random, that the sky is indifferent—that, if there are to be justice and decency in the world, they have to be deliberately introduced by human beings. As Albert Camus suggested in *The Plague,* the point is not to become an accomplice of the world's injustice. The idea is to remain vigilant, consciously vigilant, against statistical thinking and distancing and carelessness and abstractness, all of which he associated with the plague.[8] We have to begin early, I believe, in education to communicate the understanding that the bombings of Hiroshima and Nagasaki and Dresden and London and Pearl Harbor and Hanoi were in no way accidental, that they were the result of human decisions and human trade-offs. The young must be brought to see that those instances of destruction would not have happened if certain persons in the world were not deliberately transmuted into objects for other people, means to other people's ends; if wealth and resources had not been transferred from social utilities to the manufacture of weapons stockpiles; if those in power had not decided it was preferable to destroy rather than to seek out spheres of negotiation, to kill rather than to relieve hunger and heal and build.

Clearly, a value consciousness must be fostered wherever education takes place. This means a sensitivity to lacks and deficiencies in the world around—and a willingness to take action to repair. Moral education demands much more than exercise in moral reasoning. Indeed, it involves a consciousness of principles—standards, norms, imperatives—that govern the way people choose to live together. Classrooms ought to be visibly norm-governed, in the sense that those engaged in teaching and learning talk about what it means to live together according to identifiable principles: freedom, let us say, decency, rationality. There ought to be a clear recognition of differences and what the alternatives are to living lives in accord with some conceptions of the "ought." It is a matter of incarnating such principles for the sake of living with others and for the sake of giving each individual life some sense. These principles provide perspectives; they allow persons to pick out what is relevant in situations when they make their choices. When, for example, a city like Memphis builds a roadblock that prevents black citizens from driving through a white neighborhood on their way home at night, a person who has incarnated a principle of fairness or equity cannot but recognize that as a situation that is fundamentally humiliating and unfair. When domination exists in school, when there is a "hidden curriculum" that enforces tracking and compliance, those who have become committed to what they understand by freedom or by self-determination are likely to perceive the situation as one that is morally wrong. Without some sense of "oughtness," deficiencies are almost never recognized; there is a kind of blank equivalence. Things simply are what they are.

But is not a matter of principle alone. It is a question of empowering young people to recognize particular situations as those that make demands on them, demands that they take some kind of action in the light of what they cherish, what they hold dear. Moral situations never come labeled; they have to be posited as situations that hold alternatives, that can be transcended and surpassed. It may be that the sense of injustice ought to be nurtured (with respect, say, to what happened at Hiroshima, what is happening in El Salvador today). It may be that human mutuality and friendship must be deliberately fostered. What seems crucial is that young people learn what it is, not simply to know and to feel, but to act: to break through what appear to be limiting situations; to find it in some sense existentially unbearable to tolerate injustice and violations and unwarranted pain. Without confrontations of this sort when they are young (and some of them may be experienced by means of encounters with art and literature), people—even purportedly virtuous people—are likely to grow up as purely abstract thinkers, reasoning well, knowing what is "right," but remaining incapable of deeply felt concern. To care when one is young, to learn what it means to be fair and to regard others' integrity and welfare, to constitute the world somehow in terms of compassion and concern, is to develop the capability of reaching beyond the immediate and the local. It may be to develop the capability to imagine a world that is truly just—a world in which bombings and torture and violations of human beings become personally offensive and intolerable to increasing numbers of people, a world in which, at last, there are moral constraints.

What is so frightening today is the fact that nuclear bombing (limited, they tell us) is becoming thinkable; and the more people are drawn into technical talk and the belief that some Other has the right to define the world, the more likely a nuclear war will be. I am cognizant of the connections between many schools and structures and the commitments of our technologized and increasingly militarized society. We need only point to the competencies orientation and the impacts of behaviorism to remind ourselves of the influence of the technological ethic, quantification, input-output thinking, and the rest. We know all too well how many practitioners treat their pupils or clients as objects or cases. The idea of letting people learn, the idea of freely chosen projects, the idea of interpretation: most of these, having little to do with efficiency, have been set aside. We all know of the learned ignorance imposed on so many young people, of the objectifications associated with too many schools. Too many teachers have internalized the existing ideology; they ask themselves few questions; they seldom think what they are doing. I believe that, if anything is to be done in our schools where wide-awakeness and reflectiveness are concerned, there must be a consciousness of the pressures, of the impinging structures, of the mystifications. When people are brought to believe that things can be otherwise, when they are urged to imagine a better state of things, they are at least likely to become aware of what is insupportable in their lived experience and at the horizon of that field. If they are enabled to identify gaps and insufficiencies within the contexts of their own situations, they may reach out to try to remake some of the structures that confine, to make alliances with individuals in the community on behalf of specific lacks (pollution, perhaps, the dearth of playgrounds, the absence of health care, the need for storefront schools, the emergency where day care is concerned), even to engage in political and peace campaigns.

The point is, however, that all this must follow from self-understanding, from an awareness of the actually lived world, from a refusal of objectness, from a decision to be with others in a sphere that is intersubjectively meaningful. On this ground there can be new beginnings, efforts to surpass, to go beyond. Working for the day-care center, people may extend their reach to the Chilean mining town, the Cambodian beach, the Lebanese frontier. Struggling against technicism in their own curriculum, they may begin to understand what was said (and not said) at Three Mile Island, how so-called security decisions are often reached. Forging their own poetry, their own images, they may catch glimpses of horizons, understanding what is not yet.

And the goal? The "fundamental objectives" of peace education? To end the suffering, to cure the plague, to humanize the world. Of course the humanizing cannot be recognized until it is achieved; and once it is, there can only be new beginnings, new pursuits of possibility. Yes, I think that the facts of defense spending should be made clear, and the obsoleteness of our economy, and the stubborn tendency to use old solutions for new problems, to reach back into a simpler past. Yes, I think the social consequences and the medical consequences and the moral consequences of nuclear stockpiling should be made clear, as should the impossibility of anyone's winning a nuclear war. People should be urged to reflect on our share of the responsibility for the arms race now going on, on the preoccupation with retaliatory weapons, on the statistical thinking that eludes all moral constraint. That is what represents the plague to me; and the kinds of calculations that account for it are precisely like those that maintain apartheid on this planet and teenage unemployment and starvation in the wealthiest cities, that demean women and blacks and even children, that ignore or regulate the jobless and the hungry and the poor. So I am suggesting that peace education be anticalculative education and that it lead to a critique of technical talk and control. I am suggesting too that young people be empowered to ponder new possibilities, alternatives to destruction and war.

They must be enabled to speak with their own voices, tell their own stories, and, yes, to love the world. I shall turn to Albert Camus for a conclusion, because his words are so very spare and pure:

> The task is endless, it's true. But we are here to pursue it. . . . We have not overcome our condition, and yet we know it better. We know that we live in contradiction, but we also know that we must refuse this contradiction and do what is needed to reduce it. Our task . . . is to find the few principles that will calm the infinite anguish of free souls. We must mend what has been torn apart, make justice imaginable again in a world so obviously unjust, give happiness a meaning once more to peoples poisoned by the misery of this century. Naturally, it is a superhuman task. But superhuman is the term for tasks men take a long time to accomplish, that's all. Let us know our aims then, holding fast to the mind, even if force puts on a thoughtful or a comfortable face in order to seduce us. The first thing is not to despair.[9]

Notes

1 Japanese Broadcasting Company, ed., *Unforgettable Fire* (New York: Pantheon Books, 1981), p. 11.

2 Ibid., p. 13.

3 Ibid., p. 52.

4 Hannah Arendt, *The Human Condition* (Chicago: The University of Chicago Press, 1958), pp. 182–84.

5 Wendell Berry, *A Continuous Harmony: Essays Cultural and Agricultural* (New York: Harcourt Brace Jovanovich, 1975), pp. 72–73.

6 "Notes and Comments," *The New Yorker*, April 27, 1981, pp. 35-36.

7 Jean-Paul Sartre, *Being and Nothingness* (New York: Philosophical Library, 1956), p. 9.

8 Albert Camus, *The Plague* (New York: Alfred A. Knopf, 1948), pp. 229–32.

9 Albert Camus, "The Almond Trees," in his *Lyrical and Critical Essays* (New York: Alfred A. Knopf, 1968), p. 135.

Disarmament Education as World Order Inquiry

BETTY REARDON
Teachers College, Columbia University

Disarmament education, the most significant current development in peace education, now comes to wider public attention than have most other developments in this field because of the launching of the World Disarmament Campaign. Through this campaign and the public discussions surrounding the United Nations Second Special Session on Disarmament (SSD II), scholars and public leaders concerned with war-peace issues have finally acknowledged the significance of education to the disarmament process. World order scholars in particular should have a special concern with disarmament education. The main objective of their inquiry—the transformation of the global order from a war system to a peace system—requires attention not only to the basic relationship between education and social change, but also and especially to the crucial relationship between the need for unprecedented social learning, which should constitute disarmament education, and the "cutting-edge inquiry" of world order. Together disarmament education and world order inquiry comprise the search for the basic and fundamental knowledge from which to derive essential strategies for the global transformation process.

World order, as it is used in this article, refers to academic inquiry, action, research, and education related to the pursuit of world order values and to the changes in the global system necessary to the fulfillment of these values. *Disarmament education* relates specifically to those learnings required to achieve the core world order value of peace. It is that education which will provide the knowledge and skills necessary to abolish the war system. For our purposes it is education for the promotion of general and complete disarmament.[1]

In that peace research and peace education have such a clear responsibility to contribute to the disarmament process, and in that disarmament is a fundamental concern of world order research, it is essential that the relationships between these fields of inquiry be explored and clarified. The

This article by Betty Reardon is based in part on the educational implication "a Prospective on the Cutting Edge of World Order Inquiry" by Saul Mendlovitz, which appears in International InterAction *8, no. 1-2 (1981): 151-60, and also as WOMP Working Paper no. 20. A version of this article has been published under coauthorship in* Gandhi Nark *as a special issue called "Arms and Survival," 1982.*

purpose of this article is to explore those relationships, hoping to provide some clarification, as a contribution to the worldwide movement for disarmament, which I view as a significant first stage in a wider global transformation movement.

ASSUMPTIONS ABOUT DISARMAMENT

In approaching disarmament education as world order inquiry it is important to emphasize that disarmament is a necessary but not a sufficient condition for the achievement of a truly just world order, defined as the fulfillment on a global scale of the values of peace, social justice, economic equity, ecological balance, and political participation. However, even though I consider disarmament to be but one substantive component of the desired global transformation, viewing the world order movement and its transformational potential from a historic perspective, it is apparent that disarmament must be accorded the movement's highest priority for this particular decade. Disarmament is the current central task of the longer range and even wider reaching global transformation espoused by world order inquiry. This central task is two-fold: to change the international security system from a war-making system to a peacekeeping system, and to transfer the resources used to maintain the war-making system to the process of fulfilling the world order values of economic equity and social justice.

Further, the disarmament process envisioned as the means of fulfilling this task will involve as well a major shift from world militarization to world demilitarization as the fundamental necessity for truly democratic political participation. The present trend toward world militarization, fueled by the arms trade, has had a direct negative effect on all world order values, but most especially on political participation and human rights. Because the present security system is so costly in expenditure of resources and so antithetical to a humane world order, the disarmament process in and of itself can contribute to the possibilities for the fulfillment of the other values. However, neither the process nor even the goal per se is adequate to achieve the changes that will be required for the kind of humane system that would assure equal expectation of enjoyment of world order values by all members of the human family. At the same time, it is quite clear that the dangers of the present arms race, most especially the dangers inherent in the nuclear arms race, as well as the deleterious effect it has on the whole range of world order values, require that disarmament be given the very highest priority in research, education, and political action. I affirm this priority as I insist that the learnings as well as the political strategies derived from disarmament research and education be placed within the context of their relationship to the other values. Indeed, I caution that the perspectives of the other values are essential in consideration of most disarmament issues. A peace system that is not committed to the equal importance of those other goals, while it may relieve the dangers of nuclear annihilation, the fear of which seems to inspire so much of the disarmament movement in the northern-tier nations, may well freeze into place many of the injustices and oppressive processes that now lead so many peoples to resort to armed conflict in the pursuit of justice. Neither can a disarmament process that does not see justice as the primary objective of political institutions contribute to a more desirable world order. While such a process may produce a more secure world order in the sense of the reduction, even abolition of organized warfare, it cannot produce a more secure world order in the sense of "people's security," the expectation of the meeting of basic needs, including the basic right to human dignity and self-determination.

FUNDAMENTAL NORMATIVE PROBLEMS

Thus, from a world order perspective, the major issue for disarmament education can be summarized in this central question: What do we need to learn ourselves, and to teach others, in order to eliminate violence and force as the major instruments for maintaining order and pursuing political goals in the international system, while simultaneously developing practical and functional mechanisms for maintaining order and assuring effective, non-violent means to pursue justice and resolve conflict?

If one views contemporary developments from the perspective of a struggle theory of history, clearly the major struggle at the level of the global system should be to transcend the oppressive legacy of the colonial system and the inequities of the current international economic structures that govern the relationships between the so-called developing and the industrialized nations.[2] Disarmament education must confront the need to help people think in terms of a variety of ways in which the oppressed may struggle for justice and oppressors may be restrained, without recourse to arms. Unless adequate attention is given to inquiry and to learning toward this end, one cannot in good conscience espouse disarmament education as a component of world order inquiry. Nor can it be expected that oppressed nations or oppressed groups will support disarmament or teach their young the need for and the means to disarmament. The primary social education required by the oppressed is about ways and means to achieve their own liberation, ways of comprehending the nature and causes of their oppression, so that strategies for transcending it can be devised and pursued. It is therefore essential for those developing disarmament education as world order inquiry to turn equal attention to those strategies. The disarmament movement and disarmament education could well appear to the oppressed, to peoples of the Third World in particular, as another device through which the First World will continue to maintain its hegemony, simply by controlling the terms of the disarmament process and the structure for maintaining peace. Smacking of other expressions of universalism and globalism, the subjects frequently are discussed in terms that exclude the issues of injustice and oppression as forms of violence equally dehumanizing and dangerous to the future survival of humanity.[3]

Some of the central questions currently considered in disarmament education would probably be viewed from a very different perspective by oppressed groups, not only in the so-called Third World, but also in impoverished and oppressed sectors of the First World.[4] There are some fundamental questions to be faced by those who devise disarmament proposals and those who teach about them. Who will disarm? When? How? For what purpose? Under what verification procedures? What substitute processes for the pursuit of conflicting values are projected for development simultaneously with the processes of reducing weaponry and the military? Will the renunciation of organized warfare and armed force call on us to make some fundamental changes in our value priorities? If so, what are those changes, and what changes will be required from other actors in the global system? Indeed, an exchange among scholars and students in secondary and university classrooms in the first and third worlds on these questions might of itself be a productive exercise in disarmament education.

North American scholars tend to see the question of identity as the crucial one in creating the climate for the achievement of disarmament and for the pursuit of global transformation. We often advocate the development of a universal human identity in which persons conceive of themselves as members of a single species. Yet we must recognize, too, that for that universal identity to have true integrity, it must comprehend the various individual and cultural identities in a context of equal value. This requires changes in perceptions and world views that should be paramount concerns of education for a global community, indeed, of all education in a planetary era. What is involved here is educating many peoples about their own human value and about the fact of their equal social worth among other individuals and other groups. And it involves educating some about the fact that they are not "more equal." It involves educating those who exercise power to understand that power is not in their hands because they are of greater worth or value. They must learn, too, that their intellectual endeavors and political theories have no more validity than those of any other individual or group and must be subjected to the same tests; must, for example, be subjected to review by a set of questions similar to those raised above.

Any authentic universal identity must be based on a fundamental concept of self, which will be augmented and enriched by awareness of the universal dimension and which, indeed, is the foundation for the universal. Most important, we must make the links between the acknowledgment of the equal value of individual and cultural identities and the right of participation in the planning of the new institutions and structures that will bring disarmament into existence and maintain the peacekeeping system.

The normative objectives of world order inquiry that thus far have been pursued in research and speculation on the new behaviors for political and institutional actors must also be transposed into the individual and personal sphere. The question of identity makes it most evident that world order inquiry, if it is to contribute to significant disarmament education, must take into consideration the major obstacles to disarmament, particularly those obstacles that relate to personal and cultural identity and to the psychic constructs of the persons and institutions who will be charged with carrying out the disarmament process.

Among the crucial psychological or perceptual obstacles to disarmament that have been identified as a result of research in this area, fear is one of the most significant. People are afraid of disarmament, not only the oppressed, for reasons previously alluded to, but the oppressors themselves. This fear reflects more than the possibility of the loss of privilege. It reflects fear of change and the inability to live with the possibility of a world in which the shape and direction of the future is unknown. The desired behavioral changes will not be achieved if those who are engaging in the research and education to produce those changes do not take the question of fear seriously and confront that fear and its relationships to the identity issue and to the way in which ignorance of alternatives in the policy field and ignorance of the multiplicity of human identities in the cultural field feed the fear. The important factor here is that it is not enough for the educators and the researchers to be able to envision alternatives, nor to be fully cognizant of the range of cultural identities and the variety of individual and cultural value systems. The obligation they hold is to transmit this knowledge to the masses of those who need to be educated both for disarmament and for participation in the wider transformation process. Without this knowledge, which now resides primarily with the scholars, some educators, and very few politicians, the people in general will not be able to participate in the process. It will thus not be a legitimate, popular process of the type espoused by world order scholars, nor will it be able to confront constructively the conflicting perceptions and priorities involved in disarmament and global transformation.[5]

In sum, the fundamental normative problems revolve around the tensions between human dignity and integrity and social and economic equity, on the one hand, and immediate survival and the desperate need to reduce levels of violence on the other. This, in fact, has been the perennial problem of those who seek knowledge to contribute to peace, indeed, of those who would pursue peace while giving equal value to justice. Given the call for and the movement toward disarmament, which now extends far beyond the peace movement and the fields of peace research and peace education, these tensions have more cogency than ever before in both the realms of research and education and the realm of politics. Those who are professionally engaged in research and education for specific political ends must begin to respond to these tensions with practical educational approaches as well as research that has practical policy applications in both the short and the long run. In that world order has been an approach to the study of peace and justice that has taken the relationship among and between problems as a fundamental component of the mode of analysis and as a basic approach to instruction, this cogency presents a special responsibility to world order scholars and educators involved in disarmament education.

CENTRAL ISSUES IN THE INQUIRY

World order scholars have recently identified seven concerns as cutting-edge issues.[6] These are issues that provide a sharper focus on the central normative problem of world order and offer a means by which that problem might be sliced into components more easily analyzed than the total problem itself. That problem, as indicated above, is actually a set of interrelated problems centering on the issue of equity between the first and third worlds, an issue that plays itself out not only in the sociopolitical system but also in the realms of research and peace action, and thereby constitutes a significant factor to be taken into consideration in any program of peace education. Each of these foci also offer insight into issues in peace education as it relates to producing an understanding of and equipment for participation in the disarmament process.

The first of these foci is what has been called "the struggle theory of history." This particular approach to the evolution of institutional change in both domestic and global society offers an especially clarifying approach to instruction for disarmament education. From the perspective of world order, the recognition of this approach as the most logical way in which to view history and the conflicts through which it evolves provides a paradigm for the study of the central normative problem of First World–Third World equity. It also provides a perspective for the study of obstacles to disarmament. One of the major obstacles to widespread understanding of issues in disarmament has been the failure to see it as either a historical evolutionary process or as a struggle waged by those who are committed to the necessity of changing the international system for conflict resolution. This struggle has been for the most part an attempt to persuade or to undermine those who believe that the present system better serves their interests and the values to which they are committed. Viewed in this way, disarmament is but one of a series of struggles in human history that have been directed toward a more humane and equitable social order, that is, a social order less characterized by violence and oppression and one that directs itself more toward values classified as human values in general, and, in this particular historic period, world order values in particular. This view is reinforced by conceiving of disarmament as the structural aspect of demilitarization, the reversal of the present trend toward authoritarian elitism imposed by armed force.

The second focus among the cutting-edge issues is in fact demilitarization. This particular focus has special relevance for disarmament education because it enables the educator to present disarmament as a reversal of a specific, extant process that can be concretely illustrated. Disarmament, as a condition that has never actually existed, is very hard to present in descriptive form other than hypothetical models or proposals. Demilitarization, however, is something that enables world order scholars to focus on specific value-realizing processes or what they have called "transition strategies." It also enables educators to demonstrate the specific circumstances and conditions that must be undone in order for the requisite concrete steps toward construction of a disarmed world to be taken. Exploration of methods and strategies of demilitarization also provides necessary argumentation for the need for disarmament and the need to understand how to achieve disarmament, both of which are essential political and pedagogic rationales that must be put forward by any advocate of disarmament education.

The process of militarization that has taken place in the world, most particularly over the past decade and a half, is but one component of the present operation of the war system that is most obviously manifested in the arms race. It is a phenomenon that demonstrates how the excesses of the war system have an impact on all sociopolitical and economic institutions. It also shows how the excesses of that system impede the potential to realize not only peace but all other world order values as well. That militarization takes resources from development can be demonstrated with data and case studies, as can the relationship of the arms trade to militarization and to the consequent rise of oppressive regimes that violate the values of social justice, economic equity, and political participation.[7] The degree to which the militarization process propelled by the arms race also endangers the ecological system can be demonstrated through an examination of the consequences of testing nuclear weapons and the evidence that the use of chemical weapons is ecologically damaging. Thus, the militarization focus makes it possible to pursue disarmament education as world order inquiry, for it is a vehicle through which to illuminate the interrelatedness of various global problems, the effects of militarization on world order values, and the impact of the arms race on all world systems.

Demilitarization also provides the most fruitful pedagogic tool for instruction about transition. For example, an examination of the process of militarization and proposals for demilitarizing both specific societies and the global system in a step-by-step approach calls for consideration of parallel steps to build a nonviolent alternative security system, the only context in which disarmament can be perceived as either acceptable or workable.

The notion of the emergence of a "global culture and global civilization," another focus of the cutting edge, is one that speaks to the need to develop the previously discussed universal identity and to emphasize that any socio-economic unit, to be a coherent community, must have some common cultural values. Thus, disarmament can be perceived as the mechanism through which the fundamental common cultural value, that is, the value placed on survival of the human species, can be pursued. It has been implied that world order values may indeed be the first stages of the emergence of a set of values that could bring together a coherent sense of a global or human culture, uniting all the peoples of the world. However, it is equally important, as we pursue both world order inquiry and disarmament education, to understand the nature of cultural differences and diversity and to understand the need for the recognition of the potential conflict that can be produced by cultural diversity as well as its potential for enrichment and strengthening of human solidarity.[8]

It is important, as one looks to the ways in which the trends toward global culture can be maximized, not to overplay the technological possibilities of the world communications systems and all of those developments that are usually pointed to as the mechanism through which the world culture will emerge. While we cannot underestimate the global communications system as a means through which global consciousness can be brought to the surface, and find expression, the nature of that global consciousness and the multicultural dimensions it must take cannot occur exclusively through a technology that has been devised primarily by the one sector of the world that has also launched and maintained the arms race. Granted, the lethal technology of the war system has brought about the potential for total annihilation as well as the communications system that makes possible the global disarmament movement. But the movement has yet to acknowledge fully the relationships of the arms race and the technological imbalance to the maintenance of the global economic inequities that condemn the majority to poverty and oppression.

Here, educators and scholars must ask the question, Can we depend on the same technology that has produced the problem to give us insights and approaches into the resolution of that problem? In that we have placed a high value on participation and on giving full voice to those persons and cultures that have been oppressed, this question is a crucial one, which must be examined in both world order inquiry and in disarmament education from the perspective of those who are oppressed. If there is to be a legitimate world culture, it cannot be dominated by the technological Western culture, which now points to its own technology as evidence of the emergence of a single world culture by virtue of the fact that it is worldwide and affects all parts of the world.[9] This particular issue raises the human and cultural dimension of the central, normative problem of equity. This cutting edge provides an insight into the issue of global community, the issue that asks these questions: Can we build world structures in which cultural diversity can be respected and preserved while human unity and solidarity are also pursued? Can we build a world community in which differences will not impede the equal access to resources and the means to human fulfillment for any member of the world society? This is basically what we mean by community, the equitable sharing of all the resources available to the society.

I would argue indeed that the fourth cutting edge, the drive to articulate a sense of global citizenship, can come about only in the presence of community. That is, the desire to participate in bringing forth a world political system, or what has been called "the global polity," will undoubtedly be conditioned by the degree to which persons and groups see that their interests will be served by such a polity. The development of citizenship in the sense of participation thus relates very closely to the central normative problem. Participation in an authentic sense usually comes only from those who feel that they can achieve equity or those who feel that they must struggle against the present order so as to increase their chances for equity. Thus, the global political order must at least articulate equity as a value, and the development of the concept of global citizenship must go hand in hand with an inquiry into the necessary institutional framework for the achievement of equity. Without such a framework, few could be expected to support the idea of disarmament. Disarmament education should involve teaching and learning for the development of the skills needed to create the framework as well as for commitment to the value of equity.

The concept of polity also raises the issues of order and security. The process of disarmament must involve the invention of functional equivalents to force and to military might for assuring security, just as disarmament education must prepare people to understand the need for establishing those functional equivalents and to participate in inventing them. Thus, disarmament education needs to be informed by a concept of global citizenship, and I would argue that such citizenship should be based on a fundamental commitment to world order values as the basic norms of the global polity.

Pursuit of such norms is the responsibility of what has been referred to as "humane governance," designated as the fifth cutting edge of world order inquiry. Given the inevitability of conflict in a culturally and ideologically diverse world, just governance is likely to depend on the maintenance of an equitable order by nonviolent conflict-resolution procedures. However, the perennial question of the balance between order and justice, and whether order can be fully maintained within a framework of justice, is paramount for those who put forward proposals for world order systems, as it is for those who put forward concepts of a disarmed world or political processes through which the world can be disarmed. Clearly, there is a danger that the disarmament process, being so difficult and potentially so menacing to the values it seeks to serve, could give rise to a form of authoritarianism rationalized by the threat to these values (i.e., freedom, equality, etc.), just as authoritarianism has arisen out of pressures caused by rapid, exogenously derived changes in developing societies or industrial societies that come to a state of social unrest as a result of value conflict and political disintegration. The process through which the global transformation takes place, most particularly that stage in which the world is disarming, will be one in which there are rapid value changes, political stress, economic dislocation, all of the conditions that have given rise to authoritarianism. Thus, the cutting edge of humane governance becomes a concern that must be brought to bear on any proposals for disarmament or alternative global systems as a criterion for not only acceptability but workability. In other words, we must insist on this focus or we may well fall into another version of the same trap from which we hope to extricate ourselves through disarmament and demilitarization.

The foci of humane governance and global citizenship are ones that shed some light on the sixth cutting edge, "the tension between the local and the global as spheres of action and perspectives on world order problems." A world order approach would insist that humane governance is highly participatory governance. It would not sacrifice efficiency for democracy but would find a way to bring those two values into balance. Similarly, it would need to bring into balance the tension between the local and global spheres as arenas for action and as perspectives from which to view issues and problems, particularly with reference to claims on resources for the equitable meeting of needs. Local-global tension in this respect could manifest itself in the process of resource reallocation. As the vast sums spent on maintaining the armed war system are reduced in the disarmament process, there undoubtedly will be conflicts and differences over the specific designation of the alternative expenditures of those resources. While there will be general agreement that the resources should be channeled into meeting human needs, the relief of poverty, and the improvement of the quality of life, nonetheless there are likely to be a great variety of proposals regarding the ways to achieve those general goals. Some of them will be for institutions and processes that operate on the global level, requiring allocation of large portions of the newly released resources to that level. Others will be for programs at the local level so long deprived of resources directed in such large sums to "national security." Thus the competition for resources may be between the two levels most neglected under the war system. Disarmament education needs to anticipate such competition and encourage speculation on appropriate criteria for deciding such issues and handling such conflicts.

Learning for disarmament will also require reconceptualizing our concepts of "global" and "local." Just as global can come to be a unit of human identity and political organization, local can also come to be something other than a specific place. Local seems now to be in a process of redefinition that relates to the locus of intimate and daily life, "the quotidian" in terms of regular human associations and most common pursuits and tasks. These redefinitions are likely to affect profoundly the patterns of human cohesion and conflict. Where both these processes were, under the war system, conducted mainly by some form of force or coercion, it is possible that intimate and daily life could be determined by assent and consent, a circumstance that will require a totally new form of social education. Disarmament education as a means of learning to transcend the war system could be as well a transition step toward that new form of education.

This local-global tension also offers to disarmament education an opportunity to contribute to learning that will dismantle the basic structures of inequity that hold the Third World in poverty and oppression. These structures, kept in place by the war system, are based on territoriality and the concepts of distance—both geographic and cultural—that belong to a historic period that died with the dawning of the "space age." World order scholars in particular have experienced this change in the patterns of intimacy and daily life that redefine "local" and offer an important form of learning for incorporation into disarmament education.

World order research has dealt more than other disciplines with these issues and can offer insights to disarmament education. Education of this sort will be essential to transcending the problem of the tensions between the geographic local and global areas, from the perspectives of analyzing problems, plotting strategies, allocating resources, developing identities, and so forth. These are going to be constant problems over the long-term transition but could also be a creative and energizing conflictual force in the transformation process. Every person is going to have to deal with the questions of identity and the quotidian, that is, Who am I? and Where is it that I spend most of my human life, most of my days? This in turn has a specific relationship to disarmament education because it also raises the question, How do I, as an individual, act or contribute to the fundamental task of achieving disarmament, which is the basic groundwork for the total transformation? In other words, I am not a full participant in that process unless I make a contribution to making it possible. The whole process cannot, I assert, be possible unless there is a commitment and movement toward general and complete disarmament, which will be the essential challenge to current concepts of local and global as well as to traditional, territorially bound education.

The seventh cutting edge, the issue of world authority—that is, structuring the review and implementation process for ensuring disarmament and for carrying out alternative processes for security maintenance and conflict resolution—raises the question, How can we assure a legitimate, functional authority that is sensitive to all of the issues raised by the other cutting-edge issues? Responding to this question will be the fundamental, practical task of institutional design, taking world order values into account to achieve the central normative goals of equity, justice, and human dignity. The response may also trigger the most explosive of the transition conflicts.

While virtually all advocates of disarmament and peace recognize the need for a world authority, there is virtually no consensus on the nature of that authority, how it should be constituted and how it should be exercised. One of the major problems that has not been resolved, even by such efforts as the World Order Models Project, is that all current models and proposals for world authority are fundamentally Western and within the European tradition of governance. Clearly, these models are not yet adequate to the criteria of cultural diversity and human solidarity I have asserted to be a fundamental requirement of a true global community. Thus, the design and mobilization of support for a legitimate world authority is a major task for the world order scholars and a fundamental need of disarmament educators. It can be the task of institutional design, which, as the major focus of those creative aspects of disarmament education, will reintroduce into intentional learning the human imagination, for so long stifled by formal education. Thus, it is clear that not only do scholarship and research call for the application of cutting edges, but that we also need radical transformation in the education process in order to carry out the purposes of disarmament education.

There is, I assert, no vehicle potentially more productive toward the pedagogic end of nurturing the creative human imagination than articulating visions of a better world, describing ways in which a culturally diverse but unified human species might live in a world in which there was indeed conflict but in which violence was counter to both norms and expectations. The expression of that vision and of what has been previously described as "the voices, visions, and the transition" components of the transformation process is also a fundamental component of the pedagogical process. Disarmament education must enable learners to understand the voices of the structurally oppressed and empower them to give voice to all who are oppressed by the arms system, every member of the human species. Disarmament education must help people understand what the various human stakes are in the arms race and the reasons various groups will benefit from disarmament. It must also help learners not only to project their own visions but also to see and comprehend the alternative visions put forward by those with different cultures and different ideological positions. What is by now "traditional" world order inquiry method calls for a comparison of alternative relevant utopias in a search for a vision of a common preferred world, and speculates on the process of transition, the political strategies, the mobilization forces, the ways in which visions can be transposed into institutions and practices can lend themselves to a disarmament learning process. People must learn to plot these strategies in order to participate in the political process just as one learns to play a musical instrument by practicing scales, or to train as an athlete with particular exercises to perfect technique and build endurance. In a sense, the movement toward a disarmed world will call on the kinds of energies and need for strength that a very intense athletic contest requires and will call as well for the sensitivity to variations and modality in the orchestration of the various cultural and ideological components of world society into a coherent expression of our common humanity.

DISARMAMENT EDUCATION AS TRANSITION STRATEGY

The relationships between world order inquiry and disarmament education are made considerably clearer when viewed in the framework of the "three systems" identified by Richard Falk.[10] The first system, the traditional international system of states, maintains the arms race while the second system, the United Nations, articulates the need of the global community to disarm and the third system, an agglomeration of grass-roots initiatives and nongovernmental organizations, pressures the first and catalyzes the second into policy change and some substantive action. The most significant examples of such action are the two special sessions of the General Assembly on disarmament, SSD I and SSD II, and UNESCO's World Congress on Disarmament Education. Each of these events reflects the significance of disarmament education as fundamental to the disarmament process. SSD I does so in its final document, which speaks to the need for public information and education and calls on UNESCO to organize the congress. The final document of that event is a basic recognition of disarmament education as a distinct field of study. The World Disarmament Campaign, an agenda item of SSD II, demonstrates the kind of collaboration between "systems two and three" that can facilitate the broad political participation we deem essential to the transformation of the global system, which comprehends all three systems.

It is important to note that disarmament education as a distinct field of study has already given some attention to the normative problems and central issues reviewed here. The final document of the World Congress on Disarmament Education, which was convened by UNESCO in Paris in June of 1980, attends to many of these issues. The congress brought together between 300 and 400 peace educators and peace researchers, who asserted the basic, fundamental, and urgent need for disarmament education. This assembly, which was itself ideologically and culturally diverse, made significant progress toward pushing the inquiry into constructive substantive areas and in so doing acknowledged the fundamental normative problem. This acknowledgment can be seen very clearly in the ten guiding principles the congress put forth to outline the field of disarmament education.

The transformational significance of disarmament is reflected in the second principle, wherein it is stated in defining disarmament that "it may also be understood as a process aimed at transforming the current system of armed nation States into a new world order of planned unarmed peace, in which war is no longer an instrument of national policy and peoples determine their own future and live in security based on justice and solidarity."[11] This clearly recognizes some of the same value priorities as those that inform world order inquiry, and it places disarmament education within the transformational context.

The document also reflects a very sensitive awareness of the local-global problem and the identity issue when it expresses in its fourth point, "To be effective . . . disarmament education should be related to the lives and concerns of the learners and to the political realities within which disarmament is taught and should provide insights into political, economic and social factors on which the security of peoples could be based."[12]

It shows, too, that those assembled in Paris understood the interrelationship of the problems in a way similar to that illuminated by world order inquiry. This is particularly clear in point 7 of the guiding principles, which designates links between human rights and development and disarmament. "As an integral part of peace education, disarmament education has a central link with human rights education and development education, insofar as each of the three terms peace, human rights, and development must be defined in relation to the other two. Moreover, disarmament education offers an occasion to elucidate emerging concepts such as the individual and collective rights to peace and to development, based on the satisfaction of material and nonmaterial human needs."[13]

Furthermore, the document reflects a concern with the need to redefine security in the terms we have previously discussed, as well as with a search for alternative security systems as part of the fundamental purpose of education toward disarmament—just as it is a fundamental purpose of world order inquiry.

That those gathered in Paris conceived of disarmament education as inquiry, not as indoctrination, is most explicitly stated in point 8, which specifies the pedagogical objectives of disarmament education: "Whether conceived as education in the spirit of disarmament, as the incorporation of relevant materials in existing disciplines, or as the development of a distinct field of study, disarmament education should apply the most imaginative educational methods, particularly those of participatory learning, geared to each specific cultural and social situation and level of action. It aims at teaching *how* to think about disarmament rather than *what* to think about it. It should therefore be problem-centered so as to develop the analytical and critical capacity to examine and evaluate practical steps towards the reduction of arms and the elimination of war as an acceptable international practice."[14]

The World Disarmament Campaign, intended to involve all the world's people in thinking about disarmament, will be a massive education effort. It is a unique and unprecedented opportunity to mold public events into transition strategies for global transformation. It is as well a challenge to world order inquiry and disarmament education to merge their common approaches and goals into one significant transition strategy.

Notes

1 Betty Reardon, "Obstacles to Disarmament Education," in *Obstacles to Disarmament*, ed. Swadesh Rana (Paris: UNESCO, 1981), pp. 113-33.

2 Saul Mendlovitz, "A Perspective on the Cutting Edge of World Order Inquiry," *International Interactions* 8, no. 1-2 (1981): 151-60.

3 Jamie Diaz, "The Arms Race and the Role of Education," in Rana, *Obstacles to Disarmament*, pp. 105-12.

4 The author acknowledges that she herself has put forth some of these "central questions."

5 See Reardon, "Obstacles to Disarmament Education."

6 See Mendlovitz, "A Perspective on the Cutting Edge."

7 For statistics on this phenomenon see Ruth Leger Sivard, *World Military and Social Expenditures 1981* (Leesburg, Va.: World Priorities Inc., 1982).

8 Betty Reardon and Djibril Diallo, "Proposal for an Institute of World Cultures," in *Basic Documents for the University for Peace* (Costa Rica: Presidential Commission for the University of Peace, 1981).

9 "The Perversion of Science and Technology," World Order Models Project (WOMP) statement on Technology (New York: Institute for World Order, July 1978).

10 Richard Falk, "Normative Initiatives and Demilitarization," WOMP Working Paper, no. 13 (New York: Institute for World Order, 1982).

11 Report and Final Document, World Congress on Disarmament Education (Paris: UNESCO, June 9–13, 1980), SS/MD/35, p. 8.

12 Ibid.

13 Ibid., p. 9.

14 Ibid.

The Peace Movement Threat

JOHN M. BROUGHTON,
MARTA K. ZAHAYKEVICH
Teachers College, Columbia University

In the United States, we have witnessed over the past year the rapid rise of a widespread "peace movement" in response to a perceived threat of nuclear war. This movement alerts us to the idea that the very survival of the human race may be in question. The contemplation of the loss of all modes of survival, including the sense that one might aspire to spiritual continuity via successive generations or through cultural products, elicits monstrous psychic representations of the discontinuity of human life and of the sudden fracture of being. Such psychic images inevitably evoke primitive threats of annihilation that psychoanalytic theorists of the "object relations" school[1] hold to be the primary source of extreme anxiety in the early development of the self in infancy. There are two ways to respond to this threat: to move in a developmentally regressive direction or, provided there are appropriate supportive objects that the self can relate to, in a developmentally progressive one. The regressive response uses defensive fragmentation and repression that foster a highly fragile and unstable self. The progressive response, on the other hand, relies on memory to build an integrated, resilient self capable of acting on the basis of autonomous judgment and a benign conscience that is directed toward nurturance and mutual preservation.

In the latter process, memories, primarily of past aggression and loss, are made conscious, relived, understood and accepted. In this process, they congeal to form a powerful core of self that is able to resist not only psychic threats from the immediate surroundings but also political manipulation of such threats that serves to encourage the coercion of individuals by the state. Here, memory serves the dual function of promoting progressive political action and progressive psychological development. Memory is the place where the psychological and the political intersect.

Simone Weil identifies the destruction of historical meaning by the modern state as the main vehicle through which coercion comes to be implemented, while resistance to coercion arises from the impulse to preserve the past in a living memory.

The authors would like to acknowledge the fact that discussion meetings of the Chevigny Group and the Group for a Radical Human Science, dealing with the topic of the nuclear threat, contributed to the development of the ideas presented here. Our thanks to Catherine Welfare for her help in the preparation of the manuscript.

> Loss of the past, whether it be collectively or individually, is the supreme human tragedy, and we have thrown ours away just like a child picking off the petals of a rose. It is above all to avoid this loss that peoples will put up a desperate resistance to being conquered. Now, the totalitarian phenomenon of the State arises through a conquest carried out by the public authorities of the people under their care, without being able to spare them the evils necessarily accompanying all conquests. . . . The State is a cold concern which cannot inspire love, but itself kills, suppresses everything that might be loved.[2]

Weil proposes that a study of history be a central educational tool to recapture a rootedness in the past. However, for her, the true study of history has to be distinctly different from the study of history as commonly conceived in terms of glorious deeds, climaxes of civilization, pinnacles of power.

> History is a tissue of base and cruel acts in the midst of which a few drops of purity sparkle at long intervals. . . . No subject is more important from the point of view of the peoples than that of war. . . . No other method exists for acquiring knowledge about the human heart than the study of history coupled with the experience of life, in a way that the two throw light upon each other. It is our duty to supply this food to the mind of youth. But it must be truth-giving food; facts must be shown in their true perspective relatively to good and evil.[3]

A history that reconstructs what is shameful, base, and cruel in a people's past can open up possibilities for love, and can simultaneously make possible a resistance to the destructive coldness of the state. The study of war, of human and material devastation, becomes a central focus in the study of history. This study must be paired with moral judgment to guide action in the present toward the future. According to Weil, it is only this reconstitution of the past in a lived historical memory that provides a base on which people can create their own future. Without historical memory, the future becomes totally manipulable by the state.

POSITIVISM AS STATE IDEOLOGY

Central to the maintenance of the regressive, defensive reaction to issues of national security is the system of ideas, concepts, values, theories, and practices used to administer military and governmental bureaucracies in modern states. This system embodies a world view that is properly called positivism. Positivism is a metatheory or philosophy of existence, knowledge, and freedom, with a corresponding set of practical orientations. It is built around the assumption that objective understanding and coherent social life can be grounded only by the scientific method of inquiry.[4] It is no coincidence that such a world view emerges at that point in history when the form of production and even of consumption becomes technological. Simultaneously, the military market has come to be dominated by high-technology weaponry and the kitchen by high-technology culinary gadgets.

Positivism is ideology in the pejorative sense of the word.[5] It is a system of ideas and methods grounded in unquestioned assumptions about being, truth, understanding, justice, and beauty, an organization of consciousness and behavior that systematically distorts reality in the interests of stabilizing state organization and power. It falsifies reality in theory, and impoverishes it in practice. It mediates a very specific set of political purposes: to shore up illegitimate authority, to justify state domination, to ease the administrative management of people and to conceal from them the possibility of thinking, feeling, or acting in any other way.

Fundamental to the positivist vision of the true and the good is the assumption that objectivity free from political interests and other biases can be obtained by a radical segregation of knowledge from subjectivity, of object from subject, and of fact from value, by assuming that facts can be directly apprehended as sense data. Morality and aesthetics are thereby trivialized. Pure objectification, apart from any meanings that things have to concrete people, is defined as the single admissible form of human understanding. Typically, this objective knowledge is achieved through the rigorous application of the scientific method of observation and experimental manipulation of isolated "variables." One understands a phenomenon when it is made into an effect, the cause or causes of which are under the power of the scientific manager, who can therefore predict and control it. Causal explanation is the sole legitimate form of understanding. Crucial to objectification and control of phenomena is the process of precise, quantitative measurement. The paradigmatic sphere of operation for science is in relation to the natural world: physical, chemical, and biological. All understanding of and control over the social world is modeled on and evaluated in terms of the methods of the natural sciences.

Since the Second World War, it is the biological wing of the natural sciences that has acquired most prestige as the source of metaphors for the positivistic mainstream in social science and policymaking. The primary metaphor is now the organismic one of naturally evolving systems. The origins of this cybernetic gloss on positivism are rooted intellectually in American functionalism and politically in the emergence of "control systems" as a chief target of research in military-industrial technology. Social control is envisaged increasingly in terms of the technical management and promotion of systems organization. This superimposition of an organismic metaphor on scientistic epistemology has produced a souped-up "systems theory" version of positivism.[6] Systems theory reduces both mind and society to a set of hierarchically ordered, self-regulating feedback systems, each functionally subordinated to the next highest level of organization. Progress is equated with differentiation, stabilization, and "upgrading" of the overall system; augmenting of its complexity, feasibility, and efficiency; and incorporation of larger and larger segments of reality into the total organization.[7] The language of systems theory has now become the dominant one in the social sciences, as well as in the political, economic, and cultural spheres.[8] The practice of systems control is pervasive; one only has to note the form and extent of advertising to realize how much domination over the culture centralized social control is now achieving.[9]

While it is not possible to explore the political significance and impact of positivism in detail here,[10] we may briefly summarize what it excludes from the conceptualization of consciousness and action. In emphasizing value-free truth at the expense of meaning and in assuming that consciousness can be reduced to its cognitive, objectifying mode, positivism effectively undermines any thought or action that is not technical, strategic decision making, problem solving, or information processing. It precludes reflection on and judgment of the conditions to be decided on or of the problems to be solved. Those modes of experience that contain a vital noncognitive moment, such as the emotional, moral, communicative, symbolic-interpretive, aesthetic, and even political, are also preempted, or reduced to a technical cognitive form. The precognitive spheres—the unconscious, intuition, the "life world," the self—are also invalidated. Finally, the interpersonal, communal, mythic, religious, and, in particular, the historical and biographical meaning of human life are removed; with them goes the possibility of freedom. So it comes to pass that according to systems-positivism the only legitimate action is the strategic, goal-directed variety. This kind of action is split off from thought. A caesura is drawn between theory and practice, between the production of knowledge and its utilization. Scientists invent; nonscientists misuse. Such a split serves to protect the scientist from criticism and conceal his complicity in the domination by the state of its people. However, this split becomes harder to maintain when scientists supervise the production of weapons, the unambiguous use value of which is difficult to conceal.

THE AESTHETIC DIMENSION

If one detects here shades of Huxley's or Kafka's dystopian vision of modern social life, this is no coincidence. As Weber[11] intimates, positivistic scientism arises as a correlate of the technologization and bureaucratization commensurate with the emergence of modern statehood, which submit social life to the exclusive rule of "instrumental rationality." It is the ascendancy of instrumental rationality, with its purely technical and strategic concerns, that is so vividly embodied in modern nuclear diplomacy.

Marcuse has referred to the hegemony of positivistic and systems theory ideology as producing, maintaining, and justifying the restriction of life under modern statehood to a "one-dimensional" existence.[12] By this he refers in particular to the elimination of the meaning of life and society by three means. First, a kind of global anesthetization removes from people's experience their aesthetic potential for binding intellectuality to the sensuous manifold, thus preempting a capacity for critical reflection on sensuous existence. Second, a process of fragmentation and privatization of society seals off the personal from the political and eliminates the possibility of communal life and language. Third, a process of dehistoricization produces a systematic amnesia for either collective history or individual biography. All three degenerative processes serve the maintenance of existing authority structures and advance the oppression of all by increasingly irrational and arbitrary state domination. All three processes progressively eclipse the possibility of personal autonomy, critical insight, and social transformation. Marcuse's colleagues, Horkheimer and Adorno,[13] point out that these repressive and oppressive tendencies are consequences of perversions of reason that the Enlightenment concepts of truth, justice, and beauty failed to protect themselves against in the quest to be free from authoritarian tradition.

Marcuse suggests that any liberation from the crushing grip of state ideology and domination will require a reversal of anesthetizing, privatizing, and dehistoricizing forces. In particular, he holds that it is the restorative power of the aesthetic dimension, of artistic and mythopoetic sensibility, that promises most for future emancipation. The aesthetic dimension permits the restoration of one's own biography through sublimation of the chaotic, conflictual inner life into a creative play of forms, which transforms the conflictual, repressed tensions into acceptable, inspiring, and life-generating forms.

PROBLEMS OF THEORY AND POLICY IN THE U.S. DISARMAMENT MOVEMENT

The recent success of the "peace movement" in mobilizing mass demonstrations and civil disobedience actions would appear to indicate that the pleas of Marcuse and Weil have been answered, large sectors of the populace already having freed themselves from the ideological paralysis that we have just described and having seized history from the authorities. Left intellectuals are already celebrating the demonstrated vulnerability of the state. However, a closer examination reveals that this is not at all the case. While combating ideologically based amnesia may be a sufficient condition for mass protest, it turns out not to be a necessary one. As we shall see, this calls into question the political viability of disarmament activism as a social movement, and the authenticity of its self-destruction as a form of resistance to illegitimate authority.

One expects to find in a peace movement a concerted and consensual push toward world peace. However, this expectation has not yet been fulfilled, and does not appear to be a likelihood in the near future. The antinuclear movement has not analyzed or brought into question the underlying assumptions on which the continued stable functioning of state authority depends. Thus, for example, despite its self-identification as a peace movement, it has failed to mount any solid argument against the NATO alliance. This appears to be on account of its tacit valuation of supranational organizations, failing to distinguish military oligopolies from truly emancipatory antinationalist collaborations.[14] This blind spot raises a legitimate fear that the bulk of the peace movement is not essentially antimilitaristic, but rather represents a nationalistic group disenchanted with specific policies that its government has proposed as guarantees of the national security. Even where there is a genuine commitment to a supranational world order,[15] this is usually conceived of positivistically as a global "system." Such a system is equivalent to a single world state. Yet this is exactly our current problem: the existence of two superpowers with pretensions to being the first world state. A world state would only reproduce the problems of nationalism on a larger scale, perhaps, one is inclined to muse, via intergalactic war. As Weil noted, it is the constitution of states themselves that is the problem.

The antinuclear movement has also failed to mount any coherent criticism of nuclear powers other than the United States. This is evident in its conspicuous failure to link its opposition to a condemnation of recent acts of aggression in the name of "self-defense" by Britain, Israel, and, in particular, the Soviet Union. Its simplistic politics conflates condemnation of Soviet aggression vis-à-vis Afghanistan and Poland with reactionary endorsement of U.S. anti-Sovietism. This is as fallacious as saying that your enemy's enemy must be your friend.[16] Such desiderata in the international antinuclear movement have already forced the Polish workers union, Solidarity—an organization with rather strong credentials in the sphere of mass public protest—to question the political viability and moral legitimacy of the peace movement. A third shortsightedness of the antinuclear movement, belied by its name, is its exclusive focus on nuclear weaponry, ignoring the possibility that a nuclear freeze could stimulate a substitute escalation of armament production for biological warfare.

One hopes that a deeper meaning can be given to the movement, one that actualizes what is as yet an unrealized potential. This alternative interpretation would construe the movement as one directed toward a worldwide collaboration opposed in principle to offensive militarism of any kind, national or supranational, mediated by weaponry of any kind. Perhaps an even more embracing interpretation would see the meaning of disarmament protest as a metonymic expression of a much broader emancipatory objective: a reintegration of fragmented social community through a transformation of the modern state involving a democratic return of authority and power to its people by creating means of direct popular participation in political discourse, policy formation, and decision making. Surely, this is one of the major lessons to be learned from the example of Solidarity. Such a "nonaligned" political culture could provide a way out of the pro-Soviet/anti-Soviet Cold War polarities that have existed between Left and Right in the United States, and thereby realize a degree and extent of consensus hitherto stymied.[17] It would also interpret the nuclear threat as a threat directed by the state *inward* against its citizens, holding them hostage to its nuclear policies.[18]

PROBLEMS OF EDUCATIONAL PRACTICE

Disappointed in the content of the current antinuclear movement's policies, one might optimistically revive the old adage "practice precedes theory" and turn instead to the form of its praxis, on the assumption that the movement may exhibit in the process of its workings a liberatory potential that it cannot yet formulate explicitly at the level of policy. At the moment, the antinuclear movement is primarily an educational institution, attempting to enlighten the public by conveying military and political information and analysis. Therefore, one might look at the precepts of its practice by inspecting its preferred pedagogical approach. In the awareness that the movement is critical of established authority and questions its country's policies, one expects to find that it uses educational methods opposite in form to those traditionally employed in the nationalistic political socialization established by the state through public education or the consumer socialization approved by the state and conveyed via commercial television and other media. In other words, one expects to find in the practices of the movement at least an implicit critique of the dominant state ideology that has been instrumental in creating and gaining public support for established national security policies.

Unfortunately, the antinuclear movement appears to have appropriated uncritically the socialization techniques endorsed by the very authorities it is "opposing." Again, the acts of protest and resistance begin to take on the appearance of piecemeal criticism and dispute over specific policies, rather than insightful opposition to the underlying forms of government that gave rise to nuclear diplomacy and legitimated it in the first place. Specifically, the antinuclear movement has tacitly assumed the adequacy of the positivistic systems world view prevalent in American society. It has committed itself almost exclusively to a technical, strategic mode of resistance grounded in the positivistic orientation we identified above as the dominant state ideology. This commitment appears to be a major reason for the various failings in the construction of theory and the formation of policy such as those just enumerated. The positivistic systems orientation of the movement is nowhere more evident than in the typical disarmament discussions,[19] where the basic political thrust is premised on a technological and instrumental analysis of nuclear strategies, defense expenditures, weapons procurement procedures, military-industrial production techniques, and networks of political and economic influence. This form of discourse dovetails perfectly with the form of discourse utilized by the U.S. Defense Department. In these "scientific" analyses we are engaged in a competitive game of one-upmanship. The nuclear mandarins will listen only to facts and figures, we are told, and it is by being better informed about facts and figures that we can beat them at their own game. The only person who can stand up to a pronuclear technocrat is an antinuclear technocrat. (One is reminded of the servants in Buñuel's "Viridiana" who dress up in the clothes of their masters while the latter are away.) Again, the rationale is that such a technocratic approach is good because it is effective. The means are justified pragmatically by the ends rather than by examining the political and moral nature of the means themselves. Rather than serious consideration being given to the meaning of the process of educational enlightenment, the competitive negativity of corporate bureaucracies is appropriated wholesale, under the assumption that disarmament ideas must be "marketed" effectively and efficiently just like any other commodity.

Education for resistance is thereby reduced to a form of social control, opposite in content from the traditional type of nationalistic political socialization, yet replicating it in form, as though to compete with it rather than change it. Conventional socialization into accepted civic attitudes depends on a strategic use of technical control mechanisms, particularly behavior modification techniques.[20] A familiar example, especially to watchers of late-night television, is the sadistic, slow-motion, Peckinpah-style shot of a car crash, or gruesome stills of the gory aftermath, used in commercials that aim to stop drunken driving. In a similar way, local television news programs regale us with grotesque stories that are of trivial social significance and minimal news value. These are simply inversions of the repetitive allurements used in ordinary commercials or by video game machines to create addictive false needs. The blatant use of shocking and lurid imagery on the public to "scare them straight" is nothing more than punitive behavior modification. The repetitive involuntary experience of blunt punishment produces a symbolic aversive conditioning, against the conscious will of the subject. This kind of rationalized violence is the basis of propaganda and brainwashing techniques.[21]

In the various uses of propagandistic behavior-modification techniques, the violation of subjects is rationalized as "the mere presentation of the facts." Like most rationalizations, this one has an apparently solid scientific and moral basis. It is scientifically sound to inform the public visually as well as auditorily. It is morally sound to frame this as an obligation on all agents of the media. Certainly it is a fact and a value that we bear witness to history as it is made, or even as it is forgotten.[22] However, this patina of factual and ethical objectivity conceals the reality that there are *different ways* to present the same information or material. As Kant reminded us, scientific issues of truth and moral concern for freedom can be synthesized only in the aesthetic modality. This century has surely taught us, if we did not learn it from previous ones, that aesthetic visions range from the beautiful to the ugly, from the uplifting and liberating to the totalitarian and fascistic.[23] Thus, the media cannot and should not hide behind a facile claim of obligation to merely "tell it like it is." There are no "brute facts" and no "brute values." The chosen mode of aesthetic presentation can transform facts and values beyond recognition. This transformation, guided by ideology and interests, is all the more effective in our generation because of the increasing anesthesia. The technical, strategic world of ordered, bureaucratized, and administered life has left us with, at best, a vestigial aesthetic sense.[24] The historically produced lack of aesthetic discrimination in modern Western culture opens up the symbolic domain to extensive exploitation, which goes undetected by a public long since dead to the possibilities of sensuous experience and reduced now to uncritical absorbers of prefabricated messages.

Our brave new world is so constituted that propagandist coercion carried in a brutal mode of aesthetic communication escapes the scissors of the media censors as long as it is "in a good cause." Small wonder, then, that the mainstream disarmament movement, eager to propagate its message, seizes upon the very time-tested techniques of evangelism prepared by established media experts. Its dominant educational device is propagandistic: the indiscriminate and repetitive use of grandiose estimates of the quantity of carnage and lurid descriptions of specific kinds of bodily and psychic damage that nuclear war would inflict, often hammered home with pictures from Hiroshima and Nagasaki. The Physicians for Social Responsibility organization exemplifies the approach most clearly. For example, Helen Caldicott's "nuclear madness" portrays the insanity of modern military fail-safe not in the context of political history and modern international relationships but in terms of descriptions of scorched and mutilated bodies, often those of children. "The living will envy the dead," we are told.[25] "Ground Zero" is a name and phrase designed not only to evoke explosive imagery but also to confine attention to a single fragmented moment in time, the perfectly ahistorical vision.[26] The educational purpose of "Ground Zero Week" was precisely to induce enactment of the devastation to be experienced in a nuclear holocaust. Such phrases, images, and descriptions serve as "fear-jerkers." The education that is supposed to produce enlightenment and understanding engenders instead a spurious, packaged emotional repulsion. This is not education for disarmament; it is the pedagogy of the oppressor.

Bludgeoning the listener with repetitive and emphatic oratory is often justified on the grounds that listeners have become apathetic and immune to objective descriptions of the current danger of our political realities. However, it is interesting to note how discrepant this rationale is with the normative psychiatric theory that responsible physicians utilize in therapeutic practice. Surely these physicians would not recommend that one treat a patient's massive denial of painful experiences by directly reciting them to the patient. Surely they would respect and attempt to interpret the defensiveness of such patients. Thus, the direct and aggressive techniques employed by the Physicians for Social Responsibility are not consistent with the same medical-psychiatric practices the members of this establishment elsewhere promote. It is inconsistencies of this kind that suggest that some kind of counter-transferential procedure is in action when medical and psychiatric experts take to the field to promote the message of disarmament. As the analyst Searles reminds his fellow analysts, it is absolutely vital in dealing with the deepest psychotic contents of consciousness to first become aware of one's own counter-transferential tendencies to project such contents out of the self and onto the patient, where it is easier and more comfortable to find them.[27]

THE ANNIHILATION OF EMANCIPATION

Those whose teaching embraces disarmament issues offer conflicting accounts of audience response. Some report that their listeners are quickly and effectively stirred to action, joining in the movement by spreading the word to various constituencies.[28] Quite how much insight these galvanized individuals have gained remains open to question; one fears that an "antinuclear Moonies" syndrome may take hold. Other teachers and lecturers report considerable apathy on the part of those whom they address.[29] Quite commonly the response is, "We can't think about it: it's too depressing."[30] It is our guess that often those who respond in this second, self-protective way are engaged in a legitimate act of self-protection. They have experienced disarmament advertising quite objectively as battering them with images of acute suffering without providing the freedom to find adequate means of understanding and interpreting the historical and psychological meaning of such suffering. They correctly intuit that something is not quite right about the didactic methods visited upon them. They are being hurt in the name of being "reached." It is not surprising, therefore, that they resist further instruction of this coercive nature. The response of these people, often sensitive and even concerned, cannot be written off as mere resistance to truth or political apathy, much as the people themselves cannot be dismissed as obstinate or "head-in-the-sand" types. It is only the arrogance of a professional-managerial elite, used to educational status and privileged knowledge, that needs to generate the illusion of an apparently mindless mass numbed to the reality before their very eyes. This is the traditional way in which a "superior" class denies its own helplessness and projects its sensed inadequacies onto an "inferior" one. Here, as often before, the derogation of the "student" is used to justify the ascendancy and power of the "teacher."[31] Ignorance and stupidity are fictive enemies, constructed by a "resistance" movement not yet able to conceptualize how the resistance to resistance lies in the loss of subjectivity and history that ideology mediates.

The behavior modification approach is a modernized and degenerate version of American pragmatism. Its ethics are crudely utilitarian. The traditional failings of utilitarian moral systems apply equally to the kind of pedagogy used by the antinuclear propagandists. Thus, when the Physicians for Social Responsibility regale their listeners with graphic images of the medical consequences of nuclear war, or when the minority disarmament groups emphasize the destructive social consequences of defense expenditures,[32] they implicitly assume that the moral good and bad of actions can be evaluated only in terms of the consequences of those actions. This seems to imply that if only nuclear war were less damaging and less expensive, it would be less immoral. If the sale of nuclear power and weaponry to other countries were to show a profit for the United States, with a consequent decline in inflation and unemployment, would this make the maintenance of nuclear threat more moral? This kind of pragmatism confirms the suspicion that large sectors of the disarmament movement have only a relativistic, strategic interest in maximizing national and personal security, not a universalizing, principled moral concern with the illegitimacy of nuclear diplomacy or aggressive militarism per se.

The problem with utilitarian ethics is not only that its pragmatic arguments can be turned around against the disarmament movement, but that they draw attention away from the fact that the meaning of actions, especially their moral meaning, inheres in their intentionality. Taking the vantage point of a temporal moment *after* colossal disaster tends to wipe out any questions about *why* it might have happened, and hence distracts attention from a historical understanding of the possible alternative courses of events. Even when the disaster presented to us is an imaginary one, the repeated emphasis on consequences tends to paralyze the listener with a sense of helplessness and divert interest away from specific courses of social action that could be taken to avert calamity. With political understanding and historical meaning precluded, there is only one action that such listeners can resort to: the compulsive repetition of the pragmatic evangelism they have just been subjected to.

Linked to pragmatic morality is the naturalistic vision of life that also inheres in the positivistic systems world view. In the response of medical and social scientists and practitioners to the nuclear threat, there is a thoroughgoing "biologization" of the problem. The leadership role played by the Physicians for Social Responsibility, with its essentially medical vision of nuclear catastrophe, has a special significance in this regard, one that unfortunately has not been noticed. We are told by the antinuclear movement that the nuclear threat is a threat to the biological survival of the human organism.[33] Even those who question the hegemony of modern nation-states and seek an alternative unitary world order tend to do so on the grounds that there is a single "species identity."[34]

Such a naturalistic reduction of protest to a plea on behalf of life has several deleterious sequelae. First, humanity is more than just another species. To ignore the cultural and historical peculiarity and emergent qualities of humanity is to deny the fact that history is made by people. It tends to encourage the evolutionary perspective that can easily turn into a vision of the future as inevitable and beyond human control. Such a position has historically served certain vested interests.[35] Indeed, evolutionary thought has played a thoroughly reactionary and oppressive role in the social sciences and elsewhere through its translation into social Darwinism and sociobiology, which have typically eventuated in the construction of scientific legitimation of racial and class discrimination and eugenicist social policy.[36]

Second, for the disarmament movement to premise its activity on the quest for mere survival fails to raise the question of survival *of what, for what?* Is it survival of our current way of life? If so, is that survival enough? If mere survival becomes the goal, then this goal is difficult to distinguish from the goal of preserving the current stratification and standard of life to which the protesters (largely middle class) have become accustomed. Again, the peace movement comes to look like a special-interest group with little interest, if any, in emancipation.

Third, the argument in favor of survival is the exact same argument employed by the governmental-military alliance. They argue in favor of current patterns of nuclear diplomacy on the grounds that it safeguards the national security. There is even a level of international agreement about maintaining the nuclear threat on the grounds that it maximizes the possibilities of survival for all. Like the pragmatic and utilitarian moral argument, the biological one is objectivistic, ahistorical, and relativistic, and can be easily turned against the disarmament argument. It is cut from the same ideological cloth as the very policies that the movement opposes.

The coercive, pragmatic, and biologistic aspects of the positivistic systems approach to disarmament are becoming increasingly embedded in the fabric of our society through the institutionalization and professionalization of disarmament work. Because of their thorough permeation by positivistic epistemology and systems thinking, medical and social scientists buy into established structures of power, much as a special-interest group voices its needs within the existing governmental lobbying system. The concealed interest of social scientists who have espoused the technical-strategic approach to protest is a desire to be assimilable into the very governmental structure that they oppose. They envisage the role of social scientists as policy advisors to the corporate structure of the state. Positivistic science is, and always has been, primarily a policy science.[37] Thus, the strategic approach to protest is a kind of coquetry aimed at luring the authorities into an alliance. A desire to be assimilated into the structures of power and participate in them is terribly attractive to that part of the scientific establishment which has traditionally failed to capitalize directly on its potential for power over the social destiny.

Needless to say, this unconscious conformism inherent in obeisance to the language and discourse of established power is seen by the powerful as a rewarding sign that they have successfully socialized their potential dissidents. Now, they are assured that they will only be pressed to modulate armamentation along "functionally efficient" lines that will not disturb either the intranational or international system of strategic action. Domination requires that slaves be happy in their chains.[38] One way in which the dominated collude in their own oppression is by accepting wholesale the form of discourse visited upon them by their oppressors, not realizing that it is in the very nature of power to take the form of the principles governing what rational discourse is taken to be.[39] It is the dubious achievement of positivistic systems ideology to have facilitated the cooptation of would-be dissenters in the academy and other professional bodies.

Such cooptation tends to generate a mirror image on the disarmament side that reverses, but otherwise faithfully replicates, the *modus operandi* of the militarists. The structural consequence of the information-oriented politics of the strategic approach to disarmament is the erection of an extensive hierarchical bureacratic system of antinuclear information flow. The flow is channeled and regulated by an elite of antinuclear experts, who, despite their good intentions, unwittingly end up vying with each other for public recognition. They rapidly become embedded in a matrix of specialized publications, each struggling for visibility. Before you know it, there is established a new and paradoxical sphere of consumption: disarmament information. Like most innovative branches of symbolic production, especially in an era of economic decline, this one is highly competitive. It undergoes the same kind of internal differentiation and upgrading that Talcott Parsons has told us occurs "naturally" in every hierarchical bureaucratic organization.[40] Given the ultimate respectability of self-righteous moral indignation, participants in this productive process do not shrink from using the well-oiled machinery of commercial publicity to mass produce their message. Unfortunately this machine, especially its advertising arm, is adapted to the purpose of smoothly generating false needs wherever this is commercially rewarding. Thus the public, legitimately concerned about annihilation of the world that it has constructed, is subjected to powerful mass-media techniques designed to turn its concern into panic. Real anxiety—a healthy sign of repressed contents about to come to conciousness—is replaced by pseudo-anxiety, which can be placated only by the pseudo-emancipation offered by more antinuclear behavior modification. Those that begin to detect the spuriousness of this "enlightenment" may be turned off to the disarmament message or dissuaded from moving forward into disarmament activities. In this manner, disarmament education can turn against itself, reproducing in subtler form the very hostility and coerciveness that it originally set out to combat.

Given these manifold problems of theory, policy, and practice that have emerged from a lack of critical reflectivity in the antinuclear movement, we now turn to an alternative orientation that we feel offers some promise of insightful understanding, education, and action with regard to the nuclear threat and disarmament.

THE PSYCHOPOLITICS OF PARANOIA AND REPARATION

The state, its constituent individuals, and the various forms of social organization that mediate the relationship between them all can be conceived of as having an interiority. In this interior lie concealed the inner workings of a symbolic or mythic kind. The current nuclear threat also possesses such inner dynamics, which contribute vitally to its character and constitute much of its particularly penetrating and dangerous significance to our civilization. This hidden dimension calls for depth interpretation. It does not yield to simple observation and analysis of either the everyday or the scientific variety. In specific, there is a general mythic and symbolic dimension to the situation of nuclear threat that has escaped examination almost entirely. This dimension has to do with the general meanings of good and evil[41] and their relationship, which underlie the more obvious and visible machinations of states engaged in nuclear diplomacy.

These deep meanings of good and evil have both a political and a personal aspect. Psychologists such as the present authors commonly feel more comfortable in and gravitate toward the personal pole. However, as we shall see below, the personal and the political are more intimately connected than is usually supposed. There are "psycho-political" unities in which mind and society have a dialectical or interpenetrating relationship. One such unity appears in the symbolic interiority of the current situation of nuclear threat, where the classic dramas of good and evil are played out again in the masks and costumes of modern warfare and weaponry. These mythic conflicts play a role in the origins of the nuclear threat, in the military and governmental maintenance of it, in the collusion of the public in it, and in the recently emerging resistance to it. The same complex of unconscious scenarios underlies all these parts of the problematic nuclear situation.

At the heart of the interior of modern nuclear weapons policy lies the subjective apperception of the nuclear threat. It is the "horror" of nuclear holocaust imagined and feared by the human person that is the fulcrum around which diplomatic leverage is exerted. This fear and its various psychic reverberations are objectified, counted on, and even manipulated by the military and governmental artificers of nuclear weapons policies. Strategy and tactics are entirely dependent on this subjective apperception. Although the bureaucratization of military and governmental life most likely enables these makers of policy and strategy to more safely defend against and ignore such horror, it seems likely that at some level of consciousness they experience similar reactions to imagined holocaust as does the rest of the population.

In seeking to comprehend the subjective component of the nuclear situation, the psychologist cannot help but be struck immediately by the parallels between the reality of our current world situation and the unreality of the psychic world of the psychotic.[42] If one is seeking vivid and highly differentiated accounts of World War III and the carnage of nuclear destruction, one does not have to resort to disarmament ideologues. One has only to attend to the vivid tales of annihilation told by psychotics. These narratives represent the breakdown of the normal boundary between fantasy and reality, with the emergence of imagined doom as though it were a directly experienced reality. This extreme dysphoria is the scar left by disastrous psychological relationships, usually in the very earliest phases of development. In "Psychoanalytic Notes on an Autobiographical Account of a Case of Paranoia," Freud interprets one such eschatological vision offered to him by a male patient: "The end of the world is the projection of this internal catastrophe; his subjective world has come to an end since he has withdrawn his love from it."[43]

Such millenary delusions are described and documented in detail by Minkowski and Gabel.[44] These authors find psychotic delusions to be composed of pervasive morbidity, fatalism, and dread. There is commonly the sense of being "crushed" by the future, as though time itself were foreshortened. There is also a fear of poison, a sense of ubiquitous fragmentation, and a habitual use of protective magic.[45] Melanie Klein describes the paranoid psychotic patient as follows:

> The essence of his fears of persecution is the feeling that there is a hostile agency which is bent on inflicting on him suffering, damage and ultimately annihilation. This persecutory agency may be represented by one or many people or even by the forces of nature. There are innumerable and in every case specific forms which the dreaded attack may take.[46]

As long as we imagine these disturbed and catastrophic visions to be contained within the sequestered world of psychotics, we feel comfortable.[47] However, it is Freud's message that we *all* experience insanity at deeper levels of what he calls "primary process," those darker and more threatening parts of the symbolic unconscious lurking ever ready to erupt through the thin patina of rational "secondary process." For example, many "normal" nonpsychotic individuals report fantasies, or at least dreams, about the end of the world, and even disclose a certain sensual pleasure afforded by the image of unleashed hostilities and rampant destructiveness.

Klein made and documented thoroughly a claim more radical even than Freud's. Her claim was that deep in the unconscious of each adult, all the more powerful by going undetected, lies a presocial "paranoid-schizoid" stratum where all the terrifying conflicts and visions of the psychotic state continue to live and have their being. Paranoid disturbances occurring in adulthood are merely local eruptions of a deep level of persecutory anxiety that exists always in all of us, remaining from the first few months of life.[48]

Thus, each of us experiences at a more or less unconscious level the sense of "a hostile agency . . . bent on inflicting suffering, damage and ultimately annihilation." This persecution is internal and external, both moieties, however, originating in the self. The internal persecution is that threat of destruction experienced from those parts of the self that feel bad (discomfort, frustration, and hatred). In these early, unintegrated phases, the proximity of good to bad, love to hate, is intolerable. The bad, hateful parts threaten to overwhelm and destroy those parts that feel good (comforted, satisfied, and loved). These are "normal" experiences for the young infant. They manifest themselves in those seemingly spontaneous and uncaused attacks of immense fear and anger that consume the infant's viscera and leave her or him tearfully raging and beyond consolation. Although the infant's "self" or "ego" is relatively unformed at this point, there are some self-protective measures that come into play. "The primordial fear of being annihilated forces the ego into action and engenders the first defences . . . splitting, denial, omnipotence and idealization."[49] In order to keep the good parts safe, the bad-feeling parts are split off and projected outward in the form of imaginary hostile external forces. This defensive maneuvering is never fully successful, and the remaining destructive impulses felt as within the self conjure up fears of retaliation from the external persons that are imagined to be harmed by them. Thus, the earliest form of conscience is quite cruel.

Idealization is the infant's best card. "The infant's relative security is based on turning the good object into an ideal one as protection against the dangerous and persecuting object."[50] The predominant defense mobilized against the projected and retaliatory hostile forces is to idealize the good inner parts, and feel them as omnipotent and invulnerable. A benign environment provided by consistent and loving care from the mother will buffer the infant from these frightening dynamics. But if the mother is idealized in order to protect her from the infant's badness, she will become the object of a consuming envy. In that instance, the infant feels omnipotent destructiveness, wishing to attack sadistically the maternal cornucopia and the rest of the external world, laying waste to everything and poisoning it for everyone forevermore.

The power that this paranoid-schizoid mentality has over us and the danger that it holds for us inhere in our difficulty in detecting it and our consequent tendency to disown it. As a result, we tend to see the chaotic and often savage battle of good and evil working itself out external to ourselves as human subjects, almost as though it were inherent in the "forces of nature," and therefore inevitable. The world of paranoid-schizoid dynamics cannot easily be owned because it originated in that phase of development prior to the formation of a "self." Correlatively, it acknowledges no "other." This is what makes it potentially so dangerous; it is entirely presocial. It is a form of unconscious experience and activity prior to the understanding of the existence of people and social relationships. When unmodulated by more mature social consciousness, it tends to move toward a world without human existence.

The more mature social consciousness anticipated by the paranoid-schizoid phase involves the emergence of self and other in the infant's experience. This forward movement is made possible by the clear identification of goods and evils, the capacity to integrate them even to the extent of acknowledging ambivalences, and the development of faith in the potential for future goods to embrace and bind past and future evils. In this more mature phase, there emerges the ability to form a whole self in relation to a whole external object of love, typically the mother. She had previously been experienced only as part objects of indeterminate agency, due to the pervasive fragmentation characteristic of schizoid consciousness. The critical psychic advance to the true sociality of the second stage has a tragic but necessary feature. It entails the possibility of losing the whole loved object. Moreover, this loss is heightened by the fact that it is experienced poignantly as the consequence of the infant's own aggressions. However, this newly acquired potential for losing the loved one is compensated by the capacity for remembering her and the nascent ability to repair the loss by acts of creative restoration, which may take all kinds of symbolic forms. Such reparative tendencies, requiring acknowledgement of the self's aggressions, form the basis of the moral impulse carried forward into adulthood. Insofar as adequate caretaking allows the successful emergence of these ontic, mnemonic, and aesthetic qualities in the second half of the first year of life, the monstrous anxieties of the earliest developmental phase can be contained and transformed, although they are never totally supplanted.

The reader may detect certain parallels between the Kleinian psychodynamic account of the world experienced as reality by the presocial infant and the world that we, contemporary adults, experience as reality. Much of the fantasy life of the mewling, puking babe appears to have been realized concretely in the structures and instruments of nuclear diplomacy. The imagery underlying nuclear weapons strategy occupies very much the same symbolic universe as the fantastic imagery of the paranoid-schizoid position. In fact, the whole domain of nuclear politics must appeal strongly to that level of our consciousness that compulsively seeks to play out again the tensions and hostilities of primitive presocial life.

The parallel between schizoid phenomena and the catastrophic politics of modern nation-states has been noted previously by a variety of social critics.[51] Some have also noted that the parallel is mediated by distorted ideological formations that bind deformed knowledge and practice into oppressive totalities.[52] Indeed, insofar as child-rearing itself is a process of tacitly introducing ideological distortion into the nascent consciousness of the child,[53] the relation between paranoia and politics is no longer a parallel. The very basis of the perversions of nuclear diplomacy conducted and supported by adults is rooted in the perversions of human relatedness engineered by the state through its control over the form and quality of child-rearing.[54] This cycle of domination capitalizes on the ever-present potential of consciousness for a regressive retreat under malignant conditions where parent and/or state are inadequate to the demands of caretaking.

Nevertheless, Klein's message, much like that of the other object relations theorists, is one of hope. In those lacunae where adequate conditions of caring manage to prevail, and where the more implacable instrumentalities of the state fail to penetrate fully, movement toward true sociality with its reparative imperative is made possible.[55] It is made possible when the cycle of repetitive intergenerational socialization into ideology is broken by a moment where critical awareness of loss and the possibilities of reparative dialogue embrace anxieties and integrate fractures from the past.

In the following section, we shall draw some analogies between recent military history and the psychodynamic phenomena that Klein has described. While the detailed connections that such heuristic parallels conceal remain to be revealed, it does appear that the dynamics of good and evil underlying Cold War politics and the recent experiences of the American people can be understood fruitfully in terms of processes such as splitting, ambivalence, and reparative integration. On this issue, Klein's ethical and metaphysical vision converges with the historical and pedagogic concerns of Simone Weil outlined at the beginning of this article, in ways that are of some relevance to the future of the peace movement.

GOOD, EVIL, AND REPARATION IN COLD WAR POLITICS

To integrate polarized visions of good and evil in Cold War politics, it is insufficient to assume that all peoples are potentially good and can merge together in one diffuse global community. This is essentially a repressive vision that fosters forgetfulness and breeds unstable and inauthentic forced loyalties. To achieve greater unity, it is necessary for divergent peoples to work through past wrongdoings in mutual discourse, to accept reciprocal judgments, and, to the best of their abilities, to work toward repairing those evils that their nations have visited upon each other. A review of past history demonstrates that a repressive attitude of forced loyalty, tolerance, and cooperation leads to persistent eruptions of repressed national rage and a desire to annihilate the other. Such a "repressive tolerance" demolishes historical conscience and whitewashes a history of moral injustice, thus stripping people of any resources for differentiating the good that they wish to preserve from the evil that they wish to oppose. Repressive tolerance breeds an ideology of "forgive and forget," whereas psychoanalysis has demonstrated the profound fact that it is possible to forgive only when one remembers. The remembrance of things past can be seen as the mission set for modern man a century ago by various prophetic writers and poets.

Probably the greatest act of repressive forgetting forced on Americans was the historical act constituting the starting point for the Cold War. This occurred during World War II, when it was demanded of Americans that they embrace the previously hated Russians as their closest allies. A proliferation of pro-Russian propaganda films was pressed on American people, forcing a highly ambivalent loyalty. At the same time, Roosevelt—in what can only be seen now as extreme grandiosity—consistently preempted British aims of preserving the autonomy of East European countries against Russian imperialistic interests. It has been argued that American policy during the war conspired with the Russians in dividing Europe between the two nations so as to create two major spheres of power.[56] In this process, Eastern Europe was virtually handed over to the Russians, and the persistent British warnings against such action were not heeded. Roosevelt committed the egregious injustice of giving East Europe away without even consulting the peoples who were given away. In our present "age of democracy," it is incumbent on the succeeding generations to remember these wrongs of the past and to attempt to compensate for the losses that these peoples have suffered. Americans must acknowledge that they took part in a brutal bartering of peoples in order to advance their hegemony over half the globe.

Since the Americans played a major role in setting the stage for the Cold War, the peace movement ought to undermine the original bipolar structure that holds this stage together. In the long run, simply joining hands in repressive cooperation with the Russians will only repress deep-seated hostilities and exacerbate the bipolar tension. Paying more careful heed to the liberation struggle of the people again caught in the middle, notably in Poland, ought to be a central concern of the peace movement. The threat emanating from the peace movement is precisely this threat of forgetting the wrongs one's nation has committed against other peoples, and forgetting that true peace can emerge only from a reparative desire, a desire to restore the full capacity for self-rule to those peoples in whose oppression one's country has conspired.

The peace movement ought not to forget that the fraternal meeting of the great powers at Potsdam coincided with the first testing of the atom bomb in New Mexico. Such contradictory dynamics permeate international politics, and the antagonistic, destructive tendencies cannot be so easily diluted. The bomb is the ultimate symbol of the modern state that pushes toward total extinction of historical memory. The violence of the Cold War seemed inevitable, as it emerged from the state's accumulation of power at the expense of millions of powerless people foundering in war-torn Europe, Asia, and Africa. The modern superstates have catapulted themselves on the path of self-annihilation, primarily because they have abandoned the moral imperative of human restitution. As far as we can judge at present, the peace movement appears to be headed solely in the direction of preserving the balance of superpowers and of maintaining the monstrous structure of the state. We wrote this article in the hope that the peace movement may seek a more emancipatory direction that will fuse its interest with that of the oppressed people who are driven to silence in the midst of the din of the powerful. When we can speak together with them in mutual dialogue, we will begin to reconstitute a shared historical memory in which peace can grow deep and lasting roots.

Notes

1 M. Rustin, "A Socialist Consideration of Kleinian Psychoanalysis," *New Left Review* 131 (1982): 71-96.

2 Simone Weil, *The Need for Roots* (London: Routledge & Kegan Paul, 1952), pp. 109-14.

3 Ibid., p. 221.

4 L. Kolakowski, *Positivist Philosophy (*Harmondsworth, England: Penguin Books, 1968); A. Giddens, ed., *Positivism and Sociology* (London: Heinemann Educational Books, 1974); and T. W. Adorno et al., *The Positivist Dispute in German Sociology* (New York: Harper & Row, 1976).

5 By "ideology" here we mean "false consciousness" in the sense first coined by K. Marx and F. Engels in *The German Ideology* (New York: International Publishers, 1947/1845), and later elaborated by G. Lukacs in *History and Class Consciousness* (Cambridge: MIT Press, 1966/1923) and the Frankfurt Institute for Social Research (see, for example, *Aspects of Sociology* [Boston: Beacon Press, 1972]). This meaning of the concept is to be distinguished sharply from the colloquial use of the term, which equates ideology with any value system, regardless of its relative distortedness or validity (see J. Gabel, *False Consciousness* [London: Basil Blackwell, 1975]; John M. Broughton, "Review of Gabel's *False Consciousness,*" *Telos* 29 [1976]: 223-35; and idem, "Ideology-Critique and the Possibility of a Critical Developmental Psychology," *Human Development* 24 [1981]: 382-411).

6 Ludwig von Bertalanffy, *General System Theory* (New York: G. Braziller, 1968).

7 T. Parsons and R. F. Bales, *Family, Socialization and Interaction Process* (Glencoe, Ill.: Free Press, 1955).

8 A. Gouldner, *The Coming Crisis of Western Sociology* (New York: Basic Books, 1970); J. Habermas, *Legitimation Crisis* (Boston: Beacon Press, 1975); C. A. Bowers, "Emergent Ideological Characteristics of Educational Policy," *Teachers College Record* 79, no. 1 (1977): 33-54; John M. Broughton and M. K. Zahaykevich, "Personality and Ideology in Ego Development," in *Actualité de la Dialectique,* ed. J. Gabel and V. Trinh van Thao (Paris: Anthropos, 1980); and John M. Broughton, "Function and Knowledge," *Human Development* 24 (1981): 257-87.

9 S. Ewen, *Captains of Consciousness* (New York: McGraw-Hill, 1976); and J. Berger, *Ways of Seeing* (Harmondsworth, England: Penguin Books, 1972).

10 For a thorough discussion see J. Habermas, *Knowledge and Human Interest* (Boston: Beacon Press, 1971); C. Taylor, "Interpretation and the Sciences of Man," *Review of Metaphysics* 25 (1971): 1-15; and B. Fay, *Social Theory and Political Practice* (London: George Allen & Unwin, 1975).

11 See H. H. Gerth and C. W. Mills, *From Max Weber: Essays in Sociology* (New York: Oxford University Press, 1946).

12 Herbert Marcuse, *One Dimensional Man* (Boston: Beacon Press, 1964). See also R. Jacoby, *Social Amnesia* (Boston: Beacon Press, 1975).

13 M. Horkheimer and T. W. Adorno, *Dialectic of Enlightenment* (New York: Herder & Herder, 1972).

14 G. Eckenberg and N. Watts, Comments on "The New Neutralism in Western Europe," Fifth Annual Meeting of the International Society for Political Psychology, Washington, D.C., June 1982.

15 See, for example, Saul Mendlovitz, "Alternatives to the Sovereign State," paper presented at the Social Scientists and Nuclear War conference, City University, New York, June 1982.

16 C. Castoriadis, "Totalitarianism and Its Significance for the Present," paper presented at the conference on Hannah Arendt, New York University, New York, October 1981.

17 E. P. Thompson, "Why the West Must Share the Blame," *The Times of London*, December 22, 1981, p. 10.

18 E. P. Thompson, "A Letter to America," in *Protest and Survive*, ed. E. P. Thompson and D. Smith (New York: Monthly Review Press, 1981).

19 See, for example, the presentations by A. Cockburn and G. Adams, "Imperatives of Military Growth in the Soviet Union and the U.S.," at the Social Scientists and Nuclear War conference, City University, New York, June 1982.

20 Bowers, "Emergent Ideological Characteristics of Educational Policy"; and P. London, *Behavior Control* (New York: Harper & Row, 1969).

21 Robert Jay Lifton, *Thought Reform and the Psychology of Totalism* (New York: W. W. Norton, 1963).

22 E. Apfelbaum, "Mis/Myth Creation in History: The Denial of the Holocaust," *Psych Critique* 2 (1982): 9–12.

23 Berger, *Ways of Seeing*.

24 Herbert Marcuse, *Eros and Civilization* (Boston: Beacon Press, 1955); idem, *The Aesthetic Dimension* (Boston: Beacon Press, 1977); cf. Maxine Greene, "The Humanities and Emancipatory Possibility," *Journal of Education* 36 (1982): 287–305.

25 Helen Caldicott, *Nuclear Madness* (New York: Bantam, 1981).

26 Ground Zero, *Nuclear War: What's in It for You?* (New York: Pocket Books, 1982).

27 H. Searles, *Countertransference* (New York: International Universities Press, 1979).

28 For example, J. Kovel, "Rationality and Irrationality in the Face of Nuclear War," paper presented at the Social Scientists and Nuclear War conference, City University, New York, June 1982; and Caldicott, *Nuclear Madness*.

29 E. P. Thompson, "European Nuclear Disarmament," address presented at Riverside Church, New York, January 1981.

30 For example, H. Gadlin, "Rationality and Irrationality in the Face of Nuclear War," paper presented at the Social Scientists and Nuclear War conference, City University, New York, June 1982.

31 Interview with Michel Foucault, *Le Monde-The Guardian*, May 30, 1976, p. 14.

32 This position has been voiced by S. Tobias, "Women and Anti-Militarism," paper presented at the Social Scientists and Nuclear War conference, City University, New York, June 1982.

33 See, for example, Caldicott, *Nuclear Madness*.

34 See, for example, Mendlovitz, "Alternatives to the Sovereign State."

35 Lukacs, *History and Class Consciousness:* and Gabel, *False Consciousness*.

36 R. Hofstadter, *Social Darwinism in American Thought* (Boston: Beacon Press, 1955); and Clarence Karier, "Testing for Order and Control in the Corporate Liberal State," *Educational Theory* 22 (1972): 154–80.

37 Fay, *Social Theory and Political Practice*.

38 G. W. F. Hegel, *The Phenomenology of Mind* (London: Macmillan, 1910); and A. Memmi, *Dominated Man* (Boston: Beacon Press, 1968).

39 Michel Foucault, *Power, Truth, Strategy* (Sydney, Australia: Feral Publications, 1979).

40 Parsons and Bales, *Family, Socialization and Interaction Process*.

41 P. Ricoeur, *The Symbolism of Evil* (Boston: Beacon Press, 1967).

42 This parallel has been noted by many writers, especially Gabel (*False Consciousness*) and, particularly relevant to the following discussion, D. Dinnerstein (*The Mermaid and the Minotaur* [New York: Harper & Row, 1976]).

43 Sigmund Freud, "Psychoanalytic Notes on an Autobiographical Account of a Case of Paranoia," in *Standard Edition of the Complete Psychological Works*, vol. 12 (London: Hogarth, 1953–1974), pp. 70–71.

44 E. Minkowski, *Lived Time* (Evanston, Ill.: Northwestern University Press, 1970); and Gabel, *False Consciousness.*

45 Such a constellation of qualities and symptoms is portrayed vividly in the character of General Jack D. Ripper, in Stanley Kubrick's film *Dr. Strangelove.*

46 Melanie Klein, *Envy and Gratitude* (New York: Dell Publishing, 1975), pp. 32–33.

47 Michel Foucault, *Madness and Civilization* (New York: New American Library, 1965).

48 M. Klein, "Our Adult World and Its Roots in Infancy," in her *Envy and Gratitude.* See also H. Segal, *Introduction to the World of Melanie Klein* (New York: Harper & Row, 1964).

49 Klein, *Envy and Gratitude*, pp. 49–57.

50 Ibid., p. 49.

51 Sigmund Freud, *Civilization and Its Discontents* (London: Hogarth Press, 1930); idem, "Why War?" *Collected Papers*, vol. 5 (New York: Basic Books, 1969); N. O. Brown, *Life against Death* (Middletown, Conn.: Wesleyan University Press, 1959); R. D. Laing, *The Divided Self* (London: Tavistock, 1960); Dinnerstein, *The Mermaid and the Minotaur;* M. Dimen and D. Moss, "Rationality and Irrationality in the Face of Nuclear War," paper presented at the Social Scientists and Nuclear War conference, City University, New York, June 1982; G. McGovern, "The New Right and the Old Paranoia," *Congressional Record*, vol. 170, December 4, 1980, reprinted in *Psych Critique* 2 (1982): 13–14; and M. Deutsch, "Psychological Perspectives on Preventing World War III," paper presented at the Social Scientists and Nuclear War conference, City University, June 1982.

52 Gabel, *False Consciousness;* and Wilhelm Reich, *The Mass Psychology of Facism* (New York: Farrar, Straus and Girout, 1970).

53 J. Kovel, "Rationalization and the Family," *Telos* 37 (1978): 5–21; and A. Harris, "Rationalization in Infancy," in *Critical Development Theory*, ed. J. M. Broughton (New York: Plenum, forthcoming).

54 Christopher Lasch, *Haven in a Heartless World* (New York: Harper & Row, 1977).

55 Rustin, "A Socialist Consideration of Kleinian Psychoanalysis."

56 Lukacs, *History and Class Consciousness.*

VOICES FROM EUROPE

Teachers, Ethical Imagination, and World Disarmament

PETER ABBS
University of Sussex

Wars are terrible things,
Blood is as frequent as water,
People are made homeless
Their houses ruined by bombs,
Hundreds of people are killed every day.
The world is a ball of fire,
I hate wars and wars seem to hate
me and everything of joy.

Poem by First-year girl,
Bristol Comprehensive School, United Kingdom

October 24 to October 31 is Disarmament Week. It might be thought that such a week has no special relevance for teachers. I believe this is a fallacy. I believe that, on the contrary, all teachers *as teachers* must now seriously attend to the threat of nuclear warfare. Indeed, it is difficult to see how teachers can stand to one side, remain merely neutral, when the government is increasing its expenditure on nuclear weapons designed to destroy millions of lives and, at the same time, savagely undermining all those educational institutions designed to enhance life and to secure a meaningful future. It is difficult to see how teachers cannot become involved when quite recently the BBC—that vital institution for the free dissemination of information and interpretation—has, once again, shown itself to be inadequate to its great task by repressing the national discussion of the nuclear issue. (Postponing the Richard Dimbleby Memorial Lecture resembles very much the earlier refusal to show *The War Game.*) It is also difficult to see how teachers can ignore the growing formation of peace groups in their own institutions. The moral problems raised by nuclear warfare will not go away and teachers, whose commitment is to meaning and value, have no choice but to engage in the controversy. It is not a matter of teachers' becoming narrowly political and ideological. In my view that would represent a menace and a perversion of education. It is rather that teachers must now respond to a comprehensive theme based on a deep and universal desire to secure life, to achieve the conditions necessary for the protection and qualitative development of life—all life—on this planet. It is, first and foremost, an ethical and an ecological matter. As teachers, we are, perhaps unconsciously, committed to a concept of a positive future in which implicit meanings slowly unfold into existential patterns. Much of our labor today is for the truth that crystallizes tomorrow. We have an investment in the future. And it is, perhaps, in this capacity, as guardians of a creative future, that we must now enter the nuclear debate.

In this article I will attempt to define my own personal position on this matter. In a sense I wish to grasp my own view, to discover where I actually stand. My hope is that such reflection may create a similar movement of reflective thought in the reader. At the same time I must admit that I am a slow learner and that it may already be time for the profession as a whole to make clear to the nation where it stands. For as a teaching profession committed to the enhancement of life (and of all lives) through the process of time, can we possibly tolerate a society that has become committed to the death instinct, that limits the very sources of ethical and intellectual growth while it invests in the appalling machinery of mass destruction and global disaster?

However, I do not want to discuss organization in this article. I want to provoke thought among teachers. I want to speak personally. I want to speak out of my own conscience and my own perceptions. At the same time, the theme is more than a personal one. For nuclear war puts all of our lives in doubt. Nuclear war endangers our whole species and the whole of the living world. The very prospect of such a war seriously damages our sense of any future tense for creation. Thus, I would claim that even before any buttons are pressed, immeasurable psychic damage has already been done. For how can we live as whole men and women with such a menacing cloud perpetually hanging over our future? Some might claim that I am exaggerating the power of nuclear weapons. It is almost impossible to be guilty of such an offense. In our own time even the most conventional of figures—Establishment characters if you like—have warned us of the possibility of imminent catastrophe. Harold Macmillan declared:

> If all this capacity for destruction is spread around the world in the hands of all kinds of different characters—dictators, reactionaries, revolutionaries, madmen—then sooner or later, and certainly I think by the end of this century, either by error or insanity, the great crime will be committed.[1]

As is well known, the late Lord Mountbatten has, likewise, written:

> In the event of a nuclear war there will be no chances, and there will be no survivors—all will be obliterated. . . . I repeat in all sincerity as a military man I can see no use for any nuclear weapons which would not end in escalation with consequences no-one can conceive.[2]

Such an ultimate catastrophe is difficult to imagine partly because such an act of genocide is pathologically sick and inherently evil and partly because we cannot envisage easily a world without consciousness, devoid of feeling, value, and meaning. To think of our world moving like a spent cinder through the silence of space chills the spine and shocks the imagination. We would prefer not to consider it. And yet we must because that which we fear most deeply—the extinction of human life—is now possible, can, for the first time in history, actually be brought about. In the brutal language of contemporary military discourse, we have reached such a point of progress in technology that we can now "overkill" the world's population forty times.

The perception that nuclear war constituted a different kind of warfare—involving cataclysmic destruction with devastating and largely unpredictable aftereffects—has accompanied nuclear research from the beginning. Yet, as we know, it did not prevent Hiroshima and Nagasaki, events to which I will return later. Henry Stimson, Roosevelt's secretary of war, in April 1945 informed President Truman (who had known nothing of the experiment to discover the A-bomb and had to be hastily informed after he had become president of the United States) of an immense project, and I quote, "looking to the development of a new explosive of almost unbelievable destructive power"; James Byrnes, the director of war mobilization, in the same apocalyptic spirit, told Truman that his country was "perfecting an explosive great enough to destroy the whole world." Oppenheimer, who was scientific director of the first atomic project, commented after the first test of the first atomic bomb in history:

> We knew the world would not be the same. A few people laughed, a few people cried. Most people were silent. I remembered the line from the Hindu scripture, the *Bhagavad Gita:* Vishnu is trying to persuade the Prince that he should do his duty and to impress him takes on his multiarmed form and says "Now I am become death, destroyer of worlds." I suppose we all thought that one way or another.[3]

George Kistiakowsky, who was also present, remarked, "I am sure that at the end of the world—in the last millisecond of the earth's existence—the last man will see what we have just seen."[4]

Symbolically, the first explosion of the atom bomb took place in a remote desert of sand called by the Mexicans Jornada del Muerte—Journey of Death.

I quote these remarks—there are, of course, many more one could quote, like that of Oppenheimer to the effect that since Hiroshima, scientists had death on their hands—to show that the cosmic destructive potentialities of nuclear war have been clearly understood and articulated since 1945. Much as we would like to avoid thinking about the possibility of total annihilation, it is there in the technology and in the psyche of man. And, if we are to be responsible to human life, we must attempt to think the unthinkable and locate ways of preventing a human and biological holocaust. Surely educational institutions provide the right contexts for such fundamental reflection? We cannot leave it to our governments, not only because their record is absolutely deplorable but, more deeply, because what happens to our lives—what we want for ourselves and for our children, for our society and the whole human race—must be the outcome of *our own* thoughts, decisions, and actions. Such responsibility for human life cannot be delegated to specialists, to military technocrats, to governments or commercial enterprises.

Consider, for example, the kind of mindlessness that Hank Schumacher, a leading American designer of nuclear weapons, sees as representative of himself and his colleagues:

> Once they're in it [military research] very few people think much about it. My colleagues who work on nuclear devises don't do it for a reason. They do it because they are nuclear physicists. And that's where the funds are. Any of us in analytical work could make important contributions to other fields. I know we could, but the money isn't there.[5]

The nuclear scientists—and 60 percent of all scientists in the United States of America are engaged in military research of some kind—do *not* think about the human consequences of their work. We cannot, therefore, delegate responsibility to them: As a professional body, they refuse to make the necessary connections. Even less can we trust politicians and commercial agents. Our century is full of deranged psychopaths who have achieved leadership of their countries. And commercial agents, as we all know, have powerful financial interests always vying with any disturbing moral perceptions. We have no choice but to become responsible ourselves. And what is now demanded of us as individuals is that we recognize the magnitude of the peril, the great crisis of our military-technological civilizations, East and West, whose experts and leaders might well choose to inflict nuclear war rather than consider more subtle and life-affirming alternatives, alternatives rooted *not* in any power complex but in a comprehensive concern for life as a whole, alternatives that lie at the very root of our work as teachers.

Albert Einstein, who was one of the first to urge research into nuclear fission, has said that nuclear energy represents a quantum leap in technology that changes everything in the world, except consciousness. One may want to question a little the "quantum leap" because the bomb can be seen also to represent the culmination of three hundred years of scientific advance divorced from ethical principles and philosophical meaning. As well as a quantum leap, perhaps, it should also be viewed as the final negative realization of Bacon's dictum that science is concerned with the effecting of all things possible. Genocide is possible and technology can now effect it. Nuclear missiles, with their sleek phallic forms, are, I believe, the ultimate symbol of male intelligence divorced from religious impulse and feminine cherishing. Psychologically, missiles are the engines of rape. But this qualification registered, Einstein's remark embodies a deep insight. The quantum leap in technology demands, on our part, a quantum leap in ethical imagination. The challenge to our undeveloped moral nature has never been greater. Have we the imagination to find a superior way forward before our bodies and our great civilizations and cultures are reduced to a desert of nuclear dust, before the journey of death has become the common, level plateau of extinction? And can schools help to engender such an imaginative act?

I have suggested that, at times, we must try to imagine the unimaginable, so that through the ethical imagination we may work to end any kind of nuclear war. I am afraid that at the moment there are many who are imagining implementing nuclear war; they are prepared to talk about "limited-theater wars," "strategic advantages," even of seeing the whole of Europe as the convenient theater for the giant confrontation between the United States and the Soviet Union. Cruise missiles—160 of which we are soon to receive into this country—are, indeed, a part of this death-centered imagining. As many have observed, there has been, in the last few years, a radical shift in ethical imagination. During the 1960s and 1970s most people thought nuclear war so morally obscene it could never happen. There was the practical sense that it could never happen, and a moral imperative that it must never happen. Thus civil defense programs seemed out of the question, for they granted the possibility that the ethical sense would not concede: that such wars might take place. Hence in the 1970s there was little conscious alarm, although the arms spiral continued to rise. Now, the feeling has changed. Survival has become a key word in the new practical mood. During the last two years civil defense programs have been widely disseminated; a highly complex system of interconnected bunkers has been erected; and ruthless programs concerning post-nuclear attack operations have been published. The arguments for neutron bombs and cruise missiles have often been based on the notion of what is called "limited-response strategy." Thus, as most industrial nations have entered a crippling period of recession, governments, like our own, have yet gone on expanding budgets for nuclear arms. Indeed, just as the first street riots began here in England, just as the underprivileged, unemployed, unengaged youths began to rampage through their ugly urban streets, so Mrs. Thatcher's government decided to allocate £5,000,000,000 to Trident, and Mr. Reagan, for his part, decided to lift the ban on chemical weapons and to go ahead with the production of the neutron bomb and the huge MX system of missiles. Such demented juxtapositions are the very essence of our daily news! What had once struck people as unacceptable—as MAD (mutually assured destruction)—now seems to be innocuously integrated into public consciousness. We would seem to have a phantasy world in which the nuclear shelter is seen as a viable alternative and in which survivors of nuclear war quickly shake themselves free of contamination and catch the first commuter train to London to continue with their old jobs.

There are many elements in this dramatic shift of ethical sensibility, but I want to focus a little more carefully on the general unreality of the imagery in popular consciousness regarding nuclear attack. I recently did some petitioning for the World Disarmament Campaign and found that many people perceived nuclear war through the lens of the Second World War. A nuclear war would be like the blitz, it was contended. Even official publications concerning civil defense seemed wedded to a sandbag-under-the-table-switching-on-the-radio mentality. Because we all have to structure anticipated experience in terms of previous experience, this is, for uninformed people, an understandable deduction. At the same time, it is a dangerous fallacy muffling the mind and blinding the eyes to the actualities. As the techniques of World War I had little relevance to World War II, so the techniques of World War II will have next to no meaning for any third world war. There is the illusion that civilization, as we know it, would continue. This is impossible. If there were to be an extensive nuclear war, the destruction, the suffering, the horror, would be on a scale unprecedented in history. As I have said, repeating thousands of eminent men and women, such a war could even bring about the end of history.

But how could we begin to understand it? The only legitimate way would be by contemplating the comparatively light, the comparatively "primitive," bombs dropped on Hiroshima on August 6, 1945, and on Nagasaki on August 9, 1945. For my description I will take Hiroshima.

As Jim Garrison put it, "The Hiroshima bomb pulverized an entire city in one single blast." The explosion was 1,000 times stronger than the biggest blockbuster. Not only was the bomb "a city-buster," it had, as we shall see, dire radiation effects that are still in evidence today, more than thirty-five years later.

The bomb was dropped on August 6 at 8:16 in the morning as children were playing in playgrounds before school, as men and women were going about their usual business. As soon as the bomb detonated there was a blinding flash of light and a savage fireball spreading half a mile in diameter. The heat at the center of the fireball was 50,000,000 degrees fahrenheit, thousands of times hotter than the surface of the sun. Out of this light and explosion of flames arose the boiling column of smoke, mushrooming out—a flash of light, a blast devastating thousands of buildings, and then a burning turbulence of fire. This was the holocaust—in which thousands were burnt to nothingness, simply and completely incinerated. It has been estimated that of the 3,483 men, women, adolescents, children, and babies within 1,500 feet of the epicenter—the initial point of detonation—only 53 survived. Also, in order to shed all

World War II comparisons, it is important to note that of the 45 hospitals, only 3 remained standing. Of the 298 doctors, 270 were killed. Of the 1,780 nurses, 1,645 were killed. These, please observe, are the insane figures *not* of full-scale nuclear war but of *one* twenty-kiloton bomb.

However, the effects of the bomb were not confined to the epicenter. As the immense blast of energy rushed outward, destroying all in its path, so, within a short span of time, air rushed into the vacuum it had created. This incoming air quickly became a tidal wave of fire, totally out of control, burning everything that it touched. In Hiroshima, the fire storm developed twenty minutes after the bomb's detonation, lasted about six hours, and completely burnt out an area of four and one-half square miles. Dr. Hanoaka described his firsthand experience of the fire storm as follows:

> Between the Red Cross Hospital and the centre of the city I saw nothing that wasn't burned to a crisp. Streetcars were standing at Kawaya-cho and Kamiya-cho and inside were dozens of bodies, blackened beyond recognition. I saw fire reservoirs filled to the brim with dead people who looked as though they had been boiled alive. In one reservoir I saw a man, horribly burned, crouching beside another man who was dead. He was drinking blood-stained water out of the reservoir. Even if I had tried to stop him, it wouldn't have done any good; he was completely out of his head. In one reservoir there were so many dead people there wasn't enough room for them to fall over: they must have died sitting in the water.
>
> Even the swimming pool at the Prefectural First Middle School was filled with dead people. They must have suffocated while they sat in the water trying to escape the fire because they didn't appear to be burned.
>
> That pool wasn't big enough to accommodate everybody who tried to get in. You could tell that by looking around the sides. I don't know how many were caught by death with their heads hanging over the edge. In one pool I saw some people who were still alive, sitting in the water with dead all around them. They were too weak to get out. People were trying to help them, but I am sure they must have died.[6]

It is sobering to reflect that the test bomb dropped on Bikini in 1954 was 750 times more powerful than the Hiroshima bomb. It is sobering to reflect that one authority on nuclear power has suggested that a twenty-megaton fireball could ignite 1,000 square miles. It is these truths that make the sandbag-and-curtain mentality criminally wrong.

Yet I am afraid we have not completed our contemplation of Hiroshima and its suffering. The survivors had then to encounter the invisible contamination caused by radiation. These effects gave a further terror to those already traumatized by what they had witnessed. A Buddhist priest remarked:

> We heard the new phrase "A-bomb disease." The fear in us became strong, especially when we could see certain things with our eyes. A man looking perfectly well as he rode by on a bicycle one morning, suddenly vomiting blood, and then dying. . . . Soon we were all worried about our health, about our bodies—whether we should live or die. And we heard if someone did get sick, there was no treatment that could help. We had nothing to rely on, there was nothing to hold us up.[7]

People were bewildered and terrified by the new invisible "disease" of radiation. As we now know, it had innumerable effects, which have been well documented: It led to leukemia (reaching its highest rates around 1950); it led to innumerable stillbirths and miscarriages; it led to babies born with various congenital defects and abnormalities; it led to cancer and thyroid tumors; it led to eye cataracts, various blood diseases, and skin disorders; and without a doubt it increased the sense of psychic dislocation and total meaninglessness that all the survivors of the bomb suffered for the rest of their lives.

Again, it must be remembered that in the case of Hiroshima the radiation was confined to that released in the initial blast. If it had been a surface burst (as opposed to an air burst) there would have been a further massive fallout of radioactive particles from the mushroom cloud. The effects of such radiation would be similar to that described before but would be much more extensive and, depending on the wind, capable of spreading up to 1,000 kilometers, as documented in the recent United Nations publication *Comprehensive Study of Nuclear Weapons.* The thin snow of death would contaminate whatever remained after the detonation of a number of bombs on key cities and nuclear sites.

I have described the effects of one nuclear bomb, a limited bomb in comparison with those that would be employed today. Yet, in a sense, there can be nothing worse than the indiscriminate mass murder and contamination of life that took place in Japan. *The terrible has already happened.* We must not let it happen again. Hiroshima must be our school from which we learn the need for permanent peace. But have we learned our lesson? If we look at the military phenomena of our century, we can see that we have gradually allowed our consciences to shift from the concept of limited war to the concept of total war. In 1907 the Hague Convention made an agreement that war should not impinge on unarmed civilians, and we find that of the numbers killed in World War I only 5 percent were civilians. In World War II we find that 48 percent were civilians. In the Korean War we find that 84 percent were civilians. In any third world war such a distinction between civilians and professionals will be utterly meaningless. Such a war would entail the indiscriminate mass destruction of life. Such a perception should deeply shock the ethical imagination, and yet we observe in our times the steady nightmarish increase and proliferation of nuclear weapons. It is calculated that the Soviet Union has 9,000 warheads targeted on Britain, Europe, and the

United States. It is estimated that NATO and the United States have, for their part, 15,000 warheads ranged against the Warsaw Pact countries. Only last summer it was revealed that the United States is planning to spend 7 billion dollars over the next five years on chemical warfare and to begin manufacturing the neutron bomb. Moreover, it is thought that such countries as Israel, India, and South Africa may already possess nuclear weapons and that many other countries (moving from nuclear reactors for "peace" to nuclear missiles for "war") are on the threshold of obtaining them: Brazil, Argentina, and Pakistan, for example. Arrogantly and paranoically, the "advanced" countries of the world stomp on the edge of the abyss. A disaster—perhaps even begun by a seemingly insignificant accident—is inevitable, unless there is a radical countermovement from the peoples of the world, claiming the right of all to live. Only a spontaneous and unceasing worldwide expression of the ethical imagination can save us. And teachers, by the nature of their work, should have an essential part to play in generating such imagination.

In conclusion, I want to raise one further question and to present one further image from the ethical imagination.

The question is this: Could there ever be cause that would justify releasing nuclear missiles in which millions of men, women, adolescents, children, babies, and the whole chain of biological life on which their lives depend would be indiscriminately destroyed?

I myself think that there could never be such a cause, *never be a sufficient reason to sanction such an indiscriminate destruction of life.* If you share my judgment, then it also follows that one could not defend any military program that would make likely or even possible such an action. One would certainly have to say no to any offensive weapons designed to inflict nuclear destruction.

If your answer to the question—Could it ever be justified?—is negative, then I think you are ethically obliged to unconditionally disown nuclear warfare—to disown it as criminal, and as totally unacceptable as a means to solve any conceivable human dispute. That is the negative form. The positive form of the same argument might well be that one must adopt against the world's arsenal of missiles a radical concept of peace, moving outward from the individual life to the nation, from the national to the international. The profession of teaching, as I have implied, may well *presuppose such a position;* this may well be *an implicit moral element of our job.* And the same is, of course, true of other professions, most obviously the medical profession.

Finally, to the image I want to present. The day we sadly remember Hiroshima is the day on which Christians also celebrate Christ's transfiguration. In the transfiguration we have the energy that is radiant and healing, a disclosure of the divine within the human. Here in these juxtaposed images of light and transformation lies, perhaps, the clue for the future. The quantum leap in technology calls out for the quantum leap in the ethical imagination—

where we find the deep energies for renewal and for hope. If we meet destructive energy with destructive energy we create havoc. If we meet destructive energy with the counter-energy of nonviolence, our own action suggests the ethical way forward.

We must define peace in terms not only of Hiroshima but also of the transfiguration symbolically understood. Peace is not merely the absence of war. Peace cannot be secured by the deterrence of nuclear terror. Peace, rather, is a condition of being that renders nuclear war wholly unacceptable.

This is both the human and the ethical response, indeed the only living response to the prospect of the nuclear holocaust. It is, therefore, the response that should emerge most powerfully from us as a teaching profession. I have suggested that we as teachers are committed to a view of human potentiality that cannot sanction any kind of indiscriminate nuclear warfare. From the impoverished classrooms and the demoralized universities, should we as teachers and lecturers now move to unconditionally disown the instruments of genocide and to insist on the creative path out of the intolerable anxiety?

Notes

1 Harold Macmillan, quoted in *New Internationalist,* no. 97, March 1981.

2 Lord Mountbatten, quoted in ibid.

3 Robert Oppenheimer, quoted in Jim Garrison, *From Hiroshima to Harrisburg* (SCM Press Ltd., 1980).

4 George Kistiakowsky, quoted in ibid.

5 Hank Schumacher, quoted in *New Internationalist.*

6 Dr. Hanoaka, quoted in Tom Stoniar, *Nuclear Disaster* (New York: Penguin, 1964).

7 A Buddish priest, quoted in Robert Jay Lifton, *Death in Life* (Weidenfield and Nicholson, 1968).

Education for Disarmament: A Topical Necessity

ADRIAN NĂSTASE
Institute of Legal Research, Bucharest, Romania

The fast-moving course involving arms production and acquisition has become at the present moment an increasingly serious source of insecurity in international relations.

The emergence of new weapons systems and their proliferation all over the world with the aim, in the view of certain states, to restore or to reestablish the military balance actually results in military insecurity and exacerbates international rivalries and tensions. Consequently, developments having occurred in the past four decades brought about a continuous process of arms stockpiling coupled with a steady decline in international security.

Thus, although the arms buildup soared beyond imagination all through the postwar period, the security of many states was not ensured. This situation is evidenced by the fact that from 1945 to this day over a hundred armed conflicts flared up, in which more than 25 million people were killed.

The paradox is that the arms race has gained momentum at a time when no fewer than 500 million people are suffering from acute malnutrition, 800 million people are illiterate, and 250 million children under fourteen have no access to education. It is an equally serious fact that this malfunctional process involves some 20 million scientists working in the military research-development sector, thereby diverting a considerable research resource from natural, peaceful utilization.

Moreover, owing to this orientation, a large number of international cooperation projects, relating in particular to the development strategy, were subordinated to military-strategic considerations. As a result of this, the policy of détente, which prevailed during the 1970s, sometimes served certain powers as an instrument of acquiring a series of strategic zones and as an economic lever manipulated on the market of international credits.

Under the circumstances, every way and means becomes necessary in order to mobilize a joint force of international pressure capable of operating as a factor designed to help achieve general disarmament.

In this respect, the Appeal for Disarmament and Peace, launched on October 30, 1981, by the Socialist Democracy and Unity Front of Romania, on the basis of the guidelines set by President Nicolae Ceauşescu, states: "We consider that the peace-loving forces everywhere, the peoples should work most energetically to make their governments, parliaments, state leaderships pursue a new, constructive policy pervaded by the highest responsibility for the fate and future of peoples, for the world peace."[1]

There exists an indissoluble link between education and the need to achieve disarmament. By its serious implications, the arms race has negative repercussions on the educational system, diverts scientific research from its natural objectives of answering mankind's vital aspirations toward material and spiritual progress, and prevents huge resources, both material and intellectual, from being released in order to meet the urgent development requirements of every nation.

The growing international interdependencies, at the global, regional, and subregional levels, in conditions of increasingly diversified national interests, of steadily widening economic gaps, and of extremely high levels of armaments and armed forces in the contemporary world make it ever more necessary to develop, on both national and international scales, adequate forms and structures of peace education, in *particular* of its fundamental component, disarmament education.[2]

The importance of disarmament education has been stressed on more than one occasion. Thus, the final document of the tenth U.N. General Assembly Special Session on Disarmament mentioned, among other things, that the educational programs in the field of disarmament and peace contribute to a better understanding and acquaintance with the problems created by the arms race, and with the need for disarmament, and as such can play an effective role in solving this capital problem of the contemporary world, by creating a public opinion movement favorable to the cessation of the arms race, the reduction of arms stockpiles, systematic cuts in military expenditures, and the achievement of disarmament.[3]

The ultimate aim of disarmament education must certainly be the promotion of disarmament. Consequently, both the decision-making factors and public opinion must be sure of the required modalities through which disarmament can contribute to the national security of every state and to international security as a whole, and, implicitly, to the maintenance of peace.

Likewise, individuals and the public must be kept informed about the efforts being exerted at the present moment in the field of disarmament.

These objectives were singled out also during the proceedings of the UNESCO-sponsored World Congress on Disarmament Education, which was held in Paris in June 1980. As the final document of the congress indicates, disarmament education must apply to all segments of society. It must contribute to international understanding, tolerance, and social justice, and encourage children and students to approach critically the disarmament question.

As laid down in the final document of the congress, the underlying concept of disarmament in relation to disarmament education includes primarily any form of international action oriented toward arms limitation, control, and reduction and, ultimately, toward general and complete disarmament, under effective international control. In this respect, the disarmament process must be considered to aim at the transformation of the present international system into a new one, in which the peoples may live in security.[4]

According to J. Martenson, under-secretary general of the United Nations, the main objective of a disarmament education program should be to explain to a large number of people, in clear and simple terms, what the realities of the present situation are and why, in the nuclear era, security does not reside in arms accumulation but in disarmament and close cooperation among nations. Cooperation and not confrontation is the answer to the problems of a divided, overpopulated, and troubled world, a world that is arming itself at the incredible price of one million dollars a minute.[5]

It should be particularly borne in mind that, from a military standpoint, whereas in the past the efficiency of a state's defense system could be verified only when its borders were actually violated by a foreign army, at the present time the defense system of a state would be inefficient in the event of an army's deciding to undertake a nuclear attack against it by using missiles or bombers. This has led to the emergence of the concept of deterrence as part of military doctrine (meaning in the main the capacity to retaliate in case of a first nuclear strike, by delivering general strikes against densely populated areas of the adversary). For this reason, the arms race tries to achieve an impossible objective: attainment of such a superiority as would secure by first strike the destruction of all nuclear military capabilities of a potential adversary.

However, international tensions are generated not only by the *existence* of weapons but also by their deployment, and by the possibilities of using them in a surprise attack, a move that is always tempting to some military powers. Consequently, in parallel with the disarmament process, special attention must be paid to confidence building in the mutual relations of states. Viewed from this angle, it is particularly important to recall the Romanian proposal concerning the convening of the European Conference on Disarmament and Confidence-Building in our continent.

The content of disarmament education is dynamic and therefore variable. It is relatively different depending on the specific zone of the planet as it reflects, among other things, specific national interests as well as the traditions and values typical of the respective people.[6]

In principle, this educational process must lay emphasis on the need for disarmament, on the essential link existing between peace and disarmament, and on the need to seek new forms of international security that are not based on armaments; it must also stress the imperative of solving all international disputes by peaceful means as well as the importance of observing all fundamental principles of contemporary international law.[7]

The educational approach to the arms race *problématique* must include primarily the relevance of such essential factors as underlie the incessant spiral, and the multiple implications, of the arms race. It must point out that the arms race represents primarily the result of a permanent competition stemming from decisional processes of a political and strategic nature related to the main actors involved—as a rule, major powers and/or military blocs. Second, that it represents a process of permanent accumulation of destructive capacities coupled with the replacement ("modernization") of dated weaponry that, once disposed of, automatically becomes exportable merchandise. It is equally important to stress that a huge number of scientists and an enormous volume of resources are used exclusively for military purposes, a fact that has extremely harmful effect on the development of all nations; the restrictive effect of the arms race on the transfer of technology must also be included in the educational process related to disarmament.

The process in question must equally comprise the analysis of the arms race trends and of the world balance of forces, stress being laid on the dangers posed to mankind by the negative effects of continued armaments.

As part of the message it conveys, disarmament education must bring to the fore the inherent connections of disarmament with other international objectives, concepts, and values, such as international peace and security, development, human rights, and the overall interdependencies between the global problems of mankind.

To mention only the link between disarmament education and human rights, it is obvious, as stressed repeatedly by the President of Romania, Comrade Nicolae Ceauşescu, that in the general framework of these rights an essential role is played by the right of every individual to peace, implicitly, to life and to development, an aspect that should be related to a greater extent to the disarmament *problématique* and to the educational process.[8]

One of the central conceptual questions relating to the content of disarmament education is, however, the very definition of the disarmament concept,[9] including the determination of the relationship and position of the various notions involved, such as "arms limitation," "arms control," "elimination of armaments," and so forth.

So far, the theoretical models concerning the national security of states have been based in the main on the need to pursue a policy of armaments. However, as shown in the final document of the 1978 U.N. General Assembly Special Session on Disarmament, in our times, the accumulation of weapons, in particular nuclear weapons, represents a threat to rather than a protection of the future of mankind.

It is therefore necessary to work out a new theory of the mutual relations of states that should propose a set of security models, at both regional and global levels, based on a gradual and balanced reduction of military forces and armaments, account being taken of the need to maintain the military balance. Such ideas must be included in disarmament education as well (see Figure 1).

Equally, disarmament must be examined from a pluri-disciplinary angle: judicial, political, economic, sociological, physiological, and otherwise, including the determination of the relationship and relevance of each of these

Figure 1

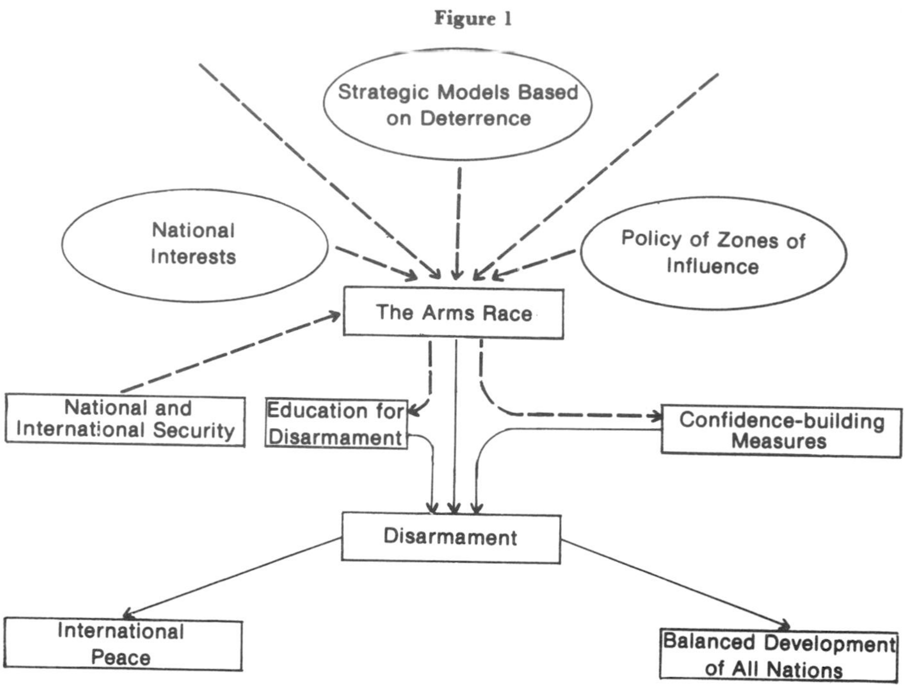

coordinates, as well as the causes of and obstacles to the attainment of disarmament.

As a result, those involved in disarmament education must pay special attention to the modalities of overcoming the obstacles to disarmament.[10] Such obstacles are *structural* (related in the main to the nature of international relationships), *conceptual* (strategic doctrines), and *cultural* (prejudice, perceptions) and include, among others, the glorification of war, the interests of the industrial-military complexes, the use of distorted military information, the manipulation of mass-media channels by transnational corporations involved in the arms production, difficulties resulting from the reconversion of military industry into civilian industry (e.g., the risk of unemployment), the exacerbation of ideologies based on violence, the susceptibility of states concerning acceptance of international arms control, malfunctions created in developing countries by the transfer of military technology, and the use in the press media of controlled information designed to amplify fear and mistrust among nations.

Disarmament education must of necessity aim at enhancing awareness of the need to achieve the closest possible cooperation among all political forces interested in disarmament.

For this reason, disarmament education must involve all age groups, in particular the younger generation, which must be oriented, in various ways and in different forms and structures, toward certain types of intersocietal and interstate behaviors, and toward specific values deriving from overall group or community interests related to the military *problématique*.

Such an education can be achieved in schools (primary and secondary), in universities, in the family, and through various mass-media channels (press, radio, television); it may involve the educators themselves in the formation of specific programs, teaching and audiovisual materials, and in general all methods considered to be the most suitable for the beneficiaries of this kind of educational process, designed to enhance understanding of the general problem of disarmament and its significant and important aspects.

This outlook on education causes the disarmament educational process to include a differentiated and phased study, knowledge, and formation of an active attitude toward the global problems of humanity, such as the maintenance of international peace and the consolidation of world security, the establishment of a new international economic order, the insurance of a balanced economic, social, and cultural development of all nations in a peaceful international environment, arms limitation, and the launching of the disarmament process.[11]

Particularly topical in this field are the ideas and conceptions evolved during the interwar period by the great Romanian diplomat Nicolae Titulescu. To Titulescu, "the foundations of peace" must be built in the conscience of the individual. "How can the edifice of peace be built without the support of the masses?" he asked.[12] By this question, he meant to reveal the important role played by public opinion in ensuring the maintenance of peace and in influencing governmental policies toward disarmament.

As far back as 1931, Titulescu remarked, "I have in mind a *moral disarmament* with the object of revising school-books so as to enhance among the youth the spirit of international solidarity."

It flows from this that one dimension of utmost importance resides in *action for disarmament,* which can be based only on the awareness of the need for disarmament and of the imperative to build a peaceful international system.

By promoting knowledge about the conditions of peace and the elimination of the causes of war in the educational system and in the mass media, disarmament education must become an active component of action for disarmament.

Similarly, governmental actions toward disarmament must be singled out in order to encourage an active behavior and to create adequate conditions for stimulating further initiatives in the field of disarmament. In our view, disarmament education in each country cannot be dissociated from the disarmament policy of the respective government, for any educational process presupposes the "reproduction" of certain systemic values, based on national interest, as they are perceived by every government.

There exists, therefore, a close link between the attitudes and actions of governments in the matter of disarmament and the *content* of disarmament education.

Thus, so far as Romania is concerned, mention should be made of the well-known initiatives taken by the Romanian government on the international plane (reduction of military expenditures by at least 10 percent until 1985, convening of a special disarmament conference in Europe, conclusion of a general pact on the renunciation of the use and threat of force, setting up of a buffer zone in Europe between NATO and the Warsaw Treaty Pact, etc.). These initiatives began with the *unilateral measures* of the Romanian state in 1979–1980 to reduce military budgets and respectively to increase the allocation for children.

Under the circumstances, it is obvious that disarmament education in Romania bears the mark of both the political will and the general will to bring about arms reduction and ultimate elimination; at the same time it plays the role of a catalyst, in an attempt to mobilize world opinion as well as foreign governments in this direction.

Along these lines, the Socialist Democracy and Unity Front of Romania, in its appeal of October 30, 1981, calls on all the men and women in our country "to tell their opinion in public meetings, organize civic rallies, demonstrations, peace marches and other mass demonstrations calling upon all states and peoples to undertake and intensify their actions so as to prevent the escalation of the arms race and the increase of military arsenals, promote concrete measures for disarmament, nuclear disarmament in the first place, free mankind from the nightmare of another war."

There exists a close interdependence between the development of science, culture, and education and the peace of mankind, since education and technical-scientific progress are both premises and consequences of peace. Hence, education based on respect for an understanding of all other peoples—therefore as education having an international vocation—not only represents a natural attribute of any educational system aspiring for humanism and rationality, which are the characteristic features of our times, but is also a fundamental prerequisite for the insurance of international peace, security, and cooperation.

Notes

1 *Scinteia,* November 1, 1981.

2 See A. Corradini, "Le Développement de l'éducation pour le désarmement en tant que domaine d'étude distinct: analyse d'introduction," paper presented at the World Congress on Disarmament Education (WCDE), June 9–13, 1980, Doc. SS-80/CONF.401/31.

3 In this respect, see A. Guha, "Disarmament Education: Why and How," a WCDE paper, June 1980.

4 Doc. UNESCO, SS-SO/CONF.401/37, p. 6.

5 Doc. UNESCO, SS-80/CONF.401/INF, 10, p. 4.

6 For a fuller analysis of the aspects, see D. Chitoran and A. Năstase, *Educatia pentru dezarmare; continut si formă* [Disarmament education: content and form], in *Revista comisiei romane pt,* UNESCO, 1980, no. 4, pp. 323–38.

7 Unfortunately, the subject matter relating to this educational process is not construed and evolved by the various educational systems in a unitary manner, coherently and in consonance with the above-mentioned objectives.

8 See also J. Vollmar Torney, *L'Éducation pour le désarmement el l'ensiegnement des droits de l'homme,* WCDE, Doc. SS/80/CONF.401/22, 1980; Theo C. Van Boven, *United Nations and Human Rights: A Critical Appraisal,* in "UN Law/Fundamental Rights," Sijthoff and Nooordhoff (1979), pp. 127f; and Th. Buergenthal, "Codification and Implementation of International Human Rights," in *Human Dignity* (New York: Oceana Publications, 1979), pp. 23f.

9 A quite ample definition of general and complete disarmament is contained in the USSR-USA Joint Declaration on Principles Agreed to Govern Disarmament Negotiations, endorsed by the UN General Assembly in its Resolution 1722/XVI of December 20, 1961. According to this declaration, general and complete disarmament must include for each state: (1) abolition of the armed forces, liquidation of military bases, cessation of the production of armaments as well as their liquidation and conversion toward peaceful purposes; (2) liquidation of all nuclear, chemical, and bacteriological stockpiles as well as other weapons of mass destruction, and cessation of the production of such weapons; (3) elimination of all vectors of weapons of mass destruction; (4) abolition of organizations and institutions designed to organize the military effort of states, cessation of military instruction, and liquidation of all military schools; and (5) cessation of military expenditures.

10 See the final report of the meeting of experts on obstacles to disarmament and the means to overcome them (Paris: UNESCO, April 1978), Doc. UNESCO SS-78/CONF.613/17, June 30, 1978, pp. 7–10. See also B. Reardon, "Obstacles to Disarmament Education," *Bulletin of Peace Proposals* 4 (1979): 336–67.

11 In this respect, see also A. Pellet, *La Part du désarment dans l'enseignement des questions internationales,* WCDE, SS-80/CONF.401/21.

12 N. Titulesco, *Progresul ideii de pact* [The progress of the idea of peace], in *Discursuri* (Bucharest: Ed. Stiintifică, 1967), pp. 346–47.

The U.S. Academy of Peace

ELISE BOULDING
Dartmouth College

It is one of the ironies of history that at the very moment when the United States is involved in the greatest peacetime military defense buildup this nation has ever known, Congress also has before it House bill H.R. 5088 and Senate bill S. 1889 proposing the establishment of a U.S. Academy of Peace. These bills are the product of more than a year of intensive work by a commission jointly appointed by President Carter, the Senate, and the House in the fall of 1979 to study the feasibility of a peace academy. The commission's report makes a strong case for the establishment of this new type of federal academy based on the following: (1) countrywide hearings to ascertain the views of a variety of relevant professional and lay publics, (2) a survey of the conflict-resolution competencies required by and available to the U.S. government, (3) and a state-of-the-art evaluation of research and training in conflict resolution and related professional fields.

The very fact that U.S. national defense policy is now being hotly debated, particularly the nuclear component of that policy, heightens interest in the question whether a new type of institution, offering a new set of tools for meeting security and defense needs, would be useful to the United States.

The idea of a national peace academy is not new. The concept has been around from the country's earliest beginnings. George Washington wrote in 1783 of the need for "a proper Peace Establishment for the U.S.," and Benjamin Rush, a signer of the Declaration of Independence, has been identified as co-author of an essay on the Constitution that laments

> that no person has taken notice of its total silence upon the subject of an office of the utmost importance to the welfare of the United States, that is, an office for promoting and preserving perpetual peace in our country. It is hoped that no objection will be made to the establishment of such an office, while we are engaged in a war with the Indians, for as the War-Office of the United States was established in the time of peace, it is equally reasonable that a Peace-Office should be established in the time of war.

The nineteenth century witnessed periodic but unsuccessful attempts to establish a peace office. Efforts in this century began in 1935, as war clouds gathered in Europe; two separate bills to establish a peace office or a bureau of peace were introduced in 1935. The present bill has its direct ancestry in bills introduced in 1945 in the context of the end of World War II, by Senator Wiley of Wisconsin and Senator Randolph of West Virginia. The fact that more than 140 bills to establish a department of peace or a national peace agency were introduced in Congress between 1935 and 1978, when the bill to appoint the recent commission of inquiry successfully passed both houses, suggests a growing awareness of the need for a nonmilitary approach to national security and international order. The concept has always had the support of important leaders in both political parties. The two most senior senators who served as co-introducers of S. 1889 are Republican Senator Mark Hatfield of Oregon and Democratic Senator Jennings Randolph of West Virginia, who first introduced a peace academy bill thirty-six years earlier. Senator Randolph thinks that it would be one of the crowning achievements of his career to see a peace academy come into being before he retires. Another key Senate figure in the groundwork for this bill has been Senator Sparks Matsunaga of Hawaii, who himself has introduced seven academy-related bills in the House and two in the Senate in his long and active career. "Sparky," as he is affectionately known, chaired the commission of inquiry and is more than any other person responsible for the final report to Congress and the present bills before it. The widespread support for the bill is evidenced by the fact that there are more than one hundred cosponsors in the House and fifty-three in the Senate. Both parties are well represented among the sponsors.

What would a peace academy mean in terms of U.S. policy? Section 2a of the Senate bill, Declaration of Findings and Purposes, states, inter alia:

—A living institution embodying the heritage, ideals and concerns of the American people for peace would be a significant response to the deep public need for the Nation to develop fully a range of effective options in addition to armed capacity, that can leash international violence and manage international conflict;

—many potentially destructive conflicts among nations and peoples have been resolved constructively and with cost efficiency at the international, national, and community levels through proper use of such techniques as negotiation, conciliation, mediation, and arbitration;

—the peacemaking activities of Americans throughout government, private enterprise, and voluntary associations can be strengthened by a national institution devoted to international peace research, education and training, and information services;

—there is a need for Federal leadership to expand and support the existing international peace and conflict resolution efforts of the Nation and to develop new comprehensive peace education and training programs, basic and applied research projects, and programs providing peace information;

—the establishment of an academy is an appropriate investment by the people of this Nation to advance the history, science, art, and practice of international peace and the resolution of conflicts among nations without the use of violence.

Clearly, then, the context of the acceptance of this bill is a commitment to the development of nonmilitary problem-solving skills for the management of conflict on the part of the U.S. government. Here is what the academy would be authorized to do (Sec. 5b):

—establish a Center for International Peace and appoint to it for periods up to two years scholars and leaders in peace from the United States and abroad to pursue scholarly inquiry and other appropriate forms of communication on international peace and conflict resolution and, as appropriate, provide stipends, grants, fellowships, and other support to the leaders and scholars;

—establish such divisions, programs, schools, and offices as the Board deems appropriate to carry out this Act;

—enter into formal and informal relationships with other institutions, public and private, for purposes not inconsistent with this Act;

—conduct research and make studies, particularly of an interdisciplinary or of a multidisciplinary nature, into the cause of war and other international conflicts and the elements of peace among the nations and peoples of the world, including peace theories, methods, techniques, programs, and systems, and into the experience of the United States and other nations in resolving conflicts with justice and dignity and without violence as they pertain to the advancement of international peace and conflict resolution;

—develop programs to make international peace and conflict resolution research, education, and training more available and useful to persons in government, private enterprise, and voluntary associations, including the creation of handbooks and other practical materials;

—provide peace education and research programs at graduate and postgraduate levels that lead to degrees as well as to certificates and other forms of recognition;

—conduct training, symposium, and continuing education programs for practitioners, policymakers, policy implementers, and citizens and noncitizens directed to developing their skills in international peace and conflict resolution;

—develop for publication or other public communication and disseminate the products of the Academy;

—establish a clearinghouse and other means for disseminating information from the field of peace learning to the public and to government personnel.

Many questions can and should be raised about the extent to which such an academy could operate with the independence required to enable it to fulfill its purposes, rather than becoming a branch of the State Department. The bill makes of the academy an independent, nonprofit national institution with a fifteen-member board appointed by Congress and the President, supported by federal funds but also able to receive private grants. The academy "shall not be considered a department, agency or instrumentality of the Federal Government" (Sec. 9a) but its budget requests to the government are subject to review by the Office of Management and Budget (OMB).

The quality of the appointments to the first board will certainly determine to a significant extent the quality of the academy itself. A strong board can help create a strong and independent academy. While the government holds the power of the purse, both through congressional appropriation and through OMB review, the fact that the academy can also receive private funds gives it more independence than regular federal agencies have.

The Senate bill was referred to the Senate Committee on Labor and Human Resources, nine of whose members are cosponsors of the bill itself. Senate hearings were held in late April, House hearings in June. Individuals and organizations from around the country were invited to testify. There is now a strong national movement in support of the bill, coordinated by an organization called the National Peace Academy Campaign. Requests for information about the hearings, and for copies of the commission report, *To Establish the United States Academy of Peace* ($5/copy), can be directed to the campaign office at 110 Maryland Avenue N.E., Suite 409, Washington, DC 20002 or to your own senators and representatives.

If it is established, there can be no guarantee that the academy of peace would function in the ways its designers have intended, as a new type of peacemaking capability for the United States. New understandings of the meaning of national security and world security both in Congress and on the part of the general public are required if the academy is to be an authentic effort to lessen our dependence on armed force. The extreme danger that nuclear weaponry represents to the survival of nations and peoples may be creating an openness to these new understandings, but changes in national habits will take time. The Peace Academy could become either another tool for the manipulation of U.S. interests around the world, or a setting for new developments in human problem solving on a global scale. It is significant that the administrators of our existing military academies, particularly Annapolis, West Point, and the Air Force Academy, are interested in the peace-academy concept and see a new sister institution as offering something our country needs, something that is missing from our present federal education and training institutions dedicated to national needs. There are risks in establishing the academy, but perhaps even greater risks in not establishing it. The consensus among those who have been involved in developing ideas for the academy is to "give the National Peace Academy a chance!"

Testimony for the U.S. Senate by Elise Boulding on a U.S. National Peace Academy

It is the business of Congress to set policy priorities for the nation, based on its best understandings of the interests of the people of the United States. It is clearly the view of a very large number of Americans of all ages and walks of life that the maintenance of peace in the face of a potentially catastrophic nuclear arms race must be the top priority of our nation today.

Military force has traditionally been the backup system for any state when its international diplomatic and problem-solving skills failed in a situation of grave conflict of interest. Military force has been seen as the last resort, never the first. Now, in 1982, our nation ought to be in a better position to exercise diplomatic and problem-solving skills in the international community than ever before, because we have resources available that were never before available. We have an educated citizenry, and provision for continuing lifelong retraining as new skills are needed. We have life-enhancing technologies to meet all human needs, and the mechanisms for creating access to them. Most valuable of all, we have a significant accumulation of social knowledge about the world in all its economic, political, cultural, linguistic, and religious diversity and an unparalleled access to new knowledge even as it is being generated. We also have a tradition of fairness, of which we are justly proud, and almost legendary skills of bargaining and mediation.

All these resources and skills are being rendered useless because of a relatively recent fascination with military technology. It is understandable that our own technological capabilities should fascinate us. Tinkering is always fun, and our society loves new models of almost anything. We have been caught unawares by this fascination, to the point where many of the top graduates of our best engineering schools go directly into one particular type of technology: weapons design. Thus, few resources are left for the systematic organization of all our problem-solving knowledge for the purpose of keeping the peace between ourselves and those we view as our competitors.

As a result we have been relying for our security on a capital-intensive military defense system that has no strategy at its disposal except confrontation diplomacy and the threat of using a mutually destroying weapons complex. A labor-intensive security system, by contrast, would consist of conflict resolution and peace maintenance strategies utilizing vast numbers of mediation and problem-solving teams in crisis settings, focused on the multiplication, not the reduction, of action possibilities. The deployment of such teams would leave adversaries less hostile and more capable of meeting the needs of their own societies without having diminished the need-meeting capability of our own nation.

The most precious resource of the United States is its human beings, whether they be soldiers, the president of our country, members of Congress, miners, teachers, scientists, children, or parents. Since there is no military technology that can now or in the future secure the lives and safety of these human beings, we must move as speedily as possible to the development of a new peace-maintenance capability. This means the establishment of the National Peace Academy, and making it operational before accidental or intentional warfare breaks out.

Such an academy could begin at once, in a matter of weeks if we so desired, to train sizable groups of people in critical sectors in the armed services, in the diplomatic service, in relevant government departments, and in the private sector, to begin to utilize all the unused conflict-resolution knowledge and skill we have available in this country. The availability of scholars, teachers, and practitioners to help make the academy operational has been amply documented in the report of the Commission on Proposals to Establish a National Peace Academy.

We have striking examples in the twentieth century of nations that have made use of conflict-resolution skills in the face of nearby deployment of great military force. In Europe we can point to Sweden, an aggressive military power in the seventeenth century but today one of the world's leading peacemaking countries and home of that important world center, the Stockholm International Peace Research Institute. There is also its neighbor Finland, which has maintained a powerful independent mediating role between Eastern and Western Europe on the basis of conflict-resolution skill alone ever since the 1950s, in spite of grave territorial threats.

Two other important examples of the deliberate choice to develop diplomacy and problem-solving skills as an alternative means to national security are found respectively in Asia and Central America. Japan, whose Peace Constitution abjures the use of force in the settlement of disputes with other nations, has to date consistently preferred to emphasize mediation skills and keep its military force at a minimum, in spite of continual pressures from the United States to increase its arms levels. Costa Rica, witnessing the use of military force to deal with social turbulence in its neighbor-states, has reaffirmed its own commitment to maintaining security without a standing army by investing its resources in the world's first University of Peace. This university has just held its inaugural ceremonies in San Jose with the blessings and support of the United Nations General Assembly, and will train students from all countries in the skills of nonmilitary conflict resolution.

Mediation, conflict resolution, and the peaceful settlement of disputes are highly labor-intensive skills that exist in small pieces here and there in the United States, in different federal and private institutions, including to a degree the military academies and the schools of diplomacy. However, they exist in such fragmented form that the critical mass needed to give our nation new international peaceful settlement capabilities is totally lacking. Only a federal peace academy can draw together the strengths available to make them usable for national needs.

I have emphasized training because that is our primary need at the moment. However, research on long-run trends and emerging alternatives in the international system that will enable the United States to contribute leadership in developing more effective mechanisms of international cooperation in the face of persisting conflicts of interest is another important function the academy can play. Furthermore, as a member of the commission that reported to Congress on the feasibility of a national peace academy I am aware of the widespread interest among institutions of higher learning in developing campus units of such an academy for on-campus research and training. This would greatly multiply the effectiveness of a national academy and create new regional capabilities for conflict resolution. I am also aware of an equally widespread interest on the part of local communities in developing local conflict-resolution resources through the good offices of a national clearinghouse that might be operated by the National Peace Academy.

The people of this country see a connection between the use of mediation and peacemaking skills in their homes and communities, and in our nation and the world. Our citizenry is suffering because local as well as international violence is on the increase. The skills to reduce violence exist, but the initiation of peace processes in the midst of conflict is difficult and demanding work. This country needs a strong federal institution committed to the development of skilled peace practitioners if we are to have a viable alternative to the increasing use of force in our time to deal with major human problems. The resources and mechanisms for establishing the National Peace Academy are available to this Congress, and I urge that positive action be taken very soon.

Activist Educators

SAM TOTTEN
Teachers College, Columbia University

The threat of nuclear war hangs over humanity's collective head like the Sword of Damocles. It is general knowledge that the United States and the Soviet Union possess the awesome destructive power to annihilate life on this planet many times over. In light of this horrific fact it seems incumbent on everyone to accept responsibility for preventing what Robert Jay Lifton of Yale University Medical School has called the "final death." Certainly a primary (or perhaps preliminary) responsibility is that of educating oneself and one's fellow human beings about the threat posed by nuclear weapons along with the consequences of nuclear war.

Most of the educational activity concerned with the threat of nuclear war is being done by activists, outside of the school setting. (While some teachers certainly allude to nuclear issues, it is reported that formal and systematic instructional efforts are rare.[1]) These "activist educators" are an eclectic, articulate, well-informed, and committed group: scientists, physicians, ex-military personnel, grass-roots organizers, politicians, artists, parents, and high school and college students. They are educating in the broadest sense. Their "classroom" is each and every city and town across the nation. Their students comprise all human beings, regardless of age, race, religion, or class. Their modes of educating are as refreshingly eclectic as they themselves are: books, articles, films, speeches, billboards, advertisements, concerts, telephone hotlines, acts of civil disobedience, convocations, television appearances, cross-country walks, and court trials. Their aims aptly fit Lawrence Cremin's definition of education: "the deliberate, systematic and sustained effort to transmit, evoke, or acquire knowledge, skills, or sensibilities as well as any outcomes of the effort."[2]

Over the course of the past year and a half I have interviewed more than seventy antinuclear activists across the nation. My purpose was to gain an insight into both the activist's own motivations, aims, frustrations, victories, defeats, and hopes and the purpose and scope of his or her organization. The following article will thus focus on both the educational endeavors of individual activist educators and those activist organizations that are working

This article refers to the current issues of education for nuclear disarmament. There is a long tradition of peace education that goes back at least to the beginning of this century, if not earlier, and that encompasses a far wider range of war-peace-educational issues than the nuclear alone.—ED.

on nuclear weapons issues. Samples of the above-mentioned interviews along with significant historical facts about the activist organizations' educational activities will be integrated into the body of the article. As the reader will come to understand, both individual activists and activist organizations have well-wrought agendas for educating the public about the threat that nuclear weapons pose to humanity. Equally evident will be the high priority that education is given in regard to their overall work.

Ironically, the first individuals to seriously teach about the threat posed by nuclear weapons were those who developed the atomic bomb—the atomic scientists. *The Bulletin of the Atomic Scientists,* first published in 1945, "began as an emergency action, undertaken by scientists who saw urgent need for an immediate educational program."[3] A primary purpose of the journal, at that time, was to educate the public about nuclear energy and what its application to war would mean for humanity. Many of the atomic scientists "anticipated that the atom bomb would be only the first of many dangerous presents from Pandora's box of modern science. Consequently it was clear that the education of man to the realities of the scientific age would be a long sustained effort."[4] To this day many of the atomic scientists—and their journal—remain at the forefront of those educating about what it means to live in the nuclear age.

There are numerous scientific organizations—the Federation of American Scientists (FAS), the Council for a Livable World, the Union of Concerned Scientists (UCS), and others—that educate about the nuclear weapons race. The Federation of American Scientists has organized the Nuclear War Education Project, which works to "promote the development of study groups, course modules, and entire courses on nuclear war; to train scientists and others to give competent presentations on nuclear war issues at schools, churches and before citizen groups; to promote the development and distribution of teaching materials on nuclear war; and to facilitate cooperation among individuals and organizations concerned with nuclear war education."[5]

Philip Morrison, a founding member of FAS and the man who was the chief engineer of the team that assembled the bomb that was dropped on Nagasaki, told me: "After the war there was a lot of attention being paid to what was being called the atomic scientists. We had a lot of voice in the public and so we kept insisting on an atomic policy. I think our great slogan was something like 'There's no defense except peace.'"[6] Concerning his own and his fellow scientists' role in educating the public about the nuclear weapons issue, he said: "I feel a sense of obligation to be working on this issue. I was responsible for these things in part, and I should be responsible for the end of them. I always was of the opinion that scientists have that degree of responsibility, or at least they can accept that degree of responsibility, to try to make known what the circumstances are. Everybody should do what he can. What I do is write books and give talks."[7]

The Council for a Livable World uses both educational and political means in order to reach a broad contingency. While the organization was founded in 1962 by the eminent nuclear physicist Leo Szilard, it was not until 1980 that the Council for a Livable World Education Fund was organized. The fund educates Americans both about the consequences of nuclear war and about such issues as the nonproliferation of nuclear technology and nuclear arms control. The mission of the fund is "to make people think about the unthinkable. Then they'll start thinking about ways to prevent it."[8]

Educating about the "unthinkable" was the express reason the Union of Concerned Scientists organized the November 11, 1981, "University Convocation on the Threat of Nuclear War." One hundred and fifty colleges and universities participated in the convocation, one of the major educational activities in 1981 about nuclear war, by showing films, sponsoring speakers, and serving as forums for debate.

Certainly the current leader in the attempt to wake Americans up to the threat of nuclear war is the organization known as the Physicians for Social Responsibility (PSR). PSR is a nonprofit, educational organization working to understand the impact of nuclear weapons and war and nuclear technology on public health. A basic part of its program is to educate the public to recognize the medical consequences of such developments.

PSR's president, Helen Caldicott, is a dynamic woman who gave up her career as a pediatrician in order to devote most of her time to educating the public about the medical consequences of nuclear war. The author of *Nuclear Madness: What You Can Do!*,[9] Caldicott is an articulate and impassioned speaker who frequently appears on nationally televised talk shows, at demonstrations, colloquia, and religious gatherings. Always searching for new ways to reach the public, she has founded a political action committee, Women's Action for Nuclear Disarmament, whose single goal is ending the nuclear arms race. More recently, she also founded the Action for Nuclear Disarmament Education Fund, which is a nonprofit organization committed to public education on the nuclear weapons issue. "I see my role," she told me, "as an educator. If you inform a democracy it functions in a responsible fashion. Also, informing the public about these issues is preventive medicine."

Physicians for Social Responsibility is not the only medical group concerned with the threat of nuclear war. The International Physicians for the Prevention of Nuclear War, founded by several physicians at Harvard Medical School, includes among its members doctors from twelve countries including the Soviet Union, Sierra Leone, France, Japan, Israel, Great Britain, and West Germany. A key member of the organization is Eugene Chazov, the personal physician of Leonid Brezhnev.

Education is a prime concern of the international physicians group. Each member has contributed to the professional and popular literature on the potentially devastating effects of nuclear war. In the Soviet Union alone, dozens of articles have been published on the medical consequences of nuclear war, and Chazov has been on Soviet television for up to an hour and a half at a time addressing such issues. James Muller, an assistant professor of cardiology and also secretary and cofounder of the organization, explained to me why he helped found the group: "What does it mean to design a new treatment for heart attack if all the people are going to be killed in a nuclear war? I think that it has to be put in the perspective that *this is the major problem*!"

An organization that is equally active, and one whose work and words are listened to by many Washington politicos, is the Center for Defense Information. The center counts among its board members such prominent ex-military and government officials as Rear Admiral Gene LaRocque (Retired); Herbert Scoville, former deputy director, CIA; and Dr. Earl C. Ravenal, former director, Asian Division (Systems Analysis), office of the secretary of defense. The center publishes and distributes the *Nuclear War Prevention Kit*, which is an educational guidebook intended for use by citizens' groups and organizations across the country that are working to prevent nuclear war. LaRocque, the director of the center, is blunt about why he thinks it is imperative that people learn about the nuclear weapons race: "Many people think nuclear weapons will never be used. But as someone who has been directly involved in U.S. nuclear planning, I can state that my country has plans and forces for actually fighting nuclear war. Our military field manuals detail the use of nuclear weapons. Our troops, airmen, and navy men train and practice for nuclear war. Nuclear war is an integral part of American military planning and the U.S. is prepared to use nuclear weapons anywhere in the world, right now in many contingencies."

Many of the activists consider grass-roots organizing the most significant type of activity since it is at this level that people are educated about how the nuclear weapons race affects them and their local community. The range of educational activities is consciously broad and diverse in method: referenda and resolution campaigns, petition drives, teach-ins, vigils, library exhibits, letter-writing campaigns, and marches.

One of the most astounding educational efforts on the nuclear weapons front has centered around the concept of the "bilateral nuclear weapons freeze," which was the brainchild of Randall Forsberg, director of the Institute for Defense and Disarmament Studies. The freeze movement, already active in forty-three states with coordinated petition campaigns in twenty states, calls on both the United States and the Soviet Union to stop the nuclear weapons race by adopting a mutual halt on the testing, production, and development of nuclear weapons and of missiles and new aircraft designed to deliver nuclear weapons. Thus far, nuclear-freeze resolutions have been passed by 309 town meetings in New England, 37 city councils from New York to California, and one or both houses in 11 state legislatures. In Washington, D.C., a freeze proposal sponsored by Senators Mark Hatfield and

Edward Kennedy, as well as others, has garnered the support of 24 senators and 166 representatives. The supporters of the freeze call it an essential, verifiable first step toward lessening the risk of nuclear war and reducing the nuclear arsenals. In many areas across the United States the petition drives are part of a larger effort to place referenda on both local and state ballots. The purpose of this is twofold: It allows the freeze proponents to conduct a massive educational effort, and it provides the "average" citizen with a vehicle by which he can voice concern about the nuclear weapons race.

Speaking of the first freeze referenda in the country, Randy Kehler, now the director of the Nuclear Weapons Freeze Campaign, told me: "We had to educate the people and to accomplish that we had newspaper ads, quarter to full page ads, that appeared all over western Massachusetts. One ad emphasized the medical consequences of nuclear war and was signed by one hundred and fifty health care professionals in Berkshire County. Another was signed by close to one hundred human service providers from Hampshire and Franklin counties. Another pointed to the religious and ethical implications of the arms race and was signed by members of the Springfield Council of Churches. We even made television commercials and radio ads, and huge billboards. We spoke at local meetings, leafletted on street corners, in supermarkets, at factory gates."

What promises to be as effective and powerful an educational tool as the freeze movement is the incipient campaign that is calling into question the federal government's civil defense plans in the event of a nuclear war. The movement, prompted by the Cambridge (Massachusetts) City Council's rejection of the government's nuclear civil defense plans, is seen by its proponents as a major educational program. As Carla Johnston, a prime activist in the movement, recently explained to me: "One way of mobilizing people is around the issue of the absurdity of civil defense in the event of a nuclear war. Through such actions as rejecting the government's plans and holding city council meetings solely for the purpose of discussing the issue you are increasing an awareness about what the effects of nuclear weapons are on communities in this country. And the Cambridge City Council plans to assist that process by holding at least one conference with other communities in order to discuss these issues. Also, it has put out a booklet on the effects of nuclear war and the lack of effectiveness of civil defense in such a situation. And, other cities around the U.S.—San Francisco, Philadelphia, Sacramento, Eugene, Boulder, Greensboro, and others—are all working in various ways to educate their citizens about the absurdity of civil defense."

Several women's groups—Womens Pentagon Action, Womens International League for Peace and Freedom, Women Strike for Peace, and the aforementioned Women's Action for Nuclear Disarmament—have played a significant role in educating, on both the grass-roots and national levels, about the nuclear threat. Women Strike for Peace, one of the oldest and most influential of the groups, has a long history when it comes to educating about the nuclear weapons race. Back in 1961, it organized a march in which 100,000 women from sixty cities marched to demand an "end to the arms race—not the human race." In 1962, 2,000 women demonstrated at the White House and the Soviet Embassy in Washington, D.C., demanding a test-ban treaty, and in 1976 the group launched a billboard campaign in seven major cities with a message that read "The nuclear arms race can make this the last generation."

A founding member of Women Strike for Peace, Madeline Duckles, apprised me of what the early days of the antinuclear movement were like: "In 1963 or 64 we thought, 'What if the Hiroshima bomb struck Civic Center in San Francisco as point zero?' The periphery of that, we figured out, would come to thirteen miles. So we we decided to march those thirteen miles to demonstrate to the people what this would mean. We started out with about 50 people in downtown San Francisco, this was a Sunday, and by the time we finished we had over a thousand coming into Civic Center."

One of the more controversial forms of education used by grass-roots educators is civil disobedience. Mavis Belisle, a native Texan and a member of the Armadillo Coalition based in Dallas, Texas, advocates the use of civil disobedience as a powerful tool of both protest and education. "So many people," she said, "in our society seem so anethesized by t.v. It takes a dramatic action to break through at all into their consciousness, and I think civil disobedience does that more than any other kind of protest. It sometimes forces people to reevaluate their values and thoughts."

Another person who sees the efficacy of civil disobedience is Robert Aldridge. Aldridge, who worked for sixteen years as an engineer for Lockheed, where he designed weapons systems and eventually quit because he could not in good conscience continue to work on building nuclear weapons, has taken part in numerous acts of civil disobedience. At one time, though, even the thought of civil disobedience was anathema to him. In an indirect way, as he explains it, it was the Berrigan brothers who taught him the value of civil disobedience: "When I was working at Lockheed, the Berrigans' civil disobedient actions turned me off enough during their protest of the Vietnam War that I started to become aware of the issues. It turned me off intellectually, but it started an awareness. I didn't approve of those actions at the time. I thought it was disgusting and unpatriotic. That's why now, I think that symbolic actions and symbolic civil disobedience are so important because they reach the feeling nature of the person."

Just as significant as the acts of civil disobedience are the pursuant trials. These trials are educational in the sense that the defendants often attempt to bring in expert witnesses—Robert Jay Lifton, Richard Falk, Robert Aldridge—expressly to address the crucial issues of the nuclear weapons race. Coverage of these trials by the media brings their messages to the attention of millions of readers and viewers across the nation.

A case in point was the trial of Sister Anne Montgomery, a member of Ploughshare Eight. Along with Dan and Phil Berrigan and others,

Montgomery was prosecuted for smashing the component of a nuclear weapon with a hammer. Speaking of her trial she remarked: "One purpose of the trial was to raise the consciousness of the people by educating them about the arms race. And, we got hundreds of letters from people from all over the country."

Coalitions made up of what were once seen to be disparate antinuclear groups are gaining in power and becoming highly effective educators. During the week of April 18–25, 1982, just such a coalition held a week of locally based, nonpartisan lectures and events throughout the country. Organized by Ground Zero, a Washington, D.C., based group, these activities were designed to educate the American people about the issue of nuclear war.

Ground Zero, consciously nonpartisan and nonpolitical, emphatically states that it does not take a position on nuclear weapons, but strongly promotes education on nuclear war. To help educators accomplish that goal, Ground Zero has developed a curriculum on nuclear war for high schools and colleges. Endorsed by the National Education Association, the curriculum package includes ten lesson plans covering topics ranging from the development of the atomic bomb to the consequences of nuclear war.

SANE (A Citizens' Organization for a Sane World), an organization that has been working for twenty-five years to bring a halt to the nuclear weapons race, believes that one cannot change public policy without also educating the public. As part of their educational program they have produced a slide show, "The Race Nobody Wins," which has been sold to over 2,000 schools and colleges. They also broadcast a weekly radio show entitled "Consider the Alternatives" through a network of over 500 radio stations nationwide.

The SANE Education Fund, which works under the auspices of SANE, produced an outstanding radio series entitled "Shadows of the Nuclear Age." The thirteen documentaries, which range in subject matter from "Hiroshima: The Decision to Use the Bomb" to "Missile Crisis" to "Nuclear Anxiety: Coping with the Eve of Destruction," were broadcast (beginning October 1, 1981) to a weekly listening audience of over five million people on nearly 700 commercial and noncommercial radio stations nationwide as well as in Guam, Puerto Rico, the Virgin Islands, Canada, and Australia.

As the nuclear weapons issue becomes more heated, more and more religious leaders are speaking out against the weapons race. (It should be noted that the traditional "peace" churches—Quakers, Mennonites, Church of the Brethren—have been speaking out against and educating about these issues since the inception of the atomic age.) Religious leaders from many faiths are referring to the weapons race as the major moral issue of modern times. Just as the support for the bilateral nuclear freeze has cut across the political spectrum, religious activity on the nuclear weapons issue cuts across faiths.

Some of the most outspoken religious leaders have included the Roman Catholic bishops. Of the 368 bishops in the United States, some 70 have gone on record as opposing the nuclear weapons race. Educating in the broadest sense—by means of speeches, position papers, sermons, and, though infrequently, civil disobedience—they have urged their parishioners to thoroughly question and examine a Christian's moral responsibility in the nuclear age. One of the most vocal bishops, Archbishop Raymond Hunthausen of Seattle, Washington, is refusing to pay 50 percent of his taxes as a protest against the weapons race, and he has urged his fellow Christians to consider doing likewise. Such actions and statements are educating tens of thousands of Catholics as well as others across the nation.

The Sojourners, an evangelical group, has published a booklet entitled *A Matter of Faith: A Study Guide for Churches on the Nuclear Arms Race.* The 108-page handbook is devised to assist churches in wrestling with the theological, historical, and contemporary ramifications of the nuclear weapons race. Likewise, the Interfaith Center to Reverse the Arms Race, working out of the Judeo-Christian tradition, has published and is disseminating a booklet entitled *The Clergy Resource Guide.* It offers a selection of materials available for use in congregational settings: scripture references, sample sermons, statements by leading figures in the religious community, and denominational statements.

Educational activities in the churches are taking a variety of forms. In New York City, the Riverside Church has an exemplary disarmament program. It publishes a monthly newsletter, *Disarming Notes;* sponsors an annual disarmament conference that draws such eminent individuals as Helen Caldicott, Studs Terkel, Bishop Leroy Matthiesen, and Riverside's own William Sloane Coffin, Jr.; and has developed a disarmament syllabus that is being used in churches and synagogues across the nation.

"I think that the nuclear weapons issues," Reverend Mr. Coffin recently told me, "is the meat and potatoes issue of the day, and it is on the plate of every Christian because we believe that God created the world and Christ redeemed the world and wanted the world to go on, and now human beings are about to put an end to God's creation. Americans need to be educated to see the dangers of leaving it up to computers to either fire or not fire nuclear weapons, and the Church can do this in its own way."

Sharing a commitment to peacemaking and seeing the bilateral nuclear weapons freeze as a feasible first step toward disarmament, the representatives of five religious groups—the Sojourners, New Call to Peacemaking, Pax Christi USA, Fellowship of Reconciliation, and World Peacemakers—began meeting in November 1980 to discuss how they could stimulate concern in U.S. churches and synagogues about the nuclear weapons race issue, particularly on the local level. The culmination of their work was the creation of "The New Abolitionist Covenant." The covenant states that those who enter into it "will become thoroughly and deeply informed about the dangers of the arms race and the steps toward peace," and "will become aware of the teaching of our religious traditions on the matter of nuclear warfare. . . . Our ignorance or passivity must be transformed into awareness and responsibility."

A unique educational endeavor is the World Peace March, which began in October 1981 and was completed in June 1982. Starting from various points around the globe, the march culminated in a major rally in New York City on June 12, coinciding with the United Nation's Second Special Session on Disarmament. Sister Clare Carter, a Buddhist nun from Boston who was the national coordinator of the march, explained the educational nature of the march to me: "Each walk had with them a portable panel of photographs of Hiroshima and Nagasaki which were used in churches, libraries, and shopping centers. They also each had a very moving slideshow of the horrors of nuclear war. The idea was to reach people in their own communities."[10]

Equally unique is the work of Barbara Reynolds, a Quaker, who is virtually a one-woman educational team. Made an honorary citizen of Hiroshima for her dedication to educating people about the horrors of the atomic destruction of Hiroshima and Nagasaki, Reynolds has been working nonstop on the issue of nuclear weapons for over twenty-five years. In the 1950s she and her family sailed into the atomic testing zone in the Pacific to lodge a protest against the tests. Reynolds also created and organized the Hiroshima/Nagasaki Memorial Collection, which is housed in the Wilmington College Peace Resource Center at Wilmington College in Ohio. Over the years she has accompanied *hibakusha* (survivors of the atomic blasts at Hiroshima and Nagasaki) around the globe in an effort to teach people about the horrors of nuclear weapons. Her latest effort in this vein was her trip across the United States with a *hibakusha* just prior to the U.N. Special Session on Disarmament. She explained to me why the *hibakusha* wish to be heard: "There's a certain syndrome that's true of all *hibakusha*. It's a deep sense of loss of trust and faith in other humans, and the goodness, I suppose, of humanity. And yet, when they speak out about their experience, it's not out of anger or bitterness or hate. They're speaking out of a deep concern for everybody. They are also speaking out of desperation because they feel that if we won't listen to them then how are we ever going to hear . . . hear about their experiences when they're dead."

Another major religious educational effort is the Nuclear Weapons Facilities Task Force, which is a network of groups, sponsored by the Fellowship of Reconciliation and the American Friends Service Committee (Quakers), that organizes locally to convert nuclear weapons facilities to socially useful production. The Colorado group, the Rocky Flats Nuclear Weapons Facilities Project, sees itself as following Gandhi's idea of *satyagraha*. *Satyagraha,* or "peaceforce," was a system of nonviolent civil disobedience Gandhi defined as "a process of educating all the elements of society and which in the end makes itself an irresistible force for change."

Educators who are activists are also increasingly becoming involved in the anti-nuclear weapons movement, and two of the most dynamic groups are the Educators for Social Responsibility (ESR), and Student/Teacher Organization to Prevent (STOP) Nuclear War. Each has a national network of locally based groups.

Formed at the Waging Peace Conference at Harvard University on May 2, 1981, Educators for Social Responsibility states that its aim is to assist in ensuring a safe future for themselves and their students by reducing the threat of nuclear war and by promoting peace. ESR networks with the Council for a Nuclear Weapons Freeze, sponsors conferences, lobbies school committees to support education for peace, and develops curricula on the nuclear weapons issue. Roberta Snow, the founder of ESR, explained to me why she founded the group: "For me, I can't understand having eighteen year olds leave the high school without having them understand what the issues are around the nuclear arms race. It is *the most pressing* issue that faces us today, and it is so irresponsible to have kids leave school and not be prepared for the biggest conflict that they're going to face and that's: 'What am I going to do about my survival in the future?' "

Reverend Jim Antal, chaplain at the Northfield-Mt. Hermon School in Northfield, Massachusetts, organized STOP Nuclear War in 1981. It has chapters in public and private schools as well as in churches and synagogues. Antal told me that the main point of STOP is "to take the guidance that the teachers can provide with the energy, idealism, enthusiasm, joie de vivre that kids have, and combine that in a way that can be an ongoing witness against nuclear weapons."

Literally scores of anti-nuclear weapons organizations have been spawned during the past year and a half. The reasons for this are probably many: the huge rallies against nuclear weapons that began in Europe, the bellicose comments by U.S. officials about the possibility of fighting and surviving a "limited nuclear war," as well as the interest created by the Bilateral Nuclear Freeze Campaign and the U.N. Second Special Session on Disarmament. The very names of the various organizations—Lawyers for Nuclear Arms Control, Business Alert to Nuclear War, Communicators for Nuclear Disarmament, Artists for Disarmament, Dancers for Disarmament, Musicians for Social Responsibility, The New Manhattan Project, Blacks Against Nukes, Children's Campaign for Nuclear Disarmament, Parents and Friends for Children's Survival, The Nurse's Alliance for the Prevention of Nuclear War, United Campuses to Prevent Nuclear War—attest to the diverse constituency working on the nuclear weapons issue. Each group is not only working on the issue, but educating about it in its own unique way.

While the various groups of activist educators may have a difference of opinion as to the best tactics and policies to use in order to accomplish their goals, they all share a deep and abiding concern about the threat of nuclear war. Concomitantly, while the effectiveness of the various organizations' educational work is yet to be determined, there is no doubt that for these activist educators the words that Einstein spoke over three decades ago were an admonition to heed. "When we released the energy from the atom everything changed except our way of thinking. Because of that we drift towards unparalleled disaster. We shall require a substantially new manner of thinking if mankind is to survive."

Notes

1 Stephanie DeAbreu, "Mounting Concern over Nuclear War Begins to Involve Nation's Schools," *Education Week,* April 7, 1982, p. 1.

2 Lawrence A. Cremin, *Public Education* (New York: Basic Books, 1976), p. 27.

3 Morton Grodzins and Eugene Rabinowitch, eds., *The Atomic Age* (New York: Simon & Schuster, 1965), p. v.

4 Ibid.

5 Letter to the author from the Federation of American Scientists Nuclear War Education Project.

6 Martha Wescoat Totten and Sam Totten, *Atomic Activists: Their Stories* (forthcoming).

7 Ibid.

8 Council for a Livable World, "Program for Ending the Nuclear Arms Race (Boston: Council for a Livable World, January 1982), p. 3.

9 Helen Caldicott, *Nuclear Madness: What You Can Do!* (New York: Bantam Books, 1980). Quotations from activists in the following paragraph are taken from Totten and Totten, *Atomic Activists.*

10 Fellowship of Reconciliation, "New Abolitionist Convenant," 1980.

Buberian Learning Groups: The Quest for Responsibility in Education for Peace

HAIM GORDON, JAN DEMAREST
Ben-Gurion Univesity of the Negev, Beersheva, Israel

Hillel said, Be of the disciples of Aharon; loving peace and pursuing peace; loving mankind and bringing them nigh to the Torah.

—Sayings of the Jewish Fathers, I, 13

INTRODUCTION

Cairo, Spring 1981. Israeli Jews and Arabs, students and staff of the Education for Peace project,[1] are meeting with Egyptian professors and students, members of the Egyptian Scientific Society for Group Training. During the three-hour encounter they divide into three subgroups of twenty participants, each subgroup containing an approximately equal number of Israeli Jews, Israeli Arabs, and Egyptians. Tensions are high. The four wars in three decades, the hatred and the dread, the stereotypes of the former enemy, the anguish, the rage, the fear, the suffering—all these are poignantly revived. The scarlet plush ball room of the Continental Hotel has become an existential meeting ground where participants confront their own harsh reality. Will the participants be able to benefit from such a confrontation? Or will this encounter merely be an instance of releasing explosive feelings, an exercise in futility?

These questions point to a basic problem I did not foresee in 1979 when I established the Buberian Learning Groups as the main thrust of the Education for Peace project. I then believed that dialogue could diminish existential mistrust between Jews and Arabs. The first two years of our endeavors overwhelmingly confirmed this belief. But only at the end of the first year did we learn that the diminishing of existential mistrust need not lead to active working for peace, especially in a war-clouded area such as the Mideast. Perhaps my lack of foresight reflected the fact that, at the outset, achieving Buberian dialogue between Jews and Arabs seemed almost impossible; in the past half century no such ambitious educational program has been initiated, let alone realized. Even Buber, who laid down guidelines for such dialogue, did virtually nothing to forward the possibility of its realization.[2] Thus when we were faced with success—with Jews and Arabs who could relate dialogically to each other—we suddenly encountered problems that transcended Buber's vision. The most immediate of these problems seemed to be: How should we educate persons to translate the pain discovered and expressed in dialogue into an active responsibility for furthering peace?

PART I: DIFFICULTIES

Surely We created man of the best stature
Then We reduced him to the lowest of the low,
Save those who believe and do good works, and theirs is a reward unfailing.

—The Koran, Surah XCV, 4–7

PERSONAL DIFFICULTIES: THE RESPONSE TO PAIN

In her poem "Five Songs to Pain," Nazak al Mala'ika, an Iraqi poet, writes:

We love you, O Pain,
From where does Pain come to us,
From where does he come?
He has been the brother of our vision from time immemorial
And the guide of our rhymes.[3]

Such a response to pain has been typical of the Arab peoples for millennia. It has also been typical of the Jewish people. In the Mideast pain has been the brother of vision from time immemorial. The outcry of the Biblical Psalms, the admonitions and the dreams of the Hebrew prophets, the language of the Koran, and Arabic poetry that constantly surges up out of a stifling reality—all these bear witness to the brotherhood of pain and vision. But there is also a noncreative dimension to such a brotherhood; often pain coupled with vision does not lead to *doing*, to changing the existential situation in which one finds oneself.

As Martin Buber indicated, genuine dialogue can be the first step toward a painful changing of one's existence in accordance with a vision. Dialogue is a supportive encounter in which a person may suddenly recognize some of the distortions of his mode of existence; such a recognition is usually painful, but often encouraging, because one may perceive, albeit vaguely, how to attempt to unravel these distortions and to live straightforwardly. Yet, following this first step, a person must be willing to take additional steps in which the pain emerges and is no longer hidden behind self-deceit or bad faith. Often the educator in a Buberian Learning Group will point out such bad faith and will encourage the participant to allow the pain and the distortion to emerge; then the participant can be guided to change his mode of being and to courageously challenge encompassing reality. At this point the educator and his student are going beyond genuine dialogue; they are moving into history.

The two personal responses to pain that we have found most difficult to surmount are lack of courage and lack of readiness. There seems to be no way of evading the fact that in order to change one's mode of existence a person must gather his powers and courageously leap into a new manner of relating to himself and to the world. The giving of oneself in dialogue can be the beginning of such a leap, but since the dialogue encounter is supportive and enhancing, and at times even exhilarating, it does not ensure that a person will act courageously in the I-It world. Thus some Jewish participants who have related dialogically to Arabs still hesitate to openly acknowledge these relationships in an all-Jewish social gathering. The same is true of Arab participants.

We know of no sure way of educating for courage, yet two approaches have proved helpful: We will show a person what would be the courageous response in a situation he describes and will demand that he act accordingly in similar situations. Through dialogue we have also helped many a person to realize that, like Gulliver arriving in Lilliput, he will often feel tied down by midget threads whose joint powers do not allow him to respond courageously. But, unlike Gulliver's bonds, it is a person's own freedom that empowers these threads. Thus, when a person says "I can't do that," he often means, "I do not want to sever some of the threads that bind me to my present situation."

For instance, quite a few Israeli Arabs complain that they are second-class citizens in Israel; they demand that the Jews in the project work to change this situation. We point out that although many of the demands are just, the Arab community must also be a strong driving force working for such a change; the Arabs themselves must initiate appropriate action. But once this point is accepted we have reached a major impasse. Arab participants suddenly feel that many minute threads bind them to their present existential situation rendering them inept. For example, Arab political activity in Israel is roughly divided between radical anti-Zionist elements (proterrorists, communists, etc.) and Arab "Uncle Toms" who serve Israeli political parties in return for economic or political favors. Within such a polarized situation an Arab participant finds that working peacefully for change is a threatening undertaking, especially since he is bound by social norms that reject any initiative not approved by the community elders. No wonder that many Arab participants feel frustrated!

Lack of readiness is difficult to overcome because the person often does not recognize his lack. Elsewhere I have indicated that lack of readiness is personified in Hamlet's inability, during most of the play, to make an existential decision that will help him find a way out of his sad situation.[4] In our Buberian Learning Groups, lack of readiness often takes the form of wishful thinking. Some Jews would like the Palestinian issue to disappear, without our needing to make a decision concerning these three million people and without our having to live with the outcome of that decision. And some Arabs would like Zionism to evaporate. In our attempts to counter lack of readiness we have adopted a two-dimensional approach. On the existential level we have begun to develop what we call the Rawls Workshop, which is an educational encounter based on the insights formulated by John Rawls in his book *A Theory of Justice.* On the level of knowledge we have acquainted participants with their own culture and history and with the culture and the history of the opposing national movement.

In the Rawls Workshop we ask participants to assume that they are in what Rawls termed the original position, behind a veil of ignorance:

> No one knows his place in society, his class position or social status; nor does he know his fortune in the distribution of natural assets and abilities, his intelligence and strength and the like. Nor, again, does anyone know his conception of the good, the particulars of his rational plan of life, or even the special features of his psychology such as his aversion to risk or liability to optimism or pessimism. More than this, I assume that the parties do not know the particular circumstances of their own society. They do not know its economic or political situation, or the level of civilization and culture it has been able to achieve. The persons in the original position have no information as to which generation they belong [to].[5]

We also ask participants to assume that they do not know if they are Arabs or Jews.

Behind the veil of ignorance a group of six Arabs and Jews is confronted with specific problems of the area, that is, the legitimacy of Zionist claims to the land of Israel, the authenticity of the Palestinian national movement, the justification of terrorist acts and of retribution. They are asked to find just principles (general and procedural) by which one could solve these problems. (During the discussion they are reminded again and again *not* to seek for a solution to the problem, but to concentrate on finding just principles.) Needless to say, such a discussion can be initiated only after participants relate dialogically to each other. We shall discuss the potentials of the Rawls Workshop in a forthcoming paper; at present we can point out that after three to four hours of painful discussion many participants see the possibility of jointly addressing the perturbing political and social exigencies that influence our being. And often a readiness to seek ways of mutual doing emerges.

Knowledge may bring about readiness. It may indicate new paths out of what seemed to be a dead end. Also, when a person sees the difficulties he must address and sees approaches to surmounting those difficulties, readiness may arise. Thus when an Arab understands that a fatalistic approach to life permeates his society, he may be aroused to counter this fatalism. Or when a Jew realizes that his fear of peace may be exaggerated—such a fear is often a gut response to the horrors of recent Jewish history—and that such an exaggeration may close possibilities of positive social action, he may find himself ready to counter this trend. Hence, the learning history and discussing existentialist themes in Jewish and Arab life and literature help arouse readiness.

To recapitulate: We believe that in order to work responsibly for peace in our area a person must undergo a painful educational process that is based on dialogue and in which he changes his passive mode of being. Many persons back away from such a process. They are unwilling to undergo pain, to take the leap; they lack courage, readiness. We have initiated some educational approaches that may encourage them to take the leap, but these approaches still need to be developed. Yet we have succeeded in helping many a person alter a mode of being in which

> Pain has no depth
> Because it is like oil in the surface of boredom.[6]

SOCIAL MORES AND RESPONSIBILITY

T. E. Lawrence opens *Seven Pillars of Wisdom* with a passage that is still true of much that occurs in the Mideast:

> As time went by our need to fight for the ideal increased to an unquestioning possession, riding spur and rein over our doubts. Willy-nilly it became a faith. We have sold ourselves into its slavery, manacled ourselves together in its chain gang, bowed ourselves to serve its holiness with all our good and ill content. The mentality of ordinary human slaves is terrible—they have lost the world—and we had surrendered, not body alone, but soul to the overmastering greed of victory. By our own act we were drained of morality, of volition, of responsibility, like dead leaves in the wind.[7]

Many groups in Jewish and Arab society have sold themselves into the slavery of the ideal for which they fight. A person who lives in such a milieu, even if he is not a member of such a group, often feels drained of morality, of volition, of responsibility. Frequently he succumbs to apathy, which is deepened by fatalistic trends in Arab society and by isolationist tendencies in Jewish society.

Participation in a Buberian Learning Group often helps a person to overcome such an apathy or such an enslavement to an ideal. It is a slow process, yet our experience has repeatedly affirmed Buber's basic vision that a discussion of perturbing problems in the spirit of dialogue is a revelation of one's freedom. Moreover, engaging in dialogue has at times led to friendships beyond one's group. But we have not yet found ways by which the dialogical experience may significantly diminish the power of deeply entrenched social mores. The fatalism that permeates Arab society is a case in point.

Contemporary Egyptian literature, which dominates the Arab literary scene, poignantly describes Arab fatalism. The novels of Naguib Mahfouz[8] portray the stagnation of Egyptian society; storytellers like Yusuf Idris,[9] Tewfik Al Hakim,[10] and Sonallah Ibrihim[11] convey the superficiality and lack of human sensitivity that often accompany a fatalistic approach to life. Still, one may ask: What characterizes Arab fatalism, as described by these writers, and as we have encountered it in our educational endeavors? We would formulate its main characteristic thus: an unwillingness to bring up and to cope with painful existential questions. Or, as Socrates would have argued: Arab society lacks philosophers who dare to educate!

Such a fatalism underlies the demand voiced by Arab participants that the Jew should identify with the Arab's passive suffering without prompting the Arab to face the questions the suffering brings up. In short, they would like the Jews to help them bask in social impotence. Such an attitude is especially notorious in relation to a volatile problem that seemingly has nothing to do with education for peace—the status of the Arab woman. Many young Arabs denounce the social mores that deny freedom to the Arab woman; they reject arranged marriages and decry the lack of friendships between the sexes; they explain in detail how difficult it is to build a meaningful relationship with a spouse whom they cannot meet in private before the eve of the marriage. And then, almost in the same breath, they explain that they have no choice but to go along with these customs.

Our main approach to diminishing Arab fatalism has been to bring Arab participants to see the futility of accepting passive suffering. We then prompt them to face painful existential questions concerning their society, such as the status of the Arab woman or the authenticity of Palestinian nationalism. We stress that these questions demand responses in one's way of life and not merely verbal exchanges. In a similar manner we counter Jewish isolationist tendencies, which work against developing peaceful relations with Arabs, that is, the Masadah Complex.[12] We stress that a Jew can free himself from this complex only by actually trusting Arabs in day-to-day encounters. But in these endeavors we are still in an exploratory stage. We can point out a general direction but we cannot indicate well-trodden paths that traverse this rough terrain.

DIFFICULTIES PERTAINING TO THE STRUCTURE OF ISRAELI SOCIETY

Israel is a Jewish state not only in that five-sixths of the population is Jewish, but also in its power structure. The Israeli defense force is predominantly Jewish; the economy is in Jewish hands; the great majority of the legislators are Jewish; there is only a handful of Arab judges and no Arab judge has served on the supreme court; most executive power is in Jewish hands. Hence assuming social responsibility frequently means working with a Jewish establishment.

I should perhaps make it clear that as initiator of the Education for Peace project I firmly believe that Israel should be a Jewish state, and not a Palestinian or secular state where Jews and Arabs live together. Here I need not elaborate the sources of this belief, but it is important to state that almost every Jew in Israel (and around the world) believes that Israel should be a Jewish state, with a Jewish majority and with a definite linkage to the Jewish heritage. In other words, like most of my fellow Jews, I accept the sociopolitical structure of Israel as a Jewish state in which Arab citizens will continue to be a minority whose national aspirations will not be realized.

All this brings up some genuine problems. Arab participants question the authenticity of dialogue if the Jews rule out the Arab wish to realize their national aspirations within Israel. "Furthermore," they argue, "why should we attempt to assume responsibility within a society that relegates us to minority status? And you, Haim, you attack our fatalism and then support a sociopolitical structure that forces us to succumb to our fate!"

Jewish participants see that their own national fulfillment curtails the freedom of Arabs, but they also recognize the dangers facing Israel. No few Arabs in the Mideast, including political leaders such as Qaddafi and Arafat, would gladly annihilate the Jewish state. Hence Israel needs to be wary of its Arab minority, whose members could support these leaders. Moreover, Arab terrorist attacks within Israel have often been supported, overtly or covertly, by indigenous Arabs. Thus, although security measures are often exaggerated, such as when an Arab electrical engineer cannot find employment because of "security reasons," the problems of Israel's security cannot be ignored.

Granting that there are grave injustices in the sociopolitical structure in Israel, we point out that declining to assume responsibility for change deepens a person's impotence. Furthermore, as the past half century has shown, the renunciation of responsibility for peace in favor of violence or fatalism has been personally destructive and has often led to profound suffering. We demand that each participant recognize this sad situation and begin to work painstakingly for peace. He has already learned that Buberian dialogue can strengthen him in his quest for responsibility.

We recognize that our demands must be specific and explicit. Yet, we hold that persons working together for peace can disagree on political issues. The project has no political affiliation, but radicals on both extremes of the Israeli political spectrum shy away from us. Disagreement among participants is accepted as a fact of living together, which need not counter trust. We also recognize that Jews must shoulder a greater part of the responsibility to change injustices in Israel; they are members of the majority and will be much more effective. We are currently learning the ways and means of working responsibly for peace in Israel, in the occupied territories, and in Egypt. We have also begun to outline a theoretical framework for such work. Many of the thoughts and insights developed by Jean Paul Sartre in his *Critique of*

Dialectical Reason will serve as the basis of such a framework. Our conclusions concerning the relevance of Sartre's thought will be presented in a separate essay.

INTERLUDE: THE STAFF

The strength of the Education for Peace project stems from the constitution and the commitment of the staff. The number of Arabs on the staff has grown significantly. During the first year we had one Arab staff member, this past year (1980–81) we had four. This year the staff will include at least five Arabs; each Buberian Learning Group will be led by a Jew and an Arab working together as co-leaders. At first Arabs frequently expressed themselves as an interest group; today they often take opposing stands on issues, arguing vehemently in Arabic and then translating to us their respective positions.

The staff has also matured in its way of life. Our meetings throb with a spirit of dialogue and a vitality that amaze outsiders, but that we no longer feel because "we're busy making other plans." We have begun to understand that education for peace is not and cannot be a partial commitment; rather, dialogue, self-education, and responsibility must characterize one's whole life. In short, education for peace in the spirit of dialogue means a constant renewal. One cannot rest with yesterday's achievements. As in love or creativity, one must be prepared each day to start all over again.

PART II: AN OVERVIEW OF THE PAST YEAR

No limits are set to the ascent of man, and to each and everyone the highest stands open. Here it is only your personal choice that decides.

—Martin Buber, *Ten Rungs: Hasidic Sayings*

FACTS AND FIGURES

Our difficulties in educating participants to assume responsibility in no way diminish the achievements of the past year; rather, the need to cope with these difficulties becomes all the more evident once one recognizes our success in broadening and deepening the dialogical approach to education for peace. It should be kept in mind that in presenting our activities in terms of facts, figures, and analyses we are projecting a thriving multidimensional educational process onto a two-dimensional research screen.

Eighty-seven persons applied for admission to our 1980/1981 beginner groups. Twenty-five Jews and the twenty-seven Arabs were accepted; fifteen

Jews and twenty Arabs were rejected. Our manner of selection was similar to that outlined previously,[13] except that it was formalized by using a semistructured questionnaire. The persons admitted were divided into three groups: a group of ten Jewish and ten Arab students, a similar group of teachers, and a group of five Jews and seven Arabs that will not be discussed for reasons of security. Seven out of the twenty-seven Arabs accepted were women; fourteen out of the twenty-five Jews accepted were women.

During the year two Jews and eleven Arabs left the beginner groups—eight dropped out and five could not fulfill the academic requirements. This is the second year that there is a higher dropout rate among Arabs, which we believe is due to two reasons: Arab social mores do not encourage openness, sincerity, straightforwardness, and self-education, and Arab participants find it difficult to trust a Jewish group leader who demands that they alter their way of life.

Five Arab and eight Jewish participants from the 1979/1980 beginner groups enrolled in the 1980/1981 year's advanced group. Two Jews and one Arab dropped out during the year. The eleven staff members also met as a group and studied existentialist topics related to peace. Thus, at the beginning of the year the project encompassed seventy-six persons in five Buberian Learning Groups (three beginner groups, one advanced, one staff). At the end of the year these five groups included sixty participants. Thirty-three out of the thirty-nine beginners who completed the year enrolled in the following year's advanced group; two decided to drop out and four moved out of the Beersheva area. The ten graduates of the advanced group wanted to continue to be partially involved in the project. Thus, even from the point of view of numbers success confronts us.

THE EDUCATIONAL PROCESS

In the beginner groups we followed the educational process outlined previously.[14] We succeeded in intensifying and enhancing some of the learning experiences, while other experiences were rather lax, that is, the meeting of dyads was not regular, and there were too few personal meetings between participants and group leaders. One important learning experience, added this year, was a weekly lecture on a topic that can help participants understand the existential situation in which we find ourselves. Relevant aspects of Jewish history, Arab history, Islam, Judaism, and so forth, were brought up and discussed by scholars in the field. The lectures were well attended.

The advanced group, which we intended should become a group that assumes responsibility for peace, did not achieve that goal. Our expectations for that group were probably unrealistic, especially since we have not yet developed appropriate methods to teach persons to assume responsibility for peace; but we also think that quite a few members of that group lacked courage and strength of character. It is beyond the scope of this paper to present a detailed overview of our educational endeavors during 1981; instead we will describe two educational experiences that indicate our direction of development.

The Trip to Egypt

This year's eight-day trip to Egypt was not only a testing experience through which we examined the genuineness of dialogue between Jewish and Arab participants; it was also a structured existential encounter with the Egyptian Other and with the otherness of Egypt. Participants worked in Jewish-Arab quartets, each of which received a portfolio of existential exercises and related reading material. Some exercises focused on perceiving the Egyptian Other, through dialogue and through examining his relations to his natural surroundings, to history, to religion, and to the future. In other exercises participants related to Egyptian history and present social norms. The final exercise focused on perceiving the Other in one's quartet.

For instance, the exercise dedicated to Islam commenced at the Islamic museum where participants were asked to attempt to relate dialogically to four pieces of art that appealed to them. They were then required to visit three mosques and to perceive how the architecture encourages one to relate to transcendence. They were also told to discuss religion with Egyptians whom they met; and finally they were required to relate their impressions to a story by Naguib Mahfouz that describes a religious encounter of an old bedridden woman.[15] Quite a few participants, among them Moslems, admitted that the exercise revealed aspects of Islam that they had previously overlooked, that is, its abstractness rooted in the concrete, and the equality of the worshiper before Allah and his ability to turn to Allah from every place in the mosque, or even outside it. Some participants felt that as a result of such abstractness or such equality a person may lose his ability to be a Thou—he may feel dwarfed among the many kneeling worshipers in the large mosque, much as the ancient Egyptian probably felt dwarfed in the ultra-grandeur of the Pharonic temples. In contrast, Mahfouz' story shows that in Islam (as in other religions), genuine dialogue is essential for an authentic belief in Allah, and is a source of courage for our everyday doings.

Our most significant existential encounters were two meetings with professors and students of the Egyptian Scientific Society for Group Training. The meetings, which were the first structured attempts of Egyptians and Israelis to reach genuine dialogue, deserve an in-depth analysis, which is in process. Here we will only present a general overview.

In the first meeting I tried to initiate an encounter based on my understanding of Buberian dialogue as a direct sharing of one's being and one's existential situation, and not a mere outpouring of feelings. A person can learn to relate dialogically by examining with other persons how an encounter in literature or a philosophical idea reflects his own existence. At the meeting I told a story and asked each participant to examine with his group how the story reflects his personal and national aspirations. The second meeting, which was led by our Egyptian colleagues, was in the format of group dynamics. We all agreed that the difference between the meetings was close to nil, since many participants, and especially the Egyptians, felt that without allowing them to express their feelings there is no point in attempting to reach dialogue. Thus in both meetings pent-up feelings were let loose and the atmosphere, which we described in the introduction, was often far from dialogical.

After the meetings we understood that we had not anticipated many of the difficulties that emerged. We Israelis did not appreciate that for an Egyptian to participate in such an encounter can be an act of daring, in terms of one's personal career and one's relations with the authorities. We did not foresee the need of Egyptians to release hostile feelings before they could enter into dialogue. We did not apprehend the complexity of the existential guilt Israeli Arabs and Egyptians have incurred toward each other, and that such guilt may be more difficult to absolve than the guilt incurred between armed enemies. We have not yet learned to respond to onslaughts of total mistrust, which some Egyptians expressed. (Buber gave some hints as to how one might reach dialogue in such situations, e.g., delicate humor, but we did not prepare our participants for such an encounter.) They were also ill prepared to deal with the stereotype of the aggressive Jew/Israeli that is deeply embedded in many an Egyptian's *Weltanschauung*. Some Israeli Arabs made the mistake of merely seeking identification from Jews and from Egyptians for their difficult existential situation. They did not designate the areas they have in common with Egyptians and those they have in common with Jews; such wavering limited their ability to enter into dialogue.

At the Egyptian-Israeli leaders' summary meeting we agreed that in attempting to compare our different methods while seeking dialogue we had overloaded the encounters themselves. Yet, despite the pain, the aggravation, and the unanswered questions we acknowledged the significant step made toward learning the difficulties of Israeli-Egyptian dialogue. We also agreed that a trialogue in such circumstances is overwhelmingly difficult. The dialogical method is appropriate for two distinct parties who have incurred guilt toward each other, but the method is next to impossible with three such parties, with six instances of incurring guilt. Here Sartre's insight that the gaze of the third party often robs me of my ability to relate authentically to the Other who faces me is valid.

The Changing of History

This year's final educational exercise was held in Acre, which for more than three decades has been an integrated city. Jewish and Arab homes and shops adjoin each other, the children play together, but still, mistrust abounds. Participants were divided into Jewish-Arab quartets who interviewed Jews and Arabs in the city concerning their relations with the other nationality. After reporting on the interviews, the quartet returned to two interviewees, one Jew and one Arab, and asked them how they would suggest changing their personal history so as to further trust between Jews and Arabs. The existential assumption underlying this question is that a person can change in the future only if he is willing to reassess his history. What probably impressed our participants most was the distance between their own mutual trust and the mistrust of the Jew and the Arab whom they encountered. They suddenly realized that during their year in the Buberian Learning Group they had reassessed their own history of mistrust and had entered the realm of genuine dialogue, the realm Buber calls actuality. And they were confronted with the truth of Buber's insight: "The I is actual through its participation in actuality. The more perfect the participation is the more actual the I becomes."[16]

PART III: SOME RESEARCH PROBLEMS AND FINDINGS

> *A main cause of philosophical disease—a one sided diet: one nourishes one's thinking with only one kind of example.*
>
> —Ludwig Wittgenstein, *Philosophical Investigations*

The breadth and the depth of experiences undergone in the Buberian Learning Groups provide a rich field for educational research. We are in the process of tilling that field while heeding Wittgenstein's warning: not to nourish our thinking with one kind of example. We plan to describe our research in a series of separate monographs; here we shall pose two significant questions that were dealt with during the year and indicate some findings.[17]

Is the Buberian Learning Group replicable? Or, in other words, could the Buberian Learning Group be a general approach that leads to dialogue and the diminishing of mistrust between members of adverse groups? This is a major question that needs to be dealt with broadly and in depth. As a first step toward responding to the question, one of our groups in 1980/1981 was led independently by two dialogical educators (both Jews) whom I had trained. They developed their own style of leadership, which differed somewhat from my own. There is no doubt in my mind, nor among our staff and participants, that these leaders succeeded. Mistrust between Jews and Arabs in this group was significantly diminished, participants related dialogically to each other, they acquired understanding and depth. In 1982 we will examine the replicability of our methods in three beginner groups, each of which will be co-led by a Jew and an Arab.

How do persons change as a result of participation in a Buberian Learning Group? The answer to this question is sought through periodically recording personal testimonies, administering questionnaires, and observation by the staff of persons, groups, and dyads. In our initial findings there is much agreement between the results of the different manners of evaluation. For instance, when first-year participants were asked at the end of the year if they trusted members of the other nationality in the group, about 75 percent said that the question seemed irrelevant. They trusted most persons in the group, especially persons with whom they had had a dialogical encounter, and this had nothing to do with nationality. This finding accords with our observations of the work in small groups. If mistrust emerged it occurred between Jew and Jew or between Arab and Arab as frequently as between Jew and Arab.

Eighty percent of the participants described the project as the most significant activity in which they participated during the year, and although they could not clearly define all areas in which their participation influenced them, they knew it did. ("Coming to meetings of our group was the most important event of my week.") In the beginners group thirty of the thirty-nine who completed the year advanced significantly in the Buberian scale of development, some reaching the third stage (the person who educates himself to relate dialogically).[18] But even those who did not see changes in their way of life acknowledged that they had acquired a deeper understanding of what needs to be done to live dialogically.

Although the questionnaire we administered to check the advance of first-year participants needs to be refined, it did reveal some important facts about the Arabs that are confirmed by personal testimonies. Quite a few Arab participants discovered their freedom and the possibility of living in a realm of trust and communion. In the pretest being suspicious of the Other was a value they embraced; in the post-test they were willing to question that value. If, formerly, being reserved was important, they now understand the value of spontaniety and of expressing feelings, especially love.

We shall summarize this brief review with three abbreviated personal testimonies from members of this year's beginner's group.

Notes written periodically by a young Arab woman

> *December 1980.* Only recently, after two months in the project, I began to comprehend the direction of development of our group. Until now I lived totally without daring or courage. I now know that bashfulness won't help me. I must start taking serious opportunities for personal development which present themselves. . . .
>
> *February 1981.* I have had the opportunity here to get to know some Jews and even to get friendly with them. This probably never would have happened without the project. I must learn more about my tradition and heritage in order to challenge some of the principles and even to break some of the chains which oppress me as a woman. . . .

June 1981. I have learned in the project how wonderful it is to be open with other persons and not to take minor problems to heart. I must be less subservient to my society. What a long difficult trek still confronts me.

Excerpts from an interview with a Jewish man who decided to drop out

Q. What did you learn in the project?
A. I think I received two important things from Buber. I became aware of the fact that I perceive many persons as objects, and I acquired patience to listen to others, even those who do not interest me.
Q. What are your criticisms?
A. Personal relations developed, but we have not advanced on the national level.
Q. Do you mean to say that you would like the project to bring about a nearing of political positions?
A. Exactly. I have grave doubts if personal relations can bring about a change in political positions.
Q. Why are you leaving the project?
A. I feel that I can employ my time better in other endeavors. I don't have too much patience to listen to other people's problems.
Q. Have you become personally close to any other participant?
A. Not really, only those who sought my advice.

Excerpts from an interview with a Jewish woman

Q. Why did you join the project?
A. It was an opportunity to get to know Arabs beyond the superficial meetings I had had previously.
Q. Do you mean that the Arab-Jewish problem really bothered you?
A. Not every moment of the day, but whenever I would hear or see something relevant on the news. I would feel angry, especially since I was doing nothing to cope with this problem. When I heard about approaching Arab-Jewish relations through existentialist philosophy I was excited. Existentialism was the only philosophy that spoke to my guts, and not only to my mind. After I joined the project something in me suddenly began to grow. It was as if my true self, which had been hidden in my stomach, began to grow at least until it reached the proportions of my body.
Q. Give me some examples.
A. Well, joining the project gave me the courage to be authentic, especially in my marital and other personal relations.
Q. Be more specific.
A. I learned to listen to people; to impose myself less; to relate to the entire person confronting me. I believed in that before, but I did not do it. It was difficult, so I threw it away. Being in the project

taught me to realize these attitudes. Now when I can listen to another person, I suddenly realized that in true listening a third thing is created between us; there is not only the other person and myself but something that is created between us.

Q. Do you have Arab friends in the project?

A. Yes, two. One of them is very close. Especially when I am with her I feel that something is created between us.

CONCLUSION: THE QUEST FOR RESPONSIBILITY

For us man is characterised above all by his going beyond a situation, and by what he succeeds in making of what he has been made.

—Jean Paul Sartre, *Search for a Method*

Our situation seems clear. We have described the Education for Peace project at the close of its second year—its difficulties, its successes, its failures, its challenge. We know that our next step is to educate persons to assume responsibility for furthering peace between Jews and Arabs. Yet we seem to have reached a chasm that can be crossed only if we guide our participants out of the laboratory conditions of the project and toward a personal involvement in altering history. Will this occur? We hope so. How? We do not know yet, but we do perceive a direction.

It would be simple to state that we shall seek situations in Israel wherein our participants could assume responsibility for peace and guide them to do so, or that we plan to give our participants a broader understanding of ways of working for social justice and to demand such involvement. Of course we shall undertake such endeavors, but they would hardly suffice. As this article has shown, the chasm persons must cross in order to assume responsibility does not only exist in Israeli society, it pervades each person's innermost being. How could it be otherwise? Bombs still explode in the Galilee and in the streets of Beirut; Jews who survived Auschwitz are still gunned down by Arab terrorists; children of Arab refugees from Jaffa still run barefoot in camps in Gaza.

An ancient Jewish legend relates that when God gave Israel the Torah the angels rebelled: "Why do the unpure morals deserve such a lofty gift? Give Your Torah to us who are worthy of it!" But God stood firm. Our sages explain that only we mortals, who sin daily, can benefit from such a gift. But in order to benefit we must assume responsibility for the Torah and the realization of its commands; we must carry it with us to the degradation of our exile and return with it proudly to our holy land. And, they add, such is true of all gifts of love that enhance human existence.

Participants in our project must be willing to defy "angels and mortals" while attempting to bring about dialogue and peace. Such a coupling of defiance and dialogue will encourage a person to cross his internal chasm; it will teach him "not to be afraid to go to hell and back."[19] To assist in such a crossing remains our greatest educational challenge.

Notes

1 For an overview of the first year of the Education for Peace project see Haim Gordon, "Buberian Learning Groups: A Response to the Challenge of Education for Peace in the Mideast," *Teachers College Record* 82, no. 2 (Winter 1980): 291–310.

2 I have discussed Buber's relation to the realization of his philosophy in Haim Gordon, "Did Martin Buber Realize His Educational Thought," *Teachers College Record* 81, no. 3 (Spring 1980): 385–94. See also idem, "The Sheltered Aesthete: A New Appraisal of Martin Buber's Life," in *Buber Centenary Volume,* ed. Jochanan Bloch and Haim Gordon. The volume has been published in Hebrew by Hakibbutz Hameuchad Publishers (1981) and will soon appear in German (Herder Verlag) and in English (Ktav Publishing House).

3 Nazak al Mala'ika, "Five Songs to Pain," in *Modern Arab Poets,* trans. and ed. Issa J. Boullata (London: Heinemann, 1976), p. 12.

4 Gordon, "Did Martin Buber Realize His Educational Thought," p. 392.

5 John Rawls, *A Theory of Justice* (Cambridge: Harvard University Press, 1971), p. 137.

6 Sala 'Abd al-Sabur, "The Shadow and the Cross," in Boullata, *Modern Arab Poets,* p. 78.

7 T. E. Lawrence, *Seven Pillars of Wisdom* (Middlesex: Penguin Books, 1962), p. 27.

8 Naguib Mahfouz is the most celebrated living author of the Arab world. His novels *Midaq Alley* and *Miramar* have been translated into English (Heinemann). Other books including *A Beggar* and the first volume of *Cairo Trilogy* appeared in Hebrew. I met Mahfouz a few times in Cairo and discussed with him at length the fatalism and the lack of dialogue in Egyptian society.

9 See Yusuf Idris, *The Cheapest Nights* (London: Heinemann, 1978). Idris is a master of the short story; his stories reek with the sweat, ignorance, and lack of sensitivity that abound in country and city life in Egypt.

10 See Tewfik Al Hakim, *Fate of a Cockroach and Other Plays of Freedom* (London: Heinemann, 1978). His short stories have also been translated into Hebrew. He is an artist at humorously describing social impotence.

11 See Sonallah Ibrahim, *The Smell of It* (London: Heinemann, 1978). Ibrahim is a young author who poignantly describes the letdown in Egyptian society after the euphoria with Nasser's social reforms.

12 Masadah was a fortress on a cliff overlooking the Dead Sea during the Roman period. Jewish Zealots withstood Roman attacks on Masadah for two years and finally killed themselves rather than fall into Roman hands. The Masadah Complex is the feeling of many Jews in Israel that the entire world is against us; hence we should constantly buttress our fortress and be prepared to die rather than give up our freedom.

13 Gordon, "Buberian Learning Groups," p. 304.

14 Ibid., pp. 297–301.

15 As far as we know the story is not translated into English.In Hebrew it is called "Habikur" [The Visit].

16 Martin Buber, *I and Thou,* trans. Walter Kaufmann (New York: Scribners, 1970), p. 113.

17 We wish to express our thanks to Sarah Hyam for assisting in the research.

18 Gordon, "Buberian Learning Groups," pp. 295–97.

19 From the song "Beautiful Boy" by Yoko Ono and John Lennon in *Double Fantasy.*

Response to "Buberian Learning Groups: The Quest for Responsibility in Education for Peace" by Haim Gordon and Jan Demarest

RIFFAT HASSAN
University of Louisville, Kentucky

As the first (and thus far the only) Muslim member of the international team evaluating the Education for Peace project, I visited Beersheva for a week in March 1981. My response to the paper by Gordon and Demarest evaluating the two-year history of the project is based both on my immediate recollections of my visit (recorded in a report submitted in June 1981 to the chairman of the Project Steering Committee and Department of Education, Ben-Gurion University of the Negev, Beersheva) and my subsequent reflections on what I observed and experienced during my visit.

To conceive of an educational program such as the Education for Peace project, particularly in the setting of Israel, requires both imagination and boldness. Dr. Gordon deserves recognition and commendation for his ability to translate a number of Martin Buber's ideas about dialogue into a philosophy of education and to test this philosophy in a real-life encounter between Jews and Arabs. To me the Education for Peace project is exciting and challenging both as concept and as actuality. The fact that it has shortcomings does not diminish either its uniqueness or its significance.

When I visited the project I was struck very forcefully by the spirit of most of its members. Having grown up under the shadows of an unceasing war, these young persons—Jews and Arabs alike—seemed to me to long so deeply for peace that they were willing to endure the pain of dialogue with the other (perceived, in fact, as the "enemy") in order to overcome the fear and the hatred that lead human beings to destroy each other. I believe that most, if not all, who entered the project were earnestly in search of a solution to the complicated problem of peaceful coexistence of Jew and Arab in present-day Israeli society. I believe that the project taught them how to decrease the "existential mistrust" between Jews and Arabs and led in some cases (I observed at least two instances personally) to the establishing of an authentic one-to-one relationship between a Jew and an Arab.

Dialogue with oneself and with the other entails a confrontation with existential reality. This reality is often painful to deal with. I admire Dr. Gordon for being able to teach the project members "the art of confrontation" through which they were able to look at the pain that lay deeply embedded in their psyche. To be able to acknowledge and articulate thoughts and feelings that have been buried under mounds of defensive behavior certainly has a cathartic effect. But confronting the bitter truth, though it might make us "free" (as the Gospel of St. John 8:32 tells us), is not in and of itself the ultimate goal of dialogue. To me the ultimate goal of I-Thou dialogue is becoming whole or fully human. To achieve this goal, more than the art of confrontation is required. What is needed is the art of loving, my definition of love being that relatedness to the other which makes possible both the healing and the growing of the other.

When I visited the project I had the distinct impression that a number of members—both Jews and Arabs—felt that though they had come a long way in their journey toward better self-understanding and understanding of the other, they were now stuck in an impasse from which even Buber could not rescue them. This sense of being unable to move forward, to bridge the gap between thought and action, led to a feeling of frustration sometimes bordering on despair. To me Dr. Gordon and Dr. Demarest appear to be describing the same feeling when they identify as the project's "most immediate" problem the difficulty of translating "the pain discovered and expressed in dialogue into an active responsibility for furthering peace." I hear them saying, in other words, that although dialogue makes the project members aware of the "distortions" of their mode of existence, this awareness does not necessarily lead to an "attempt to unravel these distortions." The writers attribute this "noncreative" attitude to a "lack of courage" and a "lack of readiness," which they regard as "the two personal responses to pain that we found most difficult to surmount."

In my report I had pointed out what seemed to me to be fundamental problems with the project's orientation and management. I believe that answers to some of the basic questions raised by this paper may be found in what I stated then. Since then, however, I have reflected more deeply on what authentic dialogue is and does, and have come to see with greater clarity than I did a year ago that the main reason the Education for Peace project is unable, in fact, to educate for peace is because the dialogue that is the means of this education is, in some ways, incomplete and inauthentic.

I do not believe that I-Thou dialogue is possible between persons who are significantly unequal in their relationship. For this reason authentic dialogue is not possible between a master and a slave or between most husbands and wives. Dialogue between Jews and Arabs is a virtual impossibility in Israel given the fact that Jews and Arabs are not equal in that society and that the Israeli Arabs are in a particularly vulnerable position, being mistrusted by many among Israeli Jews as well as Palestinian Arabs.

Not only is Dr. Gordon aware of this fact of inequality between Jews and Arabs in Israel, but he is also committed to preserving that inequality. His statement on this point is clear and candid. He says: "As initiator of the Education for Peace project I firmly believe that Israel should be a Jewish state, and not a Palestinian or secular state where Jews and Arabs live together. . . . In other words, like most of my fellow Jews, I accept the sociopolitical structure of Israel as a Jewish state in which Arab citizens will continue to be a minority whose national aspirations will not be realized."

One of the basic questions that haunts a number of sensitive Jews and Arabs in the project is: If the inequality in status between Jew and Arab in the larger Israeli society is to remain unchanged, what then is the purpose of teaching Jews and Arabs in the project the art of relating to each other as if they were equal? I remember a young Jewish woman in the project telling me with a lot of agony: "I feel as if the project is a game that we play. We pretend that we are all equal while all the time we know that we are not. Sometimes I feel that it would be kinder to stop pretending, to simply accept the fact that we are living in an unfair society, an unfair world." And I also recall the words of a young Arab man who spoke perhaps for many in his group when he said, "I feel that the real purpose of the project is to give us an opportunity to express our anger so that we would be emotionally neutralized and become passive."

The I-Thou mode of relating requires that the I and the Thou treat each other justly, not being exploitative or manipulative in any way. Where justice is lacking, the I-Thou dialogue degenerates into an I-It mode of communication. I believe that all three Abrahamic faiths—Judaism, Christianity, and Islam—establish a necessary connection between justice and peace. My paramount theological and ethical problem with the Education for Peace project is that it appears to promote the view that one can educate for peace without educating for justice. It seems to me profoundly ironical that the project members are told to find "just principles" for solving Jewish-Arab problems in the context of the Rawls Workshop but not in the context of real life.

The inequality between Jew and Arab in Israeli society is reflected in the project not only in terms of the conflicting and confusing messages given to the members regarding what authentic dialogue is or should be but also in terms of its management and curriculum. At no point have the Arabs felt that they had an equal share in the project. The main reason underlying this feeling is that there have been very few Arabs in leadership positions and the attitude of at least some Jews has been overly proprietary and patronizing. The lack of suitable Islamic sources in the curriculum is another problem of serious import, as I pointed out in my report.

"We know of no one way of educating for courage" say Gordon and Demarest. I agree with them in identifying courage as essential for bringing about change in one's mode of being. But I believe that authentic dialogue does educate for courage since it makes it possible for us to discover that which fragments our inner unity or impedes our growth. For instance, a major problem that most human beings have to face is the problem of guilt. In the Education for Peace project (as in Israel) many Jews and Arabs feel guilty. Many Jews feel guilty because they see Jews as oppressing Arabs even though they are not personally responsible for the oppression. Many Arabs feel guilty because they do not see themselves as contributing effectively to the cause of the Palestinian Arabs regardless of whether they can. No human being can avoid incurring some guilt in life, but as John Sanford points out in *Between People,* it is important to distinguish between real guilt and false guilt.

> The former we need to accept because it belongs to us. The latter we need to reject because it is not ours. . . . We really are guilty when we go against our own nature. We need to accept this guilt as our own, for it belongs to us. We may not like it, but it is ours. But there is this redeeming fact: While false guilt diminishes our personality, real guilt does not. When we assume false guilt we are destroyed by it, but when we honestly carry the guilt that belongs to us we become bigger, not smaller, in personality. Of course it is painful. Any guilt is painful. We do not want to acknowledge our real guilt. We even prefer our false guilts to our real guilts because . . . the former allow us to retain our egocentricity, but the latter require us to give it up. We complain about both kinds of guilt, but we are secretly in alliance with the false guilt. Yet it is the real guilt that can heal us. If we can manage to summon up the courage to face our real omissions and failures in life, we can begin to grow. It is the painful truth that makes us free.[1]

Authentic dialogue makes possible the facing of "the real guilt" and "the painful truth" because it is rooted in that relatedness which I call love. As I mentioned in my report, during my visit to the project I felt that some staff members were emotionally sterile and did not understand how important the "heart" is in any kind of meaningful dialogue. They had learned about confrontation but not about compassion and thought that they could carry on a dialogue with the other with the detachment of a surgeon performing an operation under clinical conditions. By learning the technique of dialogue one can confront the other with the hurt within. But mere confronting of the hurt will not lead to healing. In fact, it can sometimes be very dangerous, for it can cause a person to fall apart totally under the pressure of the internal pain. Rabindra Nath Tagore said, "He only may chastise who loves." I believe that it is also correct to say that only that person may dialogue (or confront) who loves. Jesus' golden words "Love thy neighbor as thyself" are, in fact, the foundational principle of authentic dialogue, for if I could love the other as myself then I would be willing not only to confront the other with the "painful truth" but also to share in the pain.

By and large I did not feel that the primary concern in the Education for Peace project was with sharing the pain that was discovered through dialogue. Without such sharing there can be no healing and without healing there is no growth. Courage, as Rollo May points out in *The Courage to Create,* "requires a centeredness within our own being, without which we would feel ourselves to be a vacuum. The 'emptiness' within corresponds to an apathy without; and apathy adds up, in the long run to cowardice."[2] In other words, "lack of courage" as well as "lack of readiness" reflects a lack of "centeredness within our own being." Through authentic dialogue one can help the other to find wholeness, and a centeredness within the wholeness, and thereby make it possible for the other to act with courage. The word *courage* comes from the same stem as the French word *coeur,* meaning "heart." I believe that members of the Education for Peace project would act with more courage and readiness than they have done in the past if more heart were put into the project. How that is to be done I do not know. There is no magic formula for establishing authentic dialogue nor is such dialogue merely an intellectual or academic pursuit that can be conducted by technically trained personnel. "The fact that talent is plentiful but passion is lacking seems to me to be a fundamental facet of the problem of creativity in many fields today" observes Rollo May,[3] and this lack of passion is a major reason for the barrenness of so many dialogues going on in this decade of dialogue. I believe that the ability to touch the deepest levels of the other's self requires a kind of "gift from heaven." Perhaps the project needs more people with such a gift.

But one thing that can and should be done is to introduce into the curriculum the concept of "roots," leading to a deep exploration of what it means to be Jewish-Israeli and Islamic-Arabic. The religious dimension of both Jewish and Arab identity was conspicuously missing from classroom discussions when I visited the project. I was also surprised and concerned to find out that neither Jews nor Arabs in the project were clearly aware of the intimate connection between their roots and their "center." I gather from the paper that now there is a weekly lecture on subjects such as "Jewish history, Arab history, Islam, Judaism, etc." While such lectures are certainly a useful addition to the program, in-depth research needs to be done to locate sources (particularly Islamic) that can be used to sensitize the project members to each other's cultural and religious consciousness through time and space.

And, finally: What, in my judgment, is the good that has come out of the Education for Peace project? Much good, I believe, has come out of it even though it has not succeeded in a direct manner in fulfilling what was perhaps the initiator's central aim, namely, to educate for peace. With all its imperfections, the project has provided a setting—perhaps the only one in Israel—where Jews and Arabs can meet as persons and not as stereotypes. It has also taught its members the art of confronting much that is difficult to accept, thus releasing them from the bondage of repression and passive suffering. The project has made its members aware of both the need for and the possibility of acquiring deeper knowledge and wisdom as well as greater maturity and strength of character even within the constraints imposed on them by the larger reality that encompasses them. I believe that each Jew or Arab who has entered the project with commitment has learned from it and has somehow become more fully human as a result of engaging in dialogical encounter with other Jews and Arabs. All of this constitutes a considerable good and all of this I personally value. However, what is for me the highest good that has come out of the Education for Peace project is that it has provided to a few human beings—Jews and Arabs—the opportunity to transcend the enmity and alienation of the ages and to be able to love the other despite all that separates them. This seems to me to be the project's greatest vindication.

Notes

1 John Sanford, *Between People* (Ramsey, N.J.: Paulist Press, 1982), pp. 61-65.
2 Rollo May, *The Courage to Create* (New York: W. W. Norton, 1965), p. 3.
3 Ibid., p. 88.

Peace—In and Out of Our Homes: A Report on a Workshop

KIMBERLY HUSELID GLASS
Teachers College, Columbia University

> *Our strong interests have the defects of their virtues in that they narrow our focus, blind us to the obvious, and rob us of the capacity to recognize that the emperor may be quite naked. Because our values and assumptions are usually implicit and "second nature" we proceed as if the way things are is the way things could or should be. We do not act but we react and then not with the aim of changing our conceptions—or heaven forbid, our theories from which our conceptions presumably derive—but to change what is most easy to change: the engineering aspects.*
>
> Seymour B. Sarason

THE FAMILY AS A MANAGEABLE SYSTEM

Within our broken and confused world, the family, once a basic social group, has become something to manage, to engineer toward "better" ways of living. It must be, of course, that those involved in such management are well fed, clothed, and now seeking "higher" levels of individual comfort in a world that is presented as increasingly less comfortable. Methods of parenting, of being family, in our society have grown out of a decline of what were thought to be basic values. In the last thirty years we have seen growing trends in the field of relationship management. This is not surprising. The usual response toward weakening in any area of our mechanistic society is one of repair. We run in with those ideas and theories that we think will "fix" whatever appears broken. Seldom do we appreciate wholeness.

Many of the current "parenting for peace and justice" methodologies, I fear, are such attempts at repair—at remaining within existing structures (i.e., church, school) and attempting to salvage the "good" from the "bad" while in the process bringing more life to the existing broken system by never questioning its roots. However, I believe that a group of people, living together, holds much hope for our understanding of peace in our world—not in methods of relationship, but in the quality of life that can be found within relationships. There is the possibility, in families joined together, for the re-creation of the human values that we have lost somewhere in the modernization processes. These are values centered on relationship and dependent upon a nonmechanistic, holistic way of knowing the world. The family holds more hope than do other more modern institutions, as it has a rich history in which its changing meaning is played out, from which we can trace the decline of human values. Access to families is limited; indeed, there are few of our modern-day institutions that include whole families in their wings. The church, in our society, has also lost families in its appeal to the individual spirit rather than the collective. Relational identity has become secondary to individual identity.

When I was asked to lead a workshop on Peace In and Out of Our Homes, at Old Pine Presbyterian Church, I believe that the expectations of the participants were that I would provide technique—technique for making a hard life easier to bear. I am not denying the value of people's being able to share the rough spots of their lives. What I am questioning is doing so without realizing the causes, the roots of painful lives. I am questioning the place of adaptive technique within peace education. Instead, I see value in helping people to discover in themselves the reasons for the rough spots in their own lives and the relation of those to the injustice in the world. Inner awareness is of more value in this process than is outer technique.

Peace, as a positive word, connotes, I believe, lack of conflict and tension; it has lost its deeper symbolic meanings of wholeness and justice. To limit peace to its value for relationships is to lose sight of the possibility of transformation, or deep-structure change, that can come from understanding the connections between our micro and macro existences.

In going into Old Pines I took with me my own visions of hope for the church (re-created) as a center for radical social understanding. I also know that in this country, as in many others, the church has become a central emotive force in people's lives. It has become one of our centers for making sense of the world, while it must also make sense in light of the world. It is this tension that people must tend to if they are going to have any semblance of consistency in their lives. Multiple lives must make sense under nonconflicting stories, myths we tell that hold the keys to our sense-making abilities.

I did not go into the workshop with the idea of dispensing technique. I took with me questions—my own questions—about the history of the family and the meaning of families relating in and with the world. I set up the sessions on the basis of my questions, using them as a sort of discussion guide. My own goals were to make possible the self-discovery process of individuals toward understanding the power that can be realized for greater meaning in and among families; to explore the "traditional" values that seem to be stored in our myths about what families should be like; and to explore what ultimate meanings there are in being a family. As mentioned above, these were my own questions. I believe that one of the most important things an educator can do is to realize that we do tend to ask our own questions. As we do this, the questions of the people will surface as they attempt to have us make sense of their worlds. It is these questions that need our careful attention, as they hold the key to the people's understanding of their world and the stories they have created to support that world. My pointing out the contradictions between a gospel of peace and paying for war is fruitless if people do not understand the contradiction as I do. Indeed, I may appear rather naive in light of the work they are doing to keep stable, noncontradictory lives.

> If people are unable to make sense of each other, trust relations will be impossible to establish, and either escape from the setting, or more intense identity work will be necessary.[1]

> People arrange for constancy in personality and intellectual skills by arranging environments which allow for and encourage the use of particular skills they have developed.[2]

With some of the above ideas in mind, I set up four workshop sessions on peace, talk sessions that were attended by ten to fifteen adults. While the sessions were "billed" as concerned with peace in our lives, they were almost immediately interpreted as being for parents only—an interesting happening. People came with desires to know things they could do to manage their existing home lives in the name of peace. I came attempting to have them see that their situations have a lot to do with the struggles they were having, that our value of family in this society is such that only continued fragmentation—brokenness—will result.

> No matter what fantasy or ideal mobilizes some identity work its organizing powers must constantly be maintained and reinforced. As all work in psycho-cultural adaptation has indicated, habits of both thought and deed must be maintained in a world congenial to these habits, or else new ways of thinking and doing must emerge often despite considerable pain.[3]

What follows are brief descriptions of my own visions for each of the four sessions. Because of the existing expectations and classlike orientation of adult education, I was asked to structure the sessions into topic units, which I felt led to a process of fragmentation (see the Comments Section).

SESSION 1—TOWARD A FAITHFUL VISION OF FAMILY LIFE

The opening session of the workshops emphasized the history of the family in the United States and Europe. It was also an attempt to envision other alternatives to family life based on some of our ideas about how family life "should" be. Peace as a way of life that reaches the depths of our experience was stressed in contrast to peace as a tactic or a way toward salvation. I attempted to stress the relationship between our economic system and the relationships that it allows, or that are formed in its shadow. My goal here was to link the various institutions in our society in terms of their reality, in terms of the possibility there is in these institutions for talking about peace as more than something that we do, or a good way of relating.

SESSION 2—NONVIOLENCE IN AND OUT OF OUR HOMES

This session was devoted to trying to talk about violence and the roots of violence in American society. I attempted to link violence to injustice, to ways of thinking that would expand the concept beyond its physical implications. Violence as useful and valued in this society was explored, especially in our relationships to nature and to those human beings we do not "know."

We talked here about violence in the home and the usefulness of nonviolent technique. Parents are often blamed for rearing violent children—is that the case, or are there other factors? Why do we accept violence as a given and inevitable part of human nature?

SESSION 3—LIVING SIMPLY SO THAT OTHERS MIGHT SIMPLY LIVE

In the third session we discussed ideas about daily life and their connections with a holistic vision of human existence. Discussions were encouraged around the film *How Do We Live in a Hungry World,* which depicted alternative responses to the American Dream in light of concerns for deeper meanings of life than the dream offers. The American Dream and its support systems were talked about here as well as the place of the dream in each of our lives. The idea of community was explored and the limits to that as an ideal. The values of life-style change were explored in their wider implications.

SESSION 4—WHERE DO WE GO FROM HERE?

This was an open session for dialogue around concerns that had evolved over the previous three sessions. My own concern was in trying to keep the participants from concentrating on specific issues before they could come to some sense of wholeness and an awareness of history that included their own actions. An emphasis was put on the effects of fragmentation and personal adaptation on our abilities to see more clearly the meaning in our lives.

COMMENTS

The tendency in each of the sessions was toward issues that seemed fragmenting. My desire was to continually bring the group back to a larger view of their lives, to connect their concerns for issues with wholeness and meaning, respect and reverence for all of life. Peace/war was one such issue and the tendency was to link war to an innate tendency toward violence. Peace, then, becomes the control of innate urges.

The group continually asked for techniques for more peaceful lives and homes. My response was to try to get them to envision their homes as microcosms after first viewing a picture of the whole—the macrocosm. One of my questions concerned the value of technique for really helping in any of their struggles—as in techniques of nonviolence: What are the philosophies and ways of life traditionally linked to an ethos of nonviolence? Is it of value to insert nonviolent technique into already oppressive institutions? Why are we often so uncomfortable with pacifism and the way of life that accompanies it, yet choose to adopt its valuable techniques?

My sense is that my questions were much larger in the asking than they were to the receivers—or too big to be relevant in their existing view of things. Change is painful, and much work must be done among people who have a lot to lose if change is demanded, requested, or even just suggested. To hang on to issues is much easier and does not necessarily lead to a greater understanding of wholeness or connection between issues. Fragmentation, as a mode of peace education, seems to be one of the gravest enemies of such education.

In setting up the workshops as I did, I allowed for the fragmenting process to develop. My own views of Christianity and its relation to a wholeness rich with meaning and tied to a philosophy of life were well tested and seemed to be somewhat irrelevant to people who have lives, ways of thinking about their world and their places in it, to protect. The myths, stories that are told about what life is in this country, are of course endemic in our churches (one of their chief protectors). The problems that I brought before this group were countered with the reality of their lives and the stories with which it all makes sense.

My understanding, after this experience, is that peace education, in any realm, involves so much more than imparting facts and information. Ours is a society that is very well organized for making sense of the myths we hold, even in light of blatant contradictions. Meeting with a group of people as I did for four weeks gave me merely a glimpse of their lives and the questions they presented in response to my questions. Anthropologists have long understood that the best way to know a culture and a group of people is to spend time in their ways—to go in as the village idiot and to allow oneself to be taught what one needs to know in order to live among the people. Educators in America, I suspect, often assume an understanding of people's struggles and ways of knowing the world and do not have enough respect for the richness they have created in making sense of their world. Teachers often become dealers of information rather than embodiments of life worth emulating by understanding and living with people.

In order to understand the value of peace education we need to understand education in this land. It is, I posit, not valuable to further fragment knowledge by presenting information about peace in capsule form. This was my own struggle in being responsible for these workshops. We need a sense of the value of wholeness in education that would confront the existing structure of education in this society with the deeper meanings of life, rather than an emphasis on information about that life. Change might then develop from the inside out. We cannot assume that outer change will eventually affect the way we know the world; that for me is a quantum and unsound leap. The teacher needs to be present to the taught and part of the life context. We cannot, I feel, "teach" peace as we understand "teach" in this society.

> We see everywhere, evidence of what happens when the law of wholeness is transgressed: war, poverty, bloated affluence, bloated hunger, injustice, despair, guilt, poisoned food, poisoned air, poisoned water, greed, indifference. "What shall we do?" we ask. We shall begin with a concern for wholeness and proceed to an education, lifelong, which serves this in spirit and practice.[4]

Notes

1 Lois Hood, R. P. McDermott, and M. Cole, "Let's Try to Make It a Good Day," *Discourse Processes* 3 (1980): 158.

2 Ibid.

3 R. P. McDermott and Joseph Church, "Making Sense and Feeling Good: The Ethnography of Communication and Identity Work," *Communication* 2 (1976): 137.

4 Mary Caroline Richards, "The Public School and the Education of the Whole Person," *Teachers College Record* 82, no. 1 (Fall 1980): 66.

Response: Needs in Peace Education Development Identified by Glass

BETTY REARDON

Teachers College, Columbia University

Like any other field of study in the process of development, peace education is plagued with the perennial problems of definition, not the least of which is the fundamental concept of peace itself. While peace researchers for the most part seem satisfied to settle for splitting the concept in two, some avowing that most meaning can be captured by "negative peace," the absence of war, or "positive peace," the presence of justice (or whatever other conditions make for peace), those who come new to the field are still confounded by the definitional issue. It is hard to define what we do not know and have not experienced. So we tend to extrapolate from what we do know and have experienced. The family has been the most common source of peaceful experience for most human beings. There is undoubtedly in family values something that makes for peace, and should the family as institution be lost, much too would be lost of the ways of learning peacefulness. However, the very conditions noted here as eroding the family as social institution also carry the seeds of so many other changes in the social environment that even the matrix of family cannot be precisely defined.

This circumstance brings into focus other serious questions for peace education: Which institutions are peaceful? How do they instruct in the ways of peace, and what peaceful ways do they impart? Some claim that peaceful institutions do not exist. We must invent them. Some assert that the task lies in the revitalization of traditional institutions. Still others argue for the structural transformation of modern institutions on the basis of humane values, some of the very values one suspects Kimberly Glass perceives to be at the core of the peacefulness of the family.

And so we come to a third cluster of fundamental problems for peace education, the identification of peace values and the recognition and cultivation of behavior that manifests them. What are peace values, how can they be imparted, and how can we learn to practice them in lives made more coherent by an integration of ethical values and social norms? How, in other words, can we learn to know the values, to recognize the conditions that violate them, and to adopt new social behaviors so as to help transform the conditions that violate the values and pose obstacles to a peaceful society? It is these basic questions that are central to the experiment Glass undertook, and that are fundamental to any process of peace education that calls on people to see the world differently—for example, as Glass would have us look at it, holistically. It is this process that raises the fundamental problem of pedagogy: how we as educators articulate the purposes and goals of peace learning to the learners while comprehending the purposes and goals with which they come to the learning process. The difficulty of establishing this communication lies both in disjunctures in definition and in lack of convergence of goals.

Glass comes to the issue of peace with concerns and concepts of so abstract yet so humane a nature that the very difficulty she describes in the proceedings of her seminar were as instructive as they were inevitable. Making some of the abstract and humane values traditionally associated with the family into concrete, reproducible behaviors and social patterns is a challenge to peacemakers. Developing the process whereby they can be identified and learned is a challenge to peace educators. The Glass article, in posing this challenge, exemplifies the problems of working with abstract, inadequately defined terms, and contributes to designating one of the major obstacles to both peacemakers and peace educators: lack of clarity in the communication process.

TWO SCENARIOS

The Last Day of Civilization

WILLARD J. JACOBSON
Teachers College, Columbia University

Imagine five people sitting in a circle in a cave. In the center of the circle is a huge bomb. If this bomb should explode, these five individuals and all other people would be killed and everything that might be considered their civilization would be destroyed. The generations that might have been would never have the chance of existence. (Who knows, there might have been a Socrates, a Gandhi, or a supreme peacemaker among their descendants.) Each of the five people has a fuse that can ignite the bomb. Some of the five are tempted to try to expand their empires or convert others to their cause. Other members of the circle then threaten to ignite the fuse to prevent this. There are people outside eager to join the circle in the cave, and some do, but as the number in the circle grows, the deadly danger that someone will ignite the bomb increases.

Outside the cave the sun is shining. There is the laughter and dancing of children and the look of joy and peace on the countenances of adults. People are friendly and wish each other well. Outside the cave is the world of "might be." But if the bomb should go off that world will be incinerated. Occasionally, the people inside the cave hear a note or two of the laughter of a child and, perhaps, utter an inner sigh for a touch of the sunshine or feel a twinge of regret at friendships missed and peace lost. How can the prisoners of the cave reach the freedom of the sunlight?

The path from the cave to the sunlight is not well marked, but surely there must be one. As with anyone who sees a light in the distance, we know the general direction we want to go. All of us can hope, and everyone can add to the determination that we must leave the bomb in the cave and struggle into sunlight. We can try to convey our fears and hopes in more effective ways. This is such an attempt. It is a story within a story. Within these two stories there is an attempt to broaden the concern for our predicament and kindle a hope for what might be.

We were flying east. For two months international tensions had been building. Many felt that we were truly at the edge of the abyss. The threat of nuclear war hung over the head of civilization, and there were many of the knowing who feared the almost unimaginable threat that hundreds of millions of people and everything that could be called civilization might be destroyed by the interchange of several thousand nuclear-tipped, intercontinental ballistic missiles. We were on our way to Europe to consult with colleagues and to do anything possible to prevent the holocaust. Our European friends had said, "No rational human being would ever push the button to set off a nuclear war." But—

There was a flash a hundred times brighter than lightning. But we continued to fly eastward.

Five minutes later there were ten successive flashes, and I knew that the most awful thing I could imagine had indeed happened. The nuclear interchange had taken place. Ten nuclear warheads had exploded on or above New York City. Two hundred or more other American cities had probably also been bombed. I assumed that a preemptive attempt had been made to destroy the minuteman missiles siloed in North Dakota, Montana, and ten other states, but only a fraction of them would be knocked out. The rest of them would send their deadly missiles to destroy two hundred Soviet cities and possibly some of the remaining Soviet missiles. Then, there remained over a thousand nuclear weapons on the Poseidon and Trident submarines, and the Tacamo (Take Charge and Move Out) aircraft would be in the air giving the orders to launch to the submarines at sea. Then there would be Tomahawk cruise missiles launched from aircraft in the air and ships at sea that would arrive hours later to complete that act of Armageddon. I knew that hundreds of millions of children, women, and men would be incinerated and die that awful afternoon.

The first flash that we had seen I knew had been an explosion high in space designed to knock out communication systems through an electromagnetic pulse. Ever since a test explosion over Johnson Island had played havoc with communication systems in Hawaii it had been known that communication systems could be affected by an electromagnetic pulse from a nuclear explosion high in space. Most military communications utilize earth satellites. The hotline between Washington and Moscow had used two satellites, one Soviet and the other a commercial Intelsat satellite. Communications using these satellites would have been impacted. Also, I knew that the President of the United States had forty-three ways of sending out the Emergency Action Message (EAM). Forty-one of these ways were knocked out, but the systems using fiber-optics transmission are relatively impervious to electromagnetic pulses. The availability of these fiber-optic transmission lines assured that the orders for Armageddon would go out.

We had been flying east, and this saved the eyes of our pilots. On an Air France flight going west all of the pilots were blinded by the flashes. As at Hiroshima, the retinas were actually burned by the intense radiation. The Air France plane crashed into the ocean. On our airlines it had been standard operating procedures (SOP) during international crises for one pilot on each plane to wear a thick patch over one eye so that it would be possible for him to land the plane even if blinded in the other eye.

We turned west to return to New York, and we soon saw ten mushroom clouds that were beginning to merge into one. My whole body shook and I couldn't stop shaking because I had some idea of what had happened to my family, my friends, and my home in that great city. How could one set of human beings possibly inflict such utter horror on another set of human beings and then have it inflicted on them in return?

There are no experts on nuclear warfare. No one knows for sure what would happen if there were a large-scale exchange of nuclear weapons. In another sense, almost everyone is an expert because almost everyone knows that an exchange of nuclear weapons would be the greatest cataclysm, the greatest holocaust, the greatest mass murder, the greatest destruction ever to take place on this earth. It would be so awful that many people refuse even to think about it. But it is important that we do think about it. Maybe if more people become more aware they will do more to keep it from happening. No one person can prevent the planetary incineration, but, we can hope, many people can.

Many of those who have thought about the awful consequences of a nuclear explosion have depicted the effects of the explosion of one nuclear device. For example, the explosion of a one-megaton bomb in the air above New York City would burn everything and everyone within a radius of ten to twenty miles. The temperatures might reach 3000°C., and fires would be ignited within a radius of ten miles. After a nuclear explosion there would be an initial outward blast with a lethal radius of about four and one-half miles. For an explosion over the Empire State Building, this lethal area would stretch from Prospect Park in Brooklyn to Riverside Church in upper midtown Manhattan. Within this area shards of glass would become arrows of death as they were blown into and through the bodies that happened to be in their path. After the explosion there might be a rush of fire and hot air toward the center of the explosion. In these firestorms, such as the firestorm after the bombing of Dresden where winds of several hundred miles an hour were generated, most of the people in bomb shelters would be asphyxiated. Afterward there would be the rain of radioactive debris. (In Hiroshima there was a black rain of water and soil that exposed survivors to more radioactive burning.) Depending on the wind and other meteorological conditions, a radioactive cloud might drift for hundreds of miles downwind. In the D & D (Death and Destruction) scenarios, this drifting radioactive cloud from the blast over Manhattan would "do in" much of Connecticut and Long Island. It was recognized that the thinkers of the unthinkable might not foresee some of the consequences. What happens when most of the doctors and nurses in a region are killed in the first blast? What happens when many of the burn centers in a nation are destroyed? I recalled that the resources of these centers had been strained to the breaking point by the influx of patients from the collision of two airliners. Now there would be thousands of severely burned people! The thinkers of the unthinkable had tried to purvey in vividly searing scenarios the picture of piteously painful death and almost unbelievable destruction that follows the explosion of a nuclear bomb in a crowded metropolis.

But there would be not one bomb but many. In 1982, we knew that more than 50,000 nuclear weapons had been built. The United States had over 9,400 strategic nuclear weapons and over 21,000 tactical nuclear weapons. The Soviet Union had over 8,000 strategic nuclear weapons and over 15,000 tactical nuclear weapons. Britain, France, and China also had powerful nuclear forces. India had exploded a nuclear device, and it was suspected that Israel and South Africa might have nuclear weapons. What was to prevent these from being used or even exploding accidentally? (There had been one such explosion, but most people had not even heard of it.) We had begun to try to conceptualize what would happen if many nuclear bombs were exploded. (One of my colleagues wrote a piece called "The Awful Afternoon," but he had not been able to get it published.) With all those bombs poised in silos, waiting in submarines, hung in bomb bays in intercontinental bombers, or nosed in air-breathing, low-flying missiles, it seemed almost inevitable that sometime some of the bombs would be used. There might be an accident; every year there had been four or five "close calls" that we knew about. There might be proud leaders dedicated to a righteous cause or the honor of their homeland who would not hesitate to pull the nuclear trigger. Or, in the sophisticated game of "chicken" that the two major powers play, it might become necessary for one of the powers to demonstrate a "high resolve" and "that we really mean business." I knew that the ten flashes, each brighter than a dozen suns, had been nuclear explosions.

As we headed back to the coast, my mind was twisted into excruciating contortions. What was happening to the people "down there"? My son was there. I hoped that he had died, had vaporized, within one-thousandth of a second of the ignition of the fireball. Your daughter was there. What has become of her? The lady across the aisle has a husband who couldn't come with her "because he had so much work to do." It is easier to think of statistics: the explosion of ten one-megaton weapons in New York City might lead to ten million deaths directly and millions more from the rain of a radioactive death. But we had learned long ago that large numbers tend to carry less meaning than the effects on individuals that we know and love. What do ten million deaths mean? If the true meaning were conveyed, surely no one would ever launch a nuclear weapon. When we think of what a fireball, with temperatures up to 3000°C., would do to the bodies of your daughter, my son, and that lady's husband, the awful meaning becomes searingly stark. I could barely think.

As we forced ourselves to look out the airplane windows at the ten mushroom clouds that were beginning to merge, I did think: What led to this? How could living, thinking, feeling human beings do this to each other? What was it that we hadn't learned that led to this greatest of all tragedies—the killing of millions, hundreds of millions, and the complete destruction of societies and whatever civilization there had been?

We had known of the awful effects of the explosion of nuclear weapons. In August 1945 nuclear bombs were exploded over Hiroshima and Nagasaki. Two cities were destroyed. The heat rays from the explosion burned exposed human flesh two and a half miles from the explosion. In Hiroshima nine square miles of the city were burned and pulverized into ashes and dust. The two explosions killed over 200,000 people on the day of the attack or in the days that followed. Within five years, another 130,000 people died, and people might still be suffering and dying from the effects of radiation. Of course, hundreds of thousands of others were severely injured, and it is difficult to quantify their suffering.

Yes, we had known of these effects of nuclear explosions. The consequences of the nuclear bombing of Hiroshima and Nagasaki had been studied extensively—the studies would fill library shelves. The effects had been personalized—many books had been written describing the experiences of survivors. Though we knew what had happened at Hiroshima and Nagasaki, intelligent people still planned for nuclear war, talked endlessly about esoteric strategies that might give one nation a slight advantage over the other, and now the calamitous effects at Hiroshima and Nagasaki had been multiplied a thousand times over as thousands of much more powerful bombs exploded in the United States, the Soviet Union, and probably other nations. They forgot! They forgot! They forgot! For this, we have paid an unbelievable price.

The third pilot came back to the cabin and announced that the intercom system in the plane had been damaged, and that we were heading north to try to find a safe place to land.

There were still people who believed that nuclear wars could be won. In the past, when the weapons were bows and arrows or even guns and bombs, there were ways in which one side could be considered the winner and the other the loser. The unfortunates who were split by a broadax, punctured by an arrow, or blown apart by a high-velocity bullet were certainly grim losers. But the conquerors, those who viewed the tumult of battle from a safe distance behind the lines, could in some ways consider themselves winners. However, warfare had changed. Even in World War I and World War II there were few winners because most people were worse off than they would have been if the wars had not been fought. Certainly this was true of the tens of millions who died. Surely, there would be no winners of nuclear wars. General Douglas MacArthur had said, "If you lose, you are annihilated. If you win, you stand only to lose. [Nuclear] war contains the germs of double suicide." Nuclear war is not a game, not a gamble—everyone is sure to lose.

Still the service academies at West Point, Annapolis, and Colorado Springs continued to imbue their cadets with the spirit of winning. "The future leaders of our armed services are trained to win. There is no place for losers at . . ." Too often, the leaders of our armed services have busied themselves planning war complete with planes, tanks, and aircraft carriers. It has been difficult for them to comprehend that these archaic instruments no longer count.

Those who do not believe it should look out the window. The hundreds of billions of dollars spent on defense have not defended anyone from incineration. Certainly no one has won. (The chairman of the Joint Chiefs of Staff was to be at a meeting in New York City on this day. He died along with hundreds of millions of his fellow human beings.) Many had hoped that the money, resources and talents that had been allocated to defense would really provide security. Look at the security we got!

It had been proposed that there be a National Peace Academy that would provide people with the skills needed to work for conflict resolution and peace. The secretary general of the United Nations had had the temerity to suggest that nations devote one-tenth of 1 percent of what they spend on armaments on the promotion of peace. The proposal for a National Peace Academy gathered dust as a committee report. The secretary general's "extravagant" proposal had been generally dismissed, if it was heard at all, as being "impractical."

It seemed as though we had not wanted to believe some of the basic ideas of mathematics. In human activities we seldom achieve perfection, but in most ordinary activities the imperfections are more a nuisance than a catastrophe. If a thousand automobiles roll off an assembly line, a few of them will have some imperfections. If the imperfection is not caught by a quality-control inspector, the purchaser of the automobile will surely be irritated, but a loose doorknob, for example, is hardly a catastrophe. However, a small error in a nuclear weapons system could be catastrophic, and the chances of error increase as you increase the number of nuclear weapons. In 1980 a technician in a Titan II silo in Arkansas dropped a wrench socket that fell 70 feet and broke a fuel tank. The explosion that followed left a crater 250 feet across, and hurled the worker several hundred feet. The nuclear warhead did not explode. If it had we would have lost part of Arkansas. If two nations have one or two bombs each and the handling of these bombs is supervised by very knowledgeable and responsible people who know a great deal about the possible consequences of error, the chances of error are very small. But when each of two nations has several thousand bombs, the chances of serious error are very great. If a system containing 30,000 warheads is 99.9 percent perfect, there will still be thirty errors. In an automobile assembly line, these thirty errors would be a nuisance; in a nuclear weapons system they could be catastrophic.

> The greatest of human disasters that we were witnessing could have been started by an error.

Similarly, as more nations acquire nuclear weapons, the chances that nuclear weapons will be used increases. There are rulers who have been able to convince themselves that they are God's representatives on this earth (a rather easy task) and that they are justified to use whatever power is available in their "holy wars." Others have as their mission the liberation of the toiling masses from the clutches of exploiting imperialists and use whatever force is necessary even if it means the incineration of the toiling masses. (To counter this, one person has proposed the slogan "No incineration without representation.") Others have found that they have been chosen, often after a bloody coup, to save the honor and defend the glory of the motherland. The call to fight and even to give one's life for a righteous cause has been a siren call for millennia. When this patriotic call is sounded, the excruciating moans and cries of the partially incinerated and the wailing of loved ones is not imagined. It has been said that wars are begun by men without imagination; they do not begin to imagine the sufferings that they cause. Wars are waged by men without imagination; the psyche-saving rationalization of the soldier is that "it can't happen to me." Will the self-anointed men of God, the sergeants and colonels who love their country so deeply that they will send others to die for it, and all those who believe their cause is just and holy be able to resist the temptation to use the ultimate weapon?

> As the possession of nuclear weapons proliferated, the chance that some group or nation would use weapons increased to the point of certainty.
>
> I wondered whether the stupendous disaster that we were witnessing could have been started by a fanatical group smuggling a nuclear device into a Moscow subway station or the Capitol in Washington.
>
> As I looked out the window to the west, I saw a stupendously large black cloud forming. As in Hiroshima, the huge quantities of soil made radioactive by the bombs was now triggering a black rain that would burn all living things beneath it.

It has always been too easy to start wars. In the past, wars were usually declared by men who were far beyond military age and located in capitols that seemed secure from the ravages of combat. With conveniently shallow imagination, they did not need to face the gore of combat as they issued their call to battle. It has been suggested that part of the code needed for the launch of American missiles should be implanted inside the body of a volunteer. The only way that chemicals on the code card could be activated would be by the heat of burning flesh. In the attaché case containing the rest of the code there should be a flask of gasoline and a match. Before the president could initiate the launch that would incinerate tens of millions, he should have to see one human being burn to death. When this suggestion was made to the officers at the Pentagon, they were aghast. "This horrible experience might affect the president's judgment."

It seemed as if the United States and the Soviet Union had become prisoners of each other. Each country tried to deter the other from using nuclear weapons by making certain that they would know that they also would be destroyed. This was the doctrine of Mutual Assured Destruction, which had the highly appropriate acronym MAD. When one country developed a more powerful warhead, the other country had to match it. In their negotiations, they tried to prevent the development of defense systems because this might mean that some people, probably including the leaders, might survive. This would mean that total destruction would not be assured and, therefore, that that nation might not be deterred. Eventually, the intercontinental missiles became so accurate that they could hit a football field from a distance of six thousand miles, and the warheads were so powerful that it was conceivable that the U.S. missile silos might be destroyed. Suppose the enemy could knock out all of our silos before our missiles were launched? The enemy might try a first strike. (The fact that the United States had 4,600 missiles in submarines and 2,400 in bombers was often forgotten in the anxiety of the moment.

Actually, a single Poseidon submarine carried enough destructive power to destroy every city in the Soviet Union with a population over 150,000.) If our capacity to destroy the Soviet Union completely were threatened, MAD would not work.

Some strange proposals were made. It was proposed that 4,600 missile silos be constructed in the western deserts. Two hundred actual missiles and a number of fake missiles would be shuttled from silo to silo. Then, it was argued, the Soviets would not know where the deadly missiles were and would be deterred from a preemptive strike. Since the Soviets had over 8,000 strategic nuclear weapons, they simply targeted one for each of the 4,600 silos. What did it matter if most of the silos that were struck were empty? They still had 3,400 other nuclear weapons they could target on American cities and other appropriate targets. The Americans and the Soviets had become prisoners of each other. They had very little freedom of action. More and more of their creative energies and natural resources had to be devoted to threats and counterthreats, real or imagined, posed by the adversary 6,000 miles away. Their freedom had been limited, and they had much fear. Prisoners of each other!

The price that the American and Soviet people had to pay had been backbreaking. For example, in the early seventies the Americans had developed the Safeguard ballistic missile defense system. This consisted of 100 nuclear-tipped Spartan missiles that would intercept incoming ballistic missiles at a height of up to 160 miles. There was a small matter that had not been taken into account. The explosion of the nuclear tip of the Spartan missile would have generated an electromagnetic pulse (EMP) that would have knocked out most communication equipment and shut down the electric power grid. The Safeguard ballistic missile defense system, which had cost $5.7 billion, had to be abandoned. It has been estimated that this amount of money, if directed to development assistance in agriculture, might make available enough food to feed the half billion people in this world who are seriously malnourished.

Attempts had been made to limit the number of nuclear weapons. At one time the U.S. Defense Department estimated that there were 200 targets in the Soviet Union for nuclear weapons, and, if the Soviets knew that these targets would be destroyed in the event of nuclear war, they should be deterred from starting a nuclear war. A secretary of defense even suggested that 400 nuclear weapons might be enough for deterrence. The United States then proceeded to build three hydrogen bombs a day. At the latest count we had more than 40 nuclear weapons for every Soviet city of over 100,000 population, and they had more than 32 nuclear weapons for every one of our cities of over 100,000 population. With so many nuclear warheads available, some possible use had to be suggested for them in order to justify further appropriations. Lower-grade officers worked toward promotion by developing "*N*uclear warhead *U*tilization *T*argeting *S*trategies." (NUTS was the acronym applied to this work of death.*) Why build so many nuclear weapons? The only answer was, "We've got to be stronger than the Russians."

Strategic Arms Limitations Treaties (SALT) had been agreed on by the United States and the Soviet Union after long and trying discussions over many years. After two and one-half years of negotiation, SALT I was agreed to. SALT I limited the Soviet Union and the United States in their development of Anti-Ballistic Missile Systems (ABMs). In essence both countries agreed not to develop antiballistic missile systems that might make MAD less assured. There was also a general agreement to continue negotiations. SALT I was agreed to by the heads of state of both nations and ratified by the U.S. Senate.

SALT II discussions were begun in 1972, and the SALT II agreement was signed by President Carter and General Secretary Brezhnev in Vienna on June 18, 1979. It had the following provisions for each nation:

A limit of nuclear delivery systems to 2,400. This limit was to be lowered to 2,250 at the end of 1981.
A limit of 1,320 MIRVed (Multiple Independently Targetable Re-entry Vehicles) ballistic missiles and heavy bombers with long-range cruise missiles.
A limit of 1,200 launchers of MIRVed missiles.
A limit of 820 launchers of ICBMs (Inter-Continental Ballistic Missiles).
Banned construction of additional fixed ICBM launchers.
Banned heavy mobile ICBM launchers, SLBM (Submarine-Launched Ballistic Missiles) launchers, and ASM (Air-to-Surface Ballistic Missile) launchers.
Banned flight testing of new types of ICBMs.
Banned increasing the number of warheads on existing ICBMs.
Placed ceilings on the launch weight and throw weight of strategic ballistic missiles.
Banned the Soviet SS 16 ICBM.
Banned rapid-reload ICBM systems.
Banned some possible new systems such as launchers on ships and on seabeds.
Agreed to give advance notice of certain ICBM test launches.
Agreed on a data base for systems.

**It is interesting to note how many acronyms are used in discussions of arms control and disarmament. One educator has in fact suggested that, at the very least, we should teach future citizens the meanings of these acronyms so that they can understand the discussion of matters that are of life-and-death interest for them. Sometimes the liberal use of acronyms made the deadly business seem like a game. For example, "MAD depends on the enemy's knowing that our MIRVed ICBMs, ALCMs, GLCMs, and SLBMs will not be detected by their ASATs and penetrate their ABM shield before their SS-20s can be launched and Backfires take off" (translation: 100 million dead).*

The SALT II treaty was submitted to the Senate of the United States, but it was never ratified. However, both nations had de facto abided by the SALT II agreements.

Out of the windows of our plane I saw two mushroom clouds where New London, Connecticut, had been. New London had been the home of the Electric Boat Company, which built most of the American nuclear submarines. One of these submarines, the Trident, carried such awesome destructive power that the commander of a Trident was said to be the third most powerful person in the world.

"We want security!" There had been very little discussion of what was meant by security. I had always thought it meant a feeling of freedom from danger or an assurance of safety. Some of our vaunted leaders had talked about national security and asserted that the only way we could have security was through overwhelming military power. But it seemed as if the more military power we acquired, the less secure we became. We became less secure as more nations acquired nuclear weapons and more leaders were tempted to use nuclear weapons to achieve ends they had long espoused. We became less secure as the chance of a stygian accident increased as the number of warheads and delivery systems multiplied. We became less secure as the very laws of mathematics foredoomed catastrophe because even the smallest conceivable probability meant that the unthinkable would eventually occur.

There was always a danger of accidents, and the more nuclear weapons we had the greater the chance of something going wrong. There had been the B-52 laden with a hydrogen bomb that had crashed in North Carolina. Of the six switches that had to be closed for the device to explode, five had been closed as a result of the crash. If the sixth had closed, we would have had to say goodbye to part of North Carolina. A nuclear device was dropped in Spain. It did not explode, but a huge cleanup operation was required. A nuclear device was lost and never found off Thule, Greenland. Then there are the problems of the men who keep the weapons. There are many who drink, some who use drugs, a few with psychological problems—and all eventually get bored as they wait and wait, go through exercise after exercise after exercise. We knew something about these problems in the U.S. armed services. How about the Soviet soldiers and sailors in their silos and submarines? Did they ever drink, use drugs, or get awfully bored? These were not realizations that led to a feeling of freedom from danger or an assurance of safety.

More and more nuclear weapons had become instruments employed in diplomatic negotiations. It was easy to show the flag, shoot down a couple of airplanes, or call attention once again to the large nuclear arsenals. We implied a willingness, while remaining dedicated to peace, to use the ultimate weapons if the provocations became too great. And there were always hardliners in the nation who called for stronger actions than responsible officials in the government were prepared to take. If American citizens are taken hostage, "we should bomb them into the stone age!" If the routes to our oil supplies are threatened, "we should threaten to use one of our bombs on their capital. The lesson would be learned." Some of the professionals interested in finding ways to peace had suggested that as many conflicts as possible should be resolved through conflict management, mediation, negotiation, and arbitration, but few had listened. Bluster and threat required less thought and seemed to satisfy the macho spirit engrained in so many. Eventually, of course, if you can bluster and threaten, you must be prepared to back up your bluster and threat with bold action. The finger on the switch must be ready to push or we will lose our credibility.

We had lost more than our credibility on this last day of civilization.

Someone had asked, "Who is the more secure—a citizen of the United States or a citizen of Costa Rica?" A citizen of the United States had more than 30,000 nuclear weapons on which to base his security; a citizen of Costa Rica had none. The United States had a large standing army, the most modern air force, and the world's largest navy; Costa Rica had practically no armed services. Who had the greater freedom from danger and assurance of safety? I hoped the mushroom clouds did not drift over lovely Costa Rica.

It turned out that one of the radios on the plane used old-fashioned electronic tubes rather than semiconductors and had not been knocked out by electromagnetic pulse from the nuclear detonation several hundred miles above the earth's surface. Similarly, one of the radio stations within our range had not been knocked out. One of its microphones is picking up the sounds of the last day of civilization. I just cannot tell you what the sounds are like.

I had always been puzzled as to why the American and Soviet people had paid the crippling price for the weapons that eventually were to destroy them. To build these weapons of supreme destruction they had:

- seen their health and medical systems deteriorate
- let their educational systems erode in quality
- watched their transportation systems rust
- lost out in competition with societies that did not have these burdensome defense costs
- had their idealism atrophy as they spent less and less to help the poor and the downtrodden of this world

They were depleted societies whose citizens did not know it.

In one episode the Americans made drastic cuts in their budgets. Many children went without hot lunches, elderly survived with reduced support, schools made do with less help, and woe betide those with the ill fortune to be on welfare. It was considered patriotic to spend less and less on those in need, and citizens were asked to tighten their belts for the sake of national security. They were surprised that all of this led to a larger federal budget: The defense budget was increased about twice what the social budget was cut. And the poor Soviet people—they had always been poor and became poorer.

While the sums invested in these stupendous weapons systems were indeed large, the investment in human energy and innovative creativity may have even been larger. At one time, the United States had been the leader in the development and manufacturing of automobiles, bicycles, buses, calculators, computers, railroad cars, answering machines, television sets, and almost everything else that you might expect a robust free economy to produce. But more and more research and development effort was devoted to building new and better weapons. Some of the largest business firms became so comfortable with cost-plus defense contracts that they no longer would or could compete in the marketplaces of the world. The effects were insidious. Engineers, for example, were no longer trained to be concerned over costs. When the incipient engineers graduated, they found that the highest salaries were paid by defense contractors who really did not have to worry very much about costs. The young engineers did not devote their intelligence to the demands of the world's marketplaces.

There had been people who called the nation's attention to the relative decline in productivity of the American labor force, the antiquated machine tools and other equipment in American industry, and the growing reliance on other nations for high technology. These critics had become rather unpopular when they suggested that the United States was coming to resemble a colony that provided raw materials such as lumber, coal, and minerals to nations that had more modern industrial plants, highly trained and motivated work forces, and research and development establishments that could continue to improve products and make procedures more efficient. The critics were certainly vocal, but few listened. Now, the people and the societies of the Soviet Union and the United States were being destroyed by the colossal weapons for which the people had sacrificed so much. A very wise young philosopher once said, "Build weapons and they will be used."

Out our windows to the west, we saw the clouds that had been Boston. A group of physicians had become deeply concerned about the threat of nuclear war, and had tried to call attention to the enormity of the holocaust that would destroy a large part (some even said all) of the human race. They reached the conclusion that it would be impossible to treat all of those that would be burned, maimed, shattered, and radiated in a nuclear war. The only possible treatment was prevention. They had even managed to hold meetings with their colleagues from other nations, including the Soviet Union. There was little disagreement among them about the enormity of the threat. They tried to communicate their fears through all possible channels. People listened and nodded agreement. But they, and all other groups that showed this deep concern, were unable to reach and convince those who had the power to make the final decisions.

They had described what would happen to Boston, and, unfortunately, it looked as if their descriptions were accurate. But, in addition to the obliteration of people and places, there would be destruction of civilization and the social infrastructure that makes human life possible.

How about food? All cities depend on shipped-in food. But railroads and roads would be destroyed along with the corner groceries, shopping-center supermarkets, and warehouses where food is stored. The food not blown up into the mushroom cloud would be radiated and useless. It would be impossible to bring in more food.

How about medical and health care? Most doctors and nurses would be killed along with everyone else. Those who survived would be dazed and shocked and would be prevented from ministering to the wounded by fire and radiation. Hospitals would be destroyed. The decaying dead bodies, destroyed sanitation systems, unsafe water, and reduced resistance to infection would almost certainly lead to epidemic disease. There would simply be no way to care for the sick and the wounded and prevent the spread of epidemic disease.

The physicians had asked us to try to imagine what it would be like to try to survive and cope with the greatest imaginable disaster without electricity, sanitary water, shelter, machines and medical supplies, ways to dispose of dead bodies, food, telephones and other means of communication, transportation, laboratories and the personnel and equipment to deal with burns and radiation from sickness.

The physicians had said that more than individuals would die—societies and civilization would perish. The doctors used the intellectual tools of their profession and came to the conclusion that the only way to deal with the threat of the tragedy of tragedies was through preventive medicine. They had tried their utmost to prevent this "last epidemic."

There appeared to be eight mushroom clouds melding as if magnetized where Boston had once been. Shed tears for civilization!

There have been those who had suggested that war itself should be eliminated. Long ago, Clausewitz had propounded that war could be considered an extension of a nation's foreign policy. But, if that extension meant the actual destruction of the nation itself, it could no longer be considered an option in any foreign policy that was in any way rational. The idea was simple: Why not do away with war?

Actually, other ideas and institutions that once had many adherents had been eliminated. The divine right of kings was, of course, an idea dear to kings, but it had also been an idea that prevailed for centuries. Men had died for their king believing that he was a representation of the divine here on earth. Outside of a stray monarch here or there, no one believes in the divine right of kings any more. To most people, the idea seems more than ridiculous. How about war?

Only a little over a hundred years ago many people conveniently believed in the cruel, inhuman institution of slavery, and it was widely practiced. Now, it is outlawed throughout the world, and few people profess a belief in it. Slavery was outlawed in almost all nations. Why not outlaw war?

The thought was an important one. The Kellogg-Briand Pact renounced war as an instrument of national policy; it was signed in 1928 by 63 nations. Eleven years later there was World War II and now the war of wars. Six decades after the Kellogg-Briand Pact it seemed as if the world might be ready to view war as indefensible and unconscionable—a ridiculous undertaking that should long ago have gone the way of the divine right of kings. But the world was not yet quite ready to renounce war.

The children still dance outside the cave. But what of the children that are not yet born—the generations to come? If in an act of ultimate madness there were an exchange of most of the nuclear warheads that are now in stockpiles of the nuclear-armed nations, the entire human race and most other living matter in the biosphere would be destroyed. Never again would there be the first cry of a newborn infant. Never again would there be a child skipping up the street on the first day of school. No more happiness; no more sorrow. No more love; no more hate. Never again would anyone feel pain or pleasure. Everything that can be called human would be over. There would be no future generations. Does one generation have the right to deprive all future generations of possible existence?

If the horror of horrors occurs, this third planet out from the sun may become literally dead. Three or more billion years of evolution will have stopped. The chances that other humanlike creatures will ever again evolve here or elsewhere are very small. There are those who fear that humankind evolved down a path that would lead to its extinction. Humans that can create great music and literature can also create the weapons that are capable of destroying the species. But if our species has this intelligence, it can surely use it in the struggle to survive. Why not use this unusual intelligence to ensure that generation after generation of children can dance outside the cave?

The First Day of Hope

BETTY REARDON
Teachers College, Columbia University

June 1990

It was cool and clear in the stadium this morning. The sunlight was so bright I felt as if I could see past and future as now. I could see places other than this huge arena thousands of miles from the New York home from which I viewed the events leading to this formal inauguration of the World Disarmament Plan. How had all this been possible when less than a decade ago we had been so close to unprecedented destruction? When did it start to happen? What was the turning point? Where did the vision come from that gave this sense of déjà vu? Only once before had I seen or experienced anything like today. As I scanned the stadium on my own side where the observers sat, the faces and garb reflecting the varieties of human diversity, so recently and so vigorously reclaimed from disappearance into the homogenization of the global military/industrial culture, I remembered the huge auditorium of the Medical Center in Mexico where the Womens Tribunal met in June 1975. And I thought of the great assembly in another part of Mexico City where the formal U.N. conference convened as I watched the delegates file into their section, many of them embracing, shaking hands, greeting each other with the enthusiasm of members of a winning team, with the energy of those revitalized by ultimate success in a long and arduous struggle. The official delegates were somewhat more decorous than we nongovernmental observers, members of a multiplicity of organizations and movements, many totally unaffiliated participants in the struggle. Most of us had contributed to "stalling traffic" in the large tunnel entrances, shouting, waving to each other, hugging, blowing kisses; no small number doing dances of joy as they sang their way to their places in the stand. Even the delegates seemed joyously celebrant. I saw again that same day in June when the official delegates to the World Conference for International Women's Year assembled for the inaugural session, the expansive bright hall festooned with the flags of the member states and the largely female assemblage comprising a glorious costume display, representing all the world's cultures.

Maybe it began there on those hot and rainy days when our feet were

All events and individuals mentioned prior to 1982 are actual as are some of the persons described as participants in the ceremony in the stadium. All of the events described as occurring after 1983 are as possible as the nuclear detonation that ends the "Last Day of Civilization."

constantly wet from waiting for the bus to take us for our nearly daily trips from the nongovernmental tribune to the official U.N. conference to lobby the delegates. We struggled to assure that some consideration of the legitimate concerns of women would be included in the politics-as-usual discourse of the nation-states. Ah, the startled look of the grey-garbed Chinese delegate as she emerged from the toilet stall to have a disarmament statement thrust at her! We were determined to focus attention on disarmament as the basic requirement for "peace" without which we saw little hope for the two other themes of that international year that became a U.N. decade, "equality" and "development."

Memory carried me, more comfortably than did the chartered Mexican buses, back to the tribune and the panel on disarmament where a Nobel Laureate received a standing ovation from the women when he told them the task was theirs. Without their persistent, global, and voluminous demand, he asserted, the male power structures of the nation-states would never disarm. "If you have to take to the streets, do it! And keep doing it until we've got an agreement for General and Complete Disarmament!" General and Complete Disarmament (GCD) was his watchword and the constantly articulated vision he and those who clearly perceived the true dangers to human security put forth as the only real hope for peace, and the fundamental need for survival. He also continuously pointed, as he did in his call to the women to articulate their demands forcefully and publicly, to the legitimate expression of popular sovereignty in public opinion; and to the potential for articulation and execution of the "will of the people" that lay in communications media free of the control of nation-states.

Maybe that is what really made the difference, the media. Certainly without it the great outpouring of revulsion at the thought of nuclear war and the rejection of further development of nuclear weapons would not have been so quickly perceived and responded to by the policymakers, especially the leaders of the nuclear states and most especially the superpowers. Yes, it was the media, and their coverage of the changes in strategic doctrine—the shift from deterrence to limited nuclear war policy, which the politicians did not expect the masses of people to notice or respond to, assuming they could continue to cover it over with arguments about national security and technical competence and all the smoke screens that for so long had kept the average person from confronting the fundamental security issues.

Surely that had an impact—the mistaken assumptions of a leadership out of touch with the people, in fact out of touch with reality. The shift startled and frightened even those of us in the peace movement, including the researchers who had closely followed arms issues and were always aware of the grave danger. It made the danger more imminent. We could see it, smell it, feel it, almost touch it. It was in our heads constantly, often crowding out all other thoughts, screaming "Do something! Act on your analysis! Live your commitment!" And that was part of it, too, the numbers of people beginning to live by their commitment to the reversal of militarization and the abolition of war. Some even willingly died for this goal, not as the innocent victims of militarism and repression to whose liberation they committed their lives, but as persons consciously embracing the ultimate risk for the sake of the ultimate value. But again, without the media would so many have known of them, a few American religious, a Dutch journalist, and the others? None of them had to be there with their lives on the line in the struggle. Nor in fact did all the others about whom we never learned because neither their lives nor their deaths were considered "newsworthy." Now people demanded to know.

Yes, it might be that public opinion can influence the media as much as the other way around. And even journalists can have commitments and be both acclaimed and reviled for them. I thought briefly of the Jonathan Schell phenomenon and the startling impact of his book on people who had never thought seriously about the problem of nuclear war;[1] the great stir in the media and conversation, the chastening effect, and then the denial, "Oh well, nothing new in it after all." "Very badly written, don't you think?" "Oh, yeah, typical *New Yorker* verbosity." "Hell, there simply can't be total devastation. Something, someone will survive to build anew." "Indeed, where there is life there is hope." Ah, but that possibility could not be fully denied. There could, in fact, be no *reflective* life left, arrogant as that may seem to roaches and rodents. That was it. It was really just the opposite. This time the hope was born out of the realization that there could be no life, out of the determination to prevent the death of the planet.

Yet none of this could have happened without the visions and the plans to make realities out of possibilities, without the strategies and policies to capitalize on the tiny flickering lights of hope in the developments running counter to the arms race and war during those very days when the trends toward global militarization were so virulent. Yesterday on the plane, in a seat separated from the others in my chapter of Educators for Social Responsibility (ESR),[2] who formed one of the many observer groups traveling to witness this culminating ceremony (though most of us know it is only the beginning), I reverted to my distant past as a student and teacher of history and jotted down a chronology of the political events that got us to today's affirmation ritual—a goal that had so often seemed at best quixotic, at worst impossible, even to those of us who kept insisting we could stop the arms race, that it was only a matter of "political will." I did not bother to record the long history of disarmament efforts from the mid-nineteenth century, so frequently reviewed with students, nor did I start with the international treaties of the nuclear age, all too often cited as proof of the effectiveness or inadequacies, depending on the perspective of the chronicler, of arms control agreements.[3] Instead, I pulled from the roots of history, read or remembered, some twentieth-century landmarks on the road toward the abolition of war, toward the popularization and realization of the notion of general and complete disarmament. My chronology, as copied here from the back of the travel preparation memo and schedule ESR had sent to our group, went like this.

1928	Kellogg Briand Pact—renounced war as an instrument of national policy—signed by fifty nations
1932	World Disarmament Conference meets in Geneva—recognized arms race as a cause of war
1945	U.N. Charter declares as its purpose putting an "end to the scourge of war." First resolution of the General Assembly prohibits the use of nuclear weapons
1945	Japan dissolves its military
1948	Costa Rica abolishes its army; transfers funds to education
1950–1963	U.N. peacekeeping actions undertaken
1975	International Womens Year (IWY) catalyzes international women's movement for disarmament
1978	U.N. First Special Session on Disarmament (SSD I) designates total elimination of national military forces as long-range goal of disarmament[4]
1979–1982	Shift in strategic doctrines discloses seriousness of possibility of nuclear war
1980	UNESCO convenes World Congress on Disarmament Education
	European women present disarmament petition with thousands of signatures to Secretary General at Women's Mid-Decade Conference
1981–1982	Massive demonstrations for nuclear disarmament take place in Europe, Japan, Australia, North America. June 1982 convening of SSD II becomes focal point for coordinated worldwide popular movement for disarmament
1983	Launching of U.N. World Disarmament campaign to educate and mobilize the general public in favor of disarmament[5]
1984–1986	U.N. Peacekeeping Force established as member states initiate reduction of arms and armed forces having adopted the Defensive Weapons System.[6] Several small states emulate Costa Rica and abolish their armies, transferring funds to education and development.
1985	Regional Development/Disarmament Councils established

in all world regions to guide economic conversion of resources and production from the military to civilian sectors and to assure security through the fulfillment of human needs

1987 SSD III outlines a basic treaty for general and complete disarmament

1990 Final ratification of the World Treaty on General and Complete Disarmament. Massive worldwide celebration—international ceremony to mark its coming into force

Long before yesterday's review, the events leading us here seemed clear to me. Even as they happened I would mark them off as landmarks on my mental map of the journey to disarmament. Still, I could not put my finger on what really made the difference. I kept looking around the stadium, searching out individual faces of people I knew had been important in the movement, and representative groups recognized as significant political forces or gadflies. I focused on the bright yellow robes of a Japanese Buddhist monk standing at one of the entrances to the playing field. He was holding a round single-skin drum of a type that had set the rhythm for another week in June. As more clergy began to cluster around him, preparing themselves to walk out onto the platform on the middle of the field where the opening religious observation was to take place, I heard again the pulse of those drums, blending into the guitars and crisp voices of the young Benedictines singing in the Cathedral of St. John the Divine in New York City. Ten thousand people representing virtually every spiritual and religious tradition crammed the entire space of the huge nave. Hearing the mental replay of those sounds reawakened the strong feelings of human solidarity and the spiritual energy released in the cathedral that June day in 1982.

The world religions have played a vital role in the struggle. More than any other single force in the movement, they demonstrated the ability to transcend cultural, political, and ideological differences, and manifested the courage to articulate fundamental moral principles in the face of political pragmatism. Their convergence into a single world force for peace and disarmament had come from small, fragmentary beginnings. I thought for an instant of a church basement in Brooklyn where another saffron-robed monk from Japan had spoken, simply but with passion, to a group of no more than fifteen people less than a year before the gathering of the ten thousand. We sat then at folding tables of the kind found in church basements and school gyms across the United States. Beside me was a Colombian Catholic priest, and next to him the Lutheran pastor of the church. I had never seen that pastor before, but we knew each other and spoke to each other from a relationship of long standing and the closeness that comes from recognition of a common struggle. The priest I had known over the decade since a small seminar in Mexico had brought together a handful of educators from the United States and Latin America to explore the possibilities of cooperative efforts in peace education. It was these small meetings, these tentative connections and common endeavors, that built a worldwide network of persons of very different backgrounds and life circumstance who shared similar hopes, fears, and visions. Although infrequently together, they had forged a community of caring through which they gave each other support and courage. The courage to continue in the face of setback after setback was undoubtedly the essential ingredient in the whole recipe of the disarmament struggle.

That courage was evident when some in the religious establishment who saw the need to return to the prophetic role of religion began to articulate what many were beginning to intuit about the meaning of nuclear weapons, and about the international system that had produced them at so great a cost to the entire human family. As nations marched blindly from one stage of military preparedness to the next "advance in weapons technology," military values took precedence over humane norms. It was in the early 1980s that the churches spoke out most forcefully against the irrationality and evil of the weapons, of the arms race, of the militarization process, giving popular voice to the ethical choice only a few scientists and philosophers had recognized in the early years of the "atomic age."[7] The churches had been in the forefront, too, in organizing the massive demonstrations against nuclear weapons and war that had taken place in cities all over the world in the early 1980s.

As the clergy gathered, preparing to file onto the platform, I noticed a young woman wearing a clerical collar above a dark blue bib. The collar made her appearance no less "feminine" than that of the older woman she was chatting with. Her companion wore a heavy cross and chain on a turtleneck sweater above a simple skirt. I took her to be a Catholic sister. Their presence in that gathering represented not only the significant merger between feminist politics and the peace movement that had confronted the conscience of the churches and the governments, but also the millions of women who had worked in their own communities to educate people to the dangers and the possibilities. I thought of the letter I had received about ten years ago from a young friend in Oxford, England, the mother of an eight-year-old girl who wanted a future for her child, who had surprised even herself, never having spoken in public, by beginning to make public speeches, first in her own village, then in other small communities across England. Together with other mothers who began to instruct themselves as they stood in the play yard watching children whose chances of becoming adults diminished with each technological weaponry advance, she formed a national movement similar to that being organized by women all over the world. In her letter she had told me of the four women who met around a kitchen table in Copenhagen about a year before the U.N. Mid-Decade Women's Conference was to meet there in

1980, and how from that conversation began the European Women for Peace movement, a high point of which was presenting a peace petition to the secretary general of the United Nations. It was indeed the women who nurtured and cultivated the grass-roots peace movement, standing on American street corners with Freeze[8] petitions, traveling across Europe in second-class night trains to meet with sisters in other cities without the benefit of formal translation or any of the professional and diplomatic support systems that facilitate international dialogue. Their support system was their own commitment to the future of their children. Their facilities were their own energies and their conviction that the struggle for women's equality and the struggle for world peace were one, an insight that for so long many in the movement, even those whose contribution was the analysis of the situation from which political strategies were derived, found hard to comprehend. Indeed, many still find it hard.

Yes, many of us in this struggle have had our blind spots to the way in which particular individual or group concerns related to the common goal. Certainly diversity and political divisions had often threatened to shatter the force we had begun to build, to dissipate the unity of efforts toward a universal objective. There were more political struggles than those between the superpowers and between the first and third worlds. Divisiveness within nations was spawned by the traditional political approaches to the problem, and was sometimes made worse by controversies among the researchers and scientists, many of whom claimed to have the "correct analysis" on which the political strategy for disarmament should be based. The peace research movement that emerged in Europe and the United States in the 1950s and 1960s certainly made an important contribution in spite of such differences as those between advocates of "arms control" and the advocates of "disarmament."

Looking over the delegates, I picked out reseachers I had known through the years who had devoted so much of their energies not only to the research, but to trying to bring their findings to the attention of the political establishment. I remembered the way in which the peace research community had worked to increase the participation and the substantive role of nongovernmental organizations in the U.N. deliberations on disarmament. From the early 1980s they had begun to act as a kind of global lobby in the interest of humankind, interacting with those in the international talks who were operating from the traditional national-interest perspective. Surely it was this sophisticated and informed lobbying that convinced the practical politicians that policy could be made in "the human interest."[9] The tenacious efforts of some of these researchers and other nongovernmental organizations in and around the United Nations had significantly changed the course of deliberations. It was wonderful to see the People's Security[10] lobby as an official delegation to the international meeting that had drafted and was now bringing into force this Treaty for General and Complete Disarmament. Many nongovernmental organizations were represented by such official delegations to this signature ceremony.

As the People's Security delegation filed into the stand, we observers jumped to our feet in a wild burst of applause, for they represented more than anything else "our victory," a victory we knew to be possible only in the kind of game where everybody wins. Among those we recognized in the delegation were the Japanese teacher from the Asian Regional ESR walking with the African, Latin American, and European educators whom we had elected to represent us officially at the ceremony. Walking together among the International Physicians against Nuclear War[11] were a neurosurgeon from the Soviet Union and a psychiatrist from the United States. The others I did not know but assumed they were from the social scientist, performing artist, and other professional groups that had begun to organize and build global networks for nuclear disarmament in the spring and summer of 1982 following the example of the churches and the physicians, just as we had in forming Educators for Social Responsibility.

For a while I believed it was really the formal educational efforts that had made the difference, helping people to see the need to change, the need expressed by President Kennedy for "mankind to put an end to war [before] war [puts] an end to mankind." Educators organizing in response to the nuclear threat had served as a catalyst to introduce peace studies into schools and all kinds of learning settings throughout the world. The work that had been developed since the early 1960s on the methods of teaching about alternatives to war, and the possibilities for nonviolent conflict resolution, began to be accepted even in some of the more conservative educational systems.[12] Even now I was sure that education was a very significant part of it, perhaps the most significant. That whole movement during the 1980s was an educative process in itself. People were trying to learn, struggling to instruct themselves in the issues related to weapons development, to national security, to means to end the arms race and possible alternatives to war. It may have been one of the most important learning experiences in human history. Indeed, I was very sure that what we had learned about the international system and how our efforts to make our nations more secure through more numerous and more powerful arms only made us more insecure was the most important of all lessons. Yet cognitive learning, understanding even so important a phenomenon as armed insecurity, simply did not explain it all. There was something more that had made the difference.

Among the People's Security delegation I also noted the American senator who had been one of those to introduce the Nuclear Freeze into the U.S. Senate. His presence there reminded me of the parallel development of education with political action and the way in which the citizens movement had influenced and in fact provided the direction for changing political policies. Yet I thought, too, of the nature of the early antinuclear efforts, particularly the Nuclear Freeze, which called for a halt to the way things were going and became a prelude to a new direction. But as the freeze was first proposed and discussed, in itself it did not propose or contain a specific positive direction. Those positive energies I recalled from the cathedral service did find a political vehicle when the antiwar movement joined the social justice movement, when the commitment to fulfilling human needs became as strong as the urgent desire to prevent human annihilation. It was that merger, which generated the really significant force, which kept us going through this last decade. It brought into the movement many who previously had not seen as their own the problem of preventing nuclear annihilation and devising alternatives to war. We began to see how these issues were inseparably related, just as the feminists came to understand that the militaristic values propelling the arms race were the very same values that kept women "in their place." So, too, the economically deprived, and the politically oppressed, began to comprehend the war system as a fundamental cause of their condition.[13] Most people came to see that system pushing us closer and closer to the last day of civilization.

The connection to economic equity, social justice, and human rights gave us something very positive to struggle for. While the researchers had been putting out annual reports showing the social costs of the arms race from the mid-seventies on,[14] it was the budget cuts in human services coming simultaneously with increasing arms expenditures to almost incomprehensible proportions that helped us put things together. Anyone following world events was painfully aware of two significant trends: severe economic crisis and unemployment on a worldwide basis, accompanied by a rising tide of global militarization. Many countries were falling under the control of the military and virtually all were building large military establishments. Arms control negotiations were stalled as one technological "advance" after another produced ever deadlier weaponry. It took years before an alternative international security system as the fundamental requirement for disarmament became clear to all. The freeze and the proposals of the Defensive Weapons System for cutting back on the big weapons helped to focus on the need for system change, and made more sweeping proposals possible. When the U.N. Second Special Session on Disarmament was convened in 1982, the general concern and growing fear brought it unprecendented public attention.

The event itself was no radical departure from the ordinary diplomatic trends and events. The opening session replicated the same atmosphere, the same procedures as innumerable other sessions. That day I sat in the section reserved for observers from nongovernmental organizations, excited and hopeful because the session was finally taking place. Looking out at the assembly at all the close-cropped male heads and dark suits I thought, "It's all the same. How can anything different come out of this?" Recalling that small core of hope overlaid by the lack of expectation of anything from the established political order, it finally came to me. It was the environment in which the session took place. It was what was happening outside the halls that began to turn the tide.

It was the women, the religious, the educators, the professionals, the researchers, those few politicians who began to understand, all of them reaching out to take strength from each other, acknowledging a belief in the possibility of a future, affirming that the human drama was not yet played out. It was that, the people taking responsibility for the future, recognizing that the structures in place were not adequate to the task. So they took it up themselves with no small degree of fear and yet with courage and even a sense of joy. That was the real turning point. For me it was marked from the particular day when the largest of all the growing number of demonstrations for nuclear disarmament took place as a gesture of solidarity and support to the delegates of the Second Special Session on Disarmament. Nearly a million people came into the streets of New York surrounding the United Nations and walked together to Central Park. The park that day was used for recreation, for celebration in a way in which it had never been before, in which perhaps no public park had ever been used. The music, the speeches, the cheers, were the initiation of this very ritual we observe today. As colorful as this crowd is, it pales by comparison with the crowd that took to the New York streets on June 12, 1982, when youngsters with the safety-pin earrings of the punk-rock generation and monks garbed in the robes of their religious orders walked together with the elderly and disabled in wheelchairs, businessmen in vests and ties, and mothers pushing baby strollers. They had come from all over the world, the young, the old, those with means, those with none, to walk together, to say with one voice, "We will live! We choose life for ourselves and our children. And we will remember how close we are at this moment of choice to the possibility of death."

June 12, 1982, was the first day of hope, a day of affirmation when we knew there was the possibility that it could be done, because of our own commitment and because of those who had risked and struggled before us. As the marchers walked by the platform near the entrance to the park on which a group of Japanese musicians sat surrounded by banners carrying the slogan "Never Again," we took up that chant, "Never again! Never again!" We knew we had to remember, to remember Hiroshima, to remember the victims of weaponry, war, and militarism. Last fall when the discussions were taking place about the venue for today's ceremony, almost the only point everyone agreed on right away was that the location should have profound significance to this commitment not to forget what we have done as well as what we almost did. It should be in one of the many places that now symbolize the dark side of ourselves, which came so close to destroying us: Guernica, Auschwitz, Hiroshima, Nagasaki, Afghanistan, My Lai, Lebanon. It was finally decided that we would come to this stadium, that we would observe that rememberance and this promise here in this place where the throats of poets were crushed, where the hands of musicians were smashed and the voices of those who cried for justice were silenced by militarism so deaf to poetry and music, so fearful of justice, that it brought us so very close to the final silence and to losing the possibility of this beginning.

Notes

1 Jonathan Schell, *The Fate of the Earth* (New York: Alfred A. Knopf, 1982).

2 Educators for Social Responsibility (Box 1711, New Rochelle, NY 10802), was founded in Brookline, Massachusetts, in 1981 (see organizations cited by Sam Totten in "Activist Educators" in this issue of the *Record*, pp. 199-209).

3 For information on this subject consult the U.N. Centre for Disarmament, United Nations, New York, NY 10017.

4 The text of the final document of SSDI is available from the U.N. Center for Disarmament.

5 Information on the World Disarmament Campaign is also available from the U.N. Centre for Disarmament.

6 For a description of such a system see Harry B. Hollins, "A Defensive Weapons System," *The Bulletin of the Atomic Scientists*, June/July 1982. For offprints write to the author at the Institute for World Order, 777 U.N. Plaza, New York, NY 10017.

7 Listings of such statements available from United Ministries in Education, c/o Church of the Brethren, 1451 Dundee Avenue, Elgin, Il. 60120.

8 Nuclear Weapons Freeze Campaign Clearing House, 4144 Lindell Blvd., Suite 404, St. Louis, Mo. 63108.

9 Robert Johansen, *The National Interest and the Human Interest: An Analysis of US Foreign Policy* (Princeton, N.J.: Princeton University Press, 1980).

10 For a definition of the concept of People's Security see Yoshikazu Sakamoto, "Report of the Secretary General," International Peace Research Association *Newsletter*, Fall 1981.

11 Physicians for Social Responsibility, P.O. Box 411, Planetarium Station, New York, NY 10024.

12 Betty Reardon, *Militarization, Security and Peace Education* (Valley Forge, Pa.: United Ministries in Education, 1982).

13 Betty Reardon, "Militarism and Sexism: Influences on Education for War," *Connexion*, vol. 9, no. 3, Fall 1981.

14 Ruth Leger Sivard, *World Military and Social Expenditures* (Leesburg, Va.: World Priorities, Inc.) (published annually 1977-1981).

AFFIRMATION

Education for the Celebration of Life: Optimism Despite It All

RENÉ DUBOS
1901–1982

Barbara Ward, who died in May 1981, was one of the most learned and sophisticated women of our times. Despite a frail constitution and long years of painful illness, she retained to the end a phenomenal ability to celebrate and enjoy life, and she knew, furthermore, that life can be celebrated and enjoyed under the most humble circumstances. "You can't live in Africa where I lived for eight years," she stated in an interview durng the 1970s, "without seeing the enormous amount of sheer unadulterated fun which comes from being with your neighbors, sitting around, talking, dancing . . . or just being." The love of parents for their children, expressive smiling faces, and the excitement caused by the pleasurable things that people of all ages find in nature have not been increased by education or civilization. I always have in mind the expression of bliss in the eyes of a young Australian aboriginal girl as she anticipated eating the delectable, fat larva she had just extracted from under the bark of a tree.

The disarray and disenchantment so common in modern technological societies reveal the extent to which many of us no longer know how to take advantage of this innate ability to appreciate the multiple wonders of life. Abundance of goods, physical comfort, and control of disease are clearly not sufficient to bring about individual happiness and harmonious social relationships—not even a feeling of being at peace with nature. A remark made to Hannibal by one of his officers at the end of the second Punic War speaks for Western civilization, especially as observed today in the United States: "You know how to win victories, Hannibal, but you do not know how to use them." Hannibal's bold generalship had enabled him to defeat Roman armies time after time, but he ultimately failed because the social institutions of Carthage did not formulate goals suited to his military genius. Similarly, while Western civilization has displayed immense ingenuity and vigor in using knowledge for the control and use of nature, modern societies are nevertheless deteriorating because they are inept in applying their scientific and technological prowess to the deepest concerns of human life.

Everywhere in industrial countries, the amenities of existence are threatened by environmental degradation and existential nausea. The mounting roster of material and psychological problems creates the impression that humankind has lost control of its affairs. The conditions in our cities, our contacts with nature, the endless futile tasks that crowd our days, and the very direction of our lives are determined more by technological imperatives than by our choice of desirable human goals.

Our societies know how to create material wealth and physical health but their ultimate success or failure will depend on their ability to shape a humanistic culture compatible with the fundamental satisfactions that have generated countless forms of celebrations of life even under the most stressful circumstances. The shift from obsession with quantitative growth—either of material goods or of abstract knowledge—to the search for more desirable and enjoyable ways of life will not be possible, however, without a profound change in attitudes with regard to social organization and education.

The Industrial Revolution placed a premium on the kind of intelligence, knowledge, and skills suited to the invention of manufactured articles as well as to their large-scale production and distribution. In contrast, a humanistic society will have to emphasize skills that facilitate better human relationships and a more pleasurable and creative interplay among technology, nature, and humankind. Such a society would prize *joie de vivre* and happiness over power and wealth.

Happiness is contagious and for this reason its expression can almost be regarded as a social service and a duty. As the Buddhist saying goes, "Only happy people can make a happy world." Since optimism and cheerful spirits are indispensable to mental health, the most valuable members of future technological societies may turn out to be not those with the greatest ability to produce and distribute material goods but rather those who, through empathy and happiness, have the gift of spreading a spirit of good will. The gift of helping other people feel happy is probably innate in part but it can almost certainly be enhanced by experience and education.

In any system of education for the celebration of life, the first obstacle to be overcome is the widespread belief that things are now going from bad to worse and that little if anything can be done to reverse the trend. Countless expressions of this defeatist mood are presently found in writings by economists, sociologists, and environmentalists. The book *Limits to Growth*, published by the Club of Rome in 1972, deserves special mention here because it set the fashion for using computer models and other big guns of science to validate a doomsday literature; in fact, this book continues to be quoted even though the world picture it presents has often been shown to be faulty, indeed by several members of the Club of Rome itself. The most recent and monumental contribution to this atmosphere of gloom assumed to be scientifically supported is the 800-page *Global 2000 Report to the President*. This was prepared in the United States by the Council on Environmental Quality and the State Department, in collaboration with fifteen other federal agencies, and published in 1980. There is nothing new in the general conclusion of this report that "if present trends continue, the world in 2000 will be more crowded, more polluted, less stable ecologically and more vulnerable to disruption than the world we live in now." All this has been heard before and repeatedly denied by other students of modern social problems. What is new, however, is that the authors of *Global 2000* acknowledge that "with one or two exceptions at the most, none of the agency experts knew anything about the assumptions, structures, requirements and uses of the other's calculation procedures"—the result being that different agencies held opposite views of the information used for the preparation of the report. As bluntly stated in Volume 2, "The executive agencies of the U.S. Government are not now capable of presenting the President with internally consistent projections of world trends in population, resources, and the environment for the next two decades." But this did not prevent the authors of *Global 2000* from using the big guns of computer technology to derive sweeping conclusions from faulty and grossly inaccurate, out-of-date information—the most spectacular example of the law of computer science "Garbage in, garbage out." (Recently, several of the contributors to the *Global 2000 Report* publicly acknowledged that, in their particular area of knowledge, the world situation is far less desperate than they had estimated in 1980.)

This is not the place to enumerate the factual fallacies and intellectual absurdities of *Global 2000*, but I shall at least say a few words concerning the psychological atmosphere in which the report emerged and the mood of despair it continues to foster.

According to Edward E. David (a past president of the American Association for the Advancement of Science who has served as science advisor to the White House), the fundamental origin of our present social problems "is a shift toward a national pessimism which dwells on failures and ignores success. . . . There is a loss of nerve, as occurred in ancient Greece at the close of the Golden Age." Dire predictions are more likely to be publicized and accepted than optimistic ones, not because they are based on better information or analysis, but because they are now fashionable, as revealed by their popularity on high school and college campuses. It is claimed, furthermore, that publicizing bad news and trying to document these stories with unsubstantiated figures is socially useful because it alerts the public and thus leads to action, although there is no real evidence for this assumption. The late Philip Handler, who was president of the National Academy of Sciences until 1981, stated in a report to Congress in the midst of the 1970 environment panic that "the nations of the world may yet pay a dreadful price for the public behavior of scientists who depart from . . . fact to indulge in hyperboles." The cynical attitude of the general public toward recommendations based on unwarranted scientific claims originates from the widespread awareness that much of what is reported as science does not correspond to really valid scientific information.

There are, of course, valid reasons for concern about the state of the world, but there are also reasons for hope. I shall begin, however, by mentioning a few aspects of modern societies that are unquestionably dangerous or at least threatening.

Surprising as it may seem, many objectionable aspects of modern life are the consequences of the ease with which human beings can usually adapt to undesirable conditions. The dangers of adaptation can be illustrated by many different medical examples: We adapt to air pollution by physiological mechanisms that eventually result in chronic pulmonary disease; we adapt to noisy environments by anatomical changes that result in impairment of hearing; we adapt to crowded environments by developing behavioral patterns that result in an impoverishment of the human encounter; most urban dwellers readily become adapted to starless skies, treeless avenues, shapeless buildings, tasteless bread, joyless celebrations—in other words, to conditions that lower the quality of life.

I could go on and on to illustrate that much of what we call adaptation is in reality a tolerance of bad conditions achieved at the cost of some biological, psychological, or social loss. The prevalence of such mutilations is evidence that the wisdom of the body and the mind is all too often a short-sighted wisdom. Three examples of dangerous social adaptations will reveal that societies, like individual human beings, commonly respond to threatening situations by attitudes or measures that appear adaptive at first but are destructive in the long run.

Every sensible person knows that the inevitable result of nuclear warfare would be not only immense suffering for humans and immeasurable damage to every living and inanimate thing on earth, but also the virtual collapse of our civilization. In an official document just published concerning the effects of the atom bombs on Hiroshima and Nagasaki, it is shown that the number of deaths up to 1950 was about 200,000 in Hiroshima alone. The postwar nuclear arms race has resulted in the accumulation of weapons thousands of times more powerful than those used in Japan and stockpiles with an explosive power millions of times greater. Even while peace lasts, the cost of nuclear and antinuclear arsenals is so great that it prevents the development of much-needed social programs. Yet, except for a few manifestations here and there, most of us behave as if we were not much concerned about the possibility of nuclear warfare—far less than we are, for example, about the questionable role of saccharin in the causation of cancer. We have adapted to the astronomical cost and the potential threat of nuclear warfare simply by not letting these dangers be active preoccupations of our minds. The only reason to retain some hope is the increase in antinuclear manifestations in Europe, Japan, and the United States during recent months.

Another situation about which many people display little concern is massive unemployment, especially of youth. Yet youth unemployment is, in my opinion, the greatest social tragedy of peacetime. I am as ignorant concerning social techniques that could solve the unemployment problems as

I am about solutions to nuclear disarmament, but I can at least express opinions that differ somewhat from those that govern present attitudes and policies.

It is generally assumed that the plight of unemployed young people can be made bearable by providing them with some form of welfare, including entertainment, but this seems to me an almost irrelevant approach to the problem. Human beings always function as parts of structured social groups. If they are not given the opportunity to function in normal society by being meaningfully employed, they will organize themselves in social groups of their own—as young unemployed people are doing now—a situation that will inevitably lead to destructive social conflict. Despite this enormous potential threat, we behave as if we had achieved a kind of social adaptation to youth unemployment by providing the unemployed with food and shelter, a shameful way of avoiding the responsibility of dealing with one of the deepest needs of human nature—namely, socialization. Yet, the success of several "youth conservation programs," either publicly or privately financed, leaves no doubt that even delinquent youth can be reintegrated into normal society by being given the opportunity for meaningful work.

As a last example of our frightening ability to adapt to bad conditions, I shall merely mention that the increase in terrorism, including the murder of Anwar Sadat, has been readily absorbed by the social order and even by the stock market—a chilling reminder of the desensitization of peoples and their institutions. There is nothing like repetition, no matter how outrageous the events, to dull the senses.

I shall now turn to creative aspects of adaptation and shall particularly emphasize technological and social adaptations to the future.

There are great tragedies in the world today. Paradoxically, however, much of contemporary gloom comes not from actual tragic situations but from the prospect of social and technological difficulties that have not yet occurred and may never materialize. We are collectively worried because we anticipate that, if demographic and technologic growth continues at the present rate, the earth will soon be overpopulated and its resources depleted; there will be catastrophic food shortages; pollution will alter the climate, spoil the environment, poison us, rot our lungs and dim our vision. I believe, as do many others, that industrial civilization will eventually collapse *if* we do not change our ways—but what a big *if* this is.

Human beings are rarely passive witnesses of threatening situations. Their responses to threats may be unwise, but they inevitably alter the course of events and make mockery of any attempt to predict the future from extrapolation of existing trends. In human affairs, the *logical* future, determined by past and present conditions, is less important than the *willed* future, which is largely brought about by deliberate choices—made by human beings. In my opinion, our societies have a good chance of remaining prosperous because they are learning to anticipate, long in advance, the shortages and dangers they *might* experience in the future if they do not take adequate preventive measures.

For example, the North American continent is far from being overpopulated; its population density is much lower than that of Europe and Asia. Yet, the fear of overpopulation in the *next century* has been one of the factors responsible for the decrease in average family size. Birthrates are below replacement rates in most American social groups. They have also fallen in many other countries and the one-child family is being advocated in China. Barring ecological disaster, the world population will certainly continue to increase for a few decades, but the rate of increase will not be as rapid as was believed only twenty years ago. Indeed, the world population is likely to reach a plateau in the course of the next century.

Environmental degradation became a widely recognized danger only during the 1960s, and most antipollution programs are barely ten years old. Yet there are many places in which environmental quality has already been vastly improved. Air pollution has markedly decreased in several large European, American, and Asian cities, for example, in London and even in Tokyo. Several streams and lakes that were so grossly polluted as to be qualified "dead" a decade ago have been brought back to a level of purity compatible with a rich and desirable aquatic life. A fish as ecologically exacting as the salmon has returned to the Thames in London, and to the Seine in Paris; various species of finfish and shellfish, including oysters, can once more be harvested in the Jamaica Bay of New York City. Forests that had been devastated are being allowed to recover spontaneously and massive reforestation programs are being carried out in several parts of Africa and Asia, especially in China. Areas that had become desertic are reacquiring a diversified flora and fauna as a result of being protected against browsing—for example, in Israel and even in some parts of North Africa and the Sahel. While environmental degradation is still increasing in many parts of the earth—particularly in the tropical rainforests and in areas undergoing desertification or being affected by acid rains—there are signs that modern societies are learning to work with nature so as to minimize the loss of agricultural soil and of biological species.

The most interesting aspect of the environmental improvements that have occurred during the past ten years is that many of them resulted from measures taken long before environmental degradation had become extreme. The air of most cities was not really poisonous at the time steps were taken to decrease urban air pollution. Most lakes and rivers were far from being dead at the time control of water pollution was begun. Environmental policies were therefore responses not to *actual* emergencies but rather to the *anticipation* of emergencies.

Furthermore, adaptation to the future is beginning to be conceived as going beyond preventing or correcting dangerous situations. The phrase "good environment" is no longer taken to mean only freedom from noxious influences; it implies also surroundings that provide emotional, aesthetic, and social satisfaction. City planners used to be almost exclusively concerned with problems of public health and with greater mobility and efficiency in the various aspects of urban economic life. They are now beginning to emphasize, in addition, factors that contribute in other ways to the quality of life, such as the improvement of parks and waterfronts, and the role of "city centers" to enhance social and cultural activities.

Adaptation to the future is also apparent in our concern for natural resources, as illustrated by the case of copper. Rich copper ore has become scarce, and even though methods have been worked out to use ores of low grade, a shortage of this metal appeared likely some ten years ago. Long before there was any real shortage, however, technologists developed substitutes for copper and established that aluminum could be used in its place—for example, in telephone wires—with, of course, appropriate modifications. Furthermore, it was recently discovered that glass optical fibers, and even synthetic fibers, can be used for the transmission of messages, and are indeed superior to copper in some respects. Cables of glass optical fibers are now used in several urban telephone systems. Copper is still as important as in the past in many technologies but a shortage of this metal is no longer an immediate danger.

There are many other examples of possible replacement of a particular metal by another one or by some synthetic product. We have entered the "age of substitutability." Whether we like it or not, plastics are likely to become more and more common in many different aspects of our lives. Admittedly, the use of substitutes often entails greater expenditure of energy but, as we shall now see, adaptation to the future is also taking place in the production and use of energy.

The evolution of policies for the production of energy constitutes a spectacular example of the rapid adaptive changes that commonly occur now in technological societies. When it became apparent that the supplies of certain fossil fuels were being depleted, especially with regard to petroleum and natural gas, industrial countries turned to nuclear reactors as sources of energy. It soon became obvious, however, that the natural supplies of uranium also are limited. In view of this fact, attention was focused on the breeder reactor, which produces nuclear fuel while generating energy. In several countries, the highest priority was therefore given to theoretical and practical research on breeder-reactor technology. During the 1960s and 1970s, however, several groups of scientists and citizens took a stand against the breeder program, not necessarily because they doubted its technical or economic feasibility but because they were alarmed by the dangers inherent in its operations—in particular by the inevitable accumulation of plutonium. Whatever its merits and dangers, the breeder program thus provides a striking illustration of the rapid effect of social forces on the evolution of energy policies.

During the early 1970s, more than 90 percent of the funds for energy research were earmarked for the nuclear program. There has not yet been any catastrophic accident resulting from this program (not even at Three Mile Island). From many points of view, in fact, nuclear technologies have *so far* been the safest method for the production of energy. Yet, public concern for the dangers inherent in them has profoundly affected many aspects of energy research, production, and use. In the budgets of all industrialized countries, an ever-increasing percentage of the funds for research is now allocated to energy sources that used to be neglected—solar, wind, wave, tide, geothermal, biomass, and so forth.

It can truly be said that the recent evolution of research policies for the production of energy has been an adaptive process determined, not by the existence of shortages nor by actual disasters, but by the *anticipation* of shortages and of disasters that have not yet materialized.

In 1933 the city of Chicago held a world's fair to celebrate its one-hundredth birthday with emphasis on the contributions of scientific technology to the "Century of Progress." One of the subtitles in the guide book to the fair was "Science finds, industry applies, man *conforms*" [italics mine]. The very etymology of the word *conform* indicated that, in the minds of the fair's organizers, humankind would from then on be molded by industrial forces. But in fact there are few people who now accept as an inevitable fate the fact that the new technologies will shape our lives; the more common view is that industry must take into consideration the constraints imposed by human nature and the maintenance of environmental quality. It has been said, of course, that environmental concern is just a passing fad and will vanish when the cost and inconvenience of effective control measures become apparent. The new fact, however, is that the right to a good environment has come to be regarded as an inalienable right for which the community is responsible. The formulation and implementation of sound environmental policies will naturally be difficult and there will be popular resentment against control measures that appear unfair, elitist, wasteful, or simply unreasonable. But these difficulties will not make people forget that they want environmental quality; there has never been a lasting retreat from the recognition of an inalienable right.

In addition to the preservation of the wilderness, the control of pollution, and better management of resources, many different schemes have been suggested to improve the earth's environmental quality. I shall limit myself to a very bold one published in 1974 by the Russian physicist Andrei D. Sakharov, an illustrious scientist then very much in the news. Sakharov suggested "a gradual . . . growth of two types of territory out of the industrial world that is overcrowded and inhospitable to human life and nature. I will conditionally term them 'Work Territory' (WT) and 'Preserve Territory' (PT)." The PT is larger in area and will be "set aside for maintaining the earth's ecological balance [and] for leisure activities."[1] The smaller and more densely populated WT (with an average population density of 300 people per square kilometer against 25 for PT) will be the area where people will spend most of their time.

This plan will have intensive agriculture, automated factories, and supercities with all modern conveniences "as well as a free and varied cultural life."[2] WT will provide opportunities for its inhabitants to spend time in the more natural surroundings of the PT, where "they will listen to the noise of a mountain stream or simply relish the silence, the wild beauty of the outdoors. . . . Their basic work [in PT] will be to preserve nature and themselves."[3]

Sakharov also suggested that a natural expansion of WT will be in outer-space cities—"artificial earth satellites with important industrial functions [which will also] serve as cosmic-research laboratories and way stations for long-distance flights."[4] He ended his description of this future world with the most exalted expression of faith in the future that I have ever read: "Humankind will find a rational solution to the complex problem of realizing the grand, necessary, and inevitable goal of progress without losing the humanness of humanity and the naturalness of nature."[5]

Many persons who are concerned with the shape of things to come have views of the future very different from those imagined by Sakharov. Yet all agree with him on three points: (1) there must be change, because it is an essential condition of life; (2) change can be successful only if it occurs within the constraints imposed by the ecological characteristics of each locality and by the unchangeable fundamental demands of human nature; and (3) change will probably be more and more rapid and therefore will increasingly tax the adaptability of humankind.

As mentioned earlier in this article, one of the dangers that is rarely emphasized is that human beings adapt all too passively to undesirable conditions with long-term consequences that are deplorable for themselves and for our planet. In several articles and in my most recent book, *Celebrations of Life,* I have tried to differentiate between passive adaptations that may be deleterious in the long run and creative adaptations that attempt to shape the world according to our wishes. Until now, educational systems have been designed to prepare young people for the world as we know it today, with each nation having its own cultural and educational criteria. From now on, however, it is likely that educational systems will have to be designed to prepare people of all ages for the futures we try to invent and to bring into being.

I must acknowledge at this point that since I have only limited experience as an educator (except in a few areas of medical research), the following remarks are purely theoretical and probably incompatible with the practical problems of education. I present them merely as statements of problems and not as formulae for solutions.

I shall start with a very conservative statement, namely the need to emphasize the three Rs, not only to prepare young people for jobs here and now, but also and even more to prepare them to learn. In the present educational system, of course, one does not only learn to learn, one actually learns. But learning to learn assumes a special importance in societies characterized by extremely rapid rates of change. To be adaptable, one must be able to learn and to relearn throughout one's life, and the three Rs are probably the best path known to this learning and relearning process.

Learning and especially relearning are ways of achieving adaptations to the future, and they inevitably imply some form of self-sufficiency because most life situations are so complex that they require multiple adaptive processes on the part of the coping person. Self-sufficiency is innate to a large extent, but it can be so influenced by the way of life that it appears almost as an acquired trait. Self-sufficiency can best be developed if the experiences of life expose the individual person to several changes of scene and of occupation, preferably during youth.

Attempts to reformulate priorities on noneconomic criteria go counter to the dominant trends in industrial societies and it may prove difficult to give young people the education that would prepare them for ways of life in which community spirit and some measure of self-sufficiency are as important as is now the acquisition and accumulation of money. The solution will not come from simple changes in the traditional school curricula or in pedagogical methods, but will require instead a new philosophy of educational systems.

Education and learning must not only be more dispersed throughout the society than they are now; they must also be spread more continuously throughout the life span in an attempt to keep pace with social and technological change. The necessity to continue learning in order to remain competent may have the advantage of exposing middle-aged people to the humanities that they had scorned during their early school years, an exposure that may become more and more valuable in the modern world.

Profound changes in the educational system will not be achieved by decrees from central authorities. They will require as many different experimental programs as possible, in the hope that the successful ones will serve as examples and eventually create a new consensus. Technological societies are so complex that they dread the risk of human error. For this reason they tend to reward those specialists who are least likely to make mistakes, whether they fly airplanes or run computers. They tend to discourage those who wish to become involved in really new ventures that might create risks and upset the sociotechnological apple cart.

Occupational and intelligence tests measure chiefly dimensions of the human mind that favor safety over creativity. Yet, societies can adapt to new conditions and really progress only by encouraging experiments, and giving license to take risks—whether in technology, land use, health, or education. In fact, this is the way nature proceeds to achieve adaptation and evolution. Nature is not efficient, it is redundant. It always does things in many different ways, a number of them awkward, rather than aiming first at perfect solutions. To improve human life instead of simply producing more goods, industrial societies will have to try many different ways of dealing with future situations instead of depending on the decisions of a few experts—because experts tend to be concerned primarily with means and efficiency rather than with goals and with the creative diversity that is essential for a richer life and the continued growth of civilization.

These theoretical views may not lend themselves readily to practical implementation in the educational system, but there is at least much evidence for their validity in everyday human life. I know from personal experience in this country and abroad that adolescents can deal effectively and responsibly with many life situations usually regarded as the province of adults. Years of association in New York City with the National Commission on Resources for Youth have revealed to me that even delinquent teenagers can be rehabilitated if they are allowed to engage in some kind of work that is meaningful for them and if they are given a chance to make existential their potentialities in creative activities. Mayor Edward I. Koch of New York City and William J. Haskins of the National Urban League have spoken feelingly of the achievements of youths, chiefly "black and Hispanic high school dropouts," who, as part of the Youth Conservation Corps, have restored at low cost dilapidated city parks and have created other urban facilities. It has now been demonstrated, furthermore, that many of the most important human attributes persist almost unaltered to the end of life. Contrary to what used to be believed, for example, the mechanisms for short-range memory do not inevitably deteriorate with age, but do so only as a result of organic disease or accidents. Even the mysterious attributes that make for creativity are less affected by age than they are by social circumstances.

Any program of education for celebrating life can therefore be based on the fact that human beings are endowed from adolescence through old age with most of the attributes that differentiate them from animals. These unchangeable aspects of our constitution are as relevant to the future as are diversity and change, both in ourselves and in the environment. The world of the future will be interesting and creative to the extent that it will provide opportunities for all age groups to express the various urges inherent in the biological and psychological nature of the human species. Bob Dylan stated an eternal truth when he sang "the times they are a-changing." But he should have added to his message that it is the same human nature and the same physical nature that are being eternally recycled during the change.

Notes

1 Andrei D. Sakharov, "Tomorrow: The View from Red Square," *Saturday Review World*, August 24, 1974, p. 13.

2 Ibid., p. 14.

3 Ibid.

4 Ibid.

5 Ibid., p. 110.

CONTRIBUTORS

PETER ABBS is lecturer in art, philosophy, and education at Sussex University. He was editor of *Tract* and among his books are *The Art of English; Reclamations: Essays on Culture; Mass Culture and the Curriculum; Roots and Blossom: Essays on the Philosophy, Practice and Politics of English Teaching, Autobiography in Education,* and, with Graham Carey, *Proposal for a New College.*

RICHARD J. BARNET, Senior Fellow of the Institute for Policy Studies, Washington, D.C., formerly served in the Arms Control and Disarmament Agency and is the author of *Roots of War; The Economy of Death; The Lean Years; Real Security;* and other books.

ELISE BOULDING is chair of the sociology department, Dartmouth College, a member of the governing board of the United Nations University, COPRED's representative on the U.S. Commission for UNESCO, and has served on the Commission on Proposals for a National Academy of Peace and Conflict Resolution.

JOHN BROUGHTON is originally from London. His doctorate from Harvard was in developmental psychology, and he is currently associate professor of psychology and education at Teachers College, Columbia University, where he directs the Developmental Psychology Program. He has recently edited two books, one on James Mark Baldwin and the other on critical approaches to the theory of development. His current interests include adolescence, the development of philosophical and political thought, the self, young people's orientation to health and illness, and the applications of Hegelian and neo-Marxian social theory to psychology.

MICHAEL J. CAREY writes a public affairs and politics column for the Anchorage *Daily News* and lives in Fairbanks, Alaska. He is writing a series of articles about social aspects of the nuclear threat.

JAN DEMAREST is a sociologist deeply interested in the tasks of peace education. She has been a leader with Haim Gordon in the Peace Project at Ben-Gurion University.

RENÉ DUBOS (1901-1982) was professor emeritus of environmental biomedicine and microbiologist at Rockefeller University. In recent years he was involved in problems bearing on the quality of the human environment. He was the author of twenty-three books, the last being *Celebrations of Life* (1981).

RANDALL FORSBERG is founder and director of the Institute for Defense and Disarmament in Boston. She is co-author with other members of the Boston Study

Group of *The Price of Defense.* She is the originator of the nuclear-freeze proposals, and the major leader in the campaign for it.

KIMBERLY HUSELID GLASS is a recent graduate of Teachers College, Columbia University, with an M.A. in Philosophy and Education and an Ed.M. in Family and Community Education. She is interested in pursuing a vision of education grounded in a respect for all of life.

HAIM GORDON is a lecturer at Ben-Gurion University of the Negev in Israel. Editor of the Buber Centenary volume, he has written various essays on Buber and on existentialism and education. Currently he is heading an education project entitled Education for Peace in the Spirit of Martin Buber's Philosophy, which will deal with enhancing the possibility of I-Thou relationships between Arabs and Jews.

MAXINE GREENE is the William F. Russell Professor in the Foundations of Education at Teachers College, Columbia University. She is now working on a book, based on her John Dewey Lecture, which will be titled *The Dialectic of Freedom.*

RIFFAT HASSAN is associate professor, Religious Studies Program, University of Louisville. She is especially interested in women in Islam, and is writing a book on women in the Qur'an. She is also interested in interreligious dialogue, and has participated in numerous interreligious conferences, including a continuing Trialogue of about twenty Jewish, Christian, and Muslim scholars that has met biannually since 1978 under the sponsorship of the Kennedy Institute of Ethics.

WILLARD J. JACOBSON is professor of natural sciences at Teachers College, Columbia University. He is an organizer of the Seminar on Education for Peace, Disarmament, and the Control of Nuclear Weapons at Teachers College, and he is the national research coordinator for the Second International Science Study. His most recent books are *Population Education—A Knowledge Base* and *Science for Children.*

ROBERT JAY LIFTON holds the Foundations' Fund for Research in Psychiatry professorship at Yale University. He has been particularly interested in the relationship between individual psychology and historical change, and in problems surrounding the extreme historical situations of our era. He has taken an active part in the formation of the new field of psychohistory. Among his books are *The Broken Connection: On Death and the Continuity of Life; Death in Life; Survivors of Hiroshima,* and with Richard Falk, *Indefensible Weapons* (Basic Books, forthcoming).

SEYMOUR MELMAN is professor of industrial engineering at Columbia University. He is co-chair of the national board of directors of SANE. Among his many books are *Pentagon Capitalism: The Political Economy of War; The Permanent War Economy: American Capitalism and Decline;* and the forthcoming *Profits without Production.*

ROBERT K. MUSIL is education director of the SANE Education Fund and lecturer in American Studies at Temple University, where he is teaching an honors course on nuclear disarmament. Dr. Musil is also co-producer of SANE's nationally syndicated public affairs program "Consider the Alternatives" and was project director of the National Endowment for the Humanities–funded radio documentary series "Shadows of the Nuclear Age: American Culture and the Bomb."

MICHAEL N. NAGLER is professor of classics and comparative literature at the

University of California, Berkeley, where he founded the Berkeley Peace Studies Project. His interests have ranged from oral poetry through myth and religion to nonviolence and peace. In addition to articles on these subjects he wrote *Spontaneity and Tradition: A Study of Homer's Oral Art* (1974) and *America without Violence* (1982) and is working on a collection of essays to be called *Peace Now or Never.*

ADRIAN NĂSTASE is a research fellow and scientific secretary of the Institute of Legal Research in Bucharest, Romania, and secretary of the International Law Section of the Romanian Association of International Law and International Relations. He has also recently been a research fellow at the International Peace Research Institute in Oslo and a researcher for the Division of Peace and Human Rights of UNESCO.

BETTY REARDON has worked in the field of peace education and world order studies for many years. She is currently associated with United Ministries in Education and the Teachers College Seminar on Education for Peace, Disarmament and the Control of Nuclear Weapons. She is the author of *Militarization Security and Peace Education: A Guide for Concerned Citizens,* published by and available from United Ministries in Education, c/o ABC, Valley Forge, PA 19481.

GENE SHARP, D. Phil. (Oxon.), is professor of political science at Southeastern Massachusetts University, and an associate of the Center for International Affairs at Harvard University. He is author of several books, including *The Politics of Nonviolent Action* and, most recently, *Social Power and Political Freedom.* His writings have been widely published and translated into several languages. He is a leading exponent of research and development of a substitute national defense policy called "civilian-based defense."

SAM TOTTEN is a doctoral candidate at Teachers College, Columbia University. He is currently completing two books on the issues of nuclear weapons and nuclear war: *Atomic Activists: Their Stories* (with Martha Wescoat Totten), and *Times of Crisis, Pilgrimages of Faith.*

MARTA ZAHAYKEVICH is an instructor in the Developmental Psychology Program at Teachers College, Columbia University, and in the Department of Psychology at Rutgers University, Newark, New Jersey. She is currently writing a book entitled "An Interpretive Psychology of Soviet Human Rights Activists."

INDEX